The Making
of an American Jewish Community

THE MAKING OF
AN AMERICAN JEWISH
COMMUNITY

☆☆

the history
of Baltimore Jewry
from
1773 to 1920

By ISAAC M. FEIN

THE JEWISH PUBLICATION SOCIETY OF AMERICA

Philadelphia

5731–1971

TO CHAYA
IN GRATITUDE AND LOVE
AND TO
MY CHILDREN AND GRANDCHILDREN
THE PRESENT AND FUTURE
BUILDERS OF THE
AMERICAN JEWISH COMMUNITY

PREFACE

It is told that far, far away there is a land called America. It is also told that in that land the passage we have just read, "Proclaim liberty throughout the land to all the inhabitants thereof" [Leviticus 25:10], *is the basic law of that land; and it is further told that the dwellers of that far, faraway land had these words engraved on a huge, huge bell. Now,* Kinder, *if when you grow up you find out that all of this is not just one more* bobe maise, *that all this is true, go there, go to America. But never, never forget us who pine here in the land of darkness. See to it that America comes also here, to Bendery. We so badly need it. And remember, no matter what, remain* getraye Yidn [loyal Jews].

These, as far as I can remember, were the words of my *rebbe*, Reb Haimke, a half-blind old man who spoke in a melodious Yiddish. His words—and I can still hear them now, over six decades later—were spoken as if he were relating a legend. Indeed, how could he, who lived in Bendery, only a few miles away from the "city of slaughter," Kishinev, possibly believe, possibly imagine that there was a land with "liberty for all its inhabitants," even Jews? On that spring day, I, a boy of about nine, heard for the first time the word *America*.

Fifteen years later, in 1923, I came to the land of my *rebbe*'s fancy. It did not take too long before I discovered that the Liberty Bell, about which my *rebbe* had spoken, even if he did not believe that it really existed, was cracked. And cracked were many of the ideas abroad in this country in the twenties. The Ku Klux Klan was raising its poisonous head. "Niggers" were lynched. Sacco and Vanzetti were in jail, and those who spoke out in defense of the two "foreigners" were branded as "Bolshevists." Attorney General A. Mitchell Palmer had begun his "Red Hunt" in 1919; only the hundred percenter was considered a loyal American. Forgotten were the immortal words: "Give me your tired, your poor, your huddled masses, yearning to breathe free. . . ." Xenophobia gave rise to immigration restrictions. And to pile discrimination upon discrimination, the immigration laws were especially severe against the countries of Southern and Eastern Europe, the lands of the most "undesirable foreigners."

It was the age of the WASPs. Henry Ford was spewing hatred

upon the "International Jew" in the pages of *The Dearborn In-dependent*. By courtesy of the automobile magnate, *The Protocols of the Elders of Zion* was read in every town and hamlet throughout the length and breadth of the country. The Roaring Twenties, the Jazz Age, as F. Scott Fitzgerald dubbed this period, was from the point of view of this immigrant an era of gloom, of shattered dreams.

And yet even in my first days in the new land, I instinctively felt what was explained to me years later by one of the finest Americans of our age, the writer Gerald W. Johnson. Upon hearing what Reb Haimke had told his students, the "philosopher of Bolton Street," as Johnson is affectionately known in Baltimore, reacted with the following words (in a letter of August 28, 1957):

> *Little as you may have suspected it, your share in the heritage of America began right there, and little as he may have suspected it, your rebbe had done himself what he counseled you boys to do—beyond space and time he had seized a bit of the best in America and gave it to you in Russia. The Bell is cracked, but what of that? . . . The Liberty that it proclaimed throughout the land and to all the inhabitants thereof is cracked, too. But . . . have no doubt about it—it can be recast, and it will be. . . .*

But when I came to this country in 1923, I did not, or perhaps I *thought* that I did not, remember my *rebbe*. Yet in spite of all that I found, I believed as he did that America is much more than a huge piece of real estate between the Atlantic and the Pacific. America is an idea, and the more you take from it, the more it grows. Reb Haimke did not hesitate to ask his *Kinder* to bring a piece of America to Bendery. I too did not hesitate to cast my lot with the America of the Bill of Rights. There was to be no retreat, no going back "home." *This* was to be home. The Liberty Bell was to be mended. The myth was to be restored.

The "Jewish bell" too demanded much mending. Above all, ob-literation of Jewish ignorance was needed. Thus began a lifelong career of teaching—teaching young and old the meaning of real Americanism and Jewish loyalty, and of the importance for Jews to realize in their own lives the blending of the two.

To teach, not to preach, demanded much knowledge about America's and American Jewry's past and present. The first attempt to do original research on the present was made in 1942 in Bridgeport, Connecticut, where I was to conduct a survey in depth of this rela-tively small Jewish community. The study was interrupted when I moved in 1943 to Baltimore. Yet the detailed questionnaire and the little interviewing that was carried out were of great help when I worked on this volume. (For more about the Bridgeport survey, see "A Study of a Jewish Community in New England,"*YIVO Bletter*, XX [1942], 242–256.)

Baltimore, with its much larger general and Jewish populations and its rich history, offered greater opportunities to learn and to teach. The Maryland Room at the Enoch Pratt Library and my students, young and old, proved to be veritable storehouses of information. In 1960 I published a study on Baltimore Jews as seen by non-Jews (*"Niles' Weekly Register* on the Jews," *PAJHS*, L [1960], 3–22). The classes on the history of Baltimore Jewry aroused a greater interest in their own past on the part of Baltimore Jews, and in 1960 a Jewish Historical Society of Maryland was organized. The following were the first officers of the organization, which brought about a greater historical awareness in the Jewish community: President, Hugo Dalsheimer; Vice-President, Dr. Harry Bard; Vice-President, Isaac Hamburger (now deceased); Treasurer, Dr. Alvin Thalheimer (now deceased); Secretary, Dr. Louis L. Kaplan; and Curator, Dr. Isaac M. Fein. My large personal collection of documents was turned over to the society. This was rapidly augmented by many contributions by individuals and organizations. For nine years, from 1960 until 1969 when I left Baltimore, I served as curator of the society. When I was in Israel for one year, collecting documents related to American Jewry found in Israeli Archives, Samuel S. Strouse ably served as replacement.

The growth of the society's archives has prompted a number of members, including myself, to write articles on the history of Baltimore Jewry. After the publication in 1961 of my study on "Baltimore Jews during the Civil War," (*AJHQ*, LI [1961], 67–96), based largely on hitherto unknown documents, I began to organize the material in the hope that some day a full history of the community would be written. It was, however, only five years later, in 1966, that the president of the Historical Society, Hugo Dalsheimer (who served for seven years in this capacity—from its inception, in 1960, to 1967), made a most generous contribution to the society, and this enabled it to commission me to write the present volume. It is very doubtful whether the book would have been possible without Mr. Dalsheimer's financial assistance.

This book is a biography of the Jews of one American city on their way to becoming a community. American Jewish history is tridimensional. First, like all other ethnic groups, Jews have been engaged in a process of adjustment to the American way of life; since they have been universally persecuted, they were more anxious than any other group to strike roots, to become "Americanized." No wonder the number of Jewish returnees to the old homelands was the smallest of all groups. Americanization was attained with a very high degree of success.

But while this process was going on the Jews refused to give up their identity. Continuity was high on their agenda. Although the forms changed, Jews succeeded in preserving old traditions. America was no *shtetl;* nor, for that matter, was life in America comparable to life in the large cities of Western and Eastern Europe. It was a new life but one in which the past was not dead. Changes were many. Much of the superfluous baggage was thrown overboard, but the melting pot idea was rejected. A different kind of melting pot was in the making. This one strove to make of the different American Jewries one: the American Jewry.

There is, finally, a third dimension to American Jewry. Jews are the only ethnic group spread all over the world. The lot of these fellow Jews has always remained the major concern of American Jews; they, the modern Josephs of Jewish history, became the providers for those in faraway lands who needed their help.

This book is the history of these three dimensions and the tensions and rifts which accompanied them, as they found their expression in the Jewish community of Baltimore, Maryland. It is a saga of a group which began with no political rights whatsoever but became sufficiently integrated to have one of its members, a son of a poor presser, attain the office of governor of the state. It is the history of poor foreigners whose descendants became captains of commerce and industry and luminaries in the academic world. In short, it is a history of integration into America.

At the same time Baltimore Jewry built important institutions. The Associated Jewish Charities is concerned with every phase of Jewish life. There are great welfare organizations, two Jewish institutions of higher learning, many houses of worship. With the rapid changes in America generally, Jewish life, too, undergoes many rapid changes. In all of these one element remains constant—a wish to continue as Jews, albeit different from those of the previous generations.

Baltimore Jewry has also distinguished itself on the international arena. Throughout its history it showed its anxiety for unity with Jews the world over.

The chief concern of the volume is the many; only those individuals absolutely essential for the understanding of the story are mentioned. Those who do not find the names of their ancestors in the index need not be disappointed. Their forebears were good people. The community was built not by leaders but by every Jew who lived in Baltimore— and it is impossible to mention all of these. The history of the community since 1920 is most fascinating. It had and has great leaders of national and even international repute. No name is mentioned in the Epilogue, nor is there a photograph of any living person in the illustrations. They will, no doubt, be written up in the next volume on Baltimore Jewry.

I did not choose the year 1920 arbitrarily. This was a milestone year in the history of Baltimore Jewry, for in that year the largest organizations united to form the Associated Jewish Charities. The Baltimore Jewish community came into being.

At all times I have tried to follow Ranke's injunction to "let the documents speak for themselves." I was, however, fully aware that if the picture was based only on existing documents, the result would be lopsided. Preservation of documents had always been a function of the "somebodys"; the "nobodys" hardly record and seldom preserve even the little that they do record. Characteristic of this is the following letter from the executive secretary of the Workmen's Circle, which speaks for itself:

Sept. 25, 1969

We do not have on record the names of the founders or any material that they may have had. I doubt whether such is available.

Benjamin Gebiner
Executive Secretary

And yet these nameless, half or fully forgotten men and women were the prime movers of history. Intelligent guesses had to be made. The history of events had to be reconstructed from what was accomplished.

Little did I know when I began to work on this book that my teacher Reb Ḥaimke's spirit would hover over it. Unknown to them, Baltimore Jewry lived up to his formula: Love American freedom and remain loyal Jews. This was not and it is not easy. And here again I feel obliged to quote the words of Gerald W. Johnson with which he concluded the above-mentioned letter:

We have sunk pretty low, but the memory remains. We have scaled the heights not once, but repeatedly, and if new heights rise before us, what then? Profane old Pierre Samuel, the original DuPont, said it in a letter to Thomas Jefferson. Contemplating the task before the infant republic, he wrote: "We are but snails, and we have to climb the Andes. By God, then, let's climb."

How comforting are these words at the time of this writing, when the condition of the bell seems to be beyond repair.

Baltimore Jewry until 1920, and from then till now, has proved that "memory remains," that the past does live in the present. It proved its desire and ability to climb and reach new heights.

This volume is dedicated to the climbers of the past and those of the future.

Erev Shavuot, 5730/June 9, 1970
Boston, Massachusetts

ACKNOWLEDGMENTS

I owe much to many who helped, in one measure or another, to make this book a reality. In addition to Hugo Dalsheimer, whom I have mentioned in the Preface, I am grateful to Louis F. Cahn, who succeeded him as president of the Historical Society. A man of vast knowledge of Baltimore's general history, author of several books on the subject—among them History of the Oheb Shalom, 1853–1953 *(Baltimore, 1953)—this friend read parts of the first draft and made valuable comments. Certain parts of the first draft were also read by Dr. Moses Aberbach, the present curator of the Society, and Robert S. Goldman, acquisitions librarian of the American Jewish Historical Society, who also made helpful comments. The most beneficial critic was my daughter-in-law Ruth B. Fein. A trained historian, she read the manuscript in its entirety. My debt to all these readers and especially to the last one is immeasurable. Needless to say, for all errors in facts as well as interpretation, the responsibility is solely mine.*

I benefited much from my talks with Dr. Isidore S. Meyer, former editor of the American Jewish Historical Quarterly.

I am grateful to those who gave me of their knowledge by means of personal interviews and to the very many individuals and groups who let me read letters, documents, and other records pertaining to the subject.

I want to thank my former gifted student Mrs. Froma Willens, for her help in researching the old issues of The Baltimore Sun, *and Dr. Rose Bodenheimer, who helped me on a number of occasions to decipher very difficult German documents written in Gothic. I also wish to record my gratitude to my first three typists: Mrs. Pearl Friedman, Carol Friedner, and Betty Sachs who worked hard decoding my own "hieroglyphs" and typed the first draft; and to Mrs. Marie Allen for her exemplary work in preparing the final draft.*

A large number of friends encouraged me time and again to go on with the research and finish the job. To the most persistent of these, Dr. Louis L. Kaplan, president of the Baltimore Hebrew College, my sincere thanks.

The spadework for the history of Baltimore Jewry was done by Isidor Blum in The Jews of Baltimore *(1910), Abraham D. Glushakow, in* A Pictorial History of Maryland Jewry *(1955), and Rabbi*

ACKNOWLEDGMENTS

Jeffrey B. Stiffman, in Prolegomena to the Study of the History of the Jewish Community of Baltimore, Maryland *(typescript, 1965). These works were carefully read and utilized.*

I am grateful to the "dean" of American Jewish historians, Professor Jacob R. Marcus. I owe him much for his constant encouragement, for the night sessions in his home in Cincinnati, as he, exhausted from a long day's work, lay on his sofa giving me sound advice on how to avoid pitfalls—especially the natural desire to record "everything." Again and again he discussed the problem of choice, the importance of differentiating between the wheat and the chaff. The American Jewish Archives, where I spent one summer, opened up a world of rare documents. Many, very many of the documents quoted in the volume are to be found in that remarkable institution at the Hebrew Union College–Jewish Institute of Religion in Cincinnati, a creation of Dr. Marcus. His associate Dr. Stanley F. Chyet was always prompt to send me microfilms and documents which I requested, and he and the wonderful staff of the Archives deserve my sincere thanks.

I am also indebted to Dr. Morris L. Radoff, director of the Maryland Hall of Records, Annapolis, Maryland, and Harold Manakee, director of the Maryland Historical Society, who together with their staffs were always willing to search for a rare document and explain obscure points.

I also enjoyed the assistance of the staffs of the following libraries: Dropsie College, Philadelphia; Jewish Theological Seminary, New York; Jewish Division of the New York Public Library, YIVO Institute for Jewish Research, New York; Maryland Room of the Enoch Pratt Library, Baltimore; The Johns Hopkins University. Above all I used the rich collection of the Jewish Historical Society of Maryland.

I am also grateful to Miss Naomi Kellman, of the Associated Jewish Charities, and to Miss Eugenia Calvert Holland, assistant curator of the Maryland Historical Society, for providing me with many illustrations.

It gives me great pleasure to thank my very able and extremely patient copy editor, Kay Powell, for her valuable suggestions and attention to the smallest details.

Many were helpful in one phase or another, at one time or another. There was, however, one who was involved in every phase of the work and at all times. It was her constant encouragement and sound advice that brought the book to a conclusion. To her, my dear wife Chaya, I owe more than words can express.

CONTENTS

CONTENTS

ILLUSTRATIONS

ILLUSTRATIONS

I

THE PIONEERING AGE:
THE COLONIAL PERIOD

THE ECONOMY
OF COLONIAL MARYLAND

For a full century and a half after the establishment of Maryland in 1634, its economy was largely agrarian and was based on a single crop—tobacco. King Tobacco ruled the province. It was shipped to England on English ships, and in return the colonial planters received goods manufactured in the mother country. It even served as the main currency in the colony. A contemporary noted in 1666 that "tobacco is the current Coin of Mary-land and will sooner purchase from Merchants than money."[1] Not only was tobacco the medium of exchange at home, but it was also the established currency in business transactions with the mother country.[2] Although it was never declared the colony's official currency, tobacco was recognized as such by the population as well as by the authorities. "All levies, parish, county and provincial, also fines and court charges were assessed in tobacco."[3]

There was an ever-growing crisis in the tobacco industry—as a result of excessive exploitation, the soil began to wear out. The crisis became so serious that the proprietor of the colony, Governor Benjamin Leonard Calvert, expressed his deep concern for the lot of the tobacco growers in a report in 1729 to his brother Charles Calvert. He wrote:

Tobacco is our staple, is our all, and indeed it leaves no room for anything else. It requires the attendance of all our hands. . . . When all is done . . . the planters can scarce get a living. . . . I heartily wish the planters' lay was better.[4]

In spite of this officially discouraging report, the colony continued to expand. New towns were forming. In the same year that the governor sent his report, the legislature passed an act establishing a new town destined to become the largest city in the province and one of the most important in America. The town of Baltimore was born on August 8, 1729, when the Maryland Assembly passed "an Act for erecting a Town on the North Side of Patapsco in Baltimore county; and for laying out into lots, sixty acres of land, in about the place whereon John Flemming now lives."[5]

Flemming's house stood near the banks of Uhler's Run, near the present intersection of Charles and Lombard Streets. The land on which "Baltimore Town" was to be established belonged to the well-known Carroll family of Maryland. Seven "commissioners," all of them tobacco planters, were appointed by the assembly to supervise the project. They were instructed to impanel a special jury to assess the value of the land, "and what sum of tobacco the said jury shall adjudge the sixty acres to be worth shall be paid the owners."[6]

By 1748 the tobacco crisis had deepened to such an extent that the planting of this crop was restricted by law. Tobacco finally gave place to wheat, and by the time of the American Revolution the economic mainstays of Maryland were wheat, lumber, and iron.[7]

Because commerce was undeveloped in the colony, Jews, whose main occupation at the time was trading, would have found Maryland most uncongenial from an economic point of view. Moreover, there were religious laws which made the colony practically out of bounds to Jews.

RELIGION
IN THE COLONY

The proprietary charter establishing the colony of "Mary-Land," named after Henrietta Maria, the wife of King Charles I, was a mixture of business and religion. The first paragraph of the document explained that Lord Baltimore was entrusted with establishing a colony because he was "excited with a laudable and pious zeal for the propagation of the Christian faith." The concluding paragraph of the charter again stressed the importance of religion and its place in the future colony.

If . . . any doubts or questions should arise, concerning the true sense of any word, clause, or sentence contained in this . . . charter, we will and ordain . . . and command that at all times . . . no interpretation shall be admitted thereof, by which God's Holy and Truly Christian religion . . . may in any thing suffer any prejudice or diminution.[8]

The middle paragraphs of the charter were devoted to the business aspect of the enterprise.

The "Truly Christian" character of the colony was by no means intended to affect Jews, for at the time of the issuance of this charter in 1632, there were no Jews legally in England—they had been expelled in 1290. Nor, for that matter, were there any Jews in North America. The first group of twenty-three Jews came to New Amsterdam some twenty-two years later, in 1654. Charles I was concerned not with Jews but rather with Christian dissenters. Yet although Jews were not mentioned in the charter and no one was likely to have thought of them in connection with the colony, their position was to be affected for a long time by the "Truly Christian" charter.

To the lord proprietor, Cecilius Calvert, the enterprise was a business venture, but for him religion too played an important role. Calvert was a devout Catholic who sacrificed much for the sake of his faith in England, where Catholics were persecuted. He had hoped to found a refuge for his coreligionists in the New World. Fearing accusations that he favored Catholics over Protestants, the lord proprietor leaned over backwards to show his impartiality. For one thing, he recruited some Protestants to be among the first settlers. The names of the two ships which brought these settlers, the *Ark* and the *Dove*, were symbolic of the harmony that he hoped would prevail between the two groups.

Calvert, however, did not leave it all to chance. In a directive to his brother Leonard, whom he appointed governor of the colony, and to the commissioners who accompanied the ships, he ordered that

they suffer no scandal, no offense to be given to any of the Protestants whereby any just complaint may hereafter be made by them . . . and that for that end, they cause all acts of Roman Catolique Religion to be done as privately as may be . . . and that the said Governor and Commissioners treate the Protestants wth as much mildness and favor as justice will permit. And this to be observed on land and at sea.[9]

The amity between these two groups, with their long tradition of animosity, lasted only a short while, as might have been expected. During the first fifteen years of the colony's existence, both groups did occupy one chapel in Saint Mary's, where the original settlers landed. Meanwhile, though, Puritans were entering the colony in large numbers. In addition, they were becoming more powerful in the mother country. The Catholics in Maryland were now in need of a law that would guarantee them religious freedom. Calvert was still strong enough to push such a law through the legislature. In 1649 the Act concerning Religion, popularly known as the "Toleration Act," became the law of the province (see Appendix I).

As in many religious pronouncements, the generalities were quite liberal, while the specifics were very harsh. The act did recognize that

the inforceing of the conscience in matters of Religion hath frequently fallen out to bee of Dangerous consequence in those common wealthes where it hath beene practised.

Nevertheless in the same breath, as it were, the act provided for the most severe punishments for dissenters:

Whatsoever pson or psons within this Province . . . [who] shall . . . deny our Saviour Jesus Christ to bee the sonne of God, or shall deny the holy Trinity . . . shalbe punished with death and confiscacōn or forfeiture of all of his or her lands and goods to the Lord Proprietary and his heires. [10]

The Toleration Act, like the restrictions in the original charter, was not directed against Jews. There were no Jews in Maryland. It did, however, serve as a warning to Jews in other colonies that Maryland was not a safe place for them.

The act was "liberalized" in 1723. No more was one to pay with his life for the first offense against the Christian religion. The new act read in part:

If any person hereafter in this province deny our Savior Jesus Christ to be the son of God or shall deny the Holy Trinity, he shall for the first offense be fined and his tongue bored.

The second offense called for branding the letter "B" on the offender's forehead, the "B" most likely standing for blasphemy. The death sentence was reserved only for those who dared to commit this crime for the third time. [11]

What all this meant for a Jew who might come to Maryland is quite obvious. In the words of a sound researcher of the period, "While it is true that Jews did not enjoy equality in the other colonies either, in Maryland their lives were in danger." [12]

Ominous as the Toleration Act sounds, it was a dead letter from the very beginning. Perhaps its very severity made it impractical and virtually impossible to enforce. Only one trial based on this act is on record. This one, strangely enough, concerned a Jew, even though when the act was issued it was intended to deal only with Christian dissenters. The Jew in question is notable for another reason: he is the first known Jew in the colony. [13]

THE FIRST KNOWN JEW
IN MARYLAND

The claim of being the first Jew in Maryland belongs to "the Jew Doctor," Jacob Lumbrozo, who came to the colony in 1656.[14] In addition, he merits, as far as is known, the distinction of being the first Jewish physician in the country.[15]

Lumbrozo was, however, much more than just a healer of people. He was also a farmer, an innkeeper, a businessman, and an Indian trader. In whatever capacity this Jack-of-all-trades engaged his versatile talents, he was frequently involved in court cases, sometimes as plaintiff, sometimes as defendant. As plaintiff, he was usually suing people for unpaid debts. As defendant, he was charged with more serious crimes. On one occasion he had to defend himself against a charge of having attempted to "force himself" upon a woman. The doctor justified this by citing passages to prove that what he did was not against "the scriptures."[16] A punishment for performing an abortion upon another woman was averted when he married her, thus disqualifying her as a witness against him.[17]

"The Jew Doctor," however, never faced a more serious charge than the one brought against him on February 23, 1658. This time he was accused of having committed "blasphemy," a crime carrying the death penalty under the Toleration Act. This inquiry took place in the Provincial Court of Saint Mary's, then the capital of the colony, in the presence of Governor Josiah Fendel. Two witnesses, Richard Reston and John Offsett, testified that about a year earlier they had a "discourse" with the accused, "the Jew Doctor . . . known by ye name of Jacob Lumbrozo." The "discourse," according to their testimony, was "concerning . . . Blessed Saviour, Christ, his resurrection, telling ye Lumbrozo that he was more than man, as did appear by his resurrection." They further testified that Lumbrozo's answer was that "such works might be done by necromancy or sorcery, or words to that purpose," and when he was asked "whether ye Jews did look for a Messias . . . they said Lumbrozo answered, yes."

In his deposition Lumbrozo stated that such a discussion did, indeed, take place. It was also true that he was asked by the witnesses to give an opinion on the subject and that he, by

7

*profession a Jew, answered to some particular demands then urged . . .
but sayd not any thing scoffingly, or in derogation by him whom
Christians acknowledge for their Messias.*

Lumbrozo's defense was of no avail. The court's order was that

*ye s^d Lumbrozo remain in ye Sheriff's custody, until he put in security,
body for body, to make answer to what shall be layd to his chrge,
concerning the blasphemous words & speeches, at the next Provincial
Court & the persons be there present to testify,* viva voce *in court.*

This court record is the first document of any kind dealing with a
definitely identified Jew in Maryland.

Luck was with "the Jew Doctor." Ten days after his arrest he was
released by an amnesty, proclaimed in honor of Richard Cromwell's
accession as lord protector of England, for all who "stood indicted,
convicted, or condemned to die."[18]

Lumbrozo's activities after his release added little luster to his name.
He, who in the face of danger had openly proclaimed himself a Jew,
now changed his name from Jacob to John. He acquired letters of
denization by giving the standard Christian oath. This is not to say
that he converted. There is no allusion to it in his will, which begins,
"I bequeath my soul to the Creator."[19] He died while under indictment for buying goods stolen from a murdered family.[20]

Lumbrozo's blasphemy case proves that, in spite of stringent religious
laws, one could live openly as a Jew in Maryland. We know of one
more Jew, David Ferera, who then lived in the state—he too was
sued by Lumbrozo for "wages for seven months' attendance."[21] After
Lumbrozo's trial he left the colony and went to New York. It was
much safer to be there than to stay in Maryland.[22] Even if Jews could
live openly in the state, it was nonetheless a precarious existence.

Lumbrozo's lesson was not lost on the Jews of the other American
colonies. The chief characteristics of Maryland in the colonial period
—the agricultural economy of the colony and the harsh religious laws
—combined to keep Jews away. After Lumbrozo's death in 1666, no
Jews appeared in Maryland for one hundred years. By that time,
however, different conditions prevailed in Maryland.

FIRST
BALTIMORE JEWS

It was only in 1773 that the first permanent Jewish settler appeared in Baltimore. On December 16 of that year, Benjamin Levy (c. 1726–1802)—whose Jewishness is attested to not by his name but by documents—announced in the local newspaper that he had

just opened store in Market street at the corner of Calvert street where he sells wholesale and retail, for ready money only all kinds of imported wines . . . all kinds of spices . . . a large assortment of corks for bottles . . . rubber for tables, tea, coffee, chocolate, buckets, pails . . . fine pickled salmon, Irish beef, rose blankets, English cloth, rugs, felt hats, silk and cloth umbrellas and sundry other articles.[23]

From the size of the advertisement—the largest in the paper—as well as from the items Levy offered for sale, it is obvious that it was quite an establishment.

Levy came to Baltimore from Philadelphia, where he had been a leading businessman, in 1768. In his former domicile he was one of a small but distinguished group of merchants who signed the Nonimportation Agreement against the British.[24] He mingled with the social leaders, and Robert Morris, the "financier of the Revolution" and a signer of the Declaration of Independence, was his close friend. The close relationship was not disrupted even after Levy moved to Baltimore. When Levy learned that Philadelphia might be abandoned by the Revolutionary forces, he dispatched a letter (dated December 13, 1776) to Morris inviting him to come to Baltimore and stay with him. Although Levy had come to Baltimore because of financial reverses in Philadelphia, he was still a man of means, and he was able to offer Morris good quarters.[25] The relationship was so close that the Levys named their son Robert Morris Levy, in honor of their friend.

Benjamin's wife, Rachel, in an appeal in behalf of her son to George Washington, described herself as "a former acquaintance" of the president. In her letter she requested that he give the boy—whom she described as one who was "nearly of age, brought up for a merchant, without a Capital to put into trade, and his father unable to assist him"—some position in the government. She, naturally, did not

9

forget to mention that Mr. Morris was "personally acquainted" with her son.[26]

During their lifetimes, Benjamin and Rachel Levy saw the slow but constant growth of the Jewish population in the city. They themselves, however, did not have anything to do with Jews. Rachel Levy's father, Nathan Levy, had bought the first Jewish burial ground in Philadelphia in 1738, and in 1793 the daughter went from Baltimore to Philadelphia to secure a plot for herself and her husband in that cemetery. Yet both of them, upon their deaths, were buried in Baltimore in a non-Jewish cemetery.[27]

A contemporary of the Levys in Baltimore was one Isaac Abrams. Unlike them he was not only Orthodox himself, but he also minded the ritual behavior of the other Jews. Once he saw a Philadelphia Jew who was visiting Baltimore shaving on the Sabbath; he reported the infraction to another Philadelphian, who in turn reported it to the authorities of the only synagogue in that city.[28]

This is the only mark the man left in history. The episode tells us, however, about some accommodation even among the most Orthodox. Shaving with a razor, even on a weekday, is forbidden by the Bible, yet the "sinner" was denounced not for this but for breaking the Sabbath. Obviously, there were many Jews who were clean-shaven, and one finds it difficult to fight the many.

Two more Jews of the eighteenth century are attested to by the court records. In 1752 a "Jew Tailor," Henry Hart of Arundel County, was accused of an illicit relationship with a maid, as had Lumbrozo a century before. He was sentenced to serve a man named McNamara for six months "for the Damage Sustained . . . on Acct. of the said Henry Hart begetting a Bastard child on the body of Susanna Talome, a Servant belonging to the said McNamara."[29] Perhaps his case and that of Lumbrozo are the stories, not of two rascals, but of two lonely men living in a society in which they had no opportunity to marry and have a normal family life.

In the other case the Jew was the plaintiff. Sampson Levy won a judgment against a non-Jew in 1755 in a Baltimore court.[30]

Naturally, one cannot use court records as the sole source of vital statistics. Most people go through life without ever appearing before a judge. Yet the available evidence makes it quite clear that at the time of the Revolution the number of Jews in Maryland as a whole, as well as in Baltimore, its largest city, was pathetically small. Even so, it did have its "Haym Salomon," who in fact was connected to that remarkable Philadelphia patriot's family by marriage. When General

Lafayette visited Baltimore in 1791 and told the population of the army's needs, the merchants of the city subscribed for a loan. At the head of that list, with the largest contribution, appeared the name of the merchant Jacob Hart, who was the father-in-law of Mordecai N. Salomon, Haym Salomon's son.[31] As one Baltimore Jew helped the Revolution with money, another helped on the battlefield. Nathaniel Levy enlisted and served under Lafayette in the Baltimore cavalry.[32]

Two more Baltimore Jews of that period deserve special attention: Abraham Peters and Wolf Samuel. Among the immigrants who crossed the ocean there were a considerable number who paid for their miserable steerage transportation by selling themselves as temporary servants. The indenture period—between four and seven years—was not considered too high a price for those who wanted to flee the poverty and misery in Europe, hoping for a brighter future in America. For Jews, however, the price *was* too high. No matter how bad their situation in Europe, they generally would not exchange it for a better life at the cost of servitude in non-Jewish homes. Peters and Samuel were exceptions, however. While we know of only these two cases, there may well have been others of this kind.

Our only record of Peters is in a newspaper advertisement of April 1, 1775, in which a Mr. Purdue offered a reward for the capture of seven of his escaped servants. One of them, Abraham Peters, was described as a twenty-eight-year-old "bearded Jew," a cripple who spoke good Dutch.[33]

Much more is known about the second redemptionist, Wolf (William) Samuel. Like Peters, he escaped from his master, one Stephen Boyd, who also advertised for the escapee and offered a reward. In a letter to his parents in Germany written before his escape, Wolf described his life on the plantation. The letter would have pleased his parents. According to it, Wolf lived a very happy life, though he was in servitude. The owner of the plantation was a Dutch Jew who had been in the United States only seventeen years and had already become a millionaire. Wolf too hoped to achieve success. In the meantime, he was serving as supervisor over ninety-four Negroes working in the plantation. He was studying English one hour a day, and his kind master was paying the teacher. The Dutch Jew had provided him with good clothing and even a special pair of shoes for the Sabbath. The food and tobacco given to him were of excellent quality. The period of his servitude would last two years, and during this period he would be able to save up a substantial sum of money. All in all, Wolf wrote, he could not wish for anything better for himself.

With the exception of the master's name, there was not a single true word in the entire letter. Stephen Boyd was not a Jew. Official documents show that Boyd had paid twenty-six dollars for Wolf's passage; Wolf was to work, not two years, but three years and two months to pay it off. In a complaint to the court he later described his unbearable living conditions and his lack of clothing and food.

The letter was no doubt written by a devoted son who wanted to lessen his parents' anxiety about him. Their son's long epistle never reached them, however; the "kind" master intercepted it, and it came to light only after Stephen Boyd's death, when it was found among his papers.[34] Had Boyd been able to read the letter, which was written in Yiddish, it might have reached the parents.

Wolf Samuel's letter can be seen as a forerunner to the endless number of letters which, a century later, were sent home to Europe by immigrants to this country—immigrants who wrote of their great success in America but who, in fact, were slaving in sweatshops and living in miserable conditions.

BALTIMORE:
A GROWING CITY

The late eighteenth century was a period of great change in Baltimore. In 1753, almost twenty-five years after its founding, Baltimore Town was a small village, with a population of about two hundred and with no more than twenty-five scattered houses, two taverns, and one church.[35] A radical change occurred in the next few years. Trade was constantly on the increase. Warehouses were built, stores were opened. The port became a busy place. It provided an export center from which German, Scottish, and Irish settlers in western Pennsylvania began to ship their produce. Commerce was brisk. Baltimore was on the ascendency as an important commercial center in the country.[36] In 1769 William Eddis, an English purveyor of the port of Annapolis, described Baltimore as "not only the most wealthy and popular town of the province, but inferior to few in this continent, either in size, number of inhabitants, or the advantages arising from a well conducted city with universal connexions."[37]

Before long, the town possessed all the attributes of an established American city of that period. There was a two-story courthouse, a jail, a whipping post, a pillory, and stocks. In 1773 the first newspaper, *The Maryland Journal and Baltimore Advertiser*, came into existence. New roads connecting Baltimore with Frederick, Reisterstown, and York, Pennsylvania, were built, and a stagecoach connected the town even with faraway Philadelphia. By 1790 the first United States census showed Baltimore to be a city of 13,503 inhabitants.[38] It nearly doubled in the next decade, when it rose to 26,114.[39] Commerce became so predominant that the people of the city were referred to as "the merchants of Baltimore."[40] The rising tide of trade attracted a number of merchants from Pennsylvania. Jewish merchants in that area were naturally aware of what was going on in the neighboring state.

In such an atmosphere of growth, of increased commerce and prosperity, people paid less attention to the national origin and religion of new settlers. Baltimore was becoming a city of immigrants. Abilities, courage, willingness to work and to take a chance counted more than a birth certificate. This attitude, coupled with greater economic opportunities, began to attract Jews.

It would still be a long time before Baltimore became a major Jewish center. There were only about 1,500 Jews at the time of the Revolution in the entire country.[41] But Baltimore had much to offer, and Jews began to drift in. The new era commenced with two remarkable families who left a permanent mark on the history of Baltimore Jewry and, indeed, on the city in general.

A TALE OF TWO WIDOWS AND THEIR SONS

The Ettings

The first of the two most prominent Jewish families in Baltimore were the Ettings. The family's progenitor in the United States was Elijah Etting (1724–1778), who hailed from Frankfurt on the Main and came to the United States in 1758. He settled in York, Pennsylvania, and became an important Indian trader. Two years after his death, his thirty-six-year-old widow, Shinah, moved with her five daughters to Baltimore. Her two sons, Reuben and Solomon, remained in York. The reason for this move is unknown, but it proved to be one that brought her family wealth and fame.

Shinah was an extremely energetic person of independent character. In her new abode, accompanied by five children aged fourteen, twelve, ten, eight, and four, she opened a boardinghouse "for gentlemen" at Market (now Baltimore) and Calvert Streets.[42] She maintained it for many years, even after her son Solomon, who subsequently also moved to Baltimore, had attained considerable wealth.[43] Shinah must have liked the city, because before long not only her two sons but also her three brothers settled there. By the time of her death, in 1822, she saw the rise of both of her sons and especially the younger, Solomon, to positions of great eminence in the community.[44]

Solomon Etting (1764–1847) was born in York. He was a gifted young man, and at the age of eighteen he already had secured for himself a place in American Jewish history. In 1782 he became the first native American to become a *shoḥet*. Of equal interest is the fact that he was granted authorization to slaughter in accordance with the ritual laws by an important Jewish leader of the eighteenth century, Barnard Gratz (1738–1811) of Philadelphia, who also acted as the ritual slaughterer for his own family. In spite of his many important businesses, this man found time to train the young son of his friend Elijah Etting in the skill of kosher slaughtering.[45]

Solomon married Rachel Simon, daughter of the prominent Indian trader Joseph Simon of Lancaster, Pennsylvania, where the newlyweds settled. Business often cemented marriages, and marriages, in turn, cemented businesses. Young Etting became his father-in-law's partner. America was still young. Its society was an open one, and neither Ettings's youth nor his religion stood in the newcomer's way. He rose in the Masonic Lodge and achieved standing in the community.[46]

Solomon Etting's wife died only seven years after their marriage, at the age of twenty-six. The young widower (he too was twenty-six) was left with four children. He moved from Lancaster to Philadelphia. A year after his wife's death in 1790, he married the second Rachel of his life, the daughter of his older friend and mentor, Barnard Gratz. Finally, there was one more move, this time to the city where his mother and her brothers lived—Baltimore.

As had his uncles, Solomon opened a hardware store at Calvert below Lovely Lane. But soon it was noticeable that this hardware

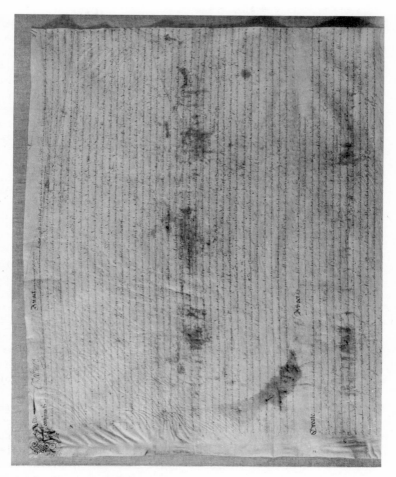

An Act Concerning Religion, 1649.
Courtesy of the Maryland Historical Society.

Mrs. Judith Cohen, 1760–1837.
Collection of the Maryland Historical Society, Frick Art
Reference Library photograph.

Mrs. Shinah Etting, 1744–1822.
Courtesy of the Maryland Historical Society.

Two widows who founded important Jewish families

storekeeper had greater ambitions and was destined for greater achieve-
ments. In 1796, while still a storekeeper—a business in which he was
to remain for another nine years—he became a director of the Union
Bank, and all the members of his family became stockholders of it.[47]

In 1795 he gave up his store and entered shipping and commerce
on a large scale. A year later he was one of a small group of Baltimoreans who established the water company of the city. Another year
—another venture. In 1807 he organized the Baltimore East India
Company, in which he invested $10,000—a considerable investment
for those days.[48] This was followed by many more important business
ventures, among them a directorship in the first American railroad
company, the Baltimore and Ohio.

No less varied than Etting's business undertakings were his civic
activities. His abilities were recognized by the community long before
he became a notable leader in the business world. He had been in the
city only two years when he was elected one of a committee of seven
leading Baltimore citizens who forwarded to President Washington a
resolution of disapproval of the John Jay treaty with Britain. In 1794
he served as a member of the standing committee of the Baltimore Republican Society. This was a Jeffersonian club, the members of which
pledged themselves "to promote Republican principles and the rights
of humanity."[49]

When Baltimore was attacked by the British in 1814, Solomon
Etting served as a representative of his ward on the citywide Committee
of Vigilance and Safety. Etting was entrusted by this committee with
especially important assignments. He was given the tasks of providing
suitable accommodations for the men in the army and founding a hospital for the sick and the wounded.[50] (His son Samuel, a young man
of eighteen at the time of the British attack, was also active on the
Vigilance and Safety Committee and served as secretary of his ward
committee. He participated in the battle at Fort McHenry, in which
he was slightly wounded.) Solomon Etting negotiated, on behalf of
the committee, with Robert Fulton and the Navy Department for the
construction of the first Fulton steam frigate.[51]

There was, in fact, hardly any cause of social importance in which
Solomon Etting was not involved. Though a native American, Etting
was quite active in the affairs of the German immigrants in the city.
He was an incorporator of the German Society of Maryland in 1817
and served as its vice-president for twenty years.[52] In 1830, at the age
of sixty-six, he was still busily engaged in civic affairs and was serving
as chairman of the Infirmary Committee in charge of the Baltimore

17

infirmary attached to the University of Maryland—the first hospital in the state. In his capacity as chairman, Etting negotiated with the secretary of the treasury to secure federal support for the infirmary.[53]

A year later, in 1831, he became a "manager" (as members of a board were called in those days) of the Maryland State Colonization Society. This group was concerned with the lot of the Negroes in the country and sought to solve the problem of freed slaves by resettling American Negroes in Africa.[54] At the head of the organization stood the most prominent contemporary Baltimorean, John B. Latrobe, a distinguished lawyer, author, painter, and great philanthropist.[55]

Although the society was for many years subsidized by the state, it accomplished little. The freed Negroes who were supposed to be sent to Africa resisted its efforts in their behalf. At a meeting held March 31, 1831, a group of Negroes passed a resolution which said:

We consider the land in which we were born and in which we have been bred our only true and appropriate home. We sincerely regret their [the Colonization Society's] effort. . . .

Out of a total of 52,938 free Negroes in 1830 and 74,723 in 1850, the society was able to recruit only 1,250—and that at a cost of over $300,000. It did establish a colony in Cape Palmas, Nigeria. In honor of the promoters of the project, the colony was named Maryland County. An Etting Street in the heart of Africa was named after the "manager."[56]

All in all, we see in Etting a dedicated citizen, one who cared and showed great concern for the welfare of the needy. It must be remembered, however, that there was one group of Baltimoreans to whom one would expect him to be the closest, but with whom he had nothing to do socially—the Jews of Baltimore.

From a handful of about thirty in 1790,[57] the number of Jews had grown to about fifteen hundred by 1847.[58] Slowly but steadily Baltimore was becoming better and better known in the Jewish world, both in America and abroad. As far back as 1813, Baltimore Jewry had acquired a reputation as a charitable community among whom a poor Jew was never lost. It is characteristically Jewish that the reputation of a community depended on the opinion of professional beggars. Through their own grapevine, people knew which community deserved the "favor" of their attention and which was to be avoided. Baltimore, it seems, was among the former. Thus when a certain shiftless *shnorrer* became dissatisfied with the "miserly" assistance given to him by the Shearith Israel Congregation in New York, he came to "terms" with it. He was given thirty dollars on the condition that he leave the city, which he did, moving from New York to the "good" Jewish community of Baltimore.[59] The city was on the Jewish map.

Yet, strange to relate, Baltimore's most prominent Jew did not have any social contact with its other Jews. A congregation was organized in 1830. A splendid synagogue was built in 1845. Various assistance societies came into being. But Etting's name does not appear among those who participated in these affairs. To be sure, he was a "pious" man and maintained a private *minyan* in his own home.[60] He remained loyal to Mikveh Israel, the Philadelphia synagogue of which he had been a seat holder while he lived in that city.[61] It was one thing to support a distant synagogue, however, but quite another matter to join a local congregation and be identified with the poor immigrants. To him these people were of little, if any, consequence.

Indeed, as far as he was concerned, they simply did not exist. In 1817 for example, when the oldest Jewish congregation in the United States, New York's Shearith Israel, asked Etting to contribute toward the rebuilding of its synagogue, Etting sent it the sum of $150, at that time a very substantial contribution. His accompanying letter noted that very little could be expected of Baltimore since there were only three Jewish families there.[62] He could live in his fashionable home on Charles and Saratoga Streets and recognize only three Baltimore Jewish families—but ignore about a hundred more.[63] He must have known that there were more Jews in the city. Indeed, sixteen years earlier he had performed an act of greatest importance for them.

One of the first problems for Jews in a new settlement was the acquisition of land for a "House of Life," as a cemetery is euphemistically called by Jews. It was difficult and at times impossible for a Jewish peddler far away from home to observe *kashrut*. He was often compelled to desecrate the Sabbath. It was sometimes difficult to secure permission to build a synagogue. An observant Jew found it hard to live under such conditions. Yet one could pray in the privacy of his own home and wait for better times when he would not have to break any of the commandments. There was, however, one problem which could not wait, which demanded an immediate solution. Since it was repugnant for a Jew to be buried in a non-Jewish cemetery, in most communities the acquisition of a cemetery even preceded the erection of a house of worship. This was true of Baltimore.

The first synagogue in the city was established in 1830, but nearly half a century before that, as far back as 1786, there was already a Jewish cemetery. It was located near the then city limits of Baltimore in Ensor Town, now north of Monument Street, between Ensor Street and Hartford Avenue. The land was the property of Charles Carroll of Carrollton, William MacMechen, and John Leggitt. In 1801 Etting and his uncle Levy Solomon bought this land, commonly called "Jews' Burying Ground."[64]

The first cemetery was the only Jewish public burial ground until 1832, when the first congregation in the city established its own cemetery. It was again in use for a very short while by the first Reform congregation in the city, formed in 1842. There is no tablet, no sign of any kind, to identify the place of this cemetery or the names of those who were buried there. We do, however, know the names of three members of one family who found their eternal rest there. When Etting granted permission to the Reform Har Sinai Verein to use the cemetery, he made two conditions. First, he forbade them "to bury non-Israelites on the cemetery." Second, the congregation was obligated to take care of the three graves of his uncles, the Solomon brothers, "buried in the center of the cemetery."[65]

Although Etting generally dissociated himself from Baltimore Jews, he was deeply conscious of his being a Jew and very sensitive to any offensive utterances directed against Jews. When his friend Senator Henry Clay made a remark on the floor of the United States Senate about a Jew which appeared to Etting to be disparaging, he immediately protested to the senator. He did not mince words and stated clearly on whose behalf he was writing.

Several of the religious society to which I belong, myself included, feel both surprized and hurt by the manner in which you introduced the expression 'The Jew' . . . evidently applying it as a reproachful designation of a man whom you consider obnoxious in character and conduct.

The correspondence between Etting and Clay reveals a new kind of relationship between Jews and non-Jews, a relationship characteristic of Jews in America. The tone of the letter is not that of an underling or even a "Court Jew." Here was a Jewish merchant writing to a senator protesting against remarks made on the floor of the Senate. Characteristic, too, was the senator's reply. It was as straightforward as Etting's letter, saying:

I regret extremely to perceive . . . that a remark of mine . . . was liable to an unfavorable interpretation in respect to Jews generally. . . . The remark was intended to describe a person and not to denounce a Nation. . . . I judge men not exclusively by their Nation, religion, ℰc, but by their individual conduct. I have always had the happiness to enjoy the friendship of many Jews . . . but I cannot doubt that there are bad Jews as well as bad Christians and bad Mahometans.[66]

Etting died in 1847 at the age of eighty-three.[67] He reaped the fruits of the attainment of political equality by the Jews in Maryland when he became one of the first two Jews elected to the City Council in 1826. His purchase of a cemetery for the Jews, his proud declaration that he belonged to the Jewish "religious society," and his struggle for Jewish equality in Maryland contrasts with his estrangement from the Jews of the city in which he lived, suggesting that if Etting was *for* the Jews, he was not *of* them. His children, unlike their father, did become active in Baltimore Jewish affairs.

Shinah Etting's elder son, Reuben (1762–1848), was not the financial success that his younger brother Solomon became.[68] He, too, married into the Gratz family. His wife, Frances Gratz, was the second Rachel Etting's first cousin. For a number of years he had a millinery store in partnership with a Mr. Kennedy at 10 Calvert Street.[69] He did not, however, strike permanent roots in this city and lived all his life intermittently in Baltimore and Philadelphia. Yet he, too, played an important role in and added to the prestige of the small Jewish group in Baltimore.

In 1798, when a war with France seemed to be imminent, Reuben Etting became captain of a company of patriots known as the Independent Blues.[70] Of far greater importance was his appointment in 1801 by Thomas Jefferson as marshal of Maryland. This was a major breakthrough for the Jews in Maryland. In a state where a Jew could not hold any public office, it was a great achievement for a Jew to be appointed by the president to an important position of trust.[71] This fact was not forgotten during the great debate on Jewish rights. It served as one more argument in favor of the Jews. By 1848, when Reuben Etting died, it was not a novelty for a Jew to hold an office of public trust in the state. His son Elijah served as district attorney of Cecil County. Others of his descendants distinguished themselves in the military as well as in civic affairs.

Eleven portraits by famous artists of members of the Etting family adorn the halls of the Maryland Historical Society.[72] They and the Etting cemetery are the visible reminders of this prominent family.[73] Solomon's own "invisible" monument, which is of greatest importance, is Jewish equality in Maryland. In this cause he was the first to raise his voice, and he continued the struggle until its successful conclusion.

The Cohens

The importance of the Ettings was matched and even surpassed by that of the Cohen family, whose history in Baltimore was also started by a widow. Israel I. Cohen (1750–1803), born in Oberdorff, Bavaria, and his wife, Judith Solomon (1760–1837), born in Bristol, England, settled in Richmond, Virginia, about 1784.[74] After Israel's death, his forty-three-year-old widow and her children, of whom the oldest, Jacob, was only fourteen years old, moved to Baltimore. During the thirty-four years she spent in the city, Judith Cohen, like Shinah Etting, witnessed the phenomenal rise of her sons and grandchildren. As in the case of the Ettings, nothing is known of the causes that made the Cohens uproot themselves and move to Baltimore. In both instances, however, it was a step that enriched the city and brought glory to the families.[75]

The first business venture of the family was into lottery, an important method of raising public funds in those days. The enterprise was a success, and a branch was opened in Philadelphia. In 1831 lottery gave way to banking. At the head of the firm stood the eldest of the brothers, Jacob (1789–1869), and the banking firm was known as Jacob I. Cohen, Jr. and Brothers.[76] It became one of the most reputable financial concerns in the country and the fiscal agent of the Rothschilds in the United States.[77] The Cohen bank proved its reliability, especially in the crisis year of 1837. It was one of the few banks that paid its depositors at the time of the suspension of specie payments.

The careers of Solomon Etting and Jacob Cohen, Jr., were very similar. Like Etting, Cohen was engaged in many important financial ventures. He too was a director of the Baltimore and Ohio Railroad. In addition, Cohen served as president of the Baltimore-Philadelphia Railroad, the Baltimore Insurance Company, and other important companies. His abilities were widely recognized. He was elected to many important public posts, including the presidency of the convention to promote the trade and commerce interests of the city of Baltimore.[78] For many years he served as secretary-treasurer of the board of the city's public schools.

Also like Etting, Jacob Cohen and his brothers were active in the German Society of Maryland. Jacob was one of its founders, his brother Benjamin served as treasurer for twenty years, and Benjamin's son Israel, in turn, succeeded him and served for more than thirty years. When the Germans in the city celebrated the 1848 revolution in their fatherland, Cohen, a native American, was the vice-chairman of the organization committee.[79] In addition, both Etting and Jacob Cohen fought the long battle for Jewish civic equality, and upon winning it both were elected to the City Council in 1826. Moreover, Cohen served as president of that body from 1845 to 1861.

Jacob Cohen followed the pattern set by Solomon Etting, who was a quarter of a century older, in other respects as well. He was a seat holder in the Mikveh Israel Synagogue in Philadelphia and assisted other out-of-town congregations.[80] He did not, however, play any part in a Baltimore congregation or in any other local Jewish organization. William Rayner, who came to Baltimore in 1840, related that when he arrived

there were about a dozen of native Jews. . . . Though of German origin, they kept to themselves, strictly apart from the newcomers, considering it rather below their dignity to have any social relations with them.[81]

The only exception was Cohen's participation in a short-lived attempt of the 1850s to establish a Sephardic congregation in the city.[82]

Both the Cohens and the Ettings established private cemeteries for their own families. The latter family acquired a plot on the north side of North and Pennsylvania Avenues in 1799. The Cohens purchased a tract for the exclusive burial of Judith Cohen and her posterity on Saratoga near Carey Street. Both cemeteries are still maintained.[83]

In the history of the Baltimore Jewish community, Jacob Cohen will be remembered primarily for the role he played in winning civic equality for the Jews. His younger brother Joshua continued the fight to eradicate from the statute books any laws which might be construed as an abridgment of Jewish equality. In 1846, twenty years after the consummation of the struggle for Jewish rights, Dr. Joshua Cohen brought about a change in an antiquated 1717 law. According to that law, a Negro was not permitted to testify in court against a white Christian. Dr. Cohen succeeded in his efforts to change that law, and the Maryland Assembly, by an act of January 23, 1847, expunged the word "Christian" from the old law. Thus, Maryland Jews were in this respect placed on a par with white Christians.[84]

Dr. Cohen continued his lobbying activities at the subsequent two state Constitutional Conventions in 1851 and 1864. On both occasions he was anxious to eradicate old discriminatory laws. When the Constitutional Convention of 1864 convened in Annapolis for the purpose of drawing up a new constitution for the state, Joshua Cohen was active in an effort to revoke the special Jewish oath. He "mentioned the subject to several of the Baltimore delegations and to some few others." In his memorandum to Governor Augustus William Bradford, a follow-up to his personal visit, he expressed the hope that Bradford would assist in removing "this last remnant of a by-gone prejudice." He suggested that the law be changed to read: "No religious test should be required as a qualification for office."[85] In this effort he, like others in later generations, succeeded only in part. Some of the old laws are still part of Maryland's legal code, even if not observed.[86]

Unlike his older brother, Jacob, Joshua did not confine his Jewish activities to the defense of Jewish political rghts. He was also very active in all local Jewish affairs, carried on a lively correspondence with Isaac Leeser, and amassed one of the finest Jewish libraries of that day.[87]

An eminent physician (one of the first ear specialists in the country), Dr. Joshua Cohen served a term as president of the Medical and Chirurgical Faculty of the University of Maryland. He was a charter member of the Maryland Historical Society and held many other important civic positions. In his obituary in *The National Medical Journal* he was praised as a great doctor, a man devoted to the "teaching and piety of the Law given to Sinai." This journal paid tribute to his broadmindedness, praising him because "no narrow boundary of creed closed around his heart, shutting out the claims and brotherhood of humanity."[88]

Two other brothers, Benjamin (1797–1845) and David (1800–1847), were founders of the Baltimore Stock Exchange in 1837. Benjamin married Solomon Etting's daughter Kitty (1799–1837), who died at the age of thirty-eight, leaving him with eleven children.

Another brother, Mendes (1796–1879), left the field of finance and retired while still a young man. For six years (1829–1835) he traveled abroad. During these years he reported in long and detailed letters to his mother and brother about subjects as far afield as the different dialects used in England and the Jewish situation in the countries he visited. (There is a wealth of information in these communications about Jews in Russia, Turkey, Palestine, and Egypt, a well as practically all countries of Central and Western Europe.)[89] Mendes Cohen was the first American to enter and investigate the Nile Valley. His collection of 689 relics collected in Egypt was given in 1884 to Johns Hopkins University. Like his older brother Jacob,

Mendes served in the government. He was a member of the Maryland legislature in 1847/1848.

The Cohens were observant Jews. They held daily services in their palatial residence on North Charles Street. When short of a *minyan,* they invited Jews from the neighborhood to participate in the services.[90] They made their observance of rituals known on appropriate occasions. Mendes Cohen took exception to an auction sale of a theater in which he was interested, for the sale took place on the Sabbath, and it was impossible for him to attend.[91] When David Cohen served on the Committee on Rules of the Baltimore Stock Exchange, he brought about the adoption of a rule that a member was not to be fined if he absented himself from a meeting on a day when his business was closed. Thus he enabled Jewish businessmen to observe their religious obligations without penalty.[92]

The early Cohens and the Ettings presented to the non-Jewish community an image of Jews as public servants, loyal and dependable people. All this, however, did not prove to be sufficient when the question of Jewish equality came up in the Maryland legislature.

THE STRUGGLE
FOR EQUALITY

The war for national independence was won. A new nation had come into being. The promise of equality to "all the inhabitants thereof" was heard in this new land, the United States of America. What was dreamed of in Philadelphia, however, remained for a long time only a dream. True, the new Constitution was adopted, but the old laws were too deeply rooted to be given up easily. The states clung jealously to the old, well-established ways of life, and where new laws came in conflict with the old, it was usually the old which prevailed. Maryland was no exception, least of all in the area of Jewish equality.

The Maryland constitution, adopted in 1776, preceded the federal Constitution by thirteen years. Its preamble, known as the Declaration of Rights, states (section 33):

It is the duty of every man to worship God in such manner as he thinks most acceptable to Him: all persons professing the Christian religion are equally entitled to protection in their religious liberty.

The test oath was stated in clear language in article 35.

No other test or qualification ought to be required on admission to any office of trust or profit than such oath of support and fidelity to the State . . . and a declaration of belief in the Christian religion.

Nothing had changed since the days of the Toleration Act of 1649! By this oath, Jews were excluded from municipal and state office. It is very doubtful whether the handful of Jews in the colony objected to this disqualification. True, it was a discriminatory law, but it did not affect any of them. None of them aspired to a government position. They were strangers, and all they wanted was to be left alone and to be given the opportunity to make a living. Political aspirations came later, with the striking of roots and with economic and social advancement. This pattern, in a general way, repeated itself with every succeeding wave of immigrants. At first the newcomer is docile, willing to accept all kinds of jobs and all kinds of insults—only to become, in the course of time, rebellious and demanding of his due. The poor Jewish peddlers and storekeepers, mostly immigrants from Bavaria, were certainly not concerned with the test oath.

Not so Solomon Etting. In him we find the first Maryland Jew who did care about civic equality. This was not because he was interested in a public position. More than that was involved. It was an insult to him, a native American, a man who was socially prominent and financially successful. In addition, one must add the influence of his father-in-law, Barnard Gratz, who in the 1790s moved from Philadelphia to Baltimore. Gratz was an old hand in the battle for Jewish equality. In Philadelphia he was one of a Jewish group who for seven years fought for—and finally, in 1790, won—civil liberties in Pennsylvania.[93] Now that he was in Baltimore, he joined his son-in-law in the struggle for Jewish rights in Maryland. This one lasted not seven but—with interruptions—a full thirty years. Gratz died in 1801 and did not live to see equality granted to Jews a quarter century later.

In 1797 "Solomon Etting and others" presented to the Maryland Assembly a petition stating that they were

a sect of people called Jews and thereby are deprived of invaluable rights of citizenship and praying to be placed on the same footing as other good citizens.[94]

In its report, the committee that had been appointed to consider it stated that the petition was "reasonable." The question, however, was not dealt with at that session of the legislature, since it was in an

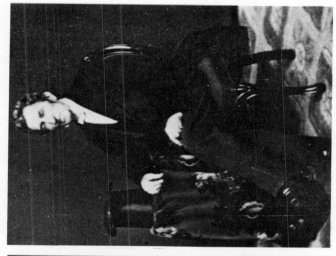

Solomon Etting, 1764–1847.
Collection of the Maryland Historical Society, Frick Art
Reference Library photograph.

Jacob I. Cohen, Jr, 1789–1869.
Courtesy of the Maryland Historical Society.

Two fighters for Jewish equality in Maryland

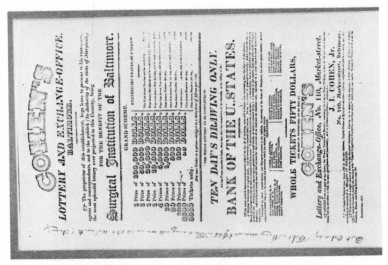

A million-dollar lottery advertisement of the Cohen bank, 1817.
Courtesy of the American Jewish Archives.

Mrs. Rachel Gratz Etting, 1764—1831.
Collection of the Maryland Historical Society, Frick Art Reference Library photograph.

"advanced stage." Subsequent petitions met with the same fate. After the defeat in 1804, the fight stopped until renewed with greater vigor fourteen years later.

By then much had changed in the position of Baltimore Jewry. In the first place, more Jews had come to the city. People met them as neighbors and did business with them. Some might have known personally or heard of Reuben Etting, whom the president himself had appointed marshal, or Simon T. Levy, the hero of Maumee Rapids (The Battle of Fallen Timbers), who was one of two Marylanders in the first class of the Military Academy at West Point.[95] Non-Jewish Masons had no doubt met Jewish Masons.[96] By this time, too, the Ettings and the Cohens played a very important role in the community. Above all else, however, was the fact that Jews were at Fort McHenry on that historic night of September 13/14, 1814, when "our flag was still there."[97]

The Jews definitely were no longer strangers to the general population of the city. One could be for them or against them, but could no longer ignore them. Among those who were strongly for Jewish equality was a Scottish immigrant who saw in the discrimination against Jews a blemish in the America of his dreams. This non-Jew, Thomas Kennedy (1776–1832), became the champion of the cause of Jewish equality in Maryland.

Kennedy, born in the year of the American Revolution, came to the United States at the age of twenty. He oriented himself quickly to the political life of the country and became a Jeffersonian.[98] In homely but sincere poetry he wrote about his ideal.

> *Few like Jefferson we find*
> *Among the sons of human kind,*
> *Friend of peace and liberty*
> *Is the son of liberty.*[99]

In 1817 Kennedy was elected to the Maryland legislature, representing Washington County. Before long, he started a historic fight which lasted a full eight years. Those were tumultuous years for Kennedy. It was an uphill battle.

On December 9, 1818, Kennedy asked for the appointment of a committee "to consider the justice and expediency of placing the Jewish inhabitants on equal footing with the Christians." A committee was appointed, with Kennedy as its chairman. The other two members were Henry Brackenridge and Ebenezer S. Thomas, both from the county of Baltimore City. Jacob Cohen, the oldest of the Cohen brothers, was Thomas's friend, and in a long letter he briefed him on the subject which the committee was to consider. Cohen stressed the point that, while Jews felt secure in Maryland and were not "insensible of the protection in . . . person and property under the law . . . ," they did object to the

obnoxious parts of the State's constitution produced only in times of darkness and prejudice [which are] blots on the present enlightened period, on the honor of the State, in direct opposition to the features and principles in the constitution of the United States.

He reminded Thomas of the Jews' most important claim to equality: "In times of peril and war the Jews had borne the privation incident to such times . . . in the defense of the common cause."

In his long letter, Cohen raised a question about a particularly dangerous form of discrimination. According to the state law, jurors and lawyers were considered state officers and were to take the test oath, which precluded a Jew from serving in either capacity. Very delicately, but at the same time very pointedly, Cohen expressed his doubts whether a full measure of justice was at all possible under such circumstances. "I wish not to be misunderstood," he wrote, "that he [a Jew] could not obtain justice, such is not my meaning . . . [but] perhaps prejudice might influence in their [the jurors'] verdict."[100]

On October 23, 1818, Kennedy presented the committee report. In his eloquent and long address (and his comments were usually extremely long), Kennedy stressed the point that religion

is a question which rests, or ought to rest between man and his Creator alone. . . . It is surely strange that a Jew who may even be raised to the highest and most honorable situation in the universe, the chief magistrate of a free people, cannot hold any office of profit or trust under the Constitution of Maryland.

He spoke with much pathos of this "peculiar" people who gave the world not only the prophets, but also "the Savior of the world." In rapture he quoted biblical passages about the restoration of the Jews in their "ancestral lands" and told the legislators in blunt words, "If we condemn them [the Jews], we condemn ourselves." It was a magnificent plea. The resolution offered by the committee said: "It is just . . . it is expedient, that Jews and Christians be placed on equal footing in regard to their civil rights."

Following the report Delegate William Pinkney drafted a bill, which declared that

no religious test, declaration or subscription of opinion as to religion, shall be required from any person or sect called Jews, as a qualification to hold or exercise any office or employment of trust in this state . . . and . . . that every oath to be administered to any person of the sect of people called Jews, shall be administered on the five books of Moses, agreeably to the religious education of that people, and not otherwise.[101]

This bill became known, as was its counterpart in England in 1753, as the "Jew Bill" and was contemptuously called "Kennedy's Jew Baby."[102] Its chief defenders besides Kennedy were Col. William G. D. Worthington, Judge Henry M. Brackenridge, and John S. Tyson, all of Baltimore City, and Ebenezer S. Thomas and the twenty-four-year-old Van Lea McMahon, both from Allegheny County.[103]

Their passionate plea for Jewish equality was based first on the law of the land, on the Constitution of the United States, which states that there shall be no religious qualification for office. This, however, was only the basic premise. The other arguments for the bill were based on an exposition of both Jewish and Christian religions. The former, it was pointed out, in no way precluded good citizenship, and the latter did not require of its followers the abridgment of the rights of the Jews. Devout Christian that he was, Kennedy went so far as to say:

I am free to declare that if Christianity cannot stand without the aid of persecution . . . let it fall; and let a new system, more rational and more benevolent, take its place.

Lest he be suspected of favoring Jews for personal reasons, Kennedy reminded the legislators that there were no Jews in the county he represented and that he was not personally acquainted with any Jew. He asserted further that his plea on behalf of the Jews was not made at their request and that "it was not even known to them that the subject would be brought forward at this time."

The legislators were not impressed by the assertion that he did not personally know any Jew. Nor were they influenced by Judge Brackenridge, who favored the bill because he had "the honor to be acquainted with a number of American Jews . . . who in point of responsibility and worth are inferior to none." Neither were they moved by the explanation that hatred of the Jews was a result of indoctrination:

Most of us have been taught from early infancy to entertain an unfavorable opinion of them [the Jews]. The books we read—the immortal Shakespeare himself—[have] been instrumental in fixing this anti-Christian hatred to a portion of our fellow men.

After prolonged debate, the question finally came up for a vote on January 13, 1819, and the bill was defeated by a vote of fifty to twenty-four. The voting was almost exclusively along party lines. The Jeffersonians were in favor; the Federalists, with the exception of two, voted against the bill.[104]

On December 3, 1822, Kennedy introduced a broader bill. In it the Jews were not mentioned at all. The all-embracing bill was "An Act to extend to the citizens of Maryland the same civil rights and privileges that are enjoyed under the Constitution of the United States." In his report on behalf of the committee, Kennedy, who was no diplomat, did not shun the Jewish angle of the bill. He stated quite clearly that while this was not a "Jew Bill," the "peculiar people with all other sects [will] benefit by it." Surprisingly, the bill passed the first reading. Since it involved a constitutional change, however, it had to be confirmed at the next session of the legislature. At that session, the opponents of the bill gathered enough strength to defeat it.

Jewish equality became a political shibboleth between the two warring political parties. In essence it was not even a struggle about Jews. Jewish emancipation happened to be the hot issue about which the two parties fought for supremacy in affairs of the state. The defenders of the bill were declared to be a danger to the community. A slanderous campaign was waged against the "Jew ticket." In the 1823 election Kennedy was opposed by one Benjamin Calloway, who, in a paid advertisement, savagely attacked Kennedy and his idea of giving Jews equality. He considered it to be

no more, no less than an attempt to bring into popular contempt the Christian religion. . . . I deprecate any change in our state government calculated to afford the least chance to the enemies of Christianity."[105]

Kennedy was defeated. He was, however, reelected in the next election.

The voice of the Jews was heard at the 1824 session, even if they did not appear personally. Col. W. G. D. Worthington presented a memorial (as petitions were called in those days) signed by Jacob Cohen, Solomon Etting (the man who had drafted the first memorial on the subject in 1797), and Etting's uncle Levi Solomon. The petitioners took a stand not only on rights for Jews but on the entire issue of rights in a free country. They made it clear that they were not seeking any special privileges,   ·

because such a privilege would be hostile, not only to the principles of our institutions, but to the express provisions of that charter which we all have sworn to support but it is equal rights that they petition; their voice is not raised in favor, but in opposition to exclusive privileges. . . . To disqualify any class of your citizens is for the people to disqualify themselves.

They urged confirmation of the bill "as fellow citizens of Maryland, as Brethren of the same human family, for the honor of the State, for the great interest of humanity. . ."[106] (see Appendix II).

In his speech before the assembly in defense of the bill, Worthington also presented a most informative document concerning the Jews in the country generally and in Maryland specifically. It consisted of questions by Worthington to which answers had been given by Solomon Etting. The latter estimated that the total Jewish population in the United States was about six thousand and that of Maryland "at least one hundred and fifty." It was also estimated that the wealth of the Jews was ten and a half million dollars. This information Worthington coupled with a warning that, should the assembly

negative the bill, who could blame those gentlemen of the Hebrew Church . . . from quitting your state, with their families, their connections, and wealth, and choose some other state, where they enjoy equal rights and favour, with all its citizens.

To strengthen his argument, the champion of the bill cited George Washington's friendly letters to various Jewish communities. He told of Judah Touro, who assisted a Protestant church when it was in need. He reminded the delegates of Jefferson's appointment of a fellow Baltimorean, Reuben Etting, to a federal post a quarter of a century earlier. Then he related the suffering of one who was known to all as a most devoted citizen, Solomon Etting. He related that the latter, "with pain in his heart and tears in his eyes," had told his son, who wanted to study law, that he would not be able to practice law in his native Maryland because a lawyer is considered a state officer, and as a Jew he could hold no state position. Worthington, like other defenders of the bill, spoke at length about Christianity, which does not approve of discrimination.

Turning to local politics, Worthington asserted that "the majority of the people in Maryland are in favour of the proposal" and insisted that "little sectional politics" should not influence the legislators. He expressed his contempt for those who

favour the Test, because it operates as a sort of monopoly of offices. The more people you disqualify, the more remain for them and their friends.

He concluded his long and masterful address with a pointed allusion to a verse from Jeremiah: "It rests with you who have the power to restore health to the daughter of her people."

Worthington was followed by John S. Tyson, who spoke of Jewish persecutions throughout the ages, of Jews

sewed up in the skins of wild beasts and thrown to the dogs in Asia, chained to the galling car for life in Africa, burned to death in Spain, flayed alive in Italy, fleeced and sentenced to banishment from time to time in England, plunged into the catacombs in France, knouted in Russia. . . .

In pain he called out: "Is not this enough? . . . Ought not the world be tired of such scenes?" He laughed at the idea expressed by some opponents of the bill that the Jews, if they were given equality, would impose their religion upon the rest of the population. He referred to this idea as "preposterous in the extreme . . . too weak to terrify even infant apprehension."

Tyson declared that he did not fear the equality of Jews but their inequality. He saw the struggle for Jewish equality merely as a symptom. The struggle, he contended, was over a most fundamental issue of concern to all, Jew and non-Jew alike.

The right to put up one religion, is the right to put down another. The right to put down one, is the right to put down all, and the right to put down all, is the right to build one upon its ruins.

In conclusion, Tyson paid homage to Kennedy who, he said,

Atlas-like bore it [the struggle for the Jew Bill] upon his shoulders at a time when it was too heavy for all other men. It fell, he raised it, it fell again, he raised it again and again.

The bill passed by a margin of one—twenty-six to twenty-five— with eighty legislators absenting themselves on that historic day of February 26, 1825. That, however, was not the end of it. It took another year before the bill was finally confirmed on January 5, 1826, by a vote of forty-five to thirty-two (see Appendix III).

The struggle for Jewish equality was over, although the final act was not identical with the original bill presented in 1818. According to the original bill, "every oath administered to any person of the sect of people called Jews shall be administered on the five books of Moses." The final bill was a compromise, according to which

every citizen . . . professing the Jewish Religion and . . . hereafter . . . appointed to any office of public trust under the state of Maryland shall in addition to the oath required to be taken by the Constitution and laws of the State or the United States, make and subscribe a declaration of his belief in a future state of rewards and punishments, in the stead of the declaration now required by the constitution and form of government of this state.[107]

Maryland was not the last state in which Jews were granted equality. In Rhode Island they secured it only in 1842, while in North Carolina they had to wait until 1868. No other struggle for their rights, however, was as protracted, as bitter, and as widely known as that in Maryland. In reporting on the Jew Bill, the national press generally followed the lead of *Niles' Weekly Register*, by far the most widely quoted periodical of the time. The editor, Hezekiah Niles, had always been outspoken in his defense of Jews. "The Jews," he wrote,

have been called the blot of the nations, yet the Redeemer was one of them and as his principles prevail and his commands are obeyed, we shall feel for both a deeper veneration and a stronger regard. The descendants of that noble and marked race . . . wherever they have power, they exert it to elevate their race. Wherever they have means, they employ them freely to spread among themselves education. . . . We trust . . . that they will meet only with a wider and warmer sympathy.[108]

As for the Jew Bill, he always favored it and referred to the constitutional restrictions imposed upon the Jews as "irreligious," "anti-Christian and anti-republican."[109] When the Jew Bill had passed, the *Register* greeted the news by announcing

the political liberation of persons held in servitude for CONSCIENCE' SAKE, *so a late and disgraceful part of our constitution is absolved.* JEWS ARE FREE.[110]

The local press generally supported the Jew Bill.[111] The Catholics of Maryland also favored the bill.[112] An expression of Catholic solidarity with the Jews came from Bishop England, the Catholic primate of South Carolina. He congratulated Tyson for "that effusion of just and spirited vindication of an injured race."[113]

Echoes of the Jew Bill debates in Annapolis were even heard abroad. Brackenridge's speech was translated into German.[114] Worthington was told by a rabbi that his speech had been translated into Hebrew.[115] Mendes Cohen was in England in 1830 while Jewish rights were being discussed in the Parliament. In letters to his mother he asked her to rush copies of the published speeches on the Jew Bill which he intended to deliver to important political leaders.[116] When the same question was debated again a quarter of a century later, in 1855, a Baltimore rabbi, Aaron Günzburg, forwarded to several parliamentarians a number of articles that appeared in Baltimore newspapers at the time of the debates on the Jew Bill.[117]

In the election for Baltimore City Council a few months after the passage of the Jew Bill, both Solomon Etting and Jacob Cohen were elected to office. This heralded the rise of Jews in government service, both in appointive as well as elective positions.[118]

THE FIRST SYNAGOGUE
IN BALTIMORE

In 1825 Solomon Etting estimated the Jewish population of Maryland, which meant almost exclusively Baltimore, to be 150, a considerable increase from the mere handful in 1780 or 1790. It was still smaller than Richmond to the south, with 200 Jews, or Philadelphia to the north, with 400; and compared with Charleston, then the largest Jewish community in the country with its 674 Jews, Baltimore was a pigmy.[119] These figures serve to remind us that 1820 was still the era of American Jewry's infancy. There were at that time in the entire United States only about 2,700 Jews.[120] In light of these figures, Baltimore, with its 150 in 1825, was already no small Jewish center.[121]

With a rapid increase in Baltimore's population, the Jewish population of the city grew as well. From 13,503 in 1790, the year of the first United States census, the population of Baltimore more than doubled in the succeeding decade to 31,514.[122] By 1820 Baltimore had become the third city in size of population in the entire country.[123]

The economic expansion of the city naturally brought a significant measure of religious tolerance. Jews had lived in the city *de facto* even when *de jure* they were not permitted. As time passed, the fact of their residence was no longer in question, although the change from tolerance to equality was still in the future. That, too, was accomplished with the passage of the Jew Bill. Thus from every point of view Baltimore held an attraction for Jews, and they responded by coming and settling in the city.

Much has been related in these pages about the Ettings and the Cohens. These Jews were important to the many Maryland Gentiles who had never met a living Jew and knew only of the Hebrews in the Bible. To them, men like Etting and Cohen served as models. This is what a Jew looks like. This is how a Jew behaves. They no doubt liked the model. And it was "good for the Jews" to have such models.

A cruel awakening was in store, however. "Plain" Jews, poor immigrants, began to arrive. These people were no bankers, no railroad magnates. They did not live in exclusive neighborhoods. They did not speak English and often lacked the "refinement" which was expected, as the saying went, from the "noble race, the seed of Abraham."

How many of them were there in Baltimore by 1830, when the first Jewish organization came into being? Who were they? Where did they come from? Where did they live and how did they make their living? These are difficult questions to answer. The majority, then as now, did not leave individual records. Important as the group of common men is, the individual in these groups remains the anonymous man about whom nothing or very little is known.

Another difficulty in understanding the period is one of semantics. The terms used in official or semiofficial documents and even in ordinary conversation are confusing to us and were not too precise even when they were in use. Thus one meets with such occupation descriptions as "dealer," "broker," "speculator." What did these terms mean? It can be established first that these terms were interchangeable and described any kind of merchant or peddler. "Ironmonger" definitely meant a hardware storekeeper; "gentleman" was a euphemism for a retired person or for one without a definite occupation. "N.G."—"not given" —gives, of course, no clue as to occupation. "Speculator" more often than not stood for storekeeper. And what is one to make of Abraham H. Cohen, who lived in Baltimore in 1817—he is listed variously as "merchant," "chymist & druggist."[124]

If the occupational problem is a confusing one, it is also quite difficult to answer questions about the immigrants' lands of origin. That they came here "from England" or "from Holland" might be correct, yet such declarations were disingenuous. An immigrant from Bavaria who stayed in England or Holland on his way to America, even for a short period, would claim to be British or Dutch. (This deception was destined to be repeated with variations in later, larger waves of immigration, when one met with Polish Jews claiming to be German. And everybody is, of course, familiar with that group which came from a place only "five minutes away from Vienna." They would naturally not mention that they meant five minutes by telephone and that they actually came from Galicia.)

In spite of all the difficulties, we do have some idea of the origins and occupational structure of early Baltimore Jewry. Most of them were immigrants from Bavaria. They lived together in East Baltimore. This area remained the Jewish center of Baltimore for well over a century. Those who prospered moved out, and new immigrants moved in. High Street, Lombard Street, Broadway, Exeter, Aisquith, and the surrounding streets were to become the teeming Jewish settlement, where poverty ruled supreme and where great institutions and organizations took care of the old and brought education and recreation to the young. All this, however, was in the future. In the meantime, the poor Bavarian immigrants, on the whole with very little education, general or Jewish, worked hard to eke out a living. Poor storekeepers kept long hours from early dawn till late at night. Peddlers made their living from the packs on their backs, carrying their wares to outlying communities in Maryland and far into Virginia.

How many of them were there? Even with all the uncertainties due to the difficulty in identifying "Jewish" names, we do have a fairly reliable answer to this question. The first United States census (1790) lists six Jewish families in Baltimore, comprising thirty-three individuals.[125] Although this is, of course, a meager number, one must remember that there were only about fifteen hundred Jews at that time in the entire country, and a city like Boston had only two Jewish families with twenty individuals.[126]

Five out of the six heads of household were merchants. One was a religious functionary, a *mohel*, about whom there is ample information. Before settling in Baltimore in 1790, Bernard Jacobs was for many years a very busy man in his chosen profession in Pennsylvania. There is no reason to believe that he came to Baltimore for professional reasons. The community was much too small for a *mohel* to practice in it, and there were no Jewish communities of any consequence nearby. There is, indeed, no record of his having performed circumcision rites

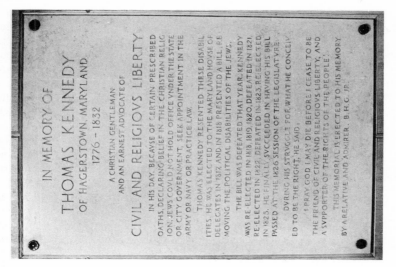

Plaque commemorating Thomas Kennedy in Sinai Hospital, Baltimore.
Courtesy of the Sinai Hospital.

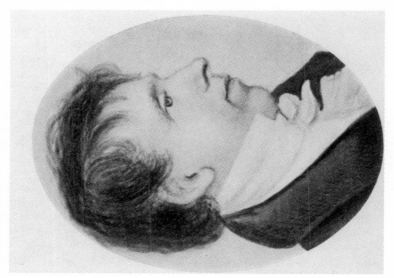

Thomas Kennedy, 1776–1832, champion of civil and religious equality.
From E. Milton Altfeld, *The Jew's Struggle for Religious and Civil Liberty in Maryland.*

Act of incorporation of the Baltimore Hebrew Congregation, the first congregation in Maryland, 1830.
Courtesy of the Baltimore Hebrew Congregation.

in Baltimore, as one would expect to find, since Jacobs was a prodigious recorder of his activities.[127]

One Baltimore Jew appeared in the Richmond listing of the census, although he more rightfully belonged in that of Baltimore. Again, we are dealing with a religious functionary of sorts. Mordecai M. Mordecai (1727–1809) occupied various minor posts in Mikveh Israel in Philadelphia and was referred to on at least one document as "Reverend Rabbi."[128] Mordecai came to Baltimore as early as 1770. The first known Litvak in the country, he was a restless individual and was for several years in and out of the city. In 1772, two years after his arrival, he acquired a ninety-nine-year lease on a piece of land on the west side of Jones Falls, now Fallsway. In the deed he was described as a "distiller."[129] The census caught up with him in Richmond. However, in June of that year he came back to Baltimore. Again, he was in and out of the city and settled permanently in 1797. He died in Baltimore in 1809.[130]

Mordecai's two sons, as well as his son-in-law, all resided in Baltimore. One of his sons, Isaac, was, like his father, a distiller. The other son was a tobacconist. Their business places were near each other on High Street in the city. Mordecai's son-in-law had a rather checkered career. Phillip Moses Russel came from England. In 1775 he enlisted in the Revolutionary army and served as a surgeon's mate— hence a legend of his being a surgeon, a position he could easily have qualified for if he were a *shohet*, a *mohel*, or even a barber.[131] On the other hand, as early as 1810 Baltimore had a *mohel*, Alexander Wertheim, who was indeed a physician.[132] In 1820 he served as health officer of Philadelphia.[133]

Another interesting Jew of the time was Elias Polack. He was a very poor man. In 1818 he estimated that all his belongings were worth no more than twenty dollars. Unable to sign his name except in Hebrew letters, he applied for a pension due him as a soldier in the War of Independence. His petition was duly approved and he was awarded eight dollars a month.[134]

After 1815 the number of Jews in the country, including Baltimore, began to increase rapidly. This influx was not a uniquely Jewish phenomenon. After the Napoleonic Wars, Central Europe was on the move. People left in droves for the legendary New World—America. It was only natural that after the Vienna Congress, where the clock of history was turned back, Jews, who suffered more from the post-1815 reaction than any other group, should want to leave the lands in which their hopes for emancipation had been dashed. And leave they did in ever-increasing numbers. Baltimore was a port of entry, and as was to be expected many of those who happened to land there remained for good.

The census of 1790 listed six Jewish households numbering thirty-three individuals; that of 1820 listed twenty-one, consisting of a hundred and twenty individuals.[135] (Seven of the householders owned among them eleven slaves and employed fifteen freedmen. Solomon Etting, the richest Jew in town, owned four slaves and employed two freedmen.)[136] The number of Jews in Baltimore increased much more rapidly after 1820.

Although there is no record of a *minyan* until 1829, there were too many Jews in the city for it to have been the first. After all, Baltimore already had a *mohel* by 1810 and a *shohet* and *mohel* in the early 1820s.[137] It can hardly be imagined that Wolf Marshutz, the *shohet*, and Gabriel Isaac, the *mohel*, failed to organize a *minyan*. Be this as it may, the first official services were held in 1829.[138]

The services were held in the house of Zalma Rhine, a newcomer, who was not really a stranger to Baltimore. As a matter of fact, he had been in the city fully forty years prior to this service. When Rhine came from Westphalia to America in 1789, he landed in Baltimore. His arrival in a city in which he was a complete stranger was later described by his nephew, Isaac Leeser (Leeser's mother was Rhine's sister), the outstanding leader of American Jewry of the mid-nineteenth century and the editor and publisher of the important Jewish monthly, *The Occident*.

Leeser's description in *The Occident* proves that a Jew is not really a stranger in a place where there are Jews, if he is only able to find them. Rhine happened to come to Baltimore on the eve of Yom Kippur.

Unacquainted, he traversed the streets of Baltimore . . . in search of Israelites to celebrate with them the holy season of our faith. He was attracted by the merchandise sign of Isaac & Levi Solomon. He entered their domicile, announced himself as a brother Israelite, who longed to spend the day with them in due solemnity and devotion, and these worthy men, and their estimable relatives [the Ettings] gladly allowed the stranger to stay with them to pray to the Throne of Grace in the society of his brothers . . . and to break with them the bread of friendship after the solemn day closed. [139]

From Baltimore, Rhine moved to Richmond, where he became a respectable merchant—Leeser clerked in his store from 1824 until 1829.[140] In 1829 Rhine came back to the city where he first landed,[141] and it was in his home, on Holiday and Pleasant Streets, that a historic *minyan* was held. It was this service that led to the formation of the first synagogue in the city.

It was Baltimore's good fortune that the seventy-two-year-old Rhine came to Baltimore. For the next fourteen years of his life, he was the moving spirit in the Jewish life in the city. Isaac Leeser frequently visited his uncle. Thanks to these visits, we have many valuable reports on the contemporary Baltimore Jewish community recorded in his magazine. Leeser, however, was much more than a reporter. He was a well-informed critic whose writings greatly influenced Baltimore Jewry.

The *minyan*, in addition to Rhine, was attended by John M. Dyer, Moses Millem, Lewis Silver, Levi Benjamin, Joseph Osterman, Joseph Ancker, Levy Collmus, Tobias Myers, and Jacob Aaron.[142] The same year, some of these men presented a petition to the legislature in the name of "sundry citizens of Baltimore," asking for a charter which would permit them to have a synagogue.

Why did the Baltimore Jews wait three full years after the passing of the Jew Bill to charter a house of worship? One can only offer a reasonable guess. They never forgot that the bill passed only with a majority of one, and they feared that their request for a charter might be rejected. As we will see later, their fears were well founded.

In December 1829 Delegate Hunt entered into the legislature a bill declaring:

Whereas the scattered Israelites of the City of Baltimore have by their petition . . . prayed that they may be incorporated with power necessary for the building of a synagogue wherein they may worship God according to the rites and customs of their Fathers . . . be it enacted . . . that John M. Dyer, Moses Millem, Lewis Silver, Levi Benjamin and Joseph Osterman of the said Congregation . . . are hereby erected into a body corporate by the name and style . . . of the Baltimore Hebrew Congregation. [143]

The third section of the bill established that the electors (as the board members were and still are called in this congregation) were not permitted to make any bylaws and regulations which are "contrary to the rights, usage and discipline of the said Synagogue." (It was this clause of the charter that later caused much trouble and eventually caused a complete break between dissidents and upholders of "the rights.")

What would seem to be a routine matter brought about an involved discussion. True, it was reported favorably by a committee

43

appointed to study it. It even passed the first reading. However, when it came up for the second reading, on February 6, 1830, it was defeated. The Jews of Baltimore would not have had a synagogue after all but for the intervention of Delegate Thomas of Saint Mary's. Together with two other members, he asked the legislature to reconsider its action on the matter. On February 25 the bill passed the House.[144] Thus the first Jewish organization in Baltimore came into being. The "Dispersed of Israel," Nidhei Israel Synagogue, was born. Who can tell whether any of the founders of the synagogue knew that the numerical value of the name they gave to their house of worship equals the number of *mitzvot* prescribed to Jews—613. Whether strictly observant or not, the Jews of Baltimore from now on had a synagogue. More than a synagogue, in fact, for following the practice to which most of the members had been accustomed when they lived in Europe, the Jews now thought of their synagogue in terms of a *ḳahal*—the governing body of a Jewish community.

II

THE FORMATIVE YEARS:
1830–1855

RELIGIOUS LIFE

The Synagogue

There were no Ettings or Cohens or anybody resembling these two wealthy and influential native Jewish families among the first thirteen members of the Baltimore Hebrew Congregation.[1] Its Hebrew name, Nidhei Israel (The Dispersed of Israel), aptly described their condition.[2] On the whole it was a group of poor, uneducated immigrants, mostly from Bavaria, with a sprinkling from Holland and England. They were eking out a very modest, if not actually a poor, living as peddlers or small storekeepers. When the congregation was organized, they were on the lowest rung of the economic ladder—which, however, some of them climbed with extraordinary rapidity. But for every one who climbed to a higher rung, another poor immigrant came; so that for many years the total complexion of the congregation did not change.[3]

The first president of the congregation, John M. Dyer, came to America in 1812. He spent eight years in New England before settling in Baltimore, where he opened a small butcher shop. It was this poor butcher who stood at the helm of the congregation for five years (1829–1834). He was one of those who prospered rather rapidly, and before long his butcher shop was converted into a packinghouse.[4]

Levi Benjamin, the treasurer of the congregation, was also one of those who attained some measure of financial success. At first a laborer, he became a peddler and advanced to become a secondhand dealer.[5] By 1837 he was so well off that he could afford to give a piece of ground to the congregation, on which it planned to build a synagogue.[6]

The most adventurous and most spectacular of the congregations' early officers was its fourth president. Leon Dyer, the son of John Dyer, enlarged his father's packinghouse. A partner in the business, he was also a "partner" in his father's synagogue. In 1835, at the age of twenty-seven, he served as trustee of the congregation. Business took him to New Orleans, where he stayed for about five years. While there, he was appointed quartermaster general of Louisiana and also served as major in the Texas war for independence. In New Orleans he also had an opportunity for a little private shooting of his own. He challenged to a duel a man who had made an insulting remark about his religion.

Upon his return to Baltimore, Leon Dyer, then only thirty-three, was elected president of the congregation and led it for seven years (1840–1847). Then he was again on the move—this time to San Francisco on business. That city had no synagogue then, so the enterprising Dyer organized and became the president of the first congregation on the West Coast (1849). Two years later he returned east where a new activity awaited him. The erstwhile Baltimore butcher was dispatched by President Fillmore on a mission to Berlin. The restless Leon Dyer died in 1883 in Louisville, Kentucky.[7]

Isadore, another son of John Dyer, was a chip off the old block. He, too, busied himself with synagogues. In 1840 he left his native city and settled in Galveston. He is credited with organizing the first congregation in Texas.[8] Thus, the pioneers of the Baltimore Hebrew Congregation became founders of congregations in distant parts of the United States.

Leon Dyer was a forerunner of many who participated in Jewish communal affairs and were at the same time active in the affairs of the general community. He was the prototype of the American Jew of later days who was simultaneously a *part of* and *apart from* America. But he was the exception in that early period of Baltimore Jewish history, for most Baltimore Jews were ordinary people, working, struggling, and adjusting themselves rather slowly to a new way of life in a new, and in many ways strange, land. Only four members of the congregation seem to have had any experience in American synagogue life.[9]

Among the congregation's members was also one of the great builders of Jewish communal life of Baltimore, Jonas Friedenwald. He came to the city in 1832 at the age of thirty and lived in the city until his death sixty-one years later. The transoceanic trip that brought Friedenwald to Baltimore was tempestuous and hazardous and took no less than four months. He brought over with him his wife and four children, the youngest an infant of two months, as well as his father, aged seventy. They were very Orthodox, and during the four months at sea they did not taste any meat.

Upon his arrival he became an umbrella mender, and subsequently he opened a grocery. Later still, he became a junk dealer and the proprietor of a hardware store. In these and in other business ventures that he undertook he prospered.[10] Always active in communal affairs, Friedenwald became the progenitor of the leading Jewish family in the city, a family of distinguished communal leaders, outstanding physicians, and professors of medicine. For many years this energetic and devoted man was active in the Baltimore Hebrew Congregation, until he left it in 1870 in protest against ritual innovations which he could not accept. In this period, he was among those who built the first congregation in the city.

All that the first thirteen members could afford as a place of worship was a rented room over a grocery. In that room on the corner of Bond and Fleet Streets the congregation met for two years. During those years the number of members more than doubled to reach twenty-nine. In 1832 the synagogue moved to larger quarters on North Exeter Street, near what is now Lexington Street. Another move was made in 1835, when the congregation already numbered fifty-five members. This time it was not just a move from one room to another. Now they occupied an entire house on High Street, between Fayette and Gay Streets. Immigrants continued to come in, and soon even the house proved to be too small. In 1837 the congregation became the owner of a three-story brick building located on the corner of Harrison Street and Etna Lane. The ground on which this building stood had been given to the congregation by Levi Benjamin. In this house the synagogue remained for a full eight years.

Membership dues provide as good a yardstick as any for measuring the economic circumstances of the Jews of the city. The dues were five dollars a year, payable in biweekly installments. That was not sufficient to maintain a synagogue, even when it was no more than one room. Additional funds were raised from an elaborate system of free offerings and fines. The normal price payable for an offering was a coin worth six and a quarter cents.[11] The "rich" would occasionally double this amount and contribute twelve and a half cents. The aliyot, that is, the calling up to the Torah, which spelled offerings and hence a fuller treasury, were auctioned off and sold to the highest bidder. It was a sign of self-reliance and increasing prosperity when the auctioneering method was given up. Leeser greeted this decision as proof of the "good progress of the Congregation."[12]

The main source of income for many years, however, was fines. The members of the congregation, most of them Bavarian Jews, came from an environment where a synagogue, though a sacred place, was nevertheless treated as if it were one's own home. This meant that people were constantly coming and going, talking to each other during the services, and altogether feeling no restraint in their behavior. America, this new strange land, changed everything. Here everything

49

was different. America demanded orderly behavior even in a synagogue. Decorum was the order of the day. Strangely enough, it was decorum, or rather the lack of it, which became a means of livelihood for the synagogue for a long time.

Although fully aware of the necessity of proper conduct in the synagogue and keenly striving for it, people could not easily give up the old ways. Hence the imposition of fines without end. There was a fine for talking during services, a fine for putting away the *tallis* before the services were over, a fine for singing louder than the *ḥazan*, a f ne for leaving the synagogue without permission of the president or ne of the officers.[13] The fines were usually twenty-five cents, a consider ble amount of money for those days. One could not become an "Amerikaner" overnight. It always took time, and occasionally it took very much time.

In one case there was a clash between two indexes of "Americanization." One would expect the people to learn not to spit on the synogogue floor. On the other hand, most good Americans chewed tobacco, and it was easy—even if at first not too pleasant—to become Americanized by following suit. (Years later chewing gum took the place of chewing tobacco as a sign of Americanization.) Between the two—permitting chewing or having a clean synagogue—the board, to its credit, preferred the latter; it forbade anyone to "shew" (chew) tobacco and imposed a fine for breaking this rule.[14] It seems, however, that the board itself never had much faith that the congregation would obey this rule— spittoons were placed near every seat. The repetition of the rules about decorum bear testimony that they were honored more in the breach than in the observance.

America was, indeed, different. In the old country a synagogue would never call on the police to help preserve order. Yet this is exactly what happened in 1852. Worshipers would leave the synagogue, especially during the reading of the Torah, and congregate on the sidewalk in front of the house of worship. The board hired two policemen to prevent such gatherings.[15] It must have helped for a while, but records tell of the repetition of this offense, leading once again to the employment of policemen.[16] The offense and the method of "curing" it were repeated many times, not only in the Baltimore Hebrew Congregation but also at virtually all the Baltimore synagogues established during that period.

Although the fines were only twenty-five or fifty cents, there is a record of one member, Joshua Greenbaum, who managed to accumulate a total of four and one-half dollars in fines. When he refused to pay, the board acted, and again in a manner that would have been inconceivable in the old country—they decided to "suit" (sue) him in a civil court. Surely no congregation in the old country would ever sue a member in a gentile court. But it did happen in Baltimore in 1853.[17]

In time even stricter rules were introduced. One was forbidden "to read or sing any prayer loud during the services."[18] This was, indeed, a complete revolution in the mode of worship. Decorum was winning out against the established European custom. The process of adjustment to the American way of life had begun, not only in immigrants' contact with "native Americans," but also in the synagogue. The leaders of the community, however, were not much better than the ordinary members. High office did not stop a president from using "a language before the Ark during Divine service [that was] uncalled for."[19] In the course of time the problem of decorum, along with many other problems, was overcome, but the adjustment process never ceased.

From its very inception, the synagogue was more than a house of worship. This was the only meeting place for Jews in the city, where people met to worship but also just to be together. The meetings (on the average, at least one a month) took place on Sunday mornings. This was when the peddlers and their suppliers had free time, for in the afternoon the packs had to be filled with merchandise for the coming week.

The meetings opened up a new world for these immigrants. Most of them had come from little towns, usually despotically ruled by established oligarchies. All communal problems had been decided by those who stood at the head of the community. But in this new land things were done differently. In the first place, the people—every member—participated in the election of the officers of the congregation. More than that, they were even called upon to debate and vote on the decisions of these officers. It was a new experience to "take the floor," to "make a motion," to "second a motion." No wonder that at first they were bewildered and their meetings were often stormy. One report reads: "The president was silenced" and "the meeting broke off without transacting any business."[20] A meeting provided an opportunity to assert oneself. The only method the members knew was to outshout, to disrupt, and thus prove to themselves and to others how important they were. It took a long time to learn and to know better. As late as 1874 the president of Har Sinai Congregation was *groblich beleidigt* (rudely insulted) at a meeting.[21]

These, then, were the Jews who laid the foundation of the Baltimore Jewish community. They were men with little or no education, as poor culturally as they were economically. The remarkable thing about it all is that somehow it worked. The meeting was a school in which one slowly learned to express oneself correctly and learned the even more difficult art of listening to what others had to say. Out of the disorder there came order, understanding, and appreciation of the democratic process.

Since the Baltimore Hebrew Congregation was the only Jewish organization in the city, it took it upon itself to provide for all the religious needs of its worshipers. This was not a *kehillah;* nothing resembling the European Jewish community ever developed in the United States. Unlike European Jewry, the American Jews were never forced by the government to belong to a Jewish communal organization. America had always been an open society. People could join or not join, remain in or withdraw from a synagogue. But since the Jews had religious needs and since there was no recognized association to take care of them, the sole Baltimore congregation acted as if it were indeed the governing body of an organized community.

The age of packaged *matzot* was a long, long way in the future. As long as the number of Jews was small, each family, or a few families banded together, took care of this need in the best way possible. As the number of Jews increased, the Baltimore Hebrew Congregation began to supervise bakers and eventually even installed a *matzot*-baking oven in the synagogue.[22]

Matzot were a once-a-year problem. The *mikve,* however, was needed all year round and so was kosher meat. All these requirements demanded daily attention. The construction and repairs of the ritual bath and the frequency with which the water was to be changed were all discussed in long and sometimes bitter debates. (It was finally decided to change the water once a week.)[23]

Kosher meat required the engagement of *shohatim* and the supervision of butchers. Again meetings, again endless debates. More than that, there were sometimes unscrupulous "kosher butchers" who took advantage of people. Someone had to step in to protect the public. Again, the congregation acted as if it had the authority to do so. We read of a butcher who was penalized by the congregation: "For six months he cannot have the killing done by our *shohatim,* because he sold *trefa* meat."[24]

There were always needy to provide for. Traditionally, charity was considered the very essence of Jewish life. In the absence of any other organization, the first synagogues did the work, which they later continued even after specialized charitable organizations had come into being. There was hardly a meeting at which some charity problem did not come up. The assistance that was rendered varied. Thus, we learn that a cord of wood was given to a poor woman who suffered from the winter cold.[25] Needless to say, help was given in case of illness. The minutes relate: "Owing to the continued illness of ———, his family is in want and the Board donates $5 to that family." No distinction was made between member and stranger when assistance was needed for a funeral. We read in the minutes that "a stranger made application to bury his child, and the Board respecting his poverty, agreed not to make any charge."[26]

A Jew would never think of himself only as a member of a single community. When in need, one community felt free to call on another for help. So it was with the first Baltimore congregation. Appeals were received from out-of-town congregations, and though the Baltimore Jews themselves were poor, they did respond as members of *Klal Israel*. To cite just one instance, when yellow fever befell the community of New Orleans in 1853, the Baltimore congregation rushed six hundred dollars, which was an extremely large sum of money in those days, to the victims.[27]

And there were, of course, endless appeals for the schools and the poor in the Holy Land. The first Palestinian *meshulah* who came to Baltimore to solicit funds for various causes was Jehiel Cohen. He came to the city in 1847 with a letter of recommendation from Isaac Lesser to his friend Dr. Joshua Cohen.[28]

In 1849 the only Baltimore rabbi, Abraham Rice, welcomed to the city the *meshulah* Aaron Selig. Rice did not limit himself to collecting money for Palestinian charities. In Selig's journal the Baltimore rabbi recorded that he had established a special society, *Mishmeret Hakodesh* (The Sacred Charge), which would in the future collect funds for "our poor brethren in the Holy City."[29] On Purim, Rice's congregation collected money for poor Jews both at home and in the Holy Land.[30] Jerusalem (as Palestine was generally referred to) was helped at times with very large sums—in 1853, for example, the extremely large sum of $1,100 was raised.[31]

One is taken aback to realize, judging from these accounts of charitable endeavors, how little people trusted each other with charity money; or perhaps it was only that they were especially careful with public funds. At any rate, they had a special charity box, which was in the charge of the sexton. The key to the box's lock, however, was in the hands of the president.[32] There was another problem too: on one occasion the treasurer received thirteen dollars in counterfeit money.[33]

More important than any other activity was the purchase of a cemetery in 1832. The three acres on Belair Road, where the first Baltimore synagogue cemetery was located, gave every member of the congregation the assurance of a Jewish funeral and burial in a Jewish cemetery. Compared with all other needs, this stood out as supreme. Even those who had been lax in their observance of daily rituals insisted on being among their brethren in death. The exceptions were, as they still are, very rare.

The First Rabbi

The period under discussion was still the "Reverend and Cantorial Age" of American Jewry. For a full 186 years after the arrival of the first Jews in 1654, there was not a single ordained rabbi in the entire country. And even half a century after the arrival of the first rabbi in 1840, a prominent American rabbi said about the condition of the American rabbinate that, "Here a man qualifies himself, ordains himself; he is his own college, his own professor, his own diploma. He is what he claims to be."[34]

A momentous event in the history of American Jews generally, but more especially in the history of Baltimore Jewry (which by that time numbered about two hundred families), took place in 1840.[35] On July 25, the German ship *Sir Isaac Newton* docked in New York. A short man limped down the gangplank. His name was Abraham Rice,[36] the first ordained rabbi to come to live in the United States. "Before Rice's arrival," Isaac Lesser wrote a dozen years later, "*Ḥazan* was the highest ecclesiastical term among us."[37] In 1845 he was still the only "licentiate Rabbi" in the whole country.[38]

Born in Gagheim, Bavaria, he had been a student in the nearby yeshiva at Würzburg, where he studied under two great talmudic scholars, Abraham Bing and Wolf Hamburger. Rice was forty years of age when he came to America. After his arrival he went to Newport, hoping to reestablish the congregation in that historic community. Having failed in this attempt (because so few Jews then lived in Newport) he returned to New York, where he met a *landsman* of his, Aaron Weglein, at that time president of the Baltimore Hebrew Congregation. Weglein could not have hoped for anything greater for his congregation than to obtain the services of a real rabbi—and the first rabbi in the country at that. Rice accepted his invitation, and on Rosh Hashanah of 1840 he preached to his new flock.

No one could possibly have foreseen that there would soon arise difficulties in the relationship between the spiritual leader and his congregants. The rabbi was Orthodox and so was the congregation. The rabbi was from Bavaria and so were the worshipers. They spoke the same language in more than one sense. It seemed to have all the earmarks of a lasting and happy union. Difficulties arose, however, soon after the rabbi's arrival.

The misunderstandings began with the question of Sabbath observance. True, the Baltimore Jews were Orthodox and would have loved to observe the Sabbath as befits traditional Jews. Peddlers, however, very often found it impossible to keep the Sabbath or, for that matter, *kashrut*. There were also members of the congregation who surreptitiously—and some even quite openly—kept their stores open on Saturdays.

Rice could not accept these double standards. Those who broke the Sabbath law were to be censured in some way. Surely such people did not deserve honors in a synagogue. The rabbi, who had greater authority in those days, directed that violators of the Sabbath should not be called up to the Torah. Rice did not reckon with the fact that there were too many such people and that an order directed against so many was not practical. He also overlooked the financial aspect of such a punishment. *Aliyot* meant offerings, which were important as income to the synagogue. The rabbi was forced to give in. Instead of his original order, he issued a milder one. Sabbath-breakers could be called up, but the congregation was not to respond with "Amen" when they recited the prescribed blessings.[39] The problem of Sabbath offenders was constantly on the agenda. The congregation as a body was trying to preserve the sanctity of the Sabbath, while individual members of the congregation were often lax.

The old ordinance about not calling up Sabbath violators to the Torah was officially done away with in 1853.[40] In any case it had been a dead letter almost from the beginning. The new order excluded those who kept their businesses open "in the city" on the Sabbath from holding office in the congregation.[41] The words "in the city" no doubt implied a recognition that peddlers were excluded from this penalty. This order, too, was widely disobeyed. The minutes relate that even the president, vice-president, and treasurer were charged with "doing business on the *shabbos*." The decision in the matter tells the whole story. In spite of the prohibition, the officers were not dismissed. Instead, it was decided "to postpone discussion on these charges indefinitely."[42]

The attitude toward Sabbath observance mirrored the general mood of the congregation. Orthodox in many ways, but. . . . It was such "buts" with which the rabbi would not compromise. He, sincere literalist that he was, required of others what he demanded of himself. It was his belief that "the heavens may vanish and the earth wear out with age, but still not an iota will vanish from our religion."[43] The observance of every "iota" was what he demanded of his congregation, and the congregation was not prepared to follow.

An uneasy peace prevailed in the congregation. Two years after Rice's arrival in the city, however, a minor revolt of great historic significance broke out. To a funeral service for a member of the congregation, one Jacob Ahrens, at which the rabbi officiated, came friends of the deceased who were members of Masonic and Odd Fellows lodges to which Ahrens belonged. These gentlemen performed at the grave certain rites customary in their societies. The rabbi remonstrated there and then.[44] In protest against Rice's action, some members left the congregation and formed the Har Sinai Verein, which was destined to become the first lasting Reform congregation organized in Baltimore and, indeed, in the United States.[45]

At first Rice was not so much concerned with the few who left the congregation. They could be written off. He fought his losing battle gallantly, but finally in 1849, totally discouraged, he gave up his position. To his friend Leeser he explained that this was a difficult decision to arrive at. But he did it, even though he was a poor man without a source of income. He was then forty-nine, and he could not, so he wrote Leeser, start a business. Yet he felt compelled to act as he did, come what may. He told Leeser that, no longer being an employee of the congregation, he now hoped to have greater influence. He concluded his letter by assuring his friend in Philadelphia that he was "always ready to fight."[46]

In what sounds like utter despair, he wrote to his former teacher Wolf Hamburger:

I dwell in complete darkness, without a teacher or companion. . . . The religious life in this land is on the lowest level, most people eat foul food and desecrate the Sabbath in public. . . . Thousands marry non-Jewish women. Under these circumstances my mind is perplexed and I wonder whether it is even permissible for a Jew to live in this land. I am tired of my life. . . . I often think of leaving and going to Paris and put my trust in the good Lord.[47]

And to his friend Leeser, he wrote two years later:

I have made it a practice not to make religion a means of livelihood. I do not want to have anything to do with Jews. . . . In Baltimore all is lost for it is "a people that has broken loose."[48]

No sooner had Rice resigned than two Christian missionaries appeared in his home. A branch of the American Society for Meliorating the Conditions of the Jews, which was a deceptive name for the missionary society, had been established in Baltimore in 1845. Later a converted Jew was stationed in the city to "labour" among the Jews.[49] Rice did his best to save people who were offered jobs and money by the missionary workers.[50] Nevertheless, the poor were attracted by their help. In response the Baltimore Hebrew Congregation decided to give poor parents three dollars a month "lest their child fall in the hands of Christian societies."[51] This sounds like blackmail, but it well describes the missionary activities in the community.

Now that Rice had resigned his position, the missionaries tried their luck with one who could be the biggest catch of all. Rice reported to Leeser the visit of the *Shpizbuben* (rascals) in every detail and asked him to publish the letter as a warning against those who wish to bring a "desecration of God's name."[52] Leeser published the whole story and protested vehemently against such "shameless" intrusions of "odious apostates. He stressed that in this country "we know nothing of a dominant church. . . . We are as much empowered by law to be Jews as they to be Christians." He urged upon the Jews "the propriety of not holding intercourse in any manner with these renegades."[53] The missionaries remained active throughout the history of the Baltimore Jewish community.[54]

Rice faithfully followed the talmudic dictum not to make the Torah "a spade to dig therewith." Thus, the first American rabbi became a businessman of sorts. At first he eked out his living from a little dry-goods store. Later he opened a grocery. His hopes of influencing his former congregation had come to naught, so in 1851 he organized a small synagogue of his own, which he served as rabbi and preacher as well as cantor. It was not a paid position, and he continued to earn his meager livelihood from his grocery. At sixty-two, he felt old and sick. In a letter to a friend he complained that he was getting weak and "cannot stand on my feet even an hour."[55] In the spring of 1862

57

his old congregation invited him to come back. He did, but too late—he died after the High Holy Days. In accordance with his instructions, his funeral was performed in the most ascetic fashion and without any eulogies.[56]

Rice had many opponents, but there were also devoted followers whose lives were influenced by him. Dr. Harry Friedenwald related that Rabbi Rice had "an important influence upon the formation of [my father's] character. . . . His loving veneration for Rice appeared in his frequent references to him."[57] The Baltimore Hebrew Congregation voted a pension of three hundred dollars annually for life to Rice's widow.[58]

Building a Synagogue

Not all Baltimore Jews belonged to the synagogue. One report relates that "more than half" did not join any Jewish organization.[59] This is most likely an exaggeration, but the centrifugal force of the American environment began to take its toll. To some Jews, Americanization meant withdrawal from Jewish life. In spite of this, the number of worshipers was constantly increasing. New immigrants were coming in and, quite naturally, were joining the synagogue. They even became a force in influencing those who had come earlier to remain within the orbit of Jewish life. Quantity was transformed into quality. The influence of the newcomers upon the "natives," the earlier arrivals, remained a tremendous force until America practically closed its doors to immigrants in 1924. It is, at bottom, the history of two opposing forces fighting for supremacy and the creation of that delicate balance known as the American-Jewish community.

The Baltimore Jewish community was no exception to this general situation. Immigrants joined the synagogue. While some old-timers withdrew just because they did not care to associate and be identified with the "foreigners," others were stimulated to become more active in the synagogue and in other Jewish communal affairs. The synagogue gained strength. There was, however, an additional outside force, one not to be minimized, which brought about the decision to utilize the strength of the synagogue and do what other non-Jewish groups in the city were doing at this time.

Baltimore in the forties was undergoing a church building boom. Various religious groups were erecting handsome houses of worship. It was only natural for the members of the congregation to become eager to do what other religious groups were doing. The time was ripe to build a *real* synagogue, one that would match the other houses of worship. The decision was made in 1841.

Following the well-established custom, an appeal was made to existing out-of-town congregations for help. We know of the response of only two congregations to the solicitation. The mother of American congregations, Shearith Israel in New York, ordered the appeal "to lie on the table."[60] But while Baltimoreans did not receive help from the nearby New York congregations, they did get a contribution of $170 from the distant congregation of Jamaica in the West Indies.[61] (A few years later, Baltimore was able to return the favor.[62])

There must have been a "building campaign" before Baltimore's leading architect, Robert Carey Long, Jr., was engaged to execute the plan. At that time Long was building numerous houses of worship. In 1842 he had completed the Alphonsus Roman Catholic Church for the German Catholics in the city. A year later he built Saint Peter's Catholic Church for the Irish. The next year two more churches were completed: the Mount Calvary Episcopal Church and the Franklin Street Presbyterian Church. In 1845 he completed another beautiful house of worship for the Baltimore Jews—the first synagogue in Maryland.

What Long built at the corner of Lloyd and Watson (then Salisbury) Streets was a large, magnificent structure in the Greek classical style popular in those days. As was to be expected in an Orthodox synagogue, there was a women's balcony which was screened off with "lattice work." There was one feature which Leeser described as "something unusual in our synagogues"[63]—the seating arrangement, which did not use the traditional open seats, but pews instead. One wonders whether in this case there was some "accommodation" to the non-Jewish architect, who convinced them that pews were the proper thing in a house of worship. One stained-glass window over the ark had a design of a Magen David, believed to be the first such motif in the country.[64]

The synagogue, now the third oldest surviving in the United States,[65] was dedicated on September 26, 1845. The ceremonies lasted three full days and were attended not only by Jews but by many non-Jews, lay people as well as clergy. In addition to Rice and A. Ansel, the cantor of the synagogue, two special speakers participated in the dedication ceremonies, Isaac Leeser from Philadelphia and the Rev. Samuel M. Isaacs from New York.[66]

There was a bitter pill in store for Rabbi Rice in connection with the celebration. A battle of the tongues, the question of English or German, started with this historic event and lasted practically till the end of the century. The man who unwittingly caused the strife was the New York speaker, Samuel Isaacs. Rice gave his sermon in German; Isaacs spoke in English. While many members of the congregation favored German over English, Rev. Isaacs made such an impression that he was offered the position of preacher in the Baltimore synagogue. He did not, however, accept the offer and Rabbi Rice remained.

Reporting on the consecration of the Baltimore synagogue, Leeser followed Aristotle's dictum that "piety requires us to honor truth above our friend," making the unpleasant remark about Rice's German sermon that

we deem it an undeniable truth, that the German language, no matter how eloquent the preacher, must soon become useless as a pulpit language, since the children of the present immigrants will soon know no other than the English language. . . . In saying this we by no means undervalue the learning and eloquence of . . . Rev. Rice . . . but only maintaining that we need another speech for the future Israelites in America.[67]

Ironically this view was also held by Rice, who, nevertheless, never mastered the English language. It was none other than Rice who pleaded with Leeser to translate the Bible into English, writing:

My friend, whom I love as my soul, the wise, the splendid author Eliezer. . . . As long as German is in power here, I know only too well that our children will not learn religion, for firstly, the children have no taste for German, secondly, no German newspaper will last which spreads true fear of God. . . . Make up your mind definitely that an English Bible be printed for us Jews. You should do it, even though you derive no benefits from it, for in this way you will be able to gain eternal life for your soul.[68]

Rice and Leeser favored English over German, not only because of the future, but also because they saw immediate danger signals. Reform Jews in this country were in close contact with their ideological friends in Germany and used only German. The constitution of the Baltimore Reform Congregation, Har Sinai, for example, was very explicit on this point: "German is to be the language of the Verein." The Minute Books of the Verein were written in German, although those of the Baltimore Hebrew Congregation were in English. The Board of Har

Sinai was called the *Kirchencommittee* (the church committee), the sexton was the *Kirchendiener* (church servant), etc. Rice and Leeser, two ideologists of traditional Judaism, displaced their antagonism from the Reform Jews to the language they used. Yet Rice continued to deliver his sermons in German, the only language both he and the congregants knew well. It was only in 1847 that he began to give one sermon a month in English.[69]

Despite its difficulties—fines, decorum, and even members leaving to form other congregations—the membership of the Baltimore Hebrew Congregation continued to grow. Because of the limited seating capacity of the synagogue, the congregation decided in 1854, when its membership reached 175, to limit membership to two hundred and to raise the entrance dues to thirty dollars.[70]

Much of what has been said about the Baltimore Hebrew Congregation was also true of the congregations that were founded later, even if to a lesser degree; the oldest congregation was the proving ground for the others. Many a battle waged in the first congregation was avoided in the others precisely because experience had already been gained and mistakes could be avoided.

Other Synagogues

Until their new building was erected, the first synagogue was generally called *Stadt Shul* (City Synagogue) to distinguish it from another located in Fell's Point, an outlying and separate district of the city. After 1845 *Stadt Shul* was known as the Lloyd Street Synagogue. The synagogue at Fell's Point was originally located in the dock area, at the foot of Broadway, where ships with immigrants aboard would dock. Some of the newcomers settled in that area. When there was a sufficient number of them, they organized a congregation of their own under the cumbersome name of Fell's Point Hebrew Friendship Congregation, Oheb Israel (Lovers of Israel), better known as *Pint* (a corruption of Point) *Shul*.[71] The congregation was chartered in 1847.[72]

As happened with the first congregation, the number of members grew and their economic situation generally improved. In 1848 the synagogue was moved from the poor location on Canton Avenue into a beautiful building erected by the congregation on Eden Street, between Lombard and Baltimore Streets. From then on until its dissolution in 1902 it was known, not by its corporate name, but as the

Eden Street *Shul*, after the street on which it was located. In the year of its consecration, the congregation engaged its own rabbi, Aaron Günzburg, who served from 1848 until 1856. The synagogue attracted many members because of its large cemetery, which is still serving Baltimore Jews. The early history of this cemetery is rather interesting. It was located halfway between Philadelphia Road and Canton Road. There was no entrance from either road to the cemetery: "When a funeral took place, they had to lift the coffin over a stone wall enclosing this land, then enter by means of ladders," the record tells us. In 1859 the congregation belatedly bought a road that provided an entrance to the cemetery.[73]

In 1849 Henry Hochheimer (1818–1912) became Baltimore's third rabbi. Like Rice, Hochheimer also came from Bavaria. He received a fine Hebrew education and was ordained in 1845. In addition, he had a doctorate in philosophy from the University of Munich, where he had even served as instructor. He was involved in the revolution of 1848, and when the revolution failed he left Germany.

Hochheimer happened to come to Baltimore at the time of Rice's resignation in 1849, and he took over the latter's position. In his inaugural sermon he spoke out against those who "will admit nothing as valued which [they] cannot comprehend with reason," as well as those who were "against every improvement, if it be so useful and necessary." On balance, it was a pronouncement against Reform. Leeser welcomed the new rabbi and published his sermon in an English translation.[74] After serving for a decade at the Lloyd Street Synagogue, he became rabbi in the Eden Street *Shul*, where he served for thirty-three years until his retirement. There were no ideological difficulties involved in Hochheimer's change of synagogues. Both congregations were Orthodox, and in both congregations there was a desire for some changes.

The situation was quite different in the third congregation, Har Sinai. It had been established in protest against extreme Orthodoxy. The small group (there were only seven people in attendance at the first meeting) was anxious to introduce changes immediately. It is doubtful, however, whether they had in mind the establishment of a Reform synagogue of the German type. The men continued to sit apart from their wives during the services. They continued to pray with their heads covered, as they had done in their old synagogues. They maintained kosher homes and observed two days of the festivals.

On the face of it, one might not have known the difference between the old Orthodox and the new "reform" group. And yet they were

Reform in the real sense of the word. They asserted that it was their privilege to decide what of the old they wanted to retain and to be free to reject what they believed ought to be rejected. They themselves wanted to be the ones to scrutinize old established traditions. Their first act, in preparation for the first services, was a foretaste of things to come—they procured an organ for use during the services. It surely did not make sense to old-timers: hats, traditional Hebrew services, men and women separated—and all this with an organ. It made sense, however, to the small group of dissenters, and this was what really mattered in the long run.

No wonder the old congregation refused to loan a Scroll of the Law to the "reformers."[75] On that memorable Shavuot, on May 15, 1842, when the first services of Har Sinai were held in the Union Hall at Baltimore Street and Union Avenue, the prescribed Torah portion was read from a printed Bible. The rift between the old and the newly established congregation became unbridgeable. The Har Sinai group established contact with the Hamburg temple, which had been established in 1816. From it they ordered prayer books for the sum of twelve dollars.

The members of Har Sinai were neither richer nor poorer than the rest of the Jews of the city. This congregation, too, at first wandered from hall to hall until it found, in December 1842, a "permanent" place on the northeast corner of Exeter Street and Eastern Avenue. It was a second-floor room in the home of one of its members, Moses Hutzler, the progenitor of a family of leading communal workers and merchants. Two years after its organization, the congregation was chartered "for the purpose of cultivating an acquaintance among the Hebrews . . . and for their mutual improvement and religious knowledge." The incorporators were Samuel Dellevie, Simon Eytinge, Max Sutro, Moses Hutzler, Joseph Simpson, and A. Nachman.

The intellectuals in the group were Simpson and Sutro. Joseph Simpson, originally from Prague, settled in Baltimore about 1828. He was a pioneer of lapidary seal engraving. A very sensitive Jew, he felt keenly about any anti-Jewish manifestation. When a Baltimore newspaper published an undignified article about Yom Kippur, Simpson published his protest in the form of a pamphlet entitled *Scapegoat*.

Simpson was especially irritated by the activities of the missionaries. When he heard that General Winfield Scott, of Mexican War fame, would preside at a missionary conference, he deemed it his duty as well as his privilege to protest to the commander-in-chief, the president of the United States. Simpson's protest tells much about the security that he and others like him found in this country. Timid immigrants at first, these people gained a sense of belonging—and hence the right to protest to the president of the country against what they considered to be improper acts of high officials. President Tyler's reply contains the explanation of why people like Simpson felt free to act in the way that he did.

The president saw nothing wrong in the general's intention to preside at a missionary meeting as long as he did not act in the capacity of army general and as long as he would "lay aside his sword and epaulets, and appear . . . in no other light than as a citizen." On matters of principle, President Tyler wrote to Simpson,

the United States have adventured upon a great and noble experiment, which is believed to have been hazarded in the absence of all previous precedent—that of total separation of Church and State. No religious establishment by law exists among us. . . . The offices of the Government are open alike to all. No tithes are levied to support an established hierarchy. . . . The Hebrew persecuted and down-trodden in other regions takes up his abode among us with none to make him afraid. He may boast as well as he can, of his descent from the Patriarchs of Old. . . . He may even turn his eye to Judea resting with confidence on the promise that is made him of his restoration to that Holy Land. . . . Such is the great experiment which we have tried . . . our system of free men would be imperfect without it.[76]

The liberal expressions of President Tyler were more than matched in deed by Joseph Simpson. A bachelor and a man of modest means, he nevertheless adopted two Christian orphans, and, though a zealous Jew, he raised them as Christians.[77] Simpson remained one of the leaders of Har Sinai until his death in 1857.[78]

While President Tyler saw no wrong in Jewish hopes and prayers for the restoration of their ancestral homeland, Max Sutro, the most learned member of Har Sinai Congregation had different thoughts on the subject. He was the reader, preacher, and teacher of the congregation. On August 8, 1845, Sutro addressed a meeting of the board of the congregation and expressed the views of one who feared to be misunderstood by non-Jews. Here was an expression of anxiety lest Jews be accused of what is now called "dual allegiance." The meeting took place before Tisha BeAv, and Sutro discussed the old custom of fasting and mourning on the ninth of the month of Av for the destruction of Jerusalem and the Temple. "We have made it our task," he said, *to examine each religious act as to its purpose before we commit it. Why mourn? Because Jerusalem, because the temple were destroyed? . . . Should we mourn because the Jewish empire perished? . . . Whatever one mourns, one wishes to possess again. Should our Christian fellow-citizen with whom we are forming one and the same social community not be of the opinion, when we are mourning the destruction of Jerusalem, that we are longing to return there and that our patriotism for our present homeland cannot be a true, genuine and fervent one? . . . Should our congregation grow and our principles become better known and more general, so that we will not have to fear any further misinterpretation, then we could always observe the Ninth [of Av], and in a suitable manner. . . .*

Sutro's suggestion was not adopted. It was "resolved that Preacher Sutro be requested to announce on the following Saturday that the divine service should take place on the Ninth of Ab and that this service should commence at 8 o'clock in the morning, if a sufficient number should turn up at the place of worship, and that the service should consist of prayer and chant."[79] The phrase "if a sufficient number should turn up at the place of worship" characterizes the situation. Not everybody, of course, was involved in ideologies like Sutro, but it was questionable whether a sufficient number of people would attend Tisha BeAv services. There is no record of a service.

A cemetery often was an index of congregational liveliness and strength. In 1845 Har Sinai was sufficiently alive to acquire its own cemetery, and by 1849, after years of wandering from building to building, the congregation was prosperous enough to build a spacious temple on High Street. The records tell us about the "crowded assemblage, consisting both of Hebrews and Christians, among the latter . . . several clergymen," who attended the dedication of the "beautiful Hebrew Temple."[80]

By this time, the moving spirit of the congregation was William S. Rayner. When he arrived in America, he was offered a position as Hebrew teacher at the Henry Street Synagogue in New York. Instead he proceeded to Baltimore, where he began working as a peddler. He was extremely successful and established a wholesale and retail dry-goods and notion business. This enterprise was followed by large real estate undertakings. In 1846, during the Mexican War, he invested heavily in United States government land claims, given by the government to participants in the war. These claims were negotiable, and Rayner made a great fortune in this investment.[81]

Rayner and Sutro led the congregation toward giving up more and more established traditions. Eventually it was resolved in 1844 that the time had come to decide which prayers were important and which were "unimportant" and therefore to be omitted.[82] Thus there developed two poles in Baltimore's Jewish religious life, Orthodoxy and Reform. In both groups, however, there were those who felt more comfortable in a middle-of-the-road synagogue. These moderate elements wanted reforms, but not Reform. The first announcement of the formation of a new synagogue appeared in an advertisement in the local English and German newspapers:

> ISRAELITES OF BALTIMORE ALL YOU WHO WISH TO JOIN AND BECOME MEMBERS OF THE NEW SYNAGOGUE WHICH IS NOW ABOUT BEING STARTED ARE REQUESTED TO ATTEND A MEETING WHICH IS TO BE HELD AT MR. PHILLIP MEYER'S, IN NORTH GAY STREET ON TO-MOR-ROW, OCT. 31ST AT 2 O'CLOCK P.M.
>
> PHILLIP HERZBERG
> CHAIRMAN[83]

Herzberg was a prominent businessman who had come to Baltimore in 1840; throughout his life he was active in various synagogues and other communal activities.[84]

On October 31, 1853, twenty-one men met at Phillip Meyer's home on North Gay Street.[85] The minutes of the new congregation show the economic improvement of Baltimore Jews. There was no more talk about six and a quarter cents, about the biweekly collection of dues. The dues of five dollars presented no problem, and each of the seventeen who attended the second meeting on November 13, 1853, paid the full amount. At this meeting, Julius Stiefel (1817–1905), a wealthy German-born businessman, was elected president of the new congregation, and he remained in that post for no less than twenty-six years.

The first services were held at 4 P.M. on Friday, November 25, 1853, on the third floor of the Schidshen Coach Factory, which was rented for one hundred dollars a year. The name of the new congregation, Oheb Shalom (Lover of Peace), first mentioned in the minutes of January 6, 1854, aptly described the philosophy of its founders. They were people who, above all, wanted to avoid religious strife. They hoped to achieve this end by dissociating themselves from extremists on the right and the left.

History repeated itself in 1853 for, like Har Sinai before it, the new congregation was refused a Scroll of the Law from the mother congregation.[86] The Eden Street *Shul* was more tolerant and lent a Scroll for one week, for which the Oheb Shalom Congregation expressed its gratitude in the press.[87] For a while, the congregation was helped out by N. H. Schloss from Georgetown, Virginia, who lent them a Scroll.[88]

Oheb Shalom was incorporated in 1854. One of its members, Isaac Hamburger, founder of an important clothing business, "gratuitously" became the *ḥazan* of the congregation, while a certain Altmeyer became the *Botschafter* (sexton), for which he was to be paid fifty dollars a year.[89] In the year of its incorporation, Oheb Shalom proved its vitality by acquiring its own cemetery.[90] In the same year it also engaged as preacher the Rev. Salomon, who, however, served the congregation for only a few months. He was accused of becoming engaged to a member of the congregation, in spite of the fact that he already had a wife. Because he had "acted against Mosaic and moral law," Salomon was "released from his office."[91]

When the "reformers" left the Baltimore Hebrew Congregation in 1842, it was believed that from then on it would be business as usual. There would be a clear-cut division of Orthodox and Reform, with each one going its own way and no more quarrels within each of the two groups. It was all wishful thinking.

There were "revolutions" where one would least expect them—at Har Sinai. Some of the members were disturbed by the innovations in the synagogue. They "longed for tradition of their fathers" and left Har Sinai to return to the mother congregation.[92] For others, the changes did not go far enough. They also left and instituted Sunday services; but after six months they returned.[93] All members of Har Sinai were Reform but some were more Reform than others, so that there was constant tension between the moderates and the extremists.

Nor was there much stability in the older congregation. There was constant friction between those Orthodox who wanted some changes and those who considered any change to be a move in the direction of Reform. In 1851 there was an outcry against Rabbi Hochheimer's introduction of confirmation for girls.[94] The opponents of the status quo were defeated when they tried to do away with the old custom of having a boy deliver a sermon at his bar mitzvah ceremony.[95] With a view to preventing any changes in the future, an amendment was adopted to the bylaws prohibiting

*alterations in the present mode of worship, and in the rites and cere-
monies now used, except with the assent of two thirds of the male
members in attendance at the regular called meeting.*[96]

There was considerable tension in the old synagogue. The members
were all Orthodox, but some were more and others less Orthodox.
There were skirmishes. These eventually brought about a split in the
congregation.

By 1855, twenty-five years after the establishment of the first
synagogue, Baltimore Jewry—4,000 strong—was religiously divided
more or less along the same lines as it is now, when it numbers over
100,000. There were, in addition to the small, private synagogue of
Rabbi Rice, four congregations: two Orthodox (one on Lloyd Street
and the other on Eden Street), a Reform Temple on High Street,
and the middle-of-the-road Oheb Shalom, which was still in its infancy.
The auspicious beginnings of the last augured well for its growth.

JEWISH EDUCATION

No doubt there was some private Jewish education in the community
before the establishment of a school. Surely the Ettings and the Cohens
and other less famous Jews provided some rudimentary Jewish education for their children, even if it was only to teach them to read the
prayers. Yet the first known document pertaining to a school is a circular letter sent out in March 1842. It was an invitation from "R.
Goldsmith, Secretary,"

*to attend the Consecration of the New School house erected by the
Hebrew and English Benevolent Academic Association of Baltimore,
in Bond street, between Pratt and Gough streets. . . .*[97]

While the invitation tells us nothing about the "erected" school,
it does reveal a bit about contemporary life. The letter was dated
March 28, and the meeting was to take place on the 30th. Not much
advance notice, but this was not needed in 1842, when the recipients
all lived in the same neighborhood and knew each other. The meeting
was called for 9 A.M., yet it was not a Sunday gathering—it took
place on Wednesday of *Ḥol haMoed Pesah.* Passover was a week
which peddlers spent at home; peddler suppliers, too, had a free week.

Some attendance was thus guaranteed. The word "erected" is no more than a figure of speech. Most likely the meeting room of the Assistance Society was used, with the word "Academic" added to the pretentious name. Nothing else is known about this school.

In 1845 there was a school at the Lloyd Street Synagogue, where Rabbi Rice taught Hebrew and another teacher taught English and German. For a long while the engagement of a teacher for English presented a special problem. True, there were some Jews who knew English; yet "three educated Christian gentlemen" were invited to examine a candidate in English.[98] The approbation of non-Jews carried great weight.

Har Sinai, too, established a school in 1845. There, a certain Mr. Brown taught the Hebrew subjects, while another teacher was engaged for English and German.[99]

For a long time the big event in the life of all children at Hebrew schools was the day of examinations. These tests were public and were attended by "parents and friends of the pupils and many visitors of different persuasions." For these occasions, too, non-Jews were invited. They were to examine children in "non-Jewish subjects."[100]

The Lloyd Street school was located in the basement of the synagogue building, and the schoolrooms were "too small, detrimental to the health of the children."[101] While there are no contemporary reports of the situation in the other schools, all later information leads one to believe that conditions were no better elsewhere. No wonder that those who could afford it engaged private teachers and that private schools were opened. In 1852 Solomon Jacobs, formerly a minister of Kingston, Jamaica, opened a school which was a boarding school for out-of-town children and a day school for Baltimore children, who lived at home. It was probably a sign of status that in addition to all regular subjects French was taught there.[102]

Boarding schools and private schools were private businesses. In the synagogue schools, the teachers were employees and were paid rather poorly. At Har Sinai, to cite one example, Mr. Brown was engaged to teach at a modified "piecework" rate—one hundred dollars for six months for thirty-three children. For every pupil above this number, he was to receive fifty cents. In view of such an income, Mr. Brown was forbidden to give private lessons.[103]

While some could afford private teachers or private schools, there were others who could not afford even the tuition of 62½ cents a month.[104] There were also a number of orphans in the city for whom the community at large felt obliged to provide some education.[105] In

1852 a society was organized whose sole function was to provide for the education of such indigent children. At first the twenty-two founders of the Society for the Education of the Poor and Orphan Children (whose motto was "To train up a child in the way it should go") opened the society's own school—the United Hebrew Select School. Later the society closed its school, and the needy orphans were placed in synagogue schools. Tuition, however, was paid by the society.[106]

All that was done during the formative years in the area of education was done in a rather primitive manner, but education in the general community itself was new and quite rudimentary. The first public school in the city opened only in 1829. It, too, was located in a room in the basement of a house of worship, the Presbyterian church. "Public" did not mean free. It was public only in the sense that tuition was very low. Parents who could not afford to pay even the one dollar tuition for the year were excused from paying upon presentation of a certificate of need.

A year later, this school was moved into a separate building in Aisquith Street, near Pratt Street. Now the public school was located in the heart of the Jewish neighborhood.[107] There were, however, no Jewish children among the 108 pupils who attended the school in 1830, its first year. The reason for this was the absence of German in the curriculum. That English was important was obvious; but German had an importance of its own. English was needed because one lived in America; German was the "native" tongue. German meant roots. German to the German Jew meant to be Jewish, to be of the Jewish group.

The seeming contradiction between this view and that of Rice and Leeser is in reality only a superficial one. These two men, like many others, feared the prevalence of German only in the religious sphere— they, too, wanted the children to know German, the language of the home. In addition, Jews at that time constituted a colony within the larger German colony, and German was all-important in their daily lives, in their intercourse with their non-Jewish German neighbors, with whom their relationship on the whole was friendly. For a long time this "native tongue" remained an integral part of the curriculum of the Jewish schools.

Rabbi Abraham Rice, 1800–1862, first rabbi in Baltimore.
Courtesy of the Lloyd Street Synagogue Museum.

Letter from Rice to Leeser (1831):
"in Baltimore all hope is lost."
Courtesy of the American Jewish Archives.

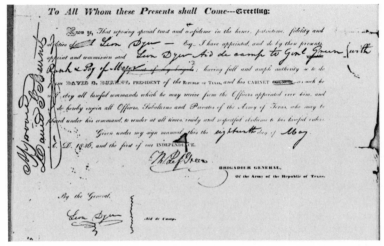

Leon Dyer, later president of the Baltimore Hebrew Congregation, is commissioned a major in the army of the Republic of Texas.
Courtesy of the American Jewish Archives.

Lloyd Street Synagogue, first synagogue built in Maryland, 1845. Legend: "Shomrei Mishmeret was inscribed in 1905."
Courtesy of the Lloyd Street Synagogue Museum.

BROADER HORIZONS—
COMMUNAL ORGANIZATIONS
OUTSIDE THE SYNAGOGUE

The synagogue was important. It took care of a Jew literally from cradle to grave. And yet there was need for an organization outside the synagogue. The congregation provided charity for the poor, but there were those who needed not charity but security in case of distress.

For the first four years of its existence (1830–1834), the Baltimore Hebrew Congregation was the only Jewish organization in the city. In 1834, however, something new was added to the life of the community, something that foreshadowed things to come. In that year forty-eight individuals joined to found a mutual assistance society—the United Hebrew Benevolent Society of Baltimore ("United," for short). Chartered on February 10, 1834, it was Baltimore's first non-synagogal Jewish organization.[108] Although officially a mutual aid society, it was in reality a charitable organization.[109] It also had, as was to be expected, some religious overtones. The charter stated that the organization could adopt a constitution and bylaws "provided, that the same shall not be contrary to . . . the Jewish Rites. . . ." The charter gave as the reason for the formation of the organization "the laudable purpose of affording relief to each other, and their respective families, in the event of sickness, distress or death."

Among the most active members of the society were Jacob Ezekiel and Levy Collmus (or Kollmus). Ezekiel, the secretary of the society, was born in Philadelphia in 1812 and came to Baltimore in 1833. He remained only a short while and made his mark in Jewish life in Richmond and, later, in Cincinnati.[110] Levy Collmus, the society's treasurer, an immigrant from Prague, settled in Baltimore in 1800. A "traveling merchant" (a euphemism for peddler), Collmus married in 1812 a Quaker girl, Frances Williams. In spite of his marriage outside the faith, he continued to be active in Jewish affairs. His ledger, a small unbound notebook, is the only known document of the "Chebra," as the name of the society appears in this booklet.[111]

The word "united" in the name of the first organization in the city may appear puzzling. Since it was the first, the society obviously could not unite with anybody. The answer is that among Jews the word had a different meaning, one which is the key to the understanding of the future development of the community. For united in this case meant that, while Jews might differ in many areas, they were united when the objective was mutual assistance.

The "United" was not only the first "secular" Jewish organization in Baltimore, it was probably the first German-Jewish society which Spanish Jews joined. It was unusual for Sephardic Jews like Benjamin Seixas and Solomon Carvalho to join an Ashkenazic synagogue. An assistance organization was quite another matter. This was the key to all future activities of various charity organizations. Charity in its widest forms was to be the unifying force of a community divided in many respects.

In the meantime, soon after the "United" came into being, other similar organizations did too. The German Hebrew Charity Society of Baltimore was organized in 1839.[112] It was followed by the Baltimore Hebrew and English Academic Association.[113] All of these were mutual assistance societies. The first purely charitable organization, the Hebrew Assistance Society, was formed in 1843. Its only objective was to render help to poor people. Five years after its formation, the Assistance Society arranged an unusual affair, the first of its kind in Baltimore. The event, a "Charity Ball," was attended not only by Jews but also by about two hundred non-Jews.[114]

In 1856 the "Assistance," as it was called, was reorganized under the name Hebrew Benevolent Society.[115] The composition of its board of directors again bears testimony to the unifying effect of charity. William S. Rayner, the leader of the Reform Jews, and Jonas Friedenwald, the extreme Orthodox Jew, could and did serve as managers of the Benevolent Society. Another manager was Dr. Joshua Cohen, who never joined any existing congregation. The biblical precept that "thy brother may live with thee" was duly observed. The Hebrew Benevolent Society remained in existence for over seven decades. From its humble beginnings and crude social work through managers, it developed in the course of time into a society with highly trained personnel, its work embracing many facets of communal life.

The poor among the Jews were given help freely, so that a leading Baltimore newspaper, writing about the conditions of the poor in the city, could state:

Inasmuch as we know, no Jew has ever asked for assistance from the general charity fund. The Jews take care of their own poor and contribute to poor of all religions.[116]

IN DEFENSE
OF THE COUNTRY

The spirit of America's "manifest destiny" was accentuated by President James K. Polk. A number of incidents brought about the invasion of Mexico by American soldiers. On May 11, 1846, Congress declared that "by act of the Republic of Mexico, a state of war exists between that government and the United States."

When the president issued a call for forty thousand volunteers, a mass war meeting was called in Baltimore. Jacob Cohen, who had courageously fought for Jewish equality, was the chairman of the meeting.[117] Enthusiasm for the defense of Texas and the Union was duly aroused, and a company bearing the name "Baltimore's Own" was mustered into the federal service. Although any Jew in the city who wished to join the company could do so, the Jews who volunteered preferred to join a special Jewish company, The First Baltimore Hebrew Guards, which was formed in 1846. The reason for this is unknown, but one may safely assume that those young men did not want to be lost in Baltimore's Own but, by creating their own independent company, to draw attention to their identity. It was their way of saying, "Yes, we are Americans and will fight for the country, but we are Jews and we want everyone to know it." With the exception of the chief officer, Captain Carroll, all officers were Jews. They were Levi Benjamin, Joseph Simpson, Samuel G. Goldsmith, S. Eytinge, and Dr. Phineas J. Horwitz.[118]

Dr. Horwitz, a surgeon, was born in Baltimore in 1822, the son of Dr. Jonathan Horwitz. Jonathan came to America in 1812 as a representative of a Jewish printing concern to examine the possibility of printing a Hebrew Bible in this country, and for this purpose he brought with him Hebrew type. The Bible was published, but Horwitz played a minor part in this enterprise.[119] He then began to study medicine at the University of Pennsylvania, and upon graduation he practiced in Philadelphia and Baltimore. Horwitz married Deborah

Andrews, Haym Salomon's granddaughter. In 1822 he settled in Baltimore, where, in addition to his work in medicine, he devoted himself to the writing of a book entitled *A Defense of the Cosmogony of Moses* (published in 1839), in which he expounded a traditional Jewish point of view. It is strange that this defender of Judaism was buried in 1852 in an Episcopalian cemetery (although there is no record of his conversion).

MAKING A LIVING

Important as all religious and social activities of Baltimore Jewry were, they were secondary to the main concern—making a living. By the end of the formative period, in the middle fifties of the last century, many of the Jews in the community had achieved a measure of economic stability. Some of the leading clothing businesses had their beginnings in those years. The majority of the immigrants, especially the recent ones, were still struggling as small storekeepers, craftsmen, or peddlers. Of these, the last was the most difficult occupation, but it was the easiest to begin. Since this was still a preindustrialized period, these immigrants could not do what their successors from Eastern Europe could so easily do at the end of the century—become "Columbus tailors" overnight. The sewing machine had not yet been invented. As for storekeeping, even the smallest store required some capital; but the penniless immigrants had absolutely nothing with which to start even the smallest business.

All that peddling required was a strong back and a pair of sturdy legs. The pack was heavy, the distances were long. The pack was filled by the supplier, who was paid for the merchandise when the peddler returned with his empty pack to the city—only to refill it and start out anew. It was a hard life. Peddlers had to be away from their families for days and at times for weeks. Although very observant at home, they were often forced by circumstances to eat non-*kasher* food on the road. They were ridiculed for their broken English, for their manners and mannerisms, in short, for being Jews. Every peddler prayed for the day when he could get rid of his heavy pack and be able to buy a horse and buggy.

The legend that every peddler achieved success and then opened a general store or even a department store is only a legend. Success stories are recorded. Failures fail even in history. Their records, like the men themselves, are forgotten. Yet, despite all the difficulties, some of the Baltimore peddlers did manage to climb the economic ladder, establish themselves, and become builders of the community. Their economic advance was not due to any Jewish "genius" for business. It was a result of hard work, coupled with the great opportunities which Baltimore offered at that period.

The formative period in the history of the Baltimore Jewish community coincided with the years of the enormous growth of Baltimore. From a city of 80,000 in 1830, it grew into a city of 170,000 in 1850.[120] The numerical growth was accompanied by a geographic expansion. By 1850 Baltimore's limits were, on the north, North Avenue; on the west, Bentalou Street; on the south, Gwynns Falls; and, on the east, East Avenue. A small town as viewed by today's standards, it was a large city by the standards of that period.

The Jewish population of the city increased even more rapidly. It more than trebled in one decade. In 1840, there were approximately two hundred families; in 1850 it numbered about seven hundred families.[121] By the end of the 1850s, Leeser believed the number of Jews in Baltimore to be "perhaps greater than that in Philadelphia, at least not much inferior."[122]

The failure of the revolution of 1848 brought large masses of Germans to America. In the decade between 1840 and 1850, 50,660 people from Germany landed in Baltimore. The following decade brought another 73,722.[123] The number of Jews was proportionately larger. They had suffered more in their "mother country" and were naturally more anxious to leave. Baltimore was a port of debarkation, although not all who landed there remained in the city. Those who settled in Baltimore found themselves, geographically speaking, in the center of the Union. It was a great railroad center, indeed, the very heart of the empire of the "iron horse." Business in the city was expanding quickly. Fortunes were made by enterprising men, especially those willing to take a chance. Many became wealthy, among them a number of Jews.

Lloyd Street, Exeter Street, High Street, and other streets in that neighborhood were the original area of Jewish settlement. Those who prospered began to move out and create new Jewish neighborhoods— a characteristic feature of areas of Jewish residence even in present-day Baltimore. Tho prosperous moved out as new poor immigrants moved in, making East Baltimore the Jewish center of the city until the nation closed its doors to further immigration.

Rabbi Isaac Mayer Wise, the leading Reform rabbi, keen observer of Jewish life that he was, described the appearance of a Jewish street on the Baltimore East Side in 1850.

> There seemed to be many Jews there, although everything is very primitive. Women in the small shops carrying children in their arms, or else knitting busily. Young men invited passers-by to enter this or that store to buy . . . M'zuzoth, Tzitzith, Talethim, Kosher cheese and Eretz Yisrael earth were on sale. On the other hand there were many prominent wholesale houses where everything was conducted in orderly and businesslike manner.[124]

Wise could not see, of course, the very many peddlers, who were scattered to all parts of Maryland and Virginia.

Where there were peddlers there were, naturally, peddler suppliers. These wholesalers developed large businesses. By 1855, the end of the formative period of the Jewish community, there were already a number of big businesses owned by Jews. These firms would develop into even greater concerns in the next quarter of a century.

There were still very few Jews in the professions. There were many who slaved for long hours in their small stores and still others who clerked in the growing clothing businesses. With the growth of these enterprises the number of drummers in faraway parts of the country grew. Economic diversity was beginning to be the norm. Leeser, who knew the community well and had observed it from close range for many years, wrote in 1851, after a visit to the city, "We hope that . . . every effort will be made . . . to unite for a common good though they worship in different synagogues."[125] He did not mention the socioeconomic divisions, which were already in existence in the 1850s and became much more pronounced in the succeeding period. Yet Leeser's hopes for unity were realized. Jewish needs at home and abroad brought together people of diverse ideologies. Diversity was there, but so was unity.

III

YEARS OF DISSENSION
AND EXPANSION:
1855–1880

DISSENSIONS

The quarter of a century following its formative period was a time of great growth for the Baltimore Jewish community, as it was for Baltimore as a whole. From a population of 188,000 in 1855, the city grew to 332,000 in 1880;[1] at the same time the Jewish community grew from 800 families[2] to no less than 10,000 souls.[3] The numerical growth was marked by accomplishments in many areas and was accompanied by great economic expansion.[4]

The Jewish geography of the city at this time also underwent a great change during this quarter century. The city of Baltimore had grown in an ever-widening arc around the original sixty acres purchased for the town in 1729. The city loomed like a hand, with Whitstone Point—at the end of which is Fort McHenry—jutting out below like a thumb, poised to clutch the northwest branch of the Patapsco River, which flows broadly southward to meet Chesapeake Bay fourteen miles away. The center of the city was the harbor. The Baltimore of the 1850s was geographically composed of three circles. The large outer circle was divided, east from west, by a turbulent stream called Jones's Falls. On the east side of this stream was another circle, the large German colony of Baltimore, and within this enclave there was a smaller area where most of the Jews of the city lived.

Although they maintained their own institutions, the Jews were a part of "little Germany." Like the German Gentiles, the Jewish Germans spoke the language of their *Vaterland;* they brought up their children in this language; and they advertised their private as well as communal affairs in Baltimore's two German dailies: *Der Deutsche Correspondent* and *Der Wecker.* The Jews were identified as Germans or German Hebrews (this was still the period when Jews designated themselves, and were designated by others, as "Hebrews" or "Israelites").

Two successive shifts in the places of residence of the Jews took place through this period. By the 1830s they were leaving the original area of settlement, moving, as their economic position improved, to the "outlying" southwest district around Hanover, Lexington, Fayette, and Saratoga Streets. In the 1870s there was a second move—this time to the area of Madison Avenue and Eutaw Place. Both times the shift was to more prosperous neighborhoods.

The first decade of the period of expansion, from 1855 until 1865, was characterized by endless dissensions and rifts. At times it seemed as if the Jewish community would be torn apart beyond repair. However, common interests proved to be stronger than differences and even animosities. They outweighed both the diversity of ideologies and the bitterness of individuals involved in the conflicts. In the center of all the clashes for several years stood the first rabbi of Har Sinai Congregation, the great leader of Reform Jewry, David Einhorn.

The Radical—David Einhorn

IN EUROPE[5]

David Einhorn was born in 1809 in the small Bavarian village of Dipseek, near Fürth. Early in his life he became a student at the famous yeshiva in Würzburg, where he studied under the renowned scholar Wolf Hamburger. (In fact, two Baltimore rabbis studied under Hamburger, both the radical Reform Jew, Einhorn, and the extreme Orthodox, Abraham Rice.) Upon ordination, the seventeen-year-old Einhorn did not immediately become a rabbi. He exchanged the hard bench of the yeshiva for that of the university and attended institutions of higher learning in Erlangen, Würzburg, and Munich. He openly expressed his liberal views on religion and rituals and was blocked from securing a post as rabbi by the Bavarian Orthodox leaders. It was only in 1842, at the age of thirty-three, that Einhorn acquired a position, and an important one at that. He became chief rabbi in Birkenfeld, in the liberal Grand Duchy of Oldenburg.

The 1840s were years of great religious controversy among Jews in Germany. Einhorn participated in rabbinical conferences in which his position on all issues was extremely radical. In 1852 he was invited to become rabbi of the Reform congregation in Pest (later part of Budapest). He had served there only two months when the government, feeling that this firebrand might prove dangerous, closed the temple altogether. Einhorn took to writing, and two years later he published his first book, *The Principles of Mosaic Faith and Its Relationship to Paganism and Rabbinic Judaism*.[6] In 1855 Einhorn received the call from Har Sinai Congregation in Baltimore. He was a man of forty-six, a man with a great reputation, when he decided to come to the New World.

FIRST STEPS IN BALTIMORE

In Baltimore, Einhorn found himself rabbi of a small and struggling congregation. On September 27, 1855, he delivered his inaugural sermon. It was much more than just a conventional religious discourse. It was an exposition of a philosophy, a platform of principles, and a call to action. He spoke of the "indisputable fact" that

the old world is fast crumbling to pieces, and a new world seeks to rise from the ruins. . . . Judaism has reached the turning point, which demands the abolition of all defunct usages.

Here was a call not for mere decorum. Although Einhorn considered it "very laudable" to make the services more attractive, he stressed the point that this alone "will and must prove unavailing." The "inward decay" could not be cured in such a manner. What Einhorn demanded was a complete revolution, a separation of "everything that is transient and corrupt, from [the] religious sphere of life." He insisted that "we must achieve for us and our children the liberation of Judaism for the sake of preventing an estrangement from Judaism."

Faith in America and in the opportunities that this country offered the Jews to develop a richer spiritual life were part of his address.

On this consecrated soil of religious liberty our community may flourish unmolested by a Pharaoh . . . where the slightest religions and their humble followers are prevented from unfolding their innate energies. Far be it from us to entertain the least doubt, that Judaism, the religion of freedom, could not endure in freedom as well as it has endured unscathed the oppression of centuries.

Finally, Einhorn spoke of his belief

in a humanity, the members of which have one and the same heavenly origin, equal in dignity of birth, in law and right, who possess the same claims for happiness and a state of blessedness which will be realized already here on earth.[7]

Those who had heard of Einhorn's activities in Europe knew that his pronouncements were a call to action, and indeed he soon proved his intentions. In this he was never alone. Although by nature a loner with a special gift for making enemies, he did attract ardent followers. The first opportunity for dissent presented itself only two weeks after Einhorn delivered his first sermon. Before long all of Baltimore Jewry became involved in the dissensions which Einhorn stirred up.

THE CLEVELAND CONFERENCE

As early as 1845, Rabbi Rice had expressed his fear that Jewish religious life in America was in danger. He believed that "though the great ocean divides us, the sparks scattered from the burning are already kindling a flame in our dwelling."[8] He was speaking, of course, about the Reform movement, which was then spreading in Germany. He saw only one solution to this danger. American Jewry was to select "a spiritual chief, or *beth din*, for the purpose of regulating our spiritual affairs and before whom all religious questions might be brought for decision."[9] Rice's call fell upon deaf ears.[10] There were no rabbis in the country to rally round him—or for that matter to oppose him. When he made his appeal, he was still the only rabbi in the entire United States.

Ten years had passed. The situation changed. There were now other rabbis, among them the organizing genius Isaac Mayer Wise, who had come to America in 1846. On August 10, 1855, Wise and eight other rabbis, among them two Baltimoreans, Hochheimer and Günzburg, issued a call for a conference "in the name of Israel's religion." The nine rabbis who issued the call requested that delegates of "Israelitisch Congregations" attend a conference on October 17 in Cleveland. One of the stated purposes of the meeting was to discuss "a plan to organize a regular synod." The conference met, and among other resolutions, adopted one asserting that:

The Bible as delivered to us by our fathers is of immediate divine origin. . . .The Talmud contains traditional legal and logical expositions of the Biblical laws, which must be expounded and practiced according to the comments of the Talmud.[11]

Einhorn, although a newcomer in the country, immediately entered the fray and issued a "protest." Joined by all the members of Har Sinai, he announced:

We do not consider the Talmudic exegesis of the Bible as legal or obligatory. . . . We also appreciate peace in Israel as a precious boon, but a peace which necessarily degrades Judaism . . . appears to us too dearly bought. . . . May the free American Israel keep a strict watch on hierarchical movements which would again forge its chains though under the most charming lullabies of peace. . . .[12]

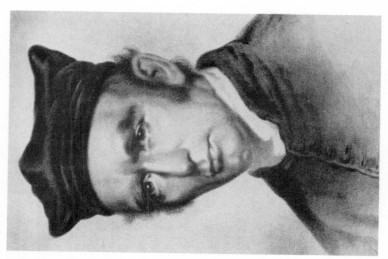

עלת תמיד

BOOK OF PRAYERS

FOR

Israelitish Congregations.

עלת תמיד העשׁיה בהר סיני לריח ניחח אשׁה ליהוה

A CONTINUAL BURNT-OFFERING, AS ORDAINED ON MOUNT SINAI FOR
A SWEET SAVOR, A SACRIFICE BY FIRE TO THE LORD.

(*Numbers XXVIII, 6.*)

FOR SALE

BY THE SEXTON OF THE CONGREGATION ADATH JESHURUN,

At their Temple in 39th St., between 7th and 8th Avenues,

NEW YORK.

Title page of Rabbi Einhorn's prayer book, Olat Tamid.
From author's collection.

Rabbi David Einhorn, 1809–1879, leading Reform rabbi, abolitionist.
Courtesy of the Har Sinai Congregation.

Title page of Rabbi Szold's prayer book, Avodat Israel.
Courtesy of the Baltimore Hebrew College.

Rabbi Benjamin Szold, 1829–1902, leading rabbi and scholar.
Courtesy of the Lloyd Street Synagogue Museum.

Einhorn was in an excellent position to disseminate his views. He had arrived in September 1855, and in February 1856 he had already begun publishing his monthly *Sinai*, subtitled *Ein Organ für Erkentniss und Veredlung des Judenthums* ("A Publication for the Understanding and Refinement of Judaism"), the motto of which was "I seek my brethren" (Gen. 37:16).

In addition to the "protest," Einhorn published a resolution of solidarity with his views by Temple Emanuel in New York, an attack on the conference by the leading Reform rabbi in Germany, Ludwig Phillipson, and his own special article on the subject—all in the first issue of *Sinai*. It was clear that the Baltimore Reform rabbi would fight against the establishment of a central religious body and against the recognition of the Talmud as an authoritative exposition of the biblical laws.

Einhorn's protest brought about a counterattack from Baltimore's Rabbi Rice. In spite of their ideological differences, there was a degree of respect between the two adversaries. Einhorn, master of sarcasm though he was, wrote of Rice that, unlike other Orthodox leaders, he was a "conscientious Orthodox."[13] And Rice, in his "Counter Protest," wrote:

Men have assumed in this country the title of Rabbis, who have put on their own heads the rabbinical cap. . . . I deem it unbecoming to contend with such men. But you, doctor, who have been familiar with the light of the Gemara *and are only too much blinded at the present moment, I think myself duty-bound to answer.*[14]

Einhorn continued his attacks on Orthodoxy, and finally Rice replied in kind:

After all it is a pity to have a religious discussion with you. For "can the Ethiopian change his skin or the leopard his spots?"; so also can you do good who are practised in doing evil? . . .[15]

Before long the Orthodox became disenchanted with their alliance with Wise, and the stillborn Cleveland Conference failed to produce the hoped-for unity of American Jewry. This effort to bring about unity among American Jews only succeeded in accentuating their differences. The discord was especially pronounced in Baltimore, where every rabbi in the community became involved. Hochheimer and Günzburg sided with Wise in his efforts to find a compromise; Einhorn fought against any conciliation with Orthodoxy, and Rice fought against any compromise with Reform. It was not, however, a quarrel among a few individuals. Each rabbi had his ardent followers. Before long the entire community was embroiled.

While all this was going on among Baltimore Jews, a political movement known as the Know-Nothings was spreading in the United States. The mass immigration of Irish and Bavarian German Catholics aroused apprehension among old-stock Americans that the country might fall into the hands of "foreigners."

The geographical concentration of the Germans and Irish in Baltimore had provided these groups with a political power base. As early as the 1820s, Germans became very prominent in the state and municipal governments. The situation in Baltimore prevailed in many other large cities as well. The rise of the Know-Nothing party in response to the fears of old-stock Americans gained momentum. It was so strong in Baltimore that it succeeded in electing its leaders, Samuel Hicks and James M. Harris, as mayor and congressman. Its clubs, the "Rednecks," "Rip-Rap," "Black Snakes," and others, "took care" of the voters. Baltimore became known as "Mob-Town."

Since the Know-Nothing party was not specifically anti-Jewish, many Jewish leaders missed the point that its antialien sentiments could ultimately affect the Jews, most of whom were newcomers.[16] Einhorn was the rare exception. Himself a foreigner and a newcomer, he dared to attack the Know-Nothings openly. As in practically all his public battles, he spoke not only for himself but for others in the community who did not have the ability or lacked the courage to express themselves publicly.

To Einhorn, this antiforeign movement represented a danger to the very existence of the country. "America," he wrote, "can exist only on moral foundations." When these bases are undermined, "it is not fit to survive, nor is it worth[y of] surviving."[17] He also saw in the struggle against the Know-Nothings a purely Jewish problem.

Once we start to evaluate people by the country of birth, next will come an evaluation by religion and in this case, surely, the Jews, the so-called crucifiers of the crucified, will be in danger.[18]

More than that, Einhorn believed that Jewish morality obliged Jews to stand up against the Know-Nothings. The defeat of this party would be a victory "of the Mosaic law of equality of the stranger with the native before the law of the land."[19]

Know-Nothingism had only a short life in American history. In spite of the fact that they attacked voters, and injured and even killed people—or perhaps because of such tactics—members of this nativist movement aroused the ire of the citizenry, and it soon went out of existence.

As for Baltimore Jews, whether they were or were not in agreement with Einhorn, they surely realized that there was among them a leader who knew no fear. There must have been many Jews in the community, however, who were apprehensive of this very quality in him. All these immigrants wanted was to make a living and not to be involved in general politics. It was one thing to fight each other on religious matters, on Jewish unity; it was quite another matter to take positions on political matters which might antagonize the neighbors, the "real" Americans. But Einhorn considered general politics also to be his business. There was fear that this man, although he might be well meaning, would endanger the position of the Jews of Baltimore, and perhaps even of the entire country.

Einhorn's fights until 1860 were, however, only a prelude to the great feud that broke out between him, the fifty-one-year-old "old-timer," and the newcomer, the thirty-year-old Benjamin Szold.

The Man of Peace and Moderation—[20]
Benjamin Szold

IN EUROPE

Benjamin Szold was born in 1829 in the village of Nemiskert, Hungary. At the age of nine he lost both his parents and was raised in the home of an uncle, who faithfully followed the will of his brother Boruch. This specified that his son Bunem (Benjamin) should attend a yeshiva, and that he "should not (God forbid) cease studying until he was at least twenty years of age."[21]

At the age of fourteen Bunem entered the yeshiva of Pressburg, where he studied for five years. He then left for Vienna in the hope of pursuing secular studies at the university. The year was 1848, the year of revolutions in Europe, and the young Szold, then nineteen years old, exchanged his books for the barricades. When the revolution was crushed, the would-be university student returned to Pressburg.

A new career awaited him. A remarkable and enterprising widow, Miryam Schaar, of the tiny village of Cziffer in Slovakia, engaged him as tutor to her six sons and four daughters. The young tutor spent six years in the company of this congenial family. He was treated as a member of the family and eventually became one in reality when he married the youngest of the daughters, Sophie. During these years he taught and studied. In 1856 he left for Breslau, where he became a student at the university and simultaneously at the Breslau Rabbinical Seminary. His teachers—among whom were such great scholars as the founder of the seminary, Zacharias Frankel, and the historian Heinrich Graetz—must have thought highly of him, for they gave him the highest recommendation when he was invited to deliver trial sermons in Stockholm.[22]

Szold was one of two candidates who were invited to deliver trial sermons; the other, Ludwig Lewysohn, was the man elected by the Stockholm community. At that time Lewysohn also received news that he had been elected rabbi of the Oheb Shalom Congregation in Baltimore,[23] but he decided to remain in Stockholm. Upon receipt of this news, the Oheb Shalom Congregation invited the great scholar Abraham Geiger to become its rabbi;[24] there is no record of Geiger's reply. Meanwhile, Lewysohn recommended Szold for the position which had been originally offered to him. When Oheb Shalom received in addition a favorable letter about him from the great scholar Zacharias Frankel, they decided to offer the position to Szold.

The president of the congregation, Julius Stiefel, and board members Jacob Rose and Joseph Sachs offered Szold the position of rabbi for five years at fifteen hundred dollars a year. They made, however, one "express stipulation": Szold "must embrace the historically moderate Reforms, which are the basis of the congregation." This generality was explained in detail.

We have an organ and a choir; the PIYUTIM *except on* Rosh Hashana *and* Yom Kippur *have been annulled. We have provisionally accepted a Hebrew prayerbook drawn up by Drs. Wise, Kalish and Rotheimer; the Torah portion is* [read] *without a melody and haphtorah is read in German. . . .*

Nothing could please the future rabbi of Oheb Shalom more than such a letter. He was a young man not given to extremes. His thinking was along the lines which are now termed "Conservative." Indeed, Szold's teacher Zacharias Frankel is considered the father of this movement, even as Szold is thought of as one of the originators of this ideology in America. He was happy to be invited by a congregation that, in the words of its officers, stood "midway between orthodoxy and ultra-reform, the last defended by Dr. Einhorn."

Szold no doubt had heard about Einhorn, but either did not expect controversy or was not afraid to meet the challenge if it came. What counted most was the letter of a congregation affirming a position dear to him.

Historical reform is a necessity here in America if the young generation is to be preserved and be inspired for Judaism, while Orthodoxy is only an empty word, which proves itself only in the synagogue through the retention of the old and fixed habits, but stands in glaring opposition to the life of the majority who follow it.[25]

Not only was the letter to the young rabbi's liking, but his mentor, Frankel, also advised him to go to America, where "the whole world will be open before you."[26]

There was one more important step to be taken before crossing the ocean. Szold married his former student Sophie Schaar, and, full of dreams and hopes, the young couple departed for a new life in the New World.

FIRST STEPS IN BALTIMORE

On September 24, 1859, only three days after his arrival, the thirty-year-old Szold delivered his inaugural sermon. Szold was an attractive speaker. His was not the Einhorn style and he pointed out that

dissensions have arisen in the midst of Israel: the spirit of the time on one side and the tradition on the other. . . . Many want to press all religious demands in obsolete garb. . . . The others again yield everything to the authority of the times. . . .

To Szold it was "evident that in neither direction the exclusive truth is contained. The truth in general, must be in a right medium. . . ."[27] The congregation was, no doubt, happy with this exposition by their rabbi. Here was one who was against Orthodoxy as well as Reform. Their hopes for a middle-of-the-road spiritual leader were fulfilled.

The Great Feud

Einhorn, who outreformed all reformers, could not possibly remain silent in the face of the new "danger." This eloquent young preacher, Szold, was even more dangerous than an outright Orthodox, for he spoke like a reformer and might be mistaken for one—which he definitely was not. He must be exposed.

With the zeal so characteristic of the man, Einhorn entered into battle. He savagely attacked Szold in a scathing article entitled "Das Schicksal der Oheb Shalom Gemeinde" (The Fate of the Oheb

Shalom Congregation), which he published in *Sinai*. It was a long article full of invective. The opening and the closing words of it were the same, "America is a land of humbug," and Einhorn's thesis was that the humbug presented by Szold might, therefore, have an appeal. It was not a criticism of Szold's philosophy of "historic Reform," but rather a bitter personal attack upon the new rabbi and his talk, which lacked *"Saft und Kraft"* (content and power). There was almost no limit to personal abuse in this "welcome" from one rabbi to another.

Herr Szold is not able to think clearly, to speak in an orderly manner, to write correctly. . . . There is only one excuse, Herr Szold does not know what he is talking about. . . . A chick barely out of the egg wants to play the role of a roaring lion. . . . a man who cannot distinguish his right hand from his left.

All this was followed by a magnanimous offer to Szold to reply, if he wished, in the *Sinai*.[28]

Szold did reply—but not in Einhorn's magazine. He published an eighteen-page, small-print brochure entitled *Der Enthülte Einhorn (Einhorn Unmasked)*. The soft-spoken Szold retorted in kind, using Einhorn's language. It began and ended with a quotation from Proverbs: "The lip of truth shall be established for ever; but a lying tongue is but for a moment." It was a call to the *Glaubensbrüder* (brothers in faith) to realize that Einhorn was "arrogant, conceited, a man without honor, who insults Judaism as no enemy of the Jews before him had ever done," and so on. Szold expressed the hope that his own name would be remembered with love, while that of Einhorn "will be execrated with an eternal curse by the entire world."[29]

The brochure concluded with a report of a "public meeting" of the Oheb Shalom Congregation held on Sunday, December 4, 1859. The meeting, so it was reported, investigated the "precious piece of Einhornism." Einhorn was identified as "the editor of the *Sinai*, who also officiates as preacher of a Sect called the Har Sinai Verein." In the report of the meeting, Einhorn's article was called a "masterpiece of unequalled insolence and shame, unbecoming a gentleman and particularly a Minister," and Szold was requested "not to condescend to notice or answer it." Yet they did answer and resolved

for the protection of our children's religious morals not [to] admit in our homes or families the keeping or reading of the so-called Sinai, edited by David Einhorn.

It was also resolved by the congregation to give the resolution the widest possible circulation by publishing it in *The Israelite*, *The Occident*, *Der Deutsche Correspondent* (*Baltimore*), and *Allgemeine Zeitung des Judenthums*. (All of this was published in the brochure in which it was recommended "not to notice or answer" Einhorn's article.) [30]

Einhorn was not the kind of man to let his adversary have the last say. He published an "*Abvertigung*" (Final Rejoinder). This was a twenty-eight page article of name-calling and ridicule of the "incompetent" Szold. "If," Einhorn wrote, "the honest Orthodox Rabbi Abraham Rice would curse me, which he does not do, I would forgive him," but, he continued, he could not forgive an "ignorant youngster." Having exhausted his invective, Einhorn finished his brochure in a tone of self-righteousness by stating, "My motto is 'Let them curse, but you shall bless.' "[31]

The altercation between the two created ill feelings, directly between the members of the two congregations involved and indirectly among other Jews in the community. The Orthodox regarded both rabbis as reformers and were only too happy to witness the falling out between them. For Jews who were not affiliated with any congregation, the constant denunciations were, no doubt, also a matter of discussion, of debate, of taking sides. The feud created turmoil in the Jewish community, which, despite ideological squabbles within each synagogue, had been otherwise placid. Now the quarrels became intra-synagogal.

The dust of this feud had hardly settled before new troubles began. This time it was a free-for-all, rabbis against rabbis, congregations against congregations, fathers against sons, brothers against brothers. The Civil War broke out. Hatred between supporters of opposing views was widespread, and what was characteristic of the country generally, including the Jews, was especially sharp in the border city of Baltimore.

Baltimore Jewry
and the Civil War[32]

There were about seven thousand Jews in Baltimore on the eve of the Civil War.[33] Their views on political issues were generally the same as those of the majority of the Germans in the city. *Der*

93

Deutsche Correspondent was the most popular German paper and was considered by the Jews as a "Jewish paper." It was in this paper, for example, and not in the English press, that the Oheb Shalom Congregation published its attack on Einhorn. The paper expressed the views of its readers and in turn molded their views. It favored the status quo on the issue of slavery. But it went a step further in reminding its readers that they were, after all, only immigrants and that they were

never to forget that the Constitution of the United States, in support of which every adopted citizen of the Republic has sworn an oath of loyalty, sanctions and protects the institution of slavery.[34]

While this was the general attitude of both the Germans and the Jews in Baltimore, there were extremists at both ends of the spectrum. On the one hand, there were those who went further than the mere acceptance of slavery as an established institution. They developed a philosophy to justify it. They considered slavery a "divine institution," with no price, including secession, too high for its retention. On the other hand, there were those who saw the Civil War as a continuation of the revolution of 1848 in Europe. They expressed their philosophy in one simple sentence: "Within the Union happy, outside the Union unhappy."[35] Paraphrasing the adage *Wie es christelt sich so juedelt es sich*, one might say about the attitude of the Baltimore Jews to the Civil War: *Wie es deutschelt sich so juedelt es sich*.

Like the bulk of the non-Jewish German immigrants, most Jews rejected both extremes. Yet the extremists did have a following, which should not be overlooked. The mood of the Jewish community was to a large degree reflected in the sermons of the rabbis. Although there were at that time many organizations, neither their Minute Books nor those of the congregations reflect conditions in the city or the inner thoughts of the people. There is hardly anything in these books which would give an inkling that a war was going on. Not that people were unconcerned about the war, but their concern was not recorded in the Minute Books.

It was generally known in the community that Rabbi Szold had secured furloughs for Jewish soldiers stationed in and around Baltimore for the High Holidays.[36] These soldiers no doubt prayed in the synagogues of the city and ate in Jewish homes. Szold was also active in the case of a Jewish private, George Kuhn, who was in great trouble—he was to be executed for desertion. Since there was no rabbi in Washington, the army sent for Szold. After he met with Kuhn, he went to the president and asked for clemency, which was denied. Szold stayed with the Jewish deserter at his execution.[37]

One of Baltimore's Jews, Moses Strauss, was a member of the delegation to protest to President Lincoln and other high government officials about General Grant's notorious order of December 17, 1862, to expel "the Jews, as a class" from the Department of the Tennessee.[38]

We know of two Jewish soldiers who were buried in the cemeteries of two Baltimore congregations.[39] Except for these few cases and an occasional remark about "unfortunate times which have befallen us,"[40] "arrears in dues," and what seems to be a natural concomitant, the reduction in the salaries of the rabbis,[41] there is nothing in the congregational records about the war. We do have the opinions of the rabbis of the city, as expressed in their sermons and writings, and the documents of a few lay people who let their feelings be known, either in writing or in deed.

Rabbi Rice at this period had his own little synagogue and had very little influence in the community at large. We know a little about his views from some of the letters he wrote to his friends. In one of them, written in the summer of 1862, he expressed apprehension and prayed, "May He, who is merciful to all, guard us in these times from all troubles and misfortunes." The "us" meant, of course, Jews. The rabbi's wife added a more specific postscript to the letter: "May God help us that the whole thing should pass peacefully for the Jews."[42]

In the oldest congregation in the city, the Baltimore Hebrew, Rabbi Bernard Illoway defended and justified slavery. While he did not go to the extreme of openly preaching secession, he did declare himself openly in sympathy with secessionists. Said Illoway:

Who can blame our brethren of the South for their being inclined to secede from a society . . . whose union is kept together . . . by . . . heavy iron ties of violence and arbitrary force? Who can blame our brethren of the South for seceding from a society whose government cannot or will not protect the property, rights and privileges of a great portion of the Union . . . ?

This statement was followed by the usual defense of states' rights. Illoway went so far as to compare the rights of states with those of foreign countries. He stated his position quite bluntly, that "we have no right to exercise violence against the institutions of other states or other countries."

All of this, however, was political doctrine. As a rabbi, Illoway felt obliged to prove that his views were based on the teachings of the Bible. He did this by posing two questions: "Why did not Moses . . . prohibit the buying or selling of slaves?" "Where was ever a greater philanthropist than Abraham, and why did he not set free his slaves?"[43]

A position of neutrality was advocated by Szold. In his sermons, he quoted the Bible and the Talmud extensively to substantiate his view that "peace is the angel of consolation." Szold had a "simple" solution: since "all . . . heartily long for . . . peace and reconciliation," all that was needed was for the warring sections to discuss the problem; because "the language . . . proves itself the harbinger of peace and reconciliation, it is in the power of this heavenly gift [language] to reconcile." The great issues of the day were reduced to statements that "the land of the free and the home of the brave is the tumultuous arena of unbridled passions, and partisans and hungry office seekers."[44] His position was very popular in Baltimore: peace, peace above all, peace at any price.

When Lincoln died, Szold eulogized him, calling him "so devoted to freedom, that we may, indeed, consider him as a son of Israel."[45] No doubt he was sincere. Szold was not anti-Negro, nor was he pro-slavery. When the war was over, Szold became active in the Baltimore Association for the Education and Moral Improvement of the Colored People.[46] He preached about "a God of love, who does not suffer men to be doomed to misery and to be enthralled in slavery."[47] During the war, however, peace was to him more precious than anything else. His belief was that only peace could preserve freedom. Similar to Szold's position was that of his personal and ideological friend, Rabbi Henry Hochheimer.[48]

Those opposed to slavery had their spokesman in Rabbi Einhorn. In his *Sinai* he denounced slavery as "the cancer of the union."[49]

Does the Negro have an iron neck that does not feel a burdensome yoke? Does he have a stiffer heart that does not bleed when . . . his beloved child is torn away from him?[50]

Einhorn published four articles[51] in answer to Rabbi Morris Jacob Raphall, who had preached in defense of slavery.[52] In bitterness and pain Einhorn wrote:

A Jew, sapling of that stem, which praises the Lord daily for deliverance out of the Egyptian yoke of slavery, undertook to defend slavery. . . . Woe to the ears that hear such things. . . . We are obliged to reject such words because they are profanation of God's name.[53]

He expected more of Jews than of others. He expected them always to "remember Egypt," and he was shocked to hear that "there are even immigrant Jews, who are so blinded as to be enthusiastic for secession and slavery."[54]

The words of a rabbi carried great weight, not only among Jews, but also in the community at large. The sermons of both Raphall and Einhorn were published and distributed by those who favored their opposing views. Raphall's sermon was quite popular in the South,[55] while one of Einhorn's patriotic sermons was disseminated in the North, the profits from its sale going to the Sanitary Commission.[56]

Einhorn was relentless in calling upon the Jews to take an active part in the Civil War. He considered it the duty of "Israel, the people of peoples . . . to fight *against* the whole world for the whole world,"[57] and in this respect he saw no difference between the Jews and the United States as a whole. Like the Jews, this country, too, had a mission.

America of the future will not rest on slave chains or belittling its adopted citizens. It will also give up its disinterestedness in the fate of other peoples of the world.[58]

This was all published by Einhorn in Baltimore, which, on the whole, was sympathetic to the South. No wonder that many Jews became concerned lest the rabbi's pronouncements endanger their position. A protest meeting of Jews was called in order to make it clear to the general community that this rabbi was speaking only for himself and did not represent the Jewish community.[59]

Einhorn was accused of showing no concern for his fellow Jews. His reply was that, on the contrary, he had always been aware that "our entire community is held responsible for the crime of one of us." It was precisely this awareness that obliged him to call upon Jews to "behave decently, to fight against prejudice."[60] He even felt it to be a service to Jews to expose without pity Jewish smugglers. In his *War with Amalek* he called upon American Jews "to make war also upon the Amalek in our own midst . . . [who] bring[s] shame and disgrace upon our religion."[61]

On April 19, 1861, federal troops on their way to Washington were attacked by a Baltimore mob. Among those arrested for "assault" was Joseph Friedenwald, son of Jonas Friedenwald.[62] On the following day the printing shops of both abolitionist publications, *Der Wecker* and *Sinai*, were demolished by the mobs. Einhorn's life was in danger, and upon the insistence of the congregation he left the city with his family on May 12. He settled in Philadelphia, where he renewed the publication of *Sinai*. In the first issue he gave a full account of the events that had led to his flight.[63] The magazine continued in Philadelphia for only one year. In the last issue, Einhorn wrote "*Sinai* dies in the battle against slavery."[64]

It is obvious that Einhorn could not have continued as rabbi as long as he did—six full years—if he had not had many supporters in his congregation. After he went to Philadelphia, those who had sided with him wanted him to return to Baltimore. But even while agreeing with the rabbi, they were much more cautious than their leader; in their letter to him they wrote that "for the sake of your own safety as well as out of consideration for the members of your congregation" they were asking him "not to comment from the pulpit on the excitable issues of the time."

How little did his followers know their rabbi if they could suggest to him that he speak only on "Judaism." He naturally rejected this invitation. A committee then went to Philadelphia to prove to him that it was only due to "sad circumstances" that they had asked him not to preach on social issues. To one of his staunchest supporters, Reuben Oppenheimer, he wrote in bitterness on August 12, 1861:

> There is nothing so loathsome, indeed, than this riffraff of bacon reformers. The light of the Rabbis becomes a destroying torch in the hands of such people.[65]

From their rabbis' sermons and writings we learn the views of Baltimore's Jewish congregations on the Civil War. There is naturally less documentation about the Jewish layman. Yet what is known tells a story of a community torn apart. Business partnerships and even families were broken up in disagreement on war issues. One Jewish merchant related in passing, as if it were an everyday occurrence: "The war broke out. One partner was a Rebel; the other a Union man. They broke up business."[66]

The majority of the Friedenwald family, leaders of the Baltimore Hebrew Congregation, agreed with their rabbi, Illoway; they were Democrats and, during the war, "strong secessionists."[67] Yet in this family, too, there was a rift. One of Jonas's sons, Dr. Aaron Friedenwald, was a Republican and "had many quarrels with his family about politics."[68] To him the Union was "a holy institution against which no tongue can speak but in blasphemy, against which no hand can be directed but in sacrilege."[69] Dr. Aaron's brother, Ike, did not merely theorize about secession, he joined the Confederate army, and Aaron's reaction to it was that he wished him "nothing else but a small shot in . . . you know where."[70]

Strange as it may seem, Dr. Aaron was arrested and charged with running the blockade. It ceases to be strange when we learn that "the real reason for his arrest was that his brother [Ike] was in the Southern army." The provost marshal demanded that Aaron say something against his brother. He refused to give the marshal any information and answered, "Do you want me to testify against my brother? Such things are not done."[71]

Dr. Friedenwald was an Orthodox Jew. He was not one of Einhorn's people. Not so his close friend Dr. Abraham B. Arnold, a member of Har Sinai, who shared his views on the Civil War. They worked together "day and night" attending to wounded soldiers.[72]

The Jewish community reflected the temper of the general community. Antagonism grew. Frame-ups became the order of the day. A leading Jewish communal worker who was a pioneer in the manufacture of ready-made clothes, Moses Wiesenfeld, a son-in-law of Jonas Friedenwald, was accused of doing business with the South. His defense was that the Confederate buttons found in his factory were planted by "disgruntled workers."[73] Wiesenfeld was convicted and spent two years in jail in Albany, New York. Circumstantial evidence indicates that the man was innocent: not only was he an active member of the Union party,[74] but the pro-Unionist Johns Hopkins was a close friend of his. More than that, the fiery abolitionist and war hero Leopold Blumenberg wrote a letter to the authorities in which he highly praised the arrested man.[75]

There were Baltimore Jews in both armies.[76] The outstanding Jew in terms of military accomplishments was Brigadier General Leopold Blumenberg (1827–1876). Born in Germany, he came to Baltimore in 1854. He joined Har Sinai, and Rabbi Einhorn was his ideological mentor. Although a successful businessman, he volunteered on September 26, 1861, and on February 8, 1862, he became a major in the militia of the state of Maryland. He gained great distinction in the bloodiest battle of the war, Antietam, where he was severely wounded. On May 18, 1863, he was appointed provost marshal of Baltimore by President Lincoln and later promoted by President Andrew Johnson to the rank of brigadier general.[77]

The Friedenwald family was not the only one that was torn apart.

The same happened to the leading Cohen family. While Mendes Cohen belonged to the Peace party (a camouflaged secessionist group) and was a delegate to the State Peace Convention,[78] his brother Edward went one step further and served in the Confederate army.[79] The third brother, Joshua, was a strong pro-Unionist.[80] Similar events happened in many Jewish families. It was a frequent occurrence that

the son who had charge of the business left it and went South, taking the money with him, which he spent in helping the Rebel cause.[81]

Most Jews were small merchants and peddlers and were hard hit in the early period of the war. There were naturally exceptions. One was a provision dealer, Mr. Rosenstock, who was able to donate five thousand pounds of the "best flour to distribute among the city poor, without distinction of faith or politics."[82]

The economic situation changed considerably with the progress of the war. Some Jews became extremely wealthy within a very short time.

Fortunes were made quickly in those days . . . there were a great deal of speculators notably among our leading coreligionists. . . . Some men arose from obscurity and became multimillionaires in a very short time.[83]

Some Baltimore Jews became real estate operators, bankers, railroad magnates, and above all manufacturers of ready-made clothes—a business which grew tremendously as a result of government orders for uniforms. The economic situation improved so much that a local correspondent wrote, "The Jews on the whole, by their intelligence and their activity, have acquired some wealth."[84]

This correspondent overlooked an entire group, although a small one, which became much poorer as a result of the war. Once the salaries of the clergy were cut, they were not raised even when conditions improved. Characteristic was the case of Cantor Leucht of the Baltimore Hebrew Congregation, whose salary was reduced "for one year" from one thousand dollars to eight hundred dollars.[85] Over four years passed but the cantor's salary was not restored. In 1865 he addressed a letter to the board of his congregation in which he asked for a raise of five hundred dollars, since contrary to all expectations "most articles of necessity are held at higher figures." Leucht made it clear that the increase was "to be discontinued . . . at such a time as a return may be had to settled and satisfactory conditions of financial affairs." Fearing that as a result of this request he might lose his position altogether, the cantor concluded the letter by saying:

While I hope that the congregation will act favorably upon my petition, I do not desire it to be understood as being unwilling . . . to abide by our present contract.[86]

The requested increase was not granted.

Constant frictions among the rabbis and their respective congregations and the rifts caused by the Civil War might have brought the community to the brink of dissolution. The community, however, proved to be strong. Writing of Baltimore, the economist Jacob Hollander remarked:

The Civil War suspended the prosperity of the city, suspended, but not destroyed. After the period of reconstruction, Baltimore emerged as an important industrial center.[87]

What Hollander has said about Baltimore generally may be applied to its Jewish community. The growing prosperity of the city was amply reflected among Baltimore Jews, quite a number of whom became wealthy and ceased to feel like immigrants. In this prosperous atmosphere communal dissensions steadily decreased, and despite occasional rifts the forces working for unity prevailed. All differences disappeared when the need arose to help fellow Jews at home or abroad. Ideologies always gave way to common concern, and in the face of Jewish needs Baltimore Jewry usually stood united.

EXPANSION

Response to Problems in Foreign Countries

The first call for united action to deal with matters other than religion came to American Jewry as early as 1840. The 40,000 Jews who lived in the country at that time were called upon to protest against a ritual blood accusation in Damascus, Syria. Although it was realized that all Jews, wherever they might find themselves, stood accused together with those in Damascus, American Jewry was unable to present a united front. It lacked the leadership to provide the necessary guidance. The larger Jewish communities in the country lodged protests, however, and succeeded in bringing about the intervention of the State Department. Baltimore Jewry at that time was still a small community and was not among those who protested the atrocities in Damascus.

Things looked different during the quarter century between 1855 and 1880. America's Jewish population grew considerably, although reliable statistics of Jews in the United States for any period are not available. (Baltimore's Rabbi Aaron Günzburg, for example, estimated the number of Jews in the country in 1850 to be 750,000, on the basis of his "study" of the U.S. Census. In the same issue of *The Occident* in which he presented his figures, Leeser made a "correction." He reduced Günzberg's figure by a full 600,000.)[88] As for Baltimore Jews in the 1850s, *The Occident* estimated in July 1855 that there were "about 12 to 15 hundred families," while for November of the same year the estimate is reduced to about 800 families.[89] Despite all these discrepancies, it is clear that Baltimore Jewry was correctly described in 1856 as one that "increased greatly in numbers and prosperity."[90] By that time, the Jewish community of Baltimore had become one to be reckoned with whenever world Jewish problems demanded action by American Jewry.

THE SWISS TREATY

In 1851 President Fillmore presented a treaty with Switzerland to the Senate for ratification. The treaty, which was to establish the rights of citizens of each country to travel and sojourn in the other country, was ratified on March 7, 1851.

There was a Jewish angle to it. Switzerland was divided into cantons, each of which was governed by its own laws. In some of these Jews were subjected to various restrictions. Switzerland was not ready to sign the American version of the compact, which would have given American Jews the same rights as those afforded to non-Jews. While the Swiss debated the issue, the restrictive cantons continued their policies of restriction of Jews, whether native or foreign. A revised treaty which did not provide equality for American Jews was ratified by President Franklin Pierce on November 6, 1854.

American Jewry became aroused. Protest meetings were held in many cities, Baltimore among them. On August 6, 1857, Einhorn wrote to the secretary of state inquiring whether "the American Jews may expect from the Washington Administration an interpretation of the treaty, which will not be prejudicial to them."[91] The reply was couched in the language of diplomacy. There was no clear-cut answer

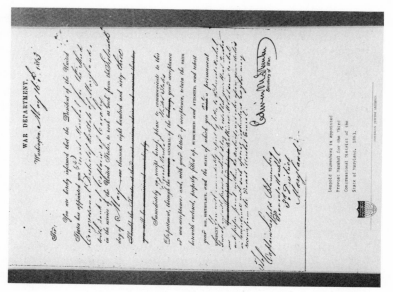

Blumenberg's appointment as provost marshal (1863).
Courtesy of the American Jewish Archives.

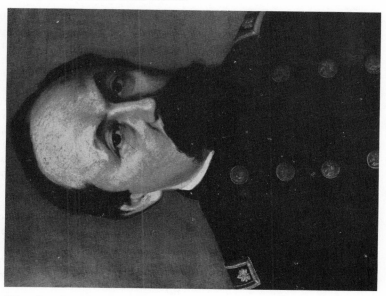

Brig. Gen. Leopold Blumenberg, 1827–1876, hero of the Civil War.
Courtesy of the Har Sinai Congregation.

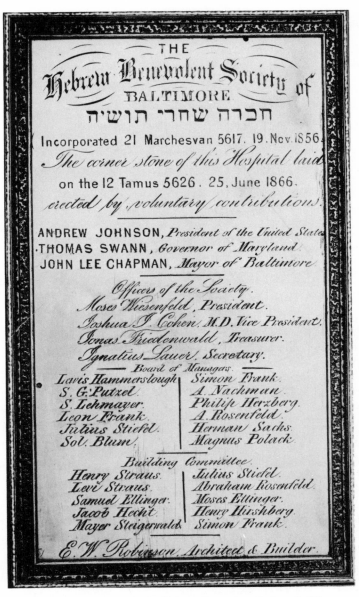

THE

Hebrew Benevolent Society of

BALTIMORE

חברה שחרי תושיה

Incorporated 21 Marchesvan 5617. 19. Nov. 1856.

The corner stone of this Hospital laid

on the 12 Tamus 5626. 25. June 1866.

erected by voluntary contributions.

ANDREW JOHNSON, *President of the United States*

THOMAS SWANN, *Governor of Maryland*

JOHN LEE CHAPMAN, *Mayor of Baltimore*

Officers of the Society.

Moses Wiesenfeld, President.

Joshua I. Cohen, M.D. Vice President.

Jonas Friedenwald, Treasurer.

Ignatius Sauer, Secretary.

Board of Managers.

Lewis Hammerslough	*Simon Frank.*
S. G. Putzel.	*A. Nachman.*
S. Lehmayer.	*Philip Herzberg.*
Leon Frank.	*A. Rosenfeld.*
Julius Stiefel.	*Herman Sachs.*
Sol. Blum.	*Magnus Polack.*

Building Committee.

Henry Straus.	*Julius Stiefel.*
Levi Straus.	*Abraham Rosenfeld.*
Samuel Ellinger.	*Moses Ellinger.*
Jacob Hecht.	*Henry Hirshberg.*
Mayer Steigerwald	*Simon Frank.*

E. W. Robinson, Architect & Builder.

Inscription on cornerstone of the Hebrew Benevolent Society Building, (5626/1866).

Courtesy of the Associated Jewish Charities. Photo by Sussman-Ochs.

to the question of Jewish rights.[92] On September 24, 1857, a Baltimore committee (consisting mainly of leading members of Einhorn's congregation, with Dr. Arnold acting as chairman) issued a call to committees from other cities to convene in Baltimore "in order to proceed in a body to Washington and to lay our grievance before his Excellency, the President of the United States."[93]

On October 29, 1857, a convention of "delegates of the Israelites from various States of the Union" was held in Baltimore. The memorial that was drafted, which was presented to the then president, James Buchanan, bears the signatures of the following Baltimoreans: M. I. Cohen, Rev. Dr. H. Hochheimer, and Phillip Herzberg.

Neither the memorial nor the subsequent delegation to Buchanan nor his vague promises to protect the rights of American Jews in Switzerland —about which he did nothing—brought about any change.[94] The treaty remained as originally worded. The interests of American Jews in Switzerland remained unprotected until 1872, when the new Swiss constitution placed the jurisdiction over aliens in the hands of the federal government.[95]

THE MORTARA CASE

The Swiss treaty issue was still on the agenda when another case attracted the attention of American Jewry. In this instance the reaction was one of pain and indignation at an outrage that had been committed against one of their own faith, even though the event took place in a faraway land.

In 1858, in Bologna, Italy, then a part of the Papal States, a six-year-old Jewish boy by the name of Edgar Mortara was forcibly taken away from his parents by the Church authorities. The child had apparently been secretly baptized by his Christian nurse when he was about one year old. This made him a Christian from the Church's point of view; hence it was considered both legal and proper to take the boy away from his parents.

Mass meetings protesting the abduction took place in every major Jewish community in the United States.[96] In Baltimore a mass meeting took place on November 28, 1859, at Independence Hall. Col. Mendes Cohen, one of the most active communal workers, presided, and A. Nachman, a leader of the Har Sinai Congregation, acted as secretary.[97]

It was a stormy meeting. Those present could not agree on a course of action. A committee of twelve was elected to draft a petition to be presented to President Buchanan. Some of the delegation members must have realized that such petitions were of little value. They remembered what had happened to their petition in the case of the Swiss treaty. Yet there was nothing else that could be done. On January 5, 1859, the petition was finally drafted; it called upon the president

to add [his] good offices to those interposed by other powers, that the Papal government may be induced to restore the . . . child . . . to his parents.[98]

The petition was signed by thirteen leading Jews of all congregations, including all the rabbis in the community. Baltimore Jewry was acting as one.

Again, all petitions were of no avail. Buchanan did issue a statement of personal regard for the Jews. He even stated that he recognized the injustice done to the Mortara family. However, political considerations outweighed the moral issue, and nothing was done by the president.[99] The Baltimore newspapers, with the exception of the Catholic ones, branded the abduction an "outrage against humanity . . . a violation of the first principle of right and justice" and called on the American Catholics "to join in protest."[100]

Einhorn was bitter about the attitude of the Catholics.[101] Neither was he kind to the president for refusing to take a stand. He described Buchanan as "sly as a fox."[102] Sarcastically he stated that after all the president was quite consistent. Indeed, how could one "who approves of slavery . . . deliver a moral sermon to the Pope?"[103]

Their attitudes toward Buchanan exemplify the differences between the two contemporary rabbis Einhorn and Szold. While the first was outspoken in his criticism, Szold described the president with a reverence shown to European monarchs. Szold wrote with pride and excitement of a chance meeting with Buchanan:

Imagine, Sophie [Mrs. Szold], he offered me his hand. . . . I looked searchingly into his face and was enchanted by his thinker's brow, his diplomatic nose and his childish mouth.[104]

Discrimination against Jews was not the only source of Jewish unity. Baltimore Jewry took note of good news about Jews, and on such occasions celebrations were in order. One such occasion was the admission of Jews to the British Parliament, which came about during the agitation about the Swiss treaty. Baltimore Jewry celebrated the event with an "enthusiastic" meeting.[105] One of the speakers at this meeting was Dr. Abraham B. Arnold, who figured prominently in many occasions of Jewish action.

Outstanding Leaders

There were now three important Jewish physicians in the city who took an active role in the life of the community. Their preeminence in the medical profession gave special significance to the fact that they were so involved in Jewish communal affairs.

The oldest of the three was Joshua Cohen, one of the famous Cohen brothers, who came to Baltimore in 1803. He was a physician of note and distinguished himself in the fields of ophthalmology and otology, of which he was a pioneer in America. He served as president of the Medical and Chirurgical Faculty of the University of Maryland (1857–1858) and wrote important medical papers.[106] In addition to being a professor of medicine, Cohen was also professor of geology and mineralogy. He was also elected member of the Royal Society of Northern Antiquaries of Copenhagen.[107] Despite all this activity, Cohen found time to carry on a lively correspondence with Leeser about Hebrew books and especially about Jewish affairs in the city, which he knew intimately and in which he remained active till his death in 1870.

The second of the trio was Abraham Arnold. Born in Germany in 1820, he came to America at the age of 12. He graduated from medical school in 1848 and settled in Baltimore a year later. He was a successful physician and in 1877–1878 served as president of the Medical and Chirurgical Faculty of the University of Maryland. Like Dr. Cohen, he too was the author of a number of medical works.[108] In addition to his professional work, until his death in 1904 Dr. Arnold found time to write on Jewish problems, to involve himself in every important Jewish affair, and later to serve for many years on the staff of the Jewish hospital.

Although an extreme Reform Jew (he was even against circumcision), Dr. Arnold enjoyed the respect of Baltimore Jewry, an honor he had earned by his devotion to the community. After having been an anti-Zionist, he had a change of heart in 1894 and wished his friend Dr. Aaron Friedenwald success in his work "for the cause of Zion."[109] Active as Dr. Arnold was in his profession and in various Jewish activities, he found time to involve himself in general politics, and he served on the State Executive Committee of the Republican party.

By far the most prominent of the three was the youngest, Aaron Friedenwald (1836–1902). Like his two older colleagues, Dr.

Friedenwald was president of the Medical and Chirurgical Faculty. He was a recognized authority on eye diseases, and for twenty-nine years he served as professor of diseases of eye and ear at the College of Physicians and Surgeons.[110] Dr. Friedenwald was an Orthodox Jew. In a letter to his son, Harry, he wrote, "Thank God, that I have not been injected with that dangerous spirit of age, which questions His existence."[111] He served as president of an Orthodox congregation, but his interests were not parochial. Both locally and nationally this member of the Friedenwald family, like his son after him, played a leading role.

There were many in the community who in one way or another emulated these outstanding physicians. The numerous institutions and organizations established in the period of expansion, some of which are still in existence, are living testimonials to those tireless workers. There was much to do. The community was growing and so were its needs. In general the activities fell into three categories: religious, welfare, and purely social.

Religious Life

SYNAGOGUES

After a visit to Baltimore in 1864, Isaac Mayer Wise reported that there were in the city "four organized synagogues and several disorganized ones, who meet in rented localities."[112] The organized congregations were Baltimore Hebrew, Hebrew Friendship (Oheb Israel), Har Sinai, and Oheb Shalom. The "disorganized" were small *minyanim* which were formed because, in Einhorn's words, "somebody wants to become a president, another wishes to be a treasurer and a third desires to play the role of a *ḥazan*."[113]

There is a record of one more "organized" synagogue during that period, although it remained in existence for only a little over two years. In 1856 the few Jews in the city who followed the Sephardic ritual established a congregation, Beth Israel, with Solomon Etting's son Samuel as president. Leeser was involved in the planning from the very beginning and conducted the first Yom Kippur service. He reported that

it was the first time the Portuguese prayers were publicly read in Baltimore, although in private worship they have been used there many years past, even before the beginning of the present century.[114]

It is strange that this group, which included some of the wealthiest Jews in the city, appealed for financial assistance to other Sephardic congregations in the country.[115] But that was the accepted way of raising funds for new synagogues, and it did not matter whether a congregation was rich or poor. The problem besetting the Sephardic congregation, however, was not a financial one. The congregation died simply because there were not enough Jews in the city who followed the Sephardic *minhag* (custom). So it "suspended its activities" in July 1859.[116] Although the congregation was only a passing phenomenon, it contributed much by establishing a new kind of Jewish school in the city.

The moving spirit of the congregation was Solomon Nunes Carvalho (1815–1894). His father, David Nunes Carvalho, had been a prominent citizen in Charleston, South Carolina. For about ten years he served as *ḥazan* of the Beth Elohim Congregation, but in 1824 he joined the group which established the Reformed Society, and he became its reader.[117] In 1828 the family moved to Baltimore. At the age of twenty, Solomon was sent to an uncle in Barbados where he spent no less than ten years. Upon his return to Baltimore he became a professional photographer and portrait painter.[118]

Carvalho gained fame when he became the official photographer of Colonel John Charles Frémont's fifth expedition to the Far West in 1853, which he later described in *Incidents of Travel and Adventure in the Far West*.[119] Upon his return to Baltimore, Carvalho became one of the most important Jewish communal leaders. Unlike his father, Solomon was an Orthodox Jew and a great friend of Leeser's, with whom he carried on a correspondence about traditional Judaism.[120] After his father's death in 1860, Solomon Carvalho moved to New York, where he continued his artistic work, attaining a measure of distinction.[121] He was also an inventor; his steam retort was utilized by the navy.[122] He died in New York in 1894.

The Carvalhos, father and son, were both writers on Jewish literary and religious themes. David Carvalho left in manuscript his "Paraphrase of the Psalms of David into English,"[123] and Solomon Carvalho wrote a volume on "Mosaic Cosmogeny"; neither work was ever published.

The impact of the short-lived Sephardic synagogue was necessarily limited. The four "organized" congregations about which Wise reported in 1864 were the ones which set the tone for the entire community during much of its history. The largest of them was the Eden Street *Shul*, with 180 members. Next in size was the Lloyd Street

(Baltimore Hebrew) Congregation, with 150 members. The Hanover Street *Shul*, Oheb Shalom, although organized only in 1853, already had 105 members, and Har Sinai Temple numbered 85 members.[124]

The last congregation to be formed by the German Jews in the city was Shearith Israel. It was established in 1879, and from the very beginning it was distinguished by its uncompromising Orthodoxy. The first synagogue of the congregation was located at Greene and German (now Redwood) Streets. After the first year Moses Strauss, the eldest of four brothers all of whom were very active in the affairs of the congregation, was its president for a quarter century. For this reason Shearith Israel became known as the Strauss synagogue. Alone among the five surviving German congregations established in the nineteenth century, Shearith Israel has remained unchanged in its staunch Orthodoxy. Even at the present time (1970) anyone who desecrates the Sabbath openly is ineligible for membership, although such a person may be a seat holder.[125]

Each congregation had its own specific problems, but all of them, and all that followed them, were always preoccupied with finances and rituals.

RABBIS AND CANTORS

Plea of poverty from a congregation does not hold ground, there is no such thing as a poor congregation. An individual may be poor but a body of men, a congregation, is never poor.[126]

In one form or another these words of a Baltimore rabbi in 1887 were the complaint of the clergy for generations. As a rule, rabbis, cantors, and teachers were underpaid. Their pleas for higher salaries were usually rejected, or at best only a minimal increase was granted. Baltimore was no exception to this universal rule. The case of Rabbi Schneeberger of Chizuk Amuno illustrates the situation. He was engaged by Chizuk Amuno Congregation in 1876 at twelve hundred dollars a year. After nine years of service he asked for an increase in his salary. The committee rejected the request since it "could find no way of increasing revenue.[127] At that time the rabbi was still a bachelor. However, when he married he felt entitled to a raise of three hundred dollars. The congregation granted only two hundred dollars. Schneeberger continued to appeal in writing and even appeared before the board; finally, after sixteen years of service his salary was raised to eighteen hundred dollars.[128] But before long there was "not enough" revenue and the salary was reduced to fifteen hundred dollars.[129] Schneeberger's was a typical case. Other rabbis had more or less similar experiences.

There was never money for a rabbi, but there always was enough to build beautiful synagogues. A Baltimore Jewish newspaper called the attention of the people to this paradoxical situation in an editorial of 1875.

We want less expensive houses of worship among both Orthodox and Reformers .... Less plush and velvet cushions, and more heartful piety would be a great remedy. ... We want more respect to our ministers. ...[130]

In light of all this it comes as a pleasant surprise to read in the Minute Books of the Baltimore Hebrew Congregation for 1856 that forty-two members requested the board to raise the salary of its rabbi. He was getting four hundred dollars a year. Those who pleaded his cause stressed that he had not received a raise for "a few years." They considered this to be an "injustice." Perhaps the real reason for their request had to do not with the "injustice" but with their sensitivity to the opinons of non-Jews. In their recommendation they stated that "it must appear to our non-coreligionists, that the Israelites do not appreciate the services of their religious leader."[131]

There was one unusual case of a rabbi about whom one wants to repeat the words of David Einhorn, *"Nur in Amerika"* (only in America). This was the case of Jacob Mayer, who served as rabbi of Har Sinai from 1874 to 1876. An engaging personality and an excellent preacher, he became very popular among Jews and non-Jews alike. All was well in Har Sinai until Rabbis Szold and Hochheimer dropped a bombshell: Mayer was a convert who worked for the Missionary Society in London. Mayer vehemently denied it. His friends refused to believe it and ascribed the accusation to jealousy. They advised their rabbi to "seek redress in court against those who defamed and injured him in the community."[132] He was given one thousand dollars by the congregation to go to Europe and produce indisputable evidence of his innocence.[133] *The Jewish Times* (New York) invited a suit; it stated bluntly, "Let convert Mayer appeal to the courts. ... We defy him or the congregation [Har Sinai] to bring a libel suit or any other suit."[134] Mayer did not sue, nor was he able to prove his innocence; finally, he resigned.

While Szold and Hochheimer were publishing the innumerable letters from people in this country and Europe who knew Mayer as a missionary, many people resigned from the congregation. The crisis was so deep that it was decided that

whereas the Har Sinai Congregation from various causes within the last few years lost a considerable number of members, it now finds itself in a position where it is necessary to apply to courts for a dissolution, as it is no longer able to maintain itself as a congregation. . . .[135]

The resolution was not carried out, and Har Sinai resumed its growth.

The "Mayer affair" brought about a reconciliation between the two old adversaries Einhorn and Szold. In reply to a friendly letter from Szold, Einhorn wrote that he was happy that "the Mayer scandal has been finished in such a way." He added, in a manner most uncharacteristic of the man of *Sturm und Drang*, "Let us not talk about former happenings between us. Let everything be forgiven and forgotten."[136]

Mayer's case was an isolated instance. Baltimore had a considerable number of distinguished rabbis. As a matter of fact, the rabbi who succeeded Mayer, Emil G. Hirsch, became one of the leading rabbis in the American Reform movement.

A synagogue needed a rabbi and perhaps even more a cantor. A good cantor drew a crowd. Since there was no rabbinic seminary in the United States, the search for rabbis was conducted through advertisements in the Jewish press in this country and in Germany and through personal contacts. These methods were also used in obtaining the services of a cantor, but there was also another method which was the most popular. Cantors would come for a Sabbath on trial, attracted by advertisements that asked for "persons deeming themselves fully qualified" to "visit Baltimore at their own expense, and perform the service on one or two Sabbaths."[137] There was no end to the "qualified" persons who appeared in the synagogues. In most cases they were poor Jews who tried their luck. As for "their own expense," they knew that a poor Jew would not be lost among Jews and that he would be helped.

In nine years (1835–1844) the Baltimore Hebrew Congregation had no less than thirteen cantors.[138] Oheb Shalom somehow managed to have on trial three cantors on one Sabbath.[139] Even as late as 1896, the Eden Street *Shul* had seventy-eight applicants for one cantorial position. Not all of them were invited, but nine cantors were given a chance to "prove themselves worthy of the position."[140]

Not only was the salary of a cantor low—usually about five hundred dollars a year—but he was expected to provide his own cantorial garb. Time and again the question of the cantor's "work clothes" was discussed.[141] One, Cantor Davidson, was willing to buy his own garb but made another request. Davidson was an unusual man—in addition to being a cantor, he was a dentist and his request was for the congregation's permission to practice dentistry. The board of the Baltimore Hebrew Congregation showed its liberalism when it decided that he "may spend his leisure time in any honorable way."[142]

Salaries for rabbis and cantors were the main expense of the synagogues and were constantly on the agenda. In spite of the constant concern about them, the economic position of the clergy was not an enviable one.

There was another matter which was perennially discussed. A natural desire to hold on to the established way of life conflicted with pressure for changes in the rituals. The necessity for change and the fear of change were regular synagogue concerns.

RELIGIOUS TRENDS

HAR SINAI

It was quite simple for Einhorn to decide which of the old rituals to retain and which to discard. He was bound not by accepted laws but by his own interpretation of them—he was his own master. He decided that one was to wear a cap and *tallis* in the synagogue, but he dispensed with the second days of the holidays.[143] Believing as he did that "the inequality of woman in the Mosaic Law forms part of the ancient priestly system of castes . . . it is our sacred duty to declare, with all emphasis, woman's perfect religious right with man . . . ,"[144] he abolished the ladies' gallery in the synagogue.[145]

There were two traditions, however, about which Einhorn would not compromise. He spoke the language of a present-day cultural pluralist when he stated his belief that each people (or, in the language of those days, race) made a distinct contribution to humanity. He stressed that "different" did not mean a division of "races" into higher and lower. Jews, he maintained, had to make their contribution; hence he opposed intermarriage, saying, "Mixed marriages are the nail in the coffin of the small Jewish race."[146] Neither would this extreme Reformer compromise about the sanctity of the Sabbath. Sabbath was the "sign" of unity between God and Israel, and he demanded that his congregants observe it.[147]

The Ninth of Av was also to be "observed," but he gave it an entirely new meaning. This was not to be a day of mourning and fasting, but rather a day of rejoicing, for on this day, *not as a disowned son thy firstborn went out into strange lands, but as thy emissary to all the families of men. . . . The one temple in Jerusalem sank into the dust, in order that countless temples might arise to thy honor and glory all over the wide surface of the globe. . . .*[148]

The rabbis who followed Einhorn introduced more and more reforms. Things reached such a point that when a parent applied in 1874 for permission to celebrate the bar mitzvah of his son in the temple, permission was denied.[149] All of this was to be expected in a Reform congregation whose members were happy to follow their Reform rabbis. It was different, of course, in the other congregations, but in all of them the problem of changes was constantly on the agenda.

BALTIMORE HEBREW

In the Baltimore Hebrew Congregation the 1852 law, according to which no reform in the worship of God could be made unless it met with the approval of two-thirds of the congregation, remained in force. The members did not actually contemplate reforms. What many of them did want was changes in matters of usage rather than of law. Every suggested change, however, met with opposition. The sanctity of custom was to be upheld. It took, for example, many meetings and endless debates before the *Mi Sheberach* and *El Mole Rahamim* "reforms" were adopted. These changes specified that when one was called up to the Torah, one could not ask for the pronouncement of blessings for more than five people and that the prayer for the dead could be recited before the ark only during the thirty days of mourning or the day of *Yahrzeit* and on Yom Kippur.[150] All of these were not matters of law but long-continued practice.

The exclusion of the *piyutim* from the prayers was also finally approved by the board. At the meeting at which this was decided, Jonas Friedenwald, with an eye to the future, demanded that it be recorded that he voted in the negative.[151]

We must always reckon with this man when speaking about the Baltimore Hebrew Congregation. He was a fighter for his ideas and was even willing to take the congregation to court to win his case. He took this unprecedented step in 1857 when he obtained a court order enjoining the congregation against renewing a contract with Rabbi Hochheimer, who was "suspect" in his eyes.[152] A compromise settlement was reached out of court. Actually, Friedenwald and his supporters won. Hochheimer's contract was renewed, but only for a few months.[153]

One should not overlook the wider implications of this case. The European way of life was disintegrating. The closed society was disappearing. A new community was arising, a community with more freedom for the individual, a community in which an individual felt that he could challenge, if necessary even in a court of law, the decisions of a synagogue board.

Friedenwald and his group were strengthened when Bernard Illoway (1814–1891) succeeded Hochheimer as rabbi of the congregation in 1859. Born in Bohemia, Illoway had a solid Jewish education under the famous talmudic scholar Moses Sopher in the yeshiva of Pressburg. He continued his studies in the rabbinical seminary of Padua. Leeser welcomed his arrival in Baltimore, expressing his hope that the new rabbi would succeed in stopping

at the very threshold a doctrine, which, should it be permitted, for ever so short a time, to remain unanswered and unrebuked . . . might greatly tend to the destruction of the most promising prospects of Judaism.[154]

Illoway did all he could to maintain Orthodoxy. His religious philosophy was that

we Yehudim have not only a belief, we have laws in addition and these laws have their origin not in the bosom of a mortal man, but they are the living word of God communicated to Israel.[155]

Strict adherence to the minutiae of the law was demanded by Illoway. He was especially strict in regard to the cemetery. He ordered the removal of images engraved on the tombstones, since "it is contrary to Mosaic law."[156] Next he forbade the planting of shrubbery, flowers, or trees on any grave.[157]

Soon after Illoway left in July 1861, the congregation adopted a new constitution, according to which "the fixed prayers shall always be read in the original Hebrew language according to the custom of the Orthodox German Jews."[158] In 1862 the congregation invited its first rabbi, Abraham Rice, to return to his post. In the few months before he died Rice continued the policies instituted by Illoway, and in regard to cemetery and burial laws he even went a step further. One of his last acts before his death was to inform the board

that according to our laws it is not allowed for ladies to step on the Burial ground at the time we bury our dead. It is therefore your duty to establish a law about this matter.[159]

The board fulfilled its "duty" and ordered the

shames *at the funeral to inform the ladies in attendance of the . . .
law and it shall be his duty to remain at the gate of the inside ground,
and not to permit any ladies within the Grounds as long as the Gentlemen are upon the Ground.*[160]

The Baltimore Hebrew seemed to be a safe Orthodox stronghold.
It was Orthodox, but there was enough of an opposition to warrant
a remark by Wise that "the majority [of the congregation] is inclined
to reform, even if they cannot agree on the precise nature of the reform
they wanted."[161] History bore him out.

The would-be "reformers" won a major victory when the board
adopted a motion made by one of its members, Leon Frank:

The Board of Managers is to make the proper Inquiries of Different
Rabbiners *belonging to the Orthodox Israelites if young ladies between
the ages of 11–14 years can assist the choir in the synagogue during
Divine Services.*[162]

There were forces working for a change in the Baltimore Hebrew
Congregation.[163] Eventually, it was the issue of a mixed choir that
proved to be fatal to the congregation. On January 2, 1870, a motion
to introduce "a choir composed of male and female voices" was defeated.[164] But half a year later the same motion was carried.[165] This
was a major breach in tradition and could not possibly go unchallenged
by the Orthodox element. It was again Jonas Friedenwald who led the
fight. On August 17, 1870, he and nineteen other members of the
congregation obtained an injunction preventing the Board of Managers
from carrying out the resolution.[166]

One name, Abraham Hofmann, is not mentioned in the injunction,
but it was he, the rabbi of the congregation, who was the prime mover
in introducing many changes. Like Rice, Hofmann was born in Bavaria
and received his rabbinic training in the yeshiva in Würzburg. This
was about all that the two men had in common. Hofmann stood for
many changes. A mixed choir was only one of them. How such a man
could become rabbi of an Orthodox congregation remains a riddle.

The case was settled out of court, and Friedenwald, together with
ten of his followers, resigned and formed their own congregation,
Chizuk Amuno. From then on reforms were the order of the day in the
Baltimore Hebrew Congregation. An organ was introduced,[167] and
the wearing of the *tallis* in the synagogue and the separation of men
from women were done away with.[168] In 1879 the traditional prayer
book was replaced by the Szold-Jastrow *Abodath Israel.*[169] While not

a Reform congregation in name, by 1880 the Baltimore Hebrew Congregation was to all intents and purposes a Reform synagogue.

OHEB SHALOM

When Oheb Shalom was organized in 1853, it was to be neither Reform nor Orthodox. Yet the mood of its members is best illustrated by the following episode. When the congregation moved into its beautiful building on Hanover Street in 1858, some members suggested the installation of an organ. The members wanted it both ways, to have an organ and to have it in a "kosher" way. They were not Reform Jews who would dare to make their own decisions. They only hoped to find authority which would interpret the law in a manner pleasing to them. As for the organ problem, a minority wanted to refer the matter to Rabbi Rice; the majority preferred to consult the leader of the American Reform movement, Rabbi Isaac Mayer Wise of Cincinnati.[170]

Wise wrote a long responsum, citing a large variety of sources, but the most important part of his answer was the very first sentence: "I say that nobody can have objections, from an Orthodox point of view, against playing the organ on the Sabbath or on any other day."[171] An organ was duly introduced, and a man was hired to operate the bellows every Sabbath for thirty-seven cents.[172] (This must have been a *Shabbes goy*. It is one thing to have an organ, and quite a different matter to operate it.)

Rabbi Szold, who came to the congregation in 1859, was in substantial agreement with Wise's religious views. He wrote to him:

Your tendencies are generally also mine. I, too, like you, am against the fresh reform. . . . People are still debating whether I am orthodox or reform. . . . I am like you . . . neither of the two or both at the same time. . . . I am a Jew and nothing Jewish is foreign to me. . . . Judaism has two constitutions, one permanent and the other changeable. Only a balance between these two brings forth the true character of Judaism.[173]

Under Szold the congregation did not become "fresh reform," but Reform it was. The second days of the holidays were abolished.[174] Later the congregation accepted the rabbi's recommendation "to omit from reading in the Torah verses concerning sacrifices . . . [of] no significance to us today," and they did away with head-covering in the synagogue.[175]

Thus by 1880 the major congregations in the city were Reform. The newly established Chizuk Amuno, which was commonly known as the Friedenwald *Shul*, was the main Orthodox synagogue. There were several others, but only small ones.

CHIZUK AMUNO

At its founding the Chizuk Amuno Congregation adopted a resolution that in their synagogue "prayer will be offered in accordance with the orthodox Rituals, the very same manner of worship, as it was inherited by us from our Forefathers."[176] In order to avoid any difficulties in the future, a most stringent law was passed.

No change or alteration or addition to our daily prayers, pijoetim, [piyutim], *jothseraus* [yotzrot], *ceremonies and customs whatsoever shall be made unless with the assent of every member belonging to this congregation, and should any member offer a motion or resolution to make any change or alteration in or in addition to the daily prayer . . . he shall ipso facto forfeit his membership.*[177]

The strict observance of rituals is best exemplified perhaps by considering the motion made by Joseph Friedenwald "to find out whether it is not against our religious law for people to sit on their cushions."[178] On December 30 a report was given that the cords of the cushion had been examined and they were "kosher." The members were accordingly permitted to sit on the cushions.

And yet, all was not quite "kosher" with all the members. How else can one explain a discussion by the board "to have some detectives appointed for undiscovered violations of religious laws"?[179] For five years Chizuk Amuno worshiped in a rented hall and functioned without a rabbi. In 1876 it moved into its beautiful Moorish-style building, only a few doors away from the Baltimore Hebrew.[180] Like all other synagogues in the city, Chizuk Amuno moved from one neighborhood to another. One thing remained constant. For many years it remained, at least officially, an Orthodox congregation.[181]

Oheb Shalom and Chizuk Amuno had a certain characteristic in common which brought about relative peace and prevented shake-ups in each congregation. There was in both of them a continuity in lay as well as in spiritual leadership. Oheb Shalom's first president, Julius Stiefel, served for twenty-six years (1853–1879) and the second, Isaac Strouse, for the next thirty years. The spiritual leadership was also constant—Rabbi Szold served the congregation for thirty-three years (1859–1892) and its cantor, Alois Kaiser, for an even longer period (1866–1908).

A similar situation prevailed at Chizuk Amuno. Its first president,

Judah Rosenwald, was Joseph Friedenwald's father-in-law. He was followed by three generations of the Friedenwald family, who served as president from 1879 until 1920 (with one interruption—from 1902 until 1911—when the president was Michael S. Levy, a member of one of the most distinguished families in the city).[182] As in the case of Oheb Shalom, Chizuk Amuno's spiritual leadership too was continuous. The first rabbi of the congregation was another "first" in the history of Baltimore Jewry. While Abraham Rice of Baltimore Hebrew had been the first ordained rabbi to come to the United States, the rabbi of Chizuk Amuno was the first native American rabbi. Henry W. Schneeberger was born in New York City in 1848. He became rabbi of the congregation in 1876 and served it for thirty-six years.[183] The cantor of the congregation, Herman Glass, served for forty-three years, from 1878 to 1921.

Continuity in leadership did not mean stagnation; it meant fewer convulsions, less danger of dissolution for the synagogue. This almost happened to the oldest congregation in the city. Indeed, because it was the proving ground for all other synagogues and also, perhaps, because it had as its rabbis Rice and Illoway, who considered the smallest of changes as Reform, there was always much bickering there, and the membership dwindled. There were 165 families who were members of the Baltimore Hebrew Congregation in 1865 but only 61 by 1874; and this came down to a mere 38 in 1888. It escaped extinction and began to grow again when it became a clear-cut Reform temple with a clearly defined ideology.

Such a definitive ideology prevailed at the Har Sinai Congregation, and there were no ideological rifts in it. Rabbis changed there quite often, each one introducing minor changes, but on the whole it was following the guidelines established by Einhorn.

OBSERVANCE OF THE SABBATH

One effort that was undertaken by all rabbis, and in which they all failed, was the preservation of the sanctity of the Sabbath. The famed traveler Benjamin II (I. J. Benjamin) relates that when he visited Baltimore in 1859, he found that Einhorn had induced the members of his congregation "to keep their places of business closed on the Sabbath."[184] This is no doubt an exaggeration, but it would seem that at least some members of Har Sinai followed their rabbi's suggestion. Another report relates Rabbi Illoway's accomplishments in this area. Under his influence, "several places have already closed the businesses" on the Sabbath.[185]

In spite of these successes, the records establish that the Sabbath was fighting for its life and that it was losing ground. In 1850, to cite only one example, no one who violated the Sabbath could serve on the board of the Baltimore Hebrew Congregation. The congregation was still Orthodox in 1857, yet in that year it was decided that one "who keeps on the Sabbath" could not serve as president or vice-president.[186] Nothing was said about any other office.

In reviewing the battle for observing the Sabbath in Baltimore, Wise called upon the Baltimore Jews

not to submit to that unjust and oppressive measure [the Sunday Law], but protest loudly and emphatically against it. . . . It is not right to be imposed upon, and bear it with lamblike meekness. Liberty must be guarded by viligance, and injustice must be replaced by sound argument.[187]

There were some protests against the Sunday closing laws, but not until much later.

THE PRAYER BOOKS

By far the most important change in ritual was the replacement of the traditional prayer book with new ones compiled in America. The two earliest of these were the work of Baltimore rabbis. The first was created by Einhorn, who started writing new prayers while still in Europe.[188] When he came to America, he continued to insist that the prayer book was to be in the "vernacular," which to him throughout his lifetime remained German. In 1856 he published his own prayer book, *Olat Tamid (Perpetual Offering)*.[189] The second prayer book was compiled by Rabbi Szold with the assistance of Rabbi Hochheimer.

When Szold came to Baltimore, he found his congregation using Wise's *Minhag America* on weekdays and the Sabbath, and the traditional prayer book on holidays. Leeser bemoaned the adoption of *Minhag America*. "The die is cast," he lamented, "and another congregation have joined themselves to the new philosophy which is now invading America."[190] Szold found the use of two different prayer books to be absurd. In 1864 his *Abodath Israel (Service of Israel)* was published. It was immediately adopted by Oheb Shalom. Subsequently it was published with Rabbi Jastrow's emendations in English and was used widely under the name *Minhag Jastrow*.

While Einhorn's and Szold's prayer books differed in many respects, they also had quite a number of similarities[191]—especially in regard to the prayers for the restoration of Zion. Szold's Ninth of Av prayers, although not as elaborate as Einhorn's, were basically the same. In both prayer books the prayers for Zion were either omitted or changed to the point where their original meaning was lost.

Einhorn considered the Exile to be a blessing, and regarded the day of the destruction of the Temple not as a day of mourning but a festive occasion. Szold did not go so far, but he did write in his special Ninth of Av service:

We do not unduly lament over the Temple that is destroyed. . . . We mourn not despairingly over the downfall of Jerusalem, for all places whither Thou hast sent us, shall be consecrated unto Thee through the worship of Thy name. . . . Thou hast given us another home in place of that which we lost in the lands of our fathers.[192]

The endless fights over observance, some insignificant and others basic, did not hurt the community. Everyone was concerned with religion, and Isaac Mayer Wise was no doubt right in his evaluation of strife related to changes in rituals. "This is one of the good effects of reform," he said, "it agitates, enlivens and rouses the dormant sentiment to active work."[193]

That was certainly true about Baltimore. It was a community concerned with all that was going on in the synagogues. As a result, religious institutions grew stronger and on occasion were able to work together for the welfare of the entire community in spite of ideological differences. Such was the case when all congregations in the city reached an agreement to "bury indigent Israelites which may die in this city devoid of friends and means . . . [and to do] this in rotation."[194]

EDUCATION

Interest in synagogue activities naturally meant an interest also in religious education, one of the principal endeavors of all congregations. Divided as they were on matters of theology and observances, all Baltimore rabbis were concerned with the education of the young. Beginning with Rice, all rabbis not only preached Jewish education but were actually engaged in teaching children. Rice, Einhorn, Szold, and all who followed them were involved in it. Szold, great scholar that he was, also found time to write a number of textbooks for elementary schools.[195]

The schools were part and parcel of the synagogues. Until the 1870s they were all-day schools, and their curricula, with slight variations, were the same. The religious program consisted of Jewish religion (each school stressing the ideology of its congregation), translation of the Bible, prayers, Hebrew language, and Jewish history. The secular program included German, English, bookkeeping, and a number of other subjects. German was the very basis of the schools. Translation and teaching were done in that language.

The dearth of teachers, especially in the beginning of this period, was matched by a lack of rabbis and appropriate textbooks. More often than not the cantor of the synagogue also taught the Jewish subjects. No wonder these "pedagogues" had great disciplinary problems. All kinds of measures were taken to improve the situation. It was decided that "the teachers will be held responsible for the conduct of their classes"[196] and that members of the school boards should visit classes to help the teachers maintain order.[197] Corporal punishment was often resorted to. While the Chizuk Amuno school board decided that "severe corporal punishment is not tolerated,"[198] that of the Baltimore Hebrew gave its teacher "the power" to use it.[199]

The financial situation of the schools was never good. Teachers were paid miserly salaries. The pupils at times engaged in helping to raise funds, usually by selling tickets for school "benefits," picnics, and the like.[200]

The situation was, of course, much better in the private schools. One of these, that of Jonas Goldsmith, was especially successful. Goldsmith, a native of Bavaria who had both a university education and a good Jewish training, came to Baltimore in 1859. He was a man of thirty-six, dedicated to his chosen profession. From the Fell's Point Congregation, where he first taught, he moved "uptown" to the Hanover Street Synagogue (Oheb Shalom). Here he worked with Rabbi Szold until 1874, when his school, like many other private schools, closed.

In the middle 1850s, a new type of Jewish school, the Sunday school, was established. It met with ridicule and scorn. Yet it struck roots and eventually became a major factor in the Jewish educational process. While the majority of children attended all-day schools, there were many who were not exposed to any Jewish education. They were to be brought into the fold.

In 1856 the Sephardic congregation opened a Sunday school, which represented a break with the established way of life. Now a child could get his Hebrew education in a one-day-a-week school. There were other peculiar features to this school. Having women teachers training children in Jewish customs and teaching the Jewish religion was strange indeed. The school was modeled after the first Sunday school in the country, established by Rebecca Gratz in Philadelphia in 1838. Sarah N. Carvalho, formerly a teacher in the Gratz school, was in charge of the Baltimore project. The most ardent workers were leading Baltimore Jews—among them a number of Ettings and Cohens. The most unusual aspect of the school, however, was the fact that it was conducted in English. This was the first time that German was challenged in a city where it enjoyed such overwhelming preference.

That there was need of such a school is best attested by the fact that before long it had as many as three hundred pupils and seventeen teachers.[201] The project was soon attacked and ridiculed. Again, it was Einhorn who began the attack, but before long the Baltimore Sunday school became a major problem and was discussed in the national press. At bottom there was, of course, much more than the problem of this particular school.

Einhorn objected to teachers of religion who did not know any Hebrew. The teachers of the Sunday school, he stated, knew Judaism as a "blind man knows colors." After a long tirade Einhorn warned parents that their children might be "crippled" by the *weibliche Theologie* (women's theology) and pleaded with them to "beware of sending [their] children to this school."[202]

Wise took issue with Einhorn. True, he too was not satisfied with Sunday schools and considered them to be "insufficient." "But," said Wise—and this "but" was and is repeated in defense of the Sunday schools down to this day—"Sunday schools provide some education and this is much better than no education." And in a light vein he added, "It is our settled opinion, that the pious efforts of ladies should always meet with man's approbation and support."[203]

Leeser had many good reasons to be happy with the Baltimore experiment. Not only were the founders of the school his personal friends, but the whole school was conducted in his spirit, being both Orthodox and conducted in English. It was only natural that he was invited to give the main address at the school's opening.[204]

The textbook used in the school was Leeser's *Catechism for Younger Children*. Einhorn was bitter in his criticism of this text. After discussing it in great detail he concluded that

NUR IN AMERIKA [*Only in America*] *could such a man* [*Leeser*], *who hardly knows the first elements of the Jewish religion, embolden himself to write a book on this subject.*[205]

At issue was the fact that the school was organized by *eingeborenen Juden* (native Jews) and that its teachers were *amerikanische Ladies.*[206] Unlike Wise and Leeser, who were oriented to America, Einhorn remained a German in spirit. To him, the teaching of the Jewish religion in English and not in German was itself an act of desecration.

It was characteristic of the age that many organizations and institutions were formed, only to die before anything important was accomplished. The intentions of the communal workers were good, but there was a lack of perseverance in the face of difficulties. The workers for a given institution gave up very readily—then found themselves working for a new one having the same aims as the one they had forsaken. The opening and closing of schools was also typical of that era.

In 1859 S. N. Carvalho and Moses Wiesenfeld opened a new Sunday school having a feature which was ahead of its time. Traditionally, a Jewish school was related to a synagogue. This school, however, was not and represented one of the first attempts to establish a Jewish communal school. A school detached from a synagogue could not possibly survive at that time (which in this respect was very similar to our own), and it failed.[207]

The community in the meantime underwent a great change. The period of recrimination was over. Since Einhorn had left the city, people found it possible to discuss communal problems, to agree or disagree, without name-calling and vindictiveness. The three rabbis in the 1860s were Szold at Oheb Shalom, Deutsch at Har Sinai, and Hochheimer at Eden Street *Shul.* The Baltimore Hebrew Congregation was without a rabbi for several years. The three rabbis, although they differed in matters of theology, found it possible to work hand in hand for the cause of Jewish education. Deutsch, in cooperation with the other two rabbis, published an undated brochure, *An die Israeliten* (*To the Israelites*), which presented a detailed discussion of Jewish education. It gave a frank account of the poor achievement in Hebrew and suggested a new plan. Their ideas have remained a topic of discussion among Jewish educators down to our own time. In view of the poor results from existing schools, they suggested that there be two types of schools or two different curricula—one for the many, another for the few. The many should acquire only rudimentary knowledge, a bare minimum. An intensive course in Hebraic studies should be offered for boys who might eventually become rabbis.

In 1867 the three rabbis went even a step further. They tried "to gather all the Hebrew youth of both sexes . . . each Sunday morning in one capacious establishment."[208] Unfortunately, the results of this attempt are not known.

Another school was organized in 1869 by Leon Dalsheimer, Dan Greenbaum, Sarah Dalsheimer, Joseph Walter, and William Schloss, who found "so few who are ready and willing to lend a helping hand."[209] As usual, there were complaints about the lack of "sufficient competent teachers."[210] (There was nothing extraordinary in the amusing resolution of the board of the Hebrew Religious School: "We do not approve of the introduction of the blackboard as we cannot see its practicability in a school of this kind. . . .")[211]

On February 2, 1868, the board of the Hebrew Religious School made a decision which was repeated in the next two decades in many other Jewish schools: "No pupils will be admitted to the school, who cannot read English." This was in a sense a historic resolution. It was the first time in Baltimore that the knowledge of English was made a prerequisite for entrance into a Jewish school. The battle between German and English was a continuing one. Even as late as 1874 the school board of Oheb Shalom Congregation passed a resolution that the Hebrew subjects taught in their school were to be translated into German.[212]

Schools reflected synagogues. The German-English problem was acute in all of them. After a debate on the subject, the board of Oheb Shalom granted Szold's request to permit him to deliver an English sermon every other Saturday. The rabbi's argument in favor of English was that "this would be more impressive for the young people."[213] English was gaining strength even in the most Germanophile congregation, Har Sinai, but its victories came only after endless debates.[214] It was a great day for the "English" on the board when it was decided that Rabbi Emil Hirsch of Har Sinai had to deliver one or, if he desired, two lectures a month in English.[215] A special bylaw to the 1874 constitution of the Baltimore Hebrew Congregation was required in order to conduct meetings in English.

The most important proponent of English in school and synagogue was the rabbi of Chizuk Amuno, Henry W. Schneeberger. It was quite natural for him, a native American, to put up a great resistance against German, which he considered "not expedient."[216] In his school English took precedence over German. It was the language of translation and the one in which teachers conversed with pupils.

Strangely, German lost its position in Baltimore not because the German element was weak but because it was strong. It was so powerful that in 1873 the school board was forced to introduce German in the public schools in German neighborhoods. Once German was available in the free public schools, it made no sense to maintain private schools. The Germans felt that they had won a great victory. Only later did it dawn on them that German as one subject in the curriculum of a public school was not the same as a thorough German education in a private German school. Along with the non-Jewish German schools, the Jewish private schools, too, closed their doors. *Lehrer* Goldsmith's school had to be closed in 1874, for instance, despite the high standards of education provided by that institution.

In the 1870s a new type of Jewish school came into being—the afternoon school, which with the Sunday and Sabbath schools became dominant factors in Jewish education.

Even during the period that Jewish all-day schools were flourishing, not all Jewish children attended them. After 1855 there were a few Jewish boys who attended Loyola College, which despite its name was also a school for younger children.[217] A considerable number of Jewish boys of well-to-do families attended the two excellent private non-Jewish schools in the city. Although under the auspices of the Lutheran Zion Church, one of these became strictly secular, under the leadership of the liberal pedagogue Heinrich Scheib, and even had among its students the sons of the ultra-Orthodox Jonas Friedenwald.[218] A second excellent private school, which taught Hebrew, was established by the '48-er, Frederick Knapp. Like the Scheib school, the F. Knapp German and English Institute was open to children of all faiths. It even advertised in *Sinai*. Both schools survived for about two decades, even after the public schools became free. The latter were overcrowded to such a degree that parents were "unwilling to endanger the health of their children" by sending them to such institutions.[219] Well-to-do people, including Jews, continued to send their children to Scheib's and Knapp's.

H. L. Mencken, himself a product of the latter school, relates that in his childhood there were about a dozen Jewish boys among its students. He saw "no enmity between the Chosen and the Goyim." Describing those "chosen" with their "Hittite noses and curly hair," he wrote that

Jewish boys of Baltimore in that innocent age [the eighties] were still palpably and unashamedly Jews . . . and had such given names as Aaron, Leon, Samuel and Isaac. I never encountered one named Irving, Sidney, Malcolm or Wesley, nor even Charles or William. . . . All Jewish boys came from well-to-do families. . . . I must add in sorrow that the Jewish boys at Knapp's were all Chazir Fresser *[pork guzzlers]*.[220]

During a quarter century of expansion, from 1855 to 1880, the Jews in Baltimore built many schools for their children. Much of the work was done haphazardly, and all too often insufficient funds were allocated for education. These negative aspects were, naturally, reflected in the achievement of the pupils. And yet the will to give the upcoming generation a good Jewish education was there, and eventually it brought results.

The synagogue was the central Jewish institution but by no means the only one. Of the 5,000 to 7,000 Jews in the city in 1860, only 525 males were members of congregations; their families comprised 3,125 individuals.[221] There were, of course, also many seat holders. But many, whether member, seat holder, or persons unaffiliated with a synagogue, found another field of activity in the Jewish community to which they devoted much of their time and energy. There were people in need, and correspondingly there were many who worked in their behalf.

CHARITY

Sixteen free white persons, above the age of twenty one years, citizens of the United States and of this State, Israelites being desirous to associate together for the purpose of providing for the relief of the destitute of their religion.[222]

The words "free" and "white" in the charter of the Hebrew Benevolent Society were part of the accepted formula in those days. At any rate, these terms did not exclude any Jews. The requirement of citizenship, however, did exclude recent immigrants—the cleavage between "old-timers" and newcomers played its role even in a Jewish charity organization. And yet the creation of the Hebrew Benevolent Society was a breakthrough. Here for the first time we find the ultra-Reformer, Rayner, the champion of Orthodoxy, Friedenwald, and others of divergent religious ideologies working hand in hand in a communal cause. Here, in the cause of charity, "natives" like Joshua Cohen were united with "immigrants"—even though they had already become citizens—like most of the other managers. Happily, Einhorn reported, "it was the first time that the wall of separation between the immigrants and the natives had fallen."[223]

From the historic date of its founding, June 25, 1856, until January 13, 1921, when all Jewish charity organizations in the city became part of the Associated Jewish Charities, the Hebrew Benevolent Society played the leading role in providing help for the needy. For a long time, the main activity of the society, like that of all charity societies of that period, was handouts. Very little or nothing was done about programs which would go beyond almsgiving.

The concept of rehabilitation, of constructive aid which would make it possible for the poor to stand on their own feet, was unknown in those days. Thus the help given to the poor did not eliminate but rather perpetuated poverty. For decades there were no professionals to evaluate and make a distinction between the poor and beggars and to treat cases on their merits. Instead, there were well-meaning "managers," people with good intentions whose piecemeal help often caused the poor to sink into beggardom. Yet the Hebrew Benevolent Society and its women's arm, the Ladies' Sewing Society (organized in 1856), helped the poor in the manner of the day by providing them with immediate necessities.

The Ladies' Sewing Society, organized by Mrs. Bernard Stern and Betsy Wiesenfeld (daughter-in-law and daughter respectively of Jonas Friedenwald)[224] to "assist poor and furnish comfortable clothing to the children of their race,"[225] took it upon itself to do much more than its name implied. In addition to providing clothes for the needy and shrouds for the dead, it had a grocery "department." One who was clothed was also to be fed. Leeser visited their "shop," which was a hall belonging to the Wiesenfelds. He examined the articles which the women were preparing for distribution and was pleased to find them "of good quality, such as no one would disdain using, if even he were to purchase them." He noted that the ladies were anxious not to embarrass their recipients, sending articles to the homes of the poor by messenger.[226]

On May 10, 1863, the Hebrew Benevolent Society called a special meeting to discuss the problem of the Jewish sick in the city. The country was at war, and Baltimore Jewry was divided into opposing camps; but all responded to the crisis in sick care. The most reliable testimony on the condition of Jewish sick in general hospitals was given by Dr. Joshua Cohen, who complained that attempts to convert them "warmed us up to the necessity of making provision to protect ourselves."[227] There was another obvious reason for the establishment of a Jewish hospital. The vast majority of Baltimore Jews were observers of the dietary laws. In the general hospitals they were fed *tref*. Moreover, Dr. Aaron Friedenwald and a "small but influential group" insisted that a Jewish hospital was needed so that young Jewish doctors could have a place to be trained like "their non-Jewish colleagues, for whom abundant hospital experience was available."[228]

Whatever the reasons, the erection of a Jewish hospital was placed on the agenda of Baltimore Jewry. Three years of fund raising preceded the laying of the cornerstone on June 25, 1866. The largest amount of money, $17,500 was raised by a "fair" conducted by the ladies' auxiliary. Another two years passed before the ten-room Hebrew Hospital and Asylum opened. Its first president was Joseph Friedenwald, who served for sixteen years.[229] The building was located on Ann Street (now Rutland Avenue), opposite the Maryland Asylum. The first patient, Jacob Schwetzer, was tubercular. In his application for admission, he stressed only that he hoped that in the Jewish hospital he "might get a diet better suited to his disease."[230] This was no doubt his way of saying that he longed to be given kosher food.

That a hospital was needed is shown by the fact that in the first year of its existence it had as many as forty-eight patients. As in other charitable organizations, the managers were all-important, admitting applicants "recommended by the Visiting Committee of physicians." The hospital was a charitable institution, and since the well-to-do would not go to public hospitals, for over two decades no one who could afford to pay came as a patient to the Hebrew Hospital. It was also nonsectarian, and there always was room for non-Jews. By 1913, 50 per cent of the patients were non-Jews.[231]

At about the same time that the community began to think about its sick, it also began to consider the problem of burying the poor. Previously this had been taken care of by collections whenever the need arose. With the growth of the Jewish population and its improved organization, the burial problem could not be left to chance. In 1869, under the leadership of Jacob Godenberg and Israel Posnansky, the Hebrew Free Burial Society was organized. The first to come with an offer of an acre of land as his contribution to the society was Johns Hopkins, the philanthropist after whom Johns Hopkins University and hospital are named. The offer was rejected. There was no intention on the part of the Jews to create a Jewish potter's field.[232]

As early as 1852 a society was formed to take care of the education of orphan children. There is no record of how the community handled the youngsters' maintenance. Most likely it was left to kind people to collect pennies and place the children in homes of poor people who needed the extra income, however small. But with the growth of the community such a situation could not be tolerated. In

1872 a Hebrew Orphan Asylum was established. Located on the outskirts of the city, it occupied the building which had formerly been the Baltimore County Almshouse. It was a gift by William S. Rayner to the community, and when it burned down a year later, he built a new building.

Rabbi Abraham Hofmann, who by that time had left his post as rabbi of the Baltimore Hebrew Congregation, became the first superintendent of the orphanage. He served in this capacity from 1873 to 1876.[233] He was succeeded by Samuel Freudenthal, who served from 1877 until his death in 1902. Like the Hebrew Hospital, the Hebrew Orphan Asylum was open to non-Jews, "in case of emergency."[234]

All these activities required money. People threw themselves into the work of fund raising. There was no end to the fairs, picnics, theatrical productions, collections at social gatherings, banquets, and balls. At the annual banquet of the Hebrew Benevolent Society "sumptuous repasts" were served; bands played music; there were dancing, toasts, speeches, and a great many donations.[235]

The balls given by the Purim Association proved to be a great source of income for charitable causes. These galas were attended not only by Jews but by "all the elite of Baltimore."[236] Joseph Friedenwald organized the association in 1868, and his brother-in-law Goody Rosenfeld was its president for the first ten years of its existence.[237] There were many other charitable organizations,[238] and their number increased, especially in the 1880s. The poor were not forgotten, but neither were they dragged out of the mire of poverty.

Charitable organizations provided opportunities for social functions and relaxation. Such amusements, however, were limited by the very character of the organizations. It was quite natural that as the economic situation improved and there was more leisure for recreation, the desire to meet for purely social reasons would grow. A large number of groups were organized for that purpose.

SOCIAL LIFE

Baltimore Jews had long been members of Masonic and Odd Fellows lodges, but in 1844 the Jeshurun, the first Baltimore B'nai B'rith lodge, was organized. The Jeshurun was the third lodge in the country for B'nai B'rith, which was organized in 1843. The Baltimore lodge grew, and by 1856 it had 160 members. But things were far from perfect with the Jeshurun. A report of their recreational activities relates that *in their clubrooms nothing else is done but playing, drinking and raising occasionally a noise for a penny or two, and this is going on, on our Sabbath, and every day alike.*[239]

The strictly Jewish character of the organization was challenged by the Emanuel Lodge, which was organized in 1850. This group claimed that the exclusion of non-Jews would "gravely prejudice" the standing of the Jews in Baltimore and that such a policy was "contrary to the enlightened spirit of the age." The problem was "resolved" when Emanuel Lodge realized that it could not possibly win and dissolved itself in 1851.[240] By 1875 there were six well-functioning B'nai B'rith lodges in the city. Although it was a purely fraternal order, the lodges were involved in some charity work.[241]

Another organization about whose aims there could be no error was the Beacon Light Literary and Pleasure Association. The character of its members as well as the hopes of those who organized the association can be inferred from its bylaws, which specified fines for "using profane language," "coming into the Hall intoxicated," and "gambling for money in the Hall."[242] Then there were the East Baltimore Hebrew Knights of Maryland, whose recreation included, of all things, military drills.[243]

There were a number of literary associations such as the Mendelssohn, the Chiosophic, and the Independent. In 1864 these three groups united in an effort to establish a National Hebrew College. With this in view, they sought the cooperation of literary societies in other cities.[244] In spite of support for the project by both Wise and Leeser, nothing came of this ambitious plan. The response from other literary societies was "to say the least, far from being satisfactory."[245] The establishment of a national institution of higher learning had to wait eleven years, until Isaac Mayer Wise founded the Hebrew Union College in Cincinnati.

The most important literary organization in the city was the Hebrew Young Men's Literary Association of Baltimore, founded in 1854. Its stated purpose was "to familiarize [members] with the important truths of the various branches of knowledge."[246] For this purpose the members met on Sunday evenings and conducted debates, lectures, and readings. Rabbi Wise's spirit hovered over every important activity in Baltimore, including this organization. The Orthodox Dr. Aaron Friedenwald, who served as the first secretary of the Literary Association, informed the Cincinnati Reform rabbi that he had been elected to an honorary membership."[247] Thanks to the painstaking "critics," as the secretaries were called, we are in possession of a detailed report of the social as well as literary activities of the organizaton from 1856 to 1858. Some of their debates sound as if they were taking place today, such as one on whether it is "just that Congress assumes the power to punish witnesses before its committee who refuse to answer questions which might betray the confidence of another."[248] Like many other organizations, the Literary Association also had its annual ball, and the proceeds were given to charity.

In 1854 a Young Men's Hebrew Association, considered to be the first "Y" in the country,[249] also functioned in Baltimore. In 1870 some opposition to the local "Y" developed, an opposition similar to one we will encounter again thirty-five years later. There seems to have been some competition between the "Y" and the synagogues, and at least one rabbi objected to the Friday night meetings.[250]

A word of encouragement came from David Philipson in Cincinnati. In a letter to Joseph Berney, an active member of the Young Men's Hebrew Association, Philipson (who a few years later became rabbi of Har Sinai) wrote that he was amazed at a rabbi's opposition to the organization. To him

all the preaching and reformed divine sermon on a Sabbath will have very little effect on the young men, as they mostly never visit the temple on a Sabbath, chained [as they are] to their stores and various offices.[251]

The attacks did not discourage the leaders of the "Y." It continued to attract young people, and in 1891 it numbered six hundred members.

Another very important Jewish social organization of the period was the Harmony Circle. It was established in 1855, and without any pretense it stated its purpose: sociability. To achieve this end it provided its members with "a reading room, a ladies' parlor and a billiard room." Sociability also found its expression in working for charity. One year after its founding it had over a hundred members and had raised quite a large sum, twenty-five hundred dollars, for charitable causes.[252] For this group, as for many others, working for charity was part of the fun. The Harmony Circle disbanded with the outbreak of the Civil War but was reorganized in 1864 under the leadership of Charles and David Hutzler. Its annual dances (at least until 1910) were important social events and a source of income to the Hebrew Benevolent Society.[253]

The "class" organization in the city was the Concordia Club. Formed in 1847 as a liberal German club, it developed into the most fashionable social center in the community. Jews played an increasingly important role in it, and eventually the Concordia became to all intents and purposes an almost exclusively Jewish club. It flourished in its handsome building on Eutaw Street at the corner of German (now Redwood) Street until it was destroyed by fire in 1910.[254]

Economic differentiation within the Jewish community naturally found its expression in every phase of Jewish life, including the social clubs. Poorer Jews were excluded by those who were wealthy. The latter, in turn, were often blackballed by members of non-Jewish clubs and societies, thus being obliged to form their own organizations.[255] By 1880 there was an abundance of all kinds of Jewish organizations. Any Jew in the city who was a "joiner" could find one to his own liking in a group that was both culturally and economically congenial.

ELITE AND MASS

In describing the economic position of Baltimore Jewry in 1865, a local correspondent wrote, "The Jews, on the whole, by their intelligence and their activity, have acquired some wealth."[256]

The correspondent, S. Manheimer, was on the whole correct. All the charity activities, the "sumptuous repasts," the balls, and the dances tell a story of well-to-do people. But by the same token all these fashionable affairs tell a story of poverty, of people who were dependent on charity. Not every peddler "acquired some wealth." And between the two extremes, the very rich and the very poor, was the large mass of peddlers, small storekeepers, clerks, and craftsmen who did not attend the "sumptuous repasts" but were not objects of charity.

It was characteristic of the economy of Baltimore in the postbellum period that the chances to advance were there, and many Jews in the city took advantage of the existing opportunities.[257] Situated as it was midway between the North and the South, linked by sea to Europe and by rail to all parts of the country, with a fairly good supply of raw material and cheap labor, Baltimore was in an excellent position to compete with other cities for commercial and industrial supremacy. Coupled with these advantages was the kinship that the people of the city have always felt for the South. At the close of the war, Baltimore capitalists invested a great deal of money in rebuilding the South. The city became known as "The Gateway to the South," and "The Trade Queen of the South."[258]

Its chief industry became ready-to-wear clothing, which the invention of the sewing machine in the 1850s made possible and huge government orders during the Civil War made popular. The industry grew apace, and by 1880 Baltimore manufacturers were successfully competing with New York in supplying clothing not only to the South, but also the Middle West. Baltimore's drummers could be found all over the country; by 1890 the city occupied sixth place in the entire country in the production of men's clothing and a decade later, in 1900, it moved up to fourth place.[259] Some who started out as wholesale clothiers became manufacturers. Others who began in very small factories developed into leading national concerns.

One of the earliest to enter the field was Moses Wiesenfeld. Born in Germany, he came to Baltimore as a lad of nineteen in 1838. He was an apprentice in the business of Jonas Friedenwald and later became his son-in-law when he married seventeen-year-old Betsy Friedenwald. In 1849 he started a wholesale clothing business, which expanded when his three brothers-in-law, Moses and Joseph Friedenwald and Bernard Stein, joined the firm. Moses Wiesenfeld and Co. became one of the leading wholesale clothiers in the country. When Moses Wiesenfeld started the business on April 22, 1849, he invested in it $5,085.91.[260] In 1860, only eleven year later, the assets of the firm were $517,589.59; and a year later the business was worth $632,-535.80.[261]

It was at this period that the foundations were laid for L. Greif & Bro., H. Sonneborn, and many other firms which before long employed thousands of workers.

Levi Greif came to this country in 1851 as a boy of fourteen. In 1859 he established a retail furnishings store. Three years later he began to manufacture overalls and, in 1865, men's suits. A year earlier his brother Max joined the firm. In 1890 the L. Greif & Bro. factory employed 250 and by 1912 as many as 3,500 workers.[262]

Henry Sonneborn came to Baltimore from Germany in 1849, at the age of twenty-three. His is another "rags to riches" story. Young Henry began peddling primarily in York, Pennsylvania. Later he opened a small men's furnishing store in Fairmount, West Virginia. It was successful, and before long he opened branches in Clarksburg, West Virginia, Janesville, Wisconsin, and Cleveland, Ohio. In 1853 he opened a store in Baltimore, which became the headquarters of his chain of establishments. Then he began to manufacture clothing for his own stores and later gave up the retail business to become a large-scale manufacturer. By 1895 the firm dominated the South in the sale of men's clothing. By 1902 it employed some twenty-five hundred people in its eight-story factory.[263]

Schloss Bros. & Co, Strouse & Bros., Isaac Hamburger & Sons,

L. & A. Frank, J. Schoeneman, Philip Kahn and Co. ("the overcoat king of America")—all these and many others who in the twentieth century employed many thousands of workers had their beginnings in that era.

While clothing was the major industry in which Jews excelled, there were also other branches of the economy in which they played an important role, especially the straw hat industry. Straw hats were little known in the country before 1870. It was the Levy family which developed this industry in Baltimore.

Michael S. Levy, the progenitor of a family that was later to be outstanding in community affairs, came to Baltimore in 1866. Originally from Posen, he came to America via England, where he lived a number of years. In Manchester he had earned a living for himself, his wife, and four children as a cap maker. In 1878 Levy began to manufacture straw hats, a relatively new industry in the city. The Baltimore hat, "The Mackinaw," became very popular throughout the country. In 1875 the total value of manufactured straw hats produced in the city was $75,000; by 1890 it had reached $1,500,000. Levy's firm was one of the leaders in the country in this rapidly expanding industry. In 1883 Michael S. Levy took his two sons into partnership, and the firm became known as M. S. Levy & Sons.[264]

Just as in industry, so it was in commerce. The foundations of a number of leading department stores in the city were laid during the quarter century between 1855 and 1880. The most outstanding among these was Hutzler Bros. Moses Hutzler came to Baltimore from Bavaria in 1836. It was at his house that Har Sinai conducted services in 1843, paying three dollars a month rent. Like many others, he started his career as a peddler. In 1858 his three sons Abram (1836–1927), Charles (1840–1907), and David (1843–1915) founded a store which eventually became the leading department store in the city. They were pioneers in introducing the one-price policy.[265] Of the three brothers, David Hutzler was especially prominent in community affairs.[266]

Craftsmen, small storekeepers, and peddlers—there were many of them, and they remain the nameless makers of history. One of them merits special distinction because of his rare craft. Selig Baumgarten (1804–1879) came to Baltimore from Germany with his wife and eight children in 1852. He was the first Jewish seal engraver in America. He engraved as many as 2,800 ambassadorial seals, as well as a seal of the state of Maryland.[267]

It is characteristic of all important Jewish businessmen of that period that they were active in Jewish charity and synagogue work. The roster of the big businessmen of Baltimore reads like the roster of the board of directors of the charity organizations and the synagogues. Moses Wiesenfeld served as president of the Lloyd Street Synagogue as well as of the Hebrew Hospital.[268] Even more active in charity work than Moses Wiesenfeld was his wife, Betsy, who survived her husband by twenty-three years (she died in 1894). Though she took care of a family of nine children and "supervised" the activities of all other Friedenwalds in the city, Betsy was always engaged in charitable activities.[269] Wiesenfeld's brother-in-law Joseph Friedenwald, a partner in the business, was extremely successful in various enterprises. In 1874 his share in the business was $185,379.14.[270] Like his sister Betsy, Joseph actively participated in many charities and was the first president of the Hebrew Orphan Asylum.[271]

The quarter of a century between 1855 and 1880 was an era of great opportunities, of which many took advantage. The accumulation of wealth created a chasm between the rich and the poor. One could easily distinguish between the elite and the masses not only in the manner in which they lived but even in how they were buried.

The Hebrew Free Burial Society took care of the burials of the very poor. No one bothered to write down the manner of burial of the ordinary Jew—there was really nothing to write about it. We do, however, have a graphic record of the burial of the well-to-do, and it comes from an unimpeachable witness. In 1876 Rabbi Szold delivered a sermon in which he expressed his great dissatisfaction with the extravagance that accompanied such dolorous occasions. He related that

during the last weeks it has frequently been our sad duty . . . to make observations on the peculiar modes in which, even in our own midst, funerals are conducted now-a-days. . . . Not a vestige is there to be detected of that heart-touching simplicity which, in by-gone times characterized such funerals. . . . The corpse is . . . dressed as if for a ball. The coffin is . . . of the costliest wood, richly upholstered, supplied with silver handles, and all imaginative ornaments . . . profusion of flowers, raised cushions, wreaths, hearts, and even in forms which are symbols of un-Jewish thoughts: anchors and crosses. . . . Why and wherefore adopt customs . . . by which the distinction between the poor and the rich is so strikingly put forward even at the all-equalizing hour of death?[272]

Although very different in life as well as in death, the elite and masses of the ten thousand Jews who lived in Baltimore by 1880 also had much in common. They spoke the same language, came from the same localities, and had the same memories. With the decline of immigration from Germany in the 1860s, the number of needy persons was constantly diminishing. There was hope that before long the unsuccessful German Jew would become, if not a Sonneborn, a Wiesenfeld, or a Friedenwald, at least a reasonably prosperous somebody who, like those who had "arrived," would participate in the balls and the "sumptuous repasts" or even become a member of the Concordia Club.

There was, however, a small group of Jews in the city who could not possibly entertain such hopes. They were newcomers whose language was different from that of the German Jews, who did not share the same memories, who were different in every way, although no one could deny that they were Jewish. These few were to be followed by many, many more. The East European Jews were coming.

IV

FROM DISCORD TO UNITY:
1880–1921

THE "RUSSIANS" ARE COMING

The Small Exodus

In a report on his visit to Baltimore in 1859, the famous Jewish traveler Benjamin II related that in the Key Street Congregation "the ritual is Polish."[1] "Polish ritual" does not necessarily mean that the congregants were of Polish origin, but there were enough Polish Jews in Baltimore by 1865 to form a congregation of their own: Bikur Cholim. With the establishment of this synagogue, the Polish Jews set a precedent followed by others for many years to come. They could have joined the Orthodox Baltimore Hebrew Congregation, but they wanted to be among their own—among people who spoke their language, Yiddish, and with whom they could reminisce about the past and share the rare joys and great sorrows that they encountered on arriving in the new country.

A synagogue needs Scrolls of the Law. Although the Polish Jews would not join a German synagogue, they did turn to the Baltimore Hebrew Congregation for help. On two previous occasions that congregation had refused similar requests, even though they had come from German Jews. Har Sinai was refused because it was Reform and Oheb Shalom because its Orthodoxy was suspect. But the Orthodoxy of the Polish Bikur Cholim was not in question, and their request was granted.[2] In addition to the Scrolls, they asked Baltimore's mother congregation to give them a piece of land in their cemetery and, with an eye to the future, asked for "the privilege of buying . . . one other half acre . . . as burying ground."[3]

Eight years later Bikur Cholim faced the kind of crisis which was to recur for many years to come. At first the East European Jews had been satisfied merely to separate themselves from the existing German congregations. But as people from a given province or even single town increased, the desire to be among one's own created split after split, and various new congregations resulted.

The first such split occurred in Bikur Cholim in 1873. By that time there were enough Litvaks among its members to secede and establish a synagogue of their own, Baltimore's second house of worship for East European Jews. This synagogue, B'nai Israel,[4] was generally known as the *Russishe Shul* (Russian synagogue). Small as this group

141

was—sixteen years after its founding it only had eighty-nine members[5] —they bought the synagogue of Chizuk Amuno in 1895, when that congregation moved uptown.[6]

Epidemics and famine in Poland and Lithuania and the extremely difficult economic conditions in Galicia brought 74,903 Jewish immigrants from these countries to the United States in the 1860s and 1870s.[7] Some who debarked in Baltimore remained in the city. By 1875 there were enough immigrants from Bialystok alone to establish a synagogue of their own, the Ohel Yakov Bialystoker *Shul*.[8] Local tradition has it that the congregation was called *Frantzoisishe Shul* (French synagogue)—a strange name for a synagogue of *landslayt* from Bialostok—because its *gabbaim* wore formal attire for Sabbath and holiday services. As the number of Jews increased, another congregation of Litvaks, the Pekroer *Shul*, named after a small town in Lithuania, came into existence in 1877. As usual, it was first housed in rented rooms, but after fifteen years the congregation built a beautiful synagogue in the heart of East Baltimore on High Street.[9]

The number of synagogues established by East European Jews at that period—and for decades to come—was not related to the number of Jews in the city. New synagogues were built for many reasons. Sometimes they resulted from the arrival of *landslayt* from a given town or because certain energetic people wanted positions of honor in a synagogue. There were various "good" reasons, but in this period they had nothing to do with a large increase in the Jewish population. By 1899 there were twenty East European synagogues in the city with a total membership of 1,081 Of these, the largest, the Beth Hamidrosh Hagadol, had 110 members.[10]

The 74,903 immigrants who came in the sixties and seventies were only a small trickle compared with the torrent of immigration in the following three decades. The 5,692 Jewish immigrants who came in 1881[11] were followed by hundreds of thousands more. The mass influx continued until the 1920s, when America shut its doors to new immigration.

The Great Exodus

On May 21, 1880, Congressman Samuel S. Cox of New York delivered a speech in the House of Representatives in behalf of persecuted Jews in various parts of the world. In speaking of the "Russian Hebrews," he read a most touching appeal from Russian Jewry "to the Israelites of America, and through them to the American people, for relief. . . ." It read:

Brethren: In this hour of all but hopeless misery, groaning under the yoke of cruel and heartless despotism, driven from our homes and firesides, persecuted by every conceivable iniquitous cruelty, our property and our means of livelihood ruthlessly torn from our grasp, our hard-toiling hands; with hearts torn with anguish, abject in soul, our manhood crushed within us, desperate and forlorn, we turn to the West, to you in your happy free homes, and we ask you to pray, we implore, we beseech you to come to our rescue; to take us out of our bondage, out of our misery; to give us a chance in your great and glorious land of liberty, whose broad and trackless acres offer an asylum and a place for weary hearts and courageous souls willing to toil and by the sweat of the brow earn their daily bread. Come, brothers of Israel in America, come to our help!

Give us the means to migrate to your shores. Let us touch with our feet the sacred soil of Washington, and with our freedom we shall become new-created for the struggle of life. . . . We do not fear work. . . . We are your suffering, but faithful brethren.[12]

The plight described in this letter was mild compared with what the Jews of Russia soon began to endure. The assassination of Czar Alexander II on March 1, 1881, signaled the beginning of a series of pogroms. The first of these attacks on the Jews, perpetrated with the blessings of the government, took place in April 1881 in Elisavetgrad, a large city in the Ukraine in which some fifteen thousand Jews lived. From there the pogroms spread to over 150 Jewish communities within a year. Even such large cities as Odessa, Kiev, and Warsaw were not spared. Several hundred Jews were massacred, and many thousands of homes and businesses were destroyed. Pogroms were followed by a series of severe restrictive laws that turned the miserable life of Russian Jewry into a nightmare. The infamous May Laws of May 3, 1882, dislodged tens of thousands of Jews. They were driven from villages and from many towns into the overcrowded Pale of Settlement.[13]

Life became unbearable. The sole means of salvation was flight, and it was to this that the Jewish masses resorted in ever-increasing numbers. They fled from Russia for their lives. The Great Exodus began. For the most part they migrated to the fabulous land across the ocean, to *the Goldene Medine* (the Golden Land—America). At first there were thousands, later hundreds of thousands who wended their way

143

across Europe to the great ports of northern Europe on their way to the promised land of liberty.

When masses of East Europeans began arriving in the United States, the German Jews in this country were already well adjusted, both economically and socially. There were very few Jewish immigrants from Germany after the 1860s, and the old-timers were at home in America. They were accepted by their non-Jewish fellow citizens as equals, as people who belonged.

And then "they" came. "They" were the East European Jews, who drew attention to themselves by being so uncouth, so untutored, so ragged, so outlandish in their manners and mannerisms in the eyes of the German Jews. Yet no matter how "native" Jews felt toward them, these immigrants were identified as their kinfolk: Jews. Resentment was coupled with fear that these newcomers, whose Jewishness no one could question, would endanger the natives' own well-established position.

The immediate reaction of the German Jews was that this immigration must be stopped. Cables to that effect were dispatched to central European Jewish agencies—in October 1881 the Hebrew Emigrant Aid Society in New York was very explicit in its cable to the Alliance Israélite Universelle in Paris. It read: SEND NO MORE IMMIGRANTS. MUST RETURN INCAPABLES.[14] But this did not help; immigrants continued to come. In June 1882 a second, sharper cable was sent: WE WILL NOT RECEIVE ANOTHER REFUGEE. FUNDS HERE EXHAUSTED. EMIGRATION MUST STOP. WILL NOT RECEIVE ANOTHER REFUGEE.[15] Similar cables were sent from a number of other cities.[16] As late as 1889 the United Jewish Charities of Rochester, New York, wrote:

They [the refugees] are a bane to the country and a curse to the Jews. The Jews [old settlers] have earned an enviable reputation in the United States, but this has been undermined by the influx of thousands who are not ripe for the enjoyment of liberty and equal rights, and all who mean well for the Jewish name should prevent them as much as possible from coming there.[17]

The established Jewish community was not the only group to oppose free immigration. Labor organizations, fearing a reduced standard of living, were also against the endless influx of foreigners. Their protests brought about a number of statutes designed to curb immigration. The first of these was passed on August 3, 1882. It provided for a head tax of fifty cents on immigrants and barred convicted criminals, the mentally incompetent, and any person who was likely to become

Two poems by Rabbi Benjamin Szold:
Above: *In Hebrew—On Purim.*
Below: *In Yiddish—The Four Periods in a Man's Life.*

Title page of Minute Book of the Shomrei Mishmeret Congregation (5650/1890).

Courtesy of the Jewish Historical Society of Maryland.

Call by Rabbi Szold to "The Inhabitants of This Land" to vote for Tilden in the presidential election of 1876.
Courtesy of the Jewish Historical Society of Maryland.

Call of "Independent Jewish Voters of the 5th Ward" against the candidate sponsored by Joseph Friedenwald, the "Idol of Uptown" (1903).
Courtesy of the Jewish Historical Society of Maryland.

Isidor Rayner, 1850—1912, served in various state positions, the House of Representatives, and in the United States Senate.
From *Addresses of Hon. Isidor Rayner*, edited by J. Frederick Essary.

a public charge.[18] The last provision was a ready weapon for immigration inspectors. Immigrants, who were generally poor, were at the mercy of the inspectors, who could easily adjudge any one of them as a candidate for public support and hence inadmissable.

In 1885 a new restrictive law was passed, the Contract Labor Law.[19] The intent of this law was to protect American workers from the importation of cheap labor. Still another restrictive measure was passed in 1891, a law requiring the medical examination of immigrants.[20] Despite protests, the legal restrictions and the abuses of them by immigration inspectors caused many tragedies; but the doors to America were still open, and immigrants by the hundreds of thousands continued to pour in annually.

Among them were many Jews who suffered almost endlessly, even if in different degrees, in the Russian Empire, Romania, and Galicia. In the first decade of the Great Exodus (1881–1890), 193,021 Jews entered the United States. This number rose to 393,516 in the second decade and to 976,243 in the decade ending in 1910. In all, during the first three decades of mass Jewish migration, 1,562,800 Jews—8.8 per cent of all immigrants—arrived in the United States.[21] The flood was interrupted by the First World War. From 1915 to 1920 an average of only 12,740 came annually, a total of 76,440 for six years.[22]

Under the Immigration Act of 1921, the number of aliens of a given nationality who could be admitted to the United States in any fiscal year was limited to 3 per cent of the number of foreign-born persons of that nationality resident in the United States, according to the United States census of 1910. The intent and effect of the law were to curb immigration from "non-Nordic" countries. Thus though Europe in the postwar period was ravaged by war and the revolutions that followed it, East European Jews found America in large measure closed to them. While 119,036 Jewish immigrants arrived in the year preceding the 1921 act, their number was cut to less than a half (53,524) in the following year.[23] This discrimination was strengthened in 1924 by the Johnson-Lodge Immigration Act, which virtually shut the doors of this country to immigrants from Eastern and Southern Europe.[24]

Immigrants in Baltimore

What was happening in the country at large was also taking place in Baltimore. The problem of the "Russians" (as the refugees became generally known, since the majority of them were from that country) [25] was high on the agenda of community leaders. Here, too, an Emigrant Aid Society was established, a very ironic name indeed, judging by the "aid" of its secretary, N. S. Weil. One of his first acts was to inform the New York committee that it should not send any refugees to Baltimore, since work could not be found for them. He further reported that those who came to Baltimore were anxious to return to Europe and that it would, of course, be more economical to send the refugees back "home" from New York than from Baltimore. [26]

Weil did indeed know some refugees who could not find work and who in despair returned to Europe. They were induced to make this tragic decision by the Emigrant Aid Society, which encouraged them to return and assisted them to do so with funds. [27] But the vast majority did not even consider such a possibility. They came here to stay.

A historic meeting which took place on August 11, 1882, gives some insight into the problem. There were 269 refugees in the city, of which 148 were totally unemployed and 44 only partially employed. Of $3,851.50 collected for aid, $1,287.60 was spent on transporting some of the immigrants to other cities and some to Europe. (In the discussion about sending people back to Europe, one communal leader, William Schloss, made a stirring demurrer. He concluded his plea with the ancient "Hear, O Israel: the Lord is our God, the Lord is One." On hearing the *Shema*, the community was so moved that it decided that refugees were not to be sent back, except in "extraordinary cases.") [28]

Just as the Baltimore Jewish community resembled other communities throughout the country, the labor organizations of the city were like the labor groups of other cities in demanding a curb to immigration. The painters' and cutters' assemblies of the Knights of Labor in Baltimore denounced the "Hebrew sweating system," which caused "pauperism" among American workers. [29] Such opinions naturally influenced the immigration inspectors, who, without much investigation and with very little hesitation, declared many immigrants likely to become public charges and therefore subject to deportation. [30]

Some immigrants were turned away for health reasons. Again the inspectors' powers were great. At one period they barred any immigrant who had red eyes, a condition alleged to be caused by trachoma. As a matter of fact it was merely a result of washing with salt water during the long voyage. Rejection on these grounds became such a major problem that the European Hebrew press warned its readers not to wash with salt water while crossing the ocean. [31]

An immigrant could be saved from deportation if a bond of one thousand dollars was deposited as a guarantee that he would not become a public charge. The bond was high; still, many were saved and were permitted to land. On one occasion fifty-eight immigrants were detained and threatened with deportation. Unable to raise bond of one thousand dollars for each one, the Jewish community offered as security the buildings of the Hebrew Hospital and the Orphan Asylum; the authorities refused the offer. Dr. Aaron Friedenwald "neglected his practice and duties to his family" in order to save the immigrants from being sent back to their native lands, the very countries where they had been so bitterly persecuted. He used his influence and finally received the cheering message: "Come and get your people."[32]

Another type of immigrant came "every year," one who was lured by unscrupulous agents and false promises. On one occasion, for example, three Russian Jews were brought by an employment agency to Baltimore. They were placed on board an oyster pungy, where they were

beaten across the jaw with a piece of iron. . . . One scarcely 20 years old had several of his teeth knocked out. . . . A colored man was ordered to pour cold water over him almost every hour of the day.

They were finally put ashore in Virginia and later brought back to Baltimore.[33] The road to freedom was not strewn with roses.

And yet immigrants continued to come in droves. In the years 1881 to 1890, 24,095 Jews landed in Baltimore,[34] a city whose Jewish population in 1880 had only been 10,000. From 1891 through 1898 another 17,367 came.[35] Immigration statistics for the following years are not complete,[36] but available figures indicate that many came. In 1907, 6,065 arrived;[37] in 1908, 2,173,[38] followed by 3,077 in 1909,[39] and so on year after year. The average annual Jewish immigration into Baltimore in the 1890s was 2,000, and from 1900 to 1905 the number rose to 5,000.[40] The numbers increased continuously. Even in 1914, the first year of World War I, 4,074 came, practically all within six months.[41]

Baltimore was a port of entry. From here the vast majority of immigrants dispersed to other places throughout the country. Still, they had to be met at the boat, provided for while they remained in the city, and often given pocket money and even tickets for their trips elsewhere. Those who remained in Baltimore naturally needed help for a longer period. For every one who became self-supporting, many others came who were in need of assistance. The German Jews, with their

149

gift for organization, threw themselves into the enormous undertaking, helping the immigrants in every way possible—by giving outright charity, by restoring health, by finding work. Many helped to diminish misery and make the newcomers self-supporting.

EXPERIMENTS IN AGRICULTURE

For very sound economic and social reasons, immigrants gravitated to Atlantic port cities. Industry flourished there. It was easier to find work, and there were better opportunities for economic advancement in the large centers. Not least important were the social opportunities these cities offered. In their bewilderment, the immigrants needed kindred souls, and it was in these places that one could find *landslayt* who had settled there earlier. Moreover, the new arrivals knew that the large city offered better educational opportunities for their children.

The leadership of American Jewry was most unhappy with this development. They feared the possible rise of anti-Jewish feelings as a result of such concentration. They also recognized that the over-crowded ghettos were disease traps. There was only one solution: disperse the immigrants throughout the country. Accordingly, the Baron de Hirsch Fund established the Industrial Removal Office in 1901 to implement a program of relocation. It was not an altogether new idea. Hezekiah Niles, a non-Jewish Baltimore editor, was one of many who had suggested it in 1817:

> *We have room enough, let them [the immigrants] come. . . . But they should press into the interior. . . . We seem too thick on the maritime frontier already. Within there is ample and profitable employment for all. . . . Strangers should be encouraged to seek it there.*[42]

After eighty years the identical idea was used by American Jewish leaders to solve the problem of Jewish immigrants.

Some refugees, like the Am Olam[43] (Eternal People) group of young Russian Jewish idealists, came to America hoping to establish agricultural settlements on free land. They founded colonies as far west as the Dakotas and Oregon, but their history in this country was a brief one. One by one most of the would-be colonists ended up in the cities. There was no Am Olam group in Baltimore, although in 1885 one of its ideologists—Dr. Alexander Harkavy—lived in the city, where he concentrated on publishing a Yiddish newspaper.[44] But there were agricultural projects planned in Baltimore—two major ones in 1882 and others later. The first involved seventy-two individuals who were sent with great fanfare to Middlesex County, Virginia, to settle on land owned by Joseph Friedenwald and David Wiesenfeld. They were provided with some cattle, agricultural implements, provisions, and a Scroll of the Law.[45] But these erstwhile *shtetl* people were left without any guidance in farming. They languished in Virginia for about five or six years; some died and the rest returned to Baltimore.[46]

A second attempt to establish an agricultural community was made by the Hebrew-Russian Aid Committee, which settled ninety individuals in a colony they named "Pisgah," in Charles County, a county in southern Maryland.[47] Despite its initial success, this experiment also failed.[48] Twenty years later, in 1902, another attempt was made by the Hebrew Colonial Society of Baltimore to settle some city dwellers on the land. A colony was established by the society on 351 acres at Halofield, three miles west of Ellicott City, about ten miles from Baltimore. In 1905 the farmers were helped by a loan of eleven thousand dollars from the Jewish Agricultural Aid Society of New York. In spite of "the spirit of freedom, cleanliness and industry" which prevailed in the colony, this attempt, like the previous ones, was doomed.[49] Indeed, all the colonies were "double trouble," as the name of one of them put it.[50] In each case, potential colonists started out with high hopes but before long were disillusioned, a typical group being twenty-five families which arrived in Baltimore after they had failed in their colonization efforts in Argentina.[51]

Salvation was not to be found on the land. For most of the immigrants, daily bread was to come from a sewing machine. In the meantime, the newcomers were in need of immediate assistance. Even those who did work quite often needed help from the community.

THAT YOUR BROTHER MAY LIVE WITH YOU

There is a degree of suffering such as no pen can describe. Emigrants arrive every day almost from Europe in such numbers . . . and expect gold to be found in the streets. But when they have come, instead of gold, the picture is changed, and they find distress of every kind meeting them at every step.[52]

This sounds like a description of the Russian immigrants. It is not. This report describes the arrival of German Jewish immigrants in 1855. In response to their plight a Baltimore rabbi, Aaron Günzburg, organized the *Unterstützungs-Verein fur Israëlitische Einwanderer* (Jewish Immigrant Aid Society) and called upon the established Jews in the city, not merely to provide immediate financial aid, but to help the newcomers establish themselves so that they could earn a living. In his call the rabbi wrote:

You know the plight of travel in steerage for weeks, nay for months and then arriving without means in a land without a language, with new customs, often without a relative or even an acquaintance. True you are doing well now, but there was a time when you were in such a situation. I call upon you: Remember those days and help the immigrants. I am asking that everyone should contribute 2¢ a week. Ich bin ein bescheidener Better [I am a modest beggar]. I want every Jew to be a member of the society.[53]

History repeated itself in the eighties. After about three decades, the poor German immigrants of the 1850s became well established, and it was their turn to mobilize and to stretch out a helping hand to Russian immigrants in the 1880s. Existing charities expanded, and many new ones came into existence. Scores of aid societies took care of people in need, literally from cradle to grave. It was a chaotic state of affairs, with many organizations doing the same work at the same time. Only the most important ones can be mentioned here.

In 1890 a branch of the Baron de Hirsch Fund, which aided Jewish immigrants from Eastern Europe, was established in Baltimore. It was headed by Aaron Friedenwald, Cyrus Adler, and Elias Rohr.[54] For many years the agent of the organization was Solomon Baroway, who served the community in many capacities for over three decades.[55] As a representative of the fund he met incoming boats and extended the first greetings to bewildered immigrants. Like all other organizations to help immigrants in the city, the Baron de Hirsch Fund was very often short of money. Baroway related that on one occasion

ninety men had crowded into his small office, and he had been very much afraid of being mobbed. There were nasty threats all around. Men told him they had no bread for their children, nothing; and his weary reply perforce had been: "Come around again in six weeks; the money for August is exhausted."[56]

The oldest and most important charity organization in the city was the Hebrew Benevolent Society, established in 1856.[57] As late as 1917 its president, Louis S. Hutzler, had this somber message for the assembled board members at the annual meeting:

Your poor are housed below a level realized by you. Your poor have insufficient clothing by day and insufficient covering at night; a condition intensified by the coldness of their habitation.[58]

152

A year later, his report was, if anything, even worse:

Many of our people are living under conditions that ought not to be permitted in a modern community. . . . We have passed through as severe a test this winter as could well be imagined. The cold has been intense, the suffering among the poor widespread.[59]

Such reports were equally true of other years.[60] All tell a tale of "insufficient earnings," "lack of work," "physical defects," and a frightfully high rate of tuberculosis. One testimony to the breakdown of family life among Jews was the commonness of desertion. Yiddish newspapers even introduced a special column for *Farshvundene Mener* (vanished husbands). Poor women, left alone and unable to support their children, placed them in asylums. For all practical purposes, such children were orphans.[61]

Those who asked for help were not *shnorrers*, not lazy good-for-nothings. In the words of the secretary of the Hebrew Benevolent Society, many "do all they can, and yet are unable to maintain themselves."[62]

WOMEN'S ORGANIZATIONS

After its organization in 1856, the Ladies' Sewing Society had provided clothes for the poor. With mass immigration, the society broadened its activities and began to provide the needy with groceries and furniture in addition to clothing. In 1885 it undertook a new project that foreshadowed things to come—it established a workshop to teach immigrant girls the seamstress trade. Work was to replace charity.[63]

A branch of the National Council of Jewish Women was organized in Baltimore in 1894. This group undertook many important projects, such as the Milk and Ice Fund, which provided milk for poor children and ice during the summer months for the needy. Crippled children were cared for by the Guild for the Crippled Children of the council. The organization was so effective that on one occasion in 1905, it raised $10,223 for refugees in ten minutes.[64] This large sum is a clue to the economic status of the members of this group. Practically all women's organizations in the city—and there were many of them—were active in charitable work. In December 1915 thirty-eight such societies, with a membership of over ten thousand persons, formed the Federation of Jewish Women. The purpose of the new organization was to coordinate their activities and bring some order to their manifold endeavors.

RESTORING HEALTH

The major task of the organized charities was to provide medical help to the sick. The Hebrew Hospital and Asylum, established in 1868, grew with the increase of the Jewish population in the city. New services were constantly being added, the first and most notable being a school for nurses in 1906. Constant increases in the number of patients required more space. The first important addition was made in 1908, when Bertha Rayner Frank, daughter of one of the pioneer builders of the community, William S. Rayner, gave the substantial sum of $84,000.[65] The Dr. Samuel Frank Building honored her husband, the late director, treasurer, and president of the hospital. In the course of time many more large contributions made possible the erection of other buildings and the provision of many new services.[66]

It was a long time before patients who could afford to pay would enter the hospital, for using such a facility was considered below the dignity of a self-supporting individual; the hospital was a place for the poor. At all times patients were given completely or partially free service. In 1916, for instance, 50 per cent of the patients were in the first category and 23 per cent in the second.[67]

From the very beginning the hospital was nonsectarian. Nevertheless, its appeals to governmental agencies for assistance were consistently rejected. The city refused to contribute anything, and the state's contribution amounted to thirty-nine cents per free hospital day, "the lowest appropriation made to any hospital in the state."[68]

Among diseases, consumption was in a class by itself. In 1910, 45 per cent of all who applied to the charities were consumptives.[69] The sickness was especially common among immigrant needleworkers. Not that these people were tubercular when they came to this country— over 90 per cent contracted the disease in Baltimore.[70] In many cases the disease proved fatal only because the poor could not afford a doctor. Also, working people feared having to quit their jobs, so that when the sick finally went into the hospital, the cure took longer and the cost—generally paid by the charity organizations—was rather high.

To complicate matters even further, tuberculosis often meant the removal of a sick parent, which, in turn, broke up a family. Again, it was the community that had to help the dislocated family. The problem did not even cease when the patient was discharged. In the words of Julius Levy, the president of the Home for the Consumptives:

It is of utmost importance that our discharged patients be looked after for a period of years if our work is to be as efficient as we desire When we realize that so many of our patients are afflicted with this dreadful disease because of the lack of proper housing, insufficient food and clothing, we must be aware of the fact that we are only in a measure doing our duty when we give institutional treatment only. . . . We must follow up our cases . . . secure positions for them which will not injuriously affect their health. . . . We must furnish . . . suitable housing . . . proper food and raiment until they can maintain themselves.[71]

In 1907 a special Home for the Consumptives was established by Jacob Epstein, a man who brought about the realization of many communal projects. In response to the great demand, new buildings were continually added. By 1910 Mount Pleasant, as it was then known, was located on a stretch of seventy-nine acres in an open area off Westminster Pike, but, in spite of its growth, there was always a long waiting list.[72]

THE ORPHAN ASYLUM

A close look at the orphanage, established in 1872, makes it possible to understand many other institutions. The activities of different charitable organizations varied, but their methods of operation were similar.

Like all other institutions, the orphanage grew with the influx of immigrants after 1881. This institution bore eloquent witness to the dangers of formal dispensation of philanthropy. The orphanage was intended to provide a loving home for those who had no home and parental love for those who lacked parents. It failed miserably in both these objectives.

The testimony of a reliable witness, a former ward of the institution, is a blistering indictment of the manner in which it was operated. "No. 73" (in the asylum the children were known by numbers, which were embroidered in red floss on each garment, rather than by name), Michael Aaronsohn, who subsequently became a rabbi, has given a detailed account of his and his sister's life in the orphanage.[73] It is a painful story of life in a beautiful building which had all the earmarks of a jail. It was

girded by walls and fences. . . . Pieces of broken glass were solidly cemented on the top of the stone walls and . . . sharp points of iron spikes studded the tops of the wooden fences.

In spite of these precautionary measures, children did escape, perhaps to avoid the frequent floggings given by the Rev. Freudenthal, the superintendent of the orphanage from 1887 till 1910.[74]

The wards could see their surviving parents only on visiting day, once every two months. They were rarely allowed outside. Visitors who were satisfied by externals—spotless cleanliness, orderliness—were very favorably impressed and wrote glowing testimonials.[75] Yet when an orphan was about to be punished because he "stole" a piece of bread, one member of the board refused to trust the account of the "theft" presented by the superintendent of the institution. Dr. Friedenwald's investigation established that the children were not given enough bread and were hungry. The good doctor declared that it was the authorities of the asylum rather than the "thief" who deserved punishment. The result was that children were thereafter permitted "as much bread at meals as they wished."[76]

Notwithstanding the harsh conditions under which the orphans lived, some of them did succeed in graduating from schools of higher learning. One of them, David Levin, received a Ph.D. degree from Columbia University in 1902. Another former ward, Eli Mayer, received his ordination at the Hebrew Union College in Cincinnati in 1903. There was a continuous tug of war between those members of the board who favored the Hebrew Union College and those who sided with the Jewish Theological Seminary, each group being anxious to send a ward who showed promise to its institution to be trained as a rabbi. Dr. Aaron Friedenwald, who far many years served on the board of the asylum, was a founder of the seminary. In one of his letters to its president, Rabbi Morais, he expressed his hope that a certain boy from the orphanage would be admitted to the seminary, because "some members of the Board of the Asylum are designing to send him to Cincinnati."[77]

SELF-HELP AMONG IMMIGRANTS

All the above-mentioned organizations and many others were formed by German Jews primarily for the immigrants. As soon as they could muster some funds, the latter established charitable associations of their own. The first of these, opened in 1890, was the Friendly Inn, a reception center for all those who needed shelter. The "inn" was filled in no time and moved several times to larger quarters. When it settled in its own roomy building at Aisquith Street, a part of it was set aside for the aged.[78]

The Friendly Inn served not only immigrants, but was also a home for transients. This was an age when many immigrants wandered from place to place, examining situations, comparing cities to find a place for permanent settlement. Others traveled from place to place because they knew that a transient would always find room and board and be provided with a ticket to move on. In 1909, for instance, the inn took care of 398 immigrants, while the number of transients was 3,617.[79]

In 1903 the immigrants organized their own Hebrew Immigrant Protective Society of Baltimore, which nine years later became a branch of the Hebrew Sheltering and Immigrant Aid Society (HIAS), established in New York in 1909.[80] The Beth Rachel Relief Association, founded in 1893, gave help to sick women, especially during confinement. It was an all-women's organization except for the president and the secretary who were males (simply because the women did not know how to conduct a meeting or write the minutes.)[81]

For death as for birth the immigrants established their own charities. Although there was a Jewish Free Burial Society, the Russians established their own *Hesed Shel Emes*, which in its first two years of existence was called upon to give free burials to about eighty people.[82]

Duplication of the charity work never bothered the Russians. There were always those who "knew how to do it better." And naturally there were those who sought office. An institution in the hands of German Jews served as a special inducement for the Russians to organize one of their own. This was the case with the Free Burial Society, and so it was with an orphanage. Although all Jewish children were accepted in the old asylum, the Russians established their own Hebrew Children's Sheltering and Protective Association in 1900.

THE MUTUAL BENEFICIAL ASSOCIATIONS

In addition to organizations dedicated exclusively to charity, there were a considerable number of mutual assistance societies, which were also semicharitable in character. The most important of these was the Hebrew Free Loan Association (*Gemilut Hasadim*). It was organized on January 4, 1898, by nine people who contributed $24 and advanced $40 as a loan. At first, loans of $5 were made to the needy, repayable without interest at the rate of 25¢ a week. The demand for loans was great, but the funds kept increasing. By 1899 the Loan Association had 119 members and the outstanding loans amounted to $396.35. In 1910 the association's capital reached $10,000, and the average loan was $20.[83] The *landsmanshaftn* and sick benefit associations were primitive versions of our present Medicare and unemployment insurance, for they provided members with some assistance during unemployment, sick benefit (usually about $3 a week), free burial, and a small amount in cash to survivors.[84]

The situation of the various charitable activities during the period was one of chaos, but a chaos which strangely enough produced results. Order—which led to much greater accomplishments—came later. In the meantime the two communities, the native and the immigrant, uptown and downtown, lived in worlds apart, although they had very much in common.

THE TWO WORLDS

Uptown—A Community of Wealth

It is difficult to picture today the almost feudal life of the Sonneborn household in those days. . . . There were eleven servants in the house. When my parents went to Long Branch for their summer vacation, they were accompanied by their coachman, stableman, carriages and horses, all conveyed in a special railroad car. The other domestics also changed residences with the family.

With the advent of the automobile Henry Sonneborn retained his horses and carriages, using them mainly for afternoon drives through Druid Hill Park. A new Pierce Arrow was used for workday jobs such as driving to and from the Company office.[85]

Obviously not all German Jews led such a "feudal" life, but there were a large number of very wealthy German Jews in the community. Many of them lived on Eutaw Place—a beautiful boulevard patterned after the Champs Élysées in Paris and Unter den Linden in Berlin— and the surrounding streets. The Joseph Friedenwalds, with their fourteen children, were neighbors of the Sonneborns. Summers they vacationed on their 1,200-acre estate near Glyndon, Maryland.[86] Near them lived the wealthy Frieds, Levys, Hutzlers, and others. Former peddlers and small storekeepers had become bankers, jobbers, department store owners, and clothing manufacturers employing thousands of workers.[87]

The upper crust of German Jews had many social events. The most important were the three "Harmony Balls," decorous occasions at which Jewish debutantes made their bows.

There was a very formal procession of debutantes in special dresses and long white gloves. The escorts in tails and also white gloves. . . .

Entertainment was provided by stars of the Metropolitan Opera performers, internationally famous stars, Paul Whiteman and his orchestra etc. The debutantes were dined and wined all winter.[88]

The Phoenix Club (established in 1866) was the meeting place of Baltimore's wealthy Jews. In 1901 the even more exclusive Suburban Club, located eight miles from the city limits, was formed. It cost $200,000.[89] Dues in both clubs were high, and the atmosphere was gay.

Most German Jews could not afford such expensive clubs. They did not have country homes, and they could neither spend the summers in a popular vacation spot like Long Branch nor take an occasional visit to Europe. Nevertheless, even poor German Jews could at least take pride in their extraction. True, they were not rich, but they were not Russians; they were not "foreigners." They belonged. If they had not made it, they had merely not made it *as yet.* After all, the Sonneborns, Friedenwalds, and other residents of Eutaw Place started out as peddlers. So the poor German Jews basked in the glory of the rich and dreamed of the day of their own success, perhaps even of their daughters' debuts.

There were Jews in Baltimore, however, who did not dream. The poor peddler or the tubercular sweatshop worker could not even dare to hope for luxuries. Yet this apparently resigned group substituted deeds for dreams. With superhuman efforts, ingenuity, endless perseverance, and a traditionally Jewish reverance for education, the poorest Jew did all he could to improve his life in the miserable ghetto.

Downtown—By the Sweat of Thy Brow

There were no boulevards in East Baltimore, the immigrant section of the city. North Exeter, one of its main streets, was

a crowded place of tenement houses, saloons, filthy shops, foul odors, hideous noises. . . . Trees, flowers, lawns . . . gardens were sorely lacking. . . . A saloon on this corner, a saloon on the opposite corner, a third saloon a few feet away . . . broken shutters and unsightly curtains.

And yet only a few years earlier North Exeter Street had been the "center of aristocratic life."[90] What happened was rather simple. The large, beautiful house of one wealthy family would become a home for many immigrants. Overcrowding did the rest. The neighborhood deteriorated and in no time became an ugly place in which to live.

A local correspondent described the effects of the neighborhood on the people:

They crowd into tenement houses, eat unwholesome food, breathe impure air, shun water and despise soap. Their children are covered with several layers of dirt. The women go unkempt, the men unwashed.[91]

The situation was, in reality, much worse. Jewish organizational leaders were able to add further ugly details:

Within the full view of public schools, hospitals, dispensaries, settlement houses, synagogues, churches, Hebrew schools and other social agencies, exist strings of bawdy houses, all night poolrooms, low dance halls, debasing moving shows and the hotels which harbor the floating and transient vice of other cities.[92]

The situation was indeed bad if one ignored the potential of the slum dwellers. Tirades against the immigrants by two distinguished Baltimore rabbis reveal this type of shortsightedness. Both mistook symptoms for essence. A Reform rabbi, Philipson of Har Sinai Congregation, spoke about the revival of "barbarism" among the immigrants. "My God," he exclaimed, "is it possible that in this late day such a custom shall be revived"—all because funds were being collected to build a *mikve*. He noted "the lack of culture, the ignorance, the superstition, the filth, the laziness" of the immigrants. Yet he granted patronizingly that "the Russian immigrant with all his faults we welcome as man, as sufferer."[93]

Henry Schneeberger, the Orthodox rabbi of Chizuk Amuno, could not object to the Orthodoxy of the immigrants, but he complained that the Russians "have so many little *shules* and not always in the best of neighborhoods."[94] Schneeberger seemed to believe that the immigrants did not want to live in the "best of neighborhoods," that they were predisposed to filth. Still, he too was tolerant and stated in a sermon that, "if the immigrants should want to join Chizuk Amuno, we should let them in."[95]

True, the Russians did not live in the "best of neighborhoods." But Schneeberger did not realize how much they hated their poverty. Moreover, they feared for the future of their children, who were becoming so outlandish, so estranged, such . . . *Amerikaner*, as their parents ended up calling them. There was good reason to be apprehensive about one's offspring. Henrietta Szold, who lived in East Baltimore, keenly described the immigrants and their children:

William Levy, 1856–1931, philanthropist.
Courtesy of the Associated Jewish Charities.

Jacob Epstein, 1864–1945, philanthropist.
Courtesy of the Jewish Historical Society of Maryland.

Education:

ראשית דעת

CATECHISM

designed for the religious instruction of

ISRAELITISH CHILDREN,

BY

Benjamin Szold,

Rabbi of the Oheb-Shalom Congregation

IN BALTIMORE.

BALTIMORE:
Published by H. F. SIEMERS, 38 W. Baltimore Street.

Text, catechism, by Rabbi Benjamin Szold (1873).
Courtesy of the Lloyd Street Synagogue Museum.

Dr. Samson Benderly, 1876–1944, founder of modern Jewish education in the United States.
Courtesy of the Jewish Historical Society of Maryland.

THE ISRAELITE.

TERMS:
One Year $1.50
Six Months 75
Three Months 40
ADVERTISEMENTS.
1 Inch, $1.00 per Month.
2 " 1.90 "
4 " 3.40 "
6 " 5.45 "
Special prices for larger
advertisements.

דער איזראעליט

אין ארגאן פיר אלללע פריונדע דעם יודענטהומם.

אום אויפקלערונג און בילדונג צו פערברייטען, און אום דען יידישען גייסט צו בעלעבען.

Der Israelit, Yiddish newspaper published in Baltimore: "An Organ for All Friends of Jewry" (1892).
From author's collection.

BALTIMORE, MARCH 28, 1842.

SIR,

You are respectfully invited to attend the CONSECRATION of the *New School-house,* erected by the *Hebrew and English Benevolent Academical Association of Baltimore,* in BOND STREET, between Pratt and Gough Streets, on Wednesday morning, the 30th inst., at 9 o'clock.

R. Goldsmith   *Secretary.*

First record of a Hebrew school in Baltimore (1842).
From author's collection.

Advertisement for Yiddish theater in Baltimore in 1892.
From author's collection.

The youngsters know only drudgery and grinding work. Their home life is not enticing. They have become Americans in naught but levity, shocking grammar, and the despicable smartness of the street and factory. . . .[96]

Overcrowded and filthy homes naturally drove youths into the streets. Delinquency became common in East Baltimore. Between 1910 and 1915 the Hebrew Benevolent Society handled 965 such cases.[97] In 1918 Dr. Flora Pollack, president of the Daughters in Israel, reported:

I go to Highlandtown three times a week and late at night on my return I see tiny youngsters swarming in the streets . . . where dope fiends, pickpockets, murderers and white slavers congregate. . . . The value of an "untouched virgin" [is] from $250 to $1000. . . .[98]

There were "numerous cases" of wayward girls.[99] The problem of "drug addiction" became "pressing."[100]

This, then, was the East Baltimore Jewish ghetto. It seemed like a place from which there was no redemption. A local Jewish publication found it "impractical . . . to believe that conditions can be altered."[101] Yet in the end the "impractical" prevailed, and conditions were improved. The immigrants did climb the rungs of Baltimore's economic and social ladder.

The rise was made possible initially by those who saw the promise beneath the "unwashed faces." One such was Henrietta Szold. She was attracted to the "lazy" Russians who worked so hard to make a living, to the "filthy" who went regularly to a *mikve* or public bathhouse, to the "ignorant" who—in the little spare time that they had—studied holy books, attended public lectures, and read newspapers and magazines in Yiddish and Hebrew. Miss Szold appreciated the "Russians" so much that she confessed:

I feel very much more drawn to these Russian Jews than to others— a prejudice as vile, doubtless, as the contrary one. Nor do I mean those, too, who are earning a competency. There is something about them. . . . I have no greater wish than to give my whole strength, time and ability to them.[102]

She awaited disembarking immigrants and "welcomed, comforted and assisted the Hebrews, who had come ashore,"[103] just as, in the 1930s at Haifa, she warmly received Youth Aliyah children from Germany and cared for them in their old-new land.

The influential local newspaper, the *Sun*, played an especially significant role in aiding the refugees. It became their champion, describing them as

exiles from oppression and just such people by which the American nation has largely been formed. They are people who have taken care of themselves at home and who have shown themselves to be industrious and law abiding.[104]

The paper defended the admission of Russian refugees because "past experience justifies . . . [the belief] that none will become public charges."[105]

The kindness of Miss Szold and others who shared her faith in the immigrants and favorable articles in the press were important. But more important was the fact that the newcomers did all they could to improve their lot, to adjust to the new environment, and to overcome their difficulties. Dr. Aaron Friedenwald observed their efforts and wrote to his son Harry in 1889:

They are becoming an important factor in the community, and it looks as if some of these days [they] will bear the same relation to the German Jews which the latter bear to the Portuguese.[106]

Friedenwald's prophecy was eventually fulfilled, and the Russian Jews in Baltimore came into their own. Still, it was many years before the immigrants extricated themselves from the poverty of ghetto life and saw their sons and daughters, not as "Americans in naught but levity," but as people of stature in the community. There were many lean years, years of agony, before this came about.

PEDDLING

By the time the new immigration began, the peddling period of American business was drawing to a close. The train had brought the farmer closer to the city. There was no more need of a traveling department store. Yet a good bit of peddling was still possible in the streets of the cities and in outlying districts, and the occupation attracted some Jewish immigrants. Among them were former storekeepers, yeshiva students, Hebrew teachers, agents of all kinds, and *inteligentn*—half-baked intellectuals who found it below their dignity to become mere factory hands. True, the life of a peddler was not an enviable one. Knocking on doors, exposure to insults, meager earnings were all bitter pills. Nevertheless, a peddler was not a *baal melokhe*. Peddling may have been "an occupation of which the peddler himself is ashamed,"[107] but for many it was easier to be ashamed than to become a worker in a factory.

Even children were peddlers. Some parents, badly in need of a few extra pennies, sent their children out with baskets of trinkets. Appeals that children be spared from growing up in the streets as semibeggars and semicheats were of no avail. The need was too great. It was even suggested that community leaders ask the legal agencies to outlaw children's peddling.[108] Nothing helped. Children continued to peddle, usually without licenses. One can easily imagine how a man like Rabbi Szold felt about it all; yet, when such children were arrested, it was he who intervened to secure their release.[109]

But the vast majority of immigrants did not make their living from the peddler's basket. They became "hands" in Baltimore's booming clothing factories.

FROM SHIP TO SHOP—FROM DARK TO DARK

On landing, immigrants were met by agents of large factories, known as "inside shops," and proprietors of small establishments, the "outside shops." Clothing manufacture had become the city's leading industry,[110] and the "green" hands were hired on the spot to help meet the great demand for ready-made clothes. In the big shops modern machines had made operations so simple that the journeyman tailor who could make a whole suit became superfluous. Work was subdivided; the big manufacturer found it economical to have material cut in his factory, with only a limited number of good tailors in his "inside shop," and to give out bundles of the cut material to contractors to produce cheap clothing.

The "bundles" were worked on outside the big factory, hence the name "outside shop." Such a shop was usually located in the contractor's tenement flat. The only capital needed for such an enterprise was about fifty dollars. What was necessary was a contact with a big shop owner—and a great deal of drive. In the ill-ventilated and unsanitary rooms worked the "manufacturer" himself, his family, and a few *landslayt*—often boarders or lodgers of the contractor. Their work days were unbearably long—sometimes as much as eighteen hours— and the wages, shockingly low.[111] "Speed up," "speed up" was the constantly repeated accompaniment to the hum of the machines. The sweatshop, born in England early in the nineteenth century and transferred to the United States during the Civil War, became the mainstay of Jewish immigrants in Baltimore in the 1880s.

With all the horrors of the system, the sweatshop nevertheless had its redeeming features. True, the air was stifling, but the atmosphere was very congenial. The Sabbath and holidays could be and were observed. People spoke the same language, both literally and figuratively. It was *heimish*. Psychologically it was the best place for a greenhorn.

There was, however, a more compelling reason to take such work. Men who had never before sewn could overnight become "Columbus tailors," as they were generally called.[112] Such "craftsmen" could get work only in such places. The inside shop needed experienced cutters and some—very few—real tailors. Not so the outside shop. Anybody could qualify, and thousands upon thousands found themselves trapped there. They knew better than anyone else that the "sweatshop is a sanitary as well as an economic evil."[113] But there was no way out, at least not for a while.

Sweatshops constantly proliferated. In 1901 there were four hundred of them in East Baltimore making more than half the clothing produced in the city.[114] Hyman Blumberg, later vice-president of the Amalgamated Workers' Union and Sidney Hillman's right hand, worked in such a shop as a child and recalled his "controversies" with his father about conditions in the sweatshops:

My father was a presser of pants making $8 a week when he worked. There were many slack weeks. Unfortunately father's job was full of stoppages. I went to work at eleven to help support the family. My father was very religious . . . he believed that everything comes from God and that all troubles will cease when the Messiah comes. When I asked father whether he was satisfied with his boss' treatment, his answer was: 'It is the will of God.'[115]

Such believers were very poor union material.

Baltimore's needle trade workers did not even have a workmen's center where they could meet and discuss their grievances. They met only at the "*Hazir Market*," (Pig Market) at the corner of Exeter and East Broadway Streets, where they came carrying their *katerinkes* (literally, music boxes), their sewing machines. Many shops in those days demanded that their workers bring their own machines and sometimes even their own thread. It was only in 1908 that this "blot upon the Jewish community," the *Hazir Market*, was removed and a labor center was established at 7 South High Street.[116] The center opened up a new chapter in the history of Baltimore's Jewish workers. They met often. They aired their complaints. They learned the meaning of solidarity and recognized that they had the power to demand a living wage.

The ranks of the needle trade workers increased considerably with the expansion of the shirt industry. By 1900 there were already twenty-five hundred persons engaged in producing $3\frac{1}{2}$ million dollars' worth of shirts.[117] This too was mostly a Jewish business. For a long time its primary base was the sweatshops, but by 1909 there were a thousand workers in one factory alone, that of Henry Strauss.[118] Shirt manufacturers had a "very strong organization," and they were the first to introduce blacklists, on which appeared the names of workers who protested existing conditions.[119]

As in many other places, strikes preceded unions in Baltimore. In 1889 Ulman's factory was struck by workers who urged:

Brothers! It is high time to consider our lot. . . . The little bread we earn by our sweat and blood is being stolen from our families. Our strength and years are ebbing away. Do not rely on miracles. Only organization can improve our situation. Unite, brothers, Jewish and Gentile workers! Join your hands in brotherhood, and only then can we hope for better things.[120]

The management's answer was curt: "Take your scissors and go home."[121] It was not enough for the company to lock out the strikers; they brought in strikebreakers from New York to carry on the work. But the supposed strikebreakers joined the striking workers and helped them to set up a semblance of a union. Twenty-four workers joined the organization, paying five cents monthly dues. But the "union" survived only a few months, and the strike accomplished very little.[122]

As time went on, there were more and more work stoppages and strikes. One thousand striking coat makers won a ten-hour work day and weekly rather than monthly payment of wages.[123] While most strikes were against the long hours of works, low wages, and lack of even elementary sanitary conditions, there were also other kinds of strikes. Workers often struck against the manufacturers' use of blacklists, which they felt endangered the very existence of the unions and curtailed freedom of speech.[124] The biggest strike—that of forty-two hundred clothing workers in 1896—was primarily against the blacklist. Although supported by other workers, the strike was a failure.[125]

Strikes, won or lost, brought workers together. Workers' organizations, weak though they were, came into existence. At the founding convention of the International Ladies' Garment Workers Union (1909), Baltimore workers in the trade—the majority of whom were

Jewish—were represented by Israel Silverman, who served as secretary of the convention and was elected a vice-president of the newly formed union. Baltimore was the fourth city in the country to receive a charter.[126]

It was nine years before this union felt strong enough to call an industry-wide strike; it lasted twenty-six weeks. One of the chief demands of the union, that employers contribute to an unemployment fund, was successful.[127] There was an extremely bitter strike at L. Greif & Bro. in 1913 which lasted four months; the police brutality it occasioned became the concern of the entire Baltimore citizenry. Important leaders of the gentile community became involved and helped the strikers financially. They were even to be found on the picket line with the workers.[128]

The last big strike in the city was that of 1915. Again there was much police brutality, but in the end both management and the newly formed Amalgamated Clothing Workers Union of America agreed to accept an old hand in labor disputes, Jacob Moses, as mediator. Sidney Hillman, the leader of the Amalgamated, came to Baltimore especially to sign the agreement. He hailed the settlement as a new day in the history of management-labor relations.[129]

Another aspect of the needle industry was the cause of much misery to workers: the work was seasonal. There was no end to the work during the busy season. But then there seemed to be no end to the long slack period. Weeks and often months of unemployment from seasonal layoffs or strikes forced many workers to turn for help to the Jewish charities. The keys to the charity treasury were often in the hands of the very people against whom the workers had been striking. The arbitrator, Jacob Moses, considered this to be "a most aggravating" situation.[130] The workers were naturally intimidated, and the factory owners could not forget that the petitioners for their aid often were workers who were striking against them or their associates.

Many factory owners must have shared the feelings of a manufacturer depicted in Sidney Nyburg's realistic novel of the period *The Chosen People*. His tirade against a striker reflects the history of most German Jewish families in Baltimore.

My father came from Bavaria when he was only 18. He could not speak one word of English. He borrowed a few dollars from another man who had come from the same village, and bought all sorts of odds and ends of dry-goods and peddled them through the country town. People laughed at him and played tricks on him. Sometimes he had to sleep by the side of the road. Often he went hungry. He did not whine about his right as a human being and the duty of the State to feed him. He kept on working till he'd saved up a few dollars of his own. Then he and my mother . . . started a little tailor shop on Exeter Street.

At first my father did nothing but mend clothes. Meanwhile he learned how to make them. By and by he saved up enough to buy a few machines. My mother helped in the shop. When they could afford to have a few helpers, they treated them just like part of the family. My mother cooked their meals for them. . . .

That little shop is what grew into the Pioneer factory. My father and mother put every bit of their lives into it. . . . They taught me to feel the same way about it. And now you come here telling me it isn't my business! Itl is my business! It's my blood in it, and the blood of my father and mother! I wouldn't let it be looted by a crowd of ignorant lawbreakers. . . .[131]

The "ignorant lawbreakers" also felt that they had put their lives into the shop. They, too, felt that they had a share in it, that they were entitled to a living wage, to reasonable hours, and to working conditions which would not shorten their lives. In such an atmosphere, it was only natural for radical movements to be very influential.

Among the immigrants who came from the large cities in Russia there were many who had been members of radical movements in their mother country. To them, radicalism was imperative. If locale had changed, the ideal remained the same—economic and political equality for all. The Baltimore radical, like those in other cities, threw himself into working for his ideals. Influential though the radicals were in East Baltimore, they were not numerous. They expressed, and expressed well, the wishes of the masses. But the masses could not join any party which showed little regard—and even expressed outright contempt—for religion.

The most vociferous group in the "great radical city,"[132] as Baltimore was dubbed, were the anarchists. They were especially prominent from 1890 to 1893, when their leader was Michael Cohn, a medical student at Hopkins. A prolific writer of newspaper articles, Cohn was also an excellent debater. His most important debate with Baltimore Orthodox elements, on September 28, 1890, was attended by over one thousand people. When Cohn asked for proof of the existence of God in the course of the debate, there were screams, and a fistfight broke out. Police rushed in and arrested ten people. Cohn was placed in solitary confinement by the police and put in *herem* by the Orthodox rabbis.

Reports in the local press[133] aroused the Jewish community. There was fear lest the importance of anarchism among Jews in the city be exaggerated. The superintendent of the Hebrew Benevolent Society, Solomon Baroway, issued an appeal in Hebrew entitled "Children Who Deal Corruptly" (an allusion to Isaiah 1:4) which urged the Jews of the city:

> Restrain yourselves and do not let your children attend meetings of the heretics [anarchists] and destroyers of the eternal order. . . . Turn away from those who call themselves anarchists.

He urged the community to isolate the anarchists, lest non-Jews believe all Russian Jews to be anarchists. He concluded his call by expressing his belief that "it would be best if they [the anarchists] would return to Russia."[134] He even attacked Yiddish as the language of the radicals, which it was—as it was also that of the Orthodox, the Zionists, the entire East European community. Baroway expressed the feeling of many maskilim who had no regard for the folk tongue. In this case there was more to it. Baroway equated Yiddish with radicalism and urged the people to teach the children the Holy Tongue, so that they would "remain Jews," and English, so that they would become "useful citizens."[135]

While at the university, Michael Cohn earned his living in a rather unusual way—as a scribe for illiterate working girls, writing letters for them to the old country. Sometimes several would come and ask him to write down the workingmen's songs popular in those days, in addition to the usual letters. As they sang, they wept, and in Cohn's words his room then looked like a vaybershe shul (ladies' synagogue). These letters made American Jewish workers' songs popular in Russia, and people there learned what life really was for an immigrant in America.[136] If the image of the Goldene Medine was thereby tarnished, the "educated" immigrants found it that much easier to adjust to the realities of life when they landed here. Thus Baltimore indirectly contributed to a better understanding of immigrant life in America.

In spite of all their disclaimers, the anarchists were Jewish. They did not engage in debates with any orthodox religionists except Jewish Orthodox. They arranged Yom Kippur balls, but it never occurred to them to demonstrate against Christians observing Christmas. They were atheists, to be sure, but they were Jewish atheists. And they did, of course, use Yiddish in their propaganda, although some of their leaders did not know the language before they came to America. They were cosmopolitans but, in a peculiar way, Jewish cosmopolitans.

If the anarchists were the most vociferous radicals, the most influential group was the socialist Bund. It gained its power by being active in the daily affairs of the workers. The anarchists were more concerned with the future, the Bund occupied itself with the present. It, too, was a small organization,[137] but its influence upon the Baltimore workers was strong.[138] Police had the party under "constant surveillance"—so constant, in fact, that the identities of the two plainclothesmen (both of them Jewish) who attended the meetings of the organization were generally known in the community.[139]

The other two Jewish radical groups in Baltimore were the Territorialists and Poalei Zion. Both were socialist, but they believed that the Jewish problem could be solved only in an independent Jewish state. The great difference between the two was that the Territorialists were willing to accept a homeland anywhere in the world, while the Poalei Zion insisted that the solution was to be found only in Zion. Although small in membership, both these groups—especially the latter—had a considerable following, although much smaller than that of the Bund.[140]

Those who sympathized with radical movements but who would not join a disciplined party formed fraternal orders which supported, but were not controlled by, the parties. They provided their members with sick benefits, some insurance, and funerals. The first to be organized in Baltimore was branch No. 9 of the national Workmen's Circle, which was formed in 1898 from an existing Men's Progressive Club. Like other Jewish organizations in the city, it met in rented rooms before buying a home at Aisquith and Lexington Streets, later known as Progressive Labor Lyceum.

The organization established a library of Yiddish and Russian books which was very popular, especially with young people. Typically the Workmen's Circle arranged lectures, debates, and concerts. In the 1920s it also maintained a children's school. It was Baltimore's only secular school conducted in Yiddish. The many activities of the Workmen's Circle and especially the soup kitchens it opened during strikes gained it both popularity and a large number of members. The organization was always the base for Bund activities in the city.[141]

The only other radical party to establish a broad base was the Poalei Zion. Their sympathizers, although not necessarily members, organized themselves in 1918 into the Jewish National Workers' Alliance (generally known as *Farband*). In regard to benefits it resembled the Workmen's Circle; ideologically they were worlds apart. Although concerned with workers' problems in Baltimore, the organization devoted much of its activity to work for the Palestinean labor movement.[142]

Protests by radicals and unionists aroused public indignation against the sweatshops. Lawmakers were compelled to establish a minimum size for workrooms and to legislate for better lighting, toilets, and ventilation.[143] Moderate as these reforms were, they could not be made by small contractors. They, too, were victims of the system and were squeezed out by large manufacturers. They could stay in business only as long as the sweatshop remained what it had always been.

While many sweatshops closed, more work opportunities were opening up in large factories. Further refinements in the sewing machine and efficient methods of production made contractors in large measure superfluous. A large-scale manufacturer could, so to speak, become his own contractor. There remained one problem which manufacturers could not or would not solve—strikes, which brought about the closure of large factories such as Sonneborn's and the removal of many others from the city. These changes, however, came only in the second decade of the century, by which time they made no appreciable difference in the lives of East Baltimore Jews. By then the vast majority of them had ceased to be "hands."

NOT BY BREAD ALONE

The life of the immigrant was a hard one. It was economically insecure, and his existence was only marginal. And yet even in the gloomy struggle for their daily bread, Jews never gave up their tradition of learning. There were Talmud classes for scholars, and weekly Bible portions and ethical literature were studied by many. The *Hasidim* had their *shtiblekh* in which wonder tales of the *rabbeim* were told and retold. *Maskilim* discussed medieval Jewish philosophers and modern Hebrew literature.

Above all, masses of people attended lectures, of which there were no end. Each of the radical parties and the Zionists invited out-of-town speakers to lecture in the city. These lectures, covering a myriad of topics, constituted a veritable folk university. Thousands filled the halls to listen to the "singer of poverty," the poet Morris Rosenfeld, the most popular bard Eliakim Zunser, the brilliant Zionist leader,

Shmaryahu Levin, the exciting Dr. Nachman Syrkin (at first a Territorialist and later a leading member of Poalei Zion), the charming Rabbi Magnes, the eloquent Stephen Wise, and many others. The Yiddish theater frequently presented plays starring the greatest actors of the New York stage.[144] Baltimore's most exciting literary event took place in 1906 when the famous Sholem Aleichem gave a reading of his works. Although the evening was arranged by the small local Territorialist group, it was attended by a thousand people, a cross section of the community.[145] Not only the audience but Sholem Aleichem, too, was quite excited about this visit. He was given all proceeds of the evening, which amounted to $210. "This," said the famed writer, "is the largest amount I ever received for one evening of work and pleasure."[146]

Baltimore's first Jewish publication, *Sinai* (1856–1861), was followed by a number of weekly newspapers in Yiddish published in the city.[147] For about two years (1890–1892) Baltimore was the home of the only Hebrew weekly in America, *Hapisga*. According to its editor, William Shur, it was "devoted to the advancement and development of the ancient Hebrew language among the American Israelites."[148]

By far the most influential Jewish publication in Baltimore was the large English weekly *The Jewish Comment* (1895–1918). At first under the editorship of several rabbis and laymen,[149] it was edited from 1899 to 1916 by Louis H. Levin; from 1916 to January 27, 1918, when it went out of existence, another board of rabbis edited it. Under Levin's editorship *The Jewish Comment* became one of the nation's leading Jewish magazines.

In addition to the local press, Baltimoreans could regularly read news about their city by Henrietta Szold (who wrote under the nom de plume "Shulamith") in the New York *Jewish Messenger* and by "Label" (Louis H. Levin's pen name) in the Philadelphia *Jewish Exponent*. Baltimore news by local correspondents was also published in German and Hebrew publications abroad.[150]

Perhaps the most important cultural institution in East Baltimore was the so-called Russian Night School. It was one of those undertakings in which Germans and Russians met and worked hand in hand. One of the many cultural groups among the immigrants was the Hebrew Literary Society, RIBAL.[151] Its members were *maskilim*. It was only natural that Henrietta Szold, who was "drawn to the Russians," should be especially drawn to this group. Their activities were cultural in character and imbued with a spirit of tradition without being

Orthodox. It was the match between *maskilim* and Miss Szold that in 1889 produced a one-room school with thirty students.

During the first semester, 150 immigrants attended classes, which dealt primarily with American history and the rudiments of English grammar, reading, and the spelling of English. The number of students kept growing, and so did the number of teachers; new, larger quarters were secured. More funds were needed. A contribution of seven hundred dollars was secured from the Baron de Hirsch Fund, and a local committee was formed to solicit for contributions from individuals.[152] Thousands of immigrants, Jews and non-Jews, attended the school from 1889 till 1897. In a sense this school never closed. It was a pioneering effort in night-school education.[153]

The importance of the school was attested to, even if in an exaggerated form, by Mr. Baroway, who served the community in different capacities for decades. "This institution," he said, "contributed more than any other single influence to make useful citizens of those thousands of Baltimore Jewish immigrants."[154] To this testimony should be added that of a prominent non-Jew from outside Baltimore who believed that the influence of the school brought him indirectly to an exalted position. When Henrietta Szold, on reaching her seventy-fifth birthday in 1935, was given the freedom of the city of New York, Mayor Fiorello La Guardia told her:

If I, the child of poor immigrant parents, am today Mayor of New York . . . it is because of you. Half a century ago you initiated that instrument of American democracy, the evening night school for the immigrants. . . . Were it not for such programs of education and Americanization at the time of our largest immigrant waves, a new slavery would have arisen in American society perhaps worse than the first.[155]

Social Life

All was not work, synagogue, or education. People socialized just for the sake of a good time, even if most social organizations had, as a part of the good time, cultural and charitable activities. Not all German Jews belonged to the Phoenix and Suburban Clubs. There were others for people who did not belong to the upper crust. Some members of the Concordia Club (destroyed by fire in 1891) established the Mercantile Club, some members of which in turn founded the Clover

Labor:

Henry Sonneborn, 1826–1918,
leading clothing manufacturer.
Courtesy of the Jewish Historical Society of
Maryland.

"Home, Sweet Home," call to the workers to establish a workers' center.
From author's collection.

Group of strikers of the Sonneborn factory (1914)
Courtesy of the Hon. Jacob Edelman.

Zionism:

Constitution of the Zion Association (1899).
From author's collection.

*Rabbi Schepsel Schaffer, 1862–1933,
the only delegate from the United States
to the First Zionist Congress.*
From Isidore Blum, *The History of the Jews of
Baltimore,* Baltimore, 1910.

*Henrietta Szold, 1860–
1945, leading Zionist,
founder of Hadassah.*

*Dr. Herman Seidel, 1884–1969, one of the founders
of the Poalei Zion in the United States.*
Courtesy of the Seidel family. Photo by Udel Bros.

Club in 1896. Each club represented a social stratum. An especially interesting group was the Society of Truth Seekers, organized by members of the Har Sinai Congregation who, so it seems from the name of their organization, needed more than the temple offered them. It was dedicated to "literary, scientific and aesthetic purposes."[156] Sociability was not necessarily a peaceful pastime. The B'rith Abraham had police stationed at the door, who entered the meeting place when "proceedings got too loud."[157] The oldest order, B'nai B'rith, sociability aside, was dedicated to alleviating "the wants of the poor and needy . . . to come to the rescue of [victims of] persecution."[158]

The reason for the founding of clubs, societies, and orders by immigrants is often found in the names of these organizations. What strangers needed when they came here was love, brotherhood, and friendship, and these three words were the motto of the popular folk organization, the Young Men's Sick Relief Association (founded in 1888).[159] The large B'rith Sholom order (founded in 1902) announced that their objective was "furthering their own lonesome life in the newly adopted country."[160] The names of their lodges are also revealing. These people were Zionists, hence a Herzl Lodge; they wished to become part of the "newly adopted country," hence a George Washington Lodge.

Synagogue Life

Rich or poor, native or immigrant, Orthodox or Reform, most Baltimore Jews had in common a strong interest in their synagogues and in the religious upbringing of their children. From 1880 to 1920 Baltimore synagogues moved from one neighborhood to another along with the Jewish community. As Jews left a neighborhood, they sold their established houses of worship to other Jews who were moving in. There was only one exception. The oldest and formerly the most Orthodox *shul*, the Lloyd Street Synagogue—which became Reform in 1870—was sold to a Lithuanian Catholic church in 1889. There is no record to explain why this beautiful synagogue was not bought by the Jews of the neighborhood. (The congregation built a magnificent and costly temple on Madison Avenue, which was dedicated in 1891.)[161]

The original Lloyd Street house of worship remained in the possession of a church until 1905, when it was reclaimed by Jews. The congregation Shomrei Mishmereth Hakodesh (Guardians of the Holy

Commandment), whose members stemmed from the province of Volhynia in the Ukraine, bought the old Jewish house of worship. Again it became the leading synagogue in East Baltimore.[162] Its Orthodoxy was characterized by a most stringent rule: "If a member wants to introduce changes which endanger the existence of the community he is to be expelled."[163] Yet even this most Orthodox synagogue had difficulty in having a daily *minyan* and was compelled to pass an ordinance obliging every member to attend these services at least once a month. Failure to do so was punishable by a fine of twenty-five cents.[164] In 1910 Abraham (Avrum) Schwartz (1871–1937) became rabbi of this congregation. His "great learning and sterling character" made him known as the "chief Rabbi of Russian Jews."[165]

The second oldest synagogue in the city, the Fell's Point Synagogue, survived until 1901. Until then its leadership had ignored the members' departure from the neighborhood; but by 1901 it became impossible to maintain the synagogue any longer. It was already too late to move to a new neighborhood, for members who had moved over the years had joined other congregations. A group of East European immigrants bought the old building and established a new synagogue, Aitz Hayim.[166]

In the 1860s the Jews lived primarily between Lloyd Street and the bridge. Twenty years later a move westward began, reaching as far as Carey Street. After the turn of the century, German Jews began to move to North Avenue, Bolton, Lanvale, and McCullogh Streets. The very wealthy settled on Eutaw Place. It was to this area that the old synagogues were transferred. All of them relocated within a radius of a few blocks. Baltimore Hebrew was on Madison Avenue. In 1894 Har Sinai moved into a new building on Bolton Street costing $100,-000. Oheb Shalom built its beautiful temple at Eutaw and Lanvale Place in 1892 at a cost of $225,000. In 1895 Chizuk Amuno moved into a new building which cost about $45,000, at McCullogh and Mosher Streets. The other synagogues moved from this area directly to the northwestern section of the city, but Chizuk Amuno moved in 1922 to a new building only a few blocks to the north, on Eutaw Place and Chauncey Street. The last German congregation in the city moved north to McCullogh and Bloom Streets in 1903, and eventually it also left for the newer Jewish section, Park Heights Avenue.

This section was opened up for Jewish settlement by a small group of Orthodox East European Jews who moved into this outlying district in 1917. Here they formed a *minyan* under the apt name of Shaarei Zion (the Gates of Zion). This district, with its spacious apartment buildings and beautiful suburban homes, became the new Jewish "ghetto," the Zion of Baltimore Jews.[167]

Another section of the city that attracted many Jews in the 1920s was Forest Park. The first synagogue to be established in this area was Beth Tfiloh, which eventually became the largest Orthodox congregation in Baltimore. The first services took place in a private home in 1921. On December 16 of that year a charter was obtained that specified that in the congregation

the form of prayer shall forever be according to the orthodox customs of the Hebrews and said customs shall not be changed or any other form of prayer be adopted without the consent of the entire Congregation.[168]

While the movement to new sections was unmistakable, the bulk of the Jewish population continued to live in East Baltimore until the 1920s. It was here that the first immigrants established their *minyanim*, their small *landsmanshaft* congregations. For a long time many synagogues bore, in addition to Hebrew names, the names of the districts or towns of origin of their founders. Many of these split, merged, and went out of existence, leaving no trace in history. Most of them were not even incorporated. Moreover, "private organizations oft[en] hire[d] unsanitary halls with unpleasant surroundings to cater to the Rosh Hashanah and Yom Kippur Jews."[169]

Some old problems continued to plague the synagogues. One might expect that by the 1880s there would no longer be a German-English language problem. By that time the German Jews spoke English, and there had hardly been any German immigrants since the 1860s to insist on the use of German. Yet German was still a concern in the uptown synagogues, although its position was constantly weakening. In 1881 Har Sinai resolved that the High Holiday services be conducted in German, although the language of the sermon was left to the rabbi.[170] That a resolution to pray in German was necessary at all indicates the waning status of that language; its use formerly had been unquestioned.

Prospective candidates for rabbinic positions were now required to exhibit their knowledge in both German and the "vernacular," that is, English.[171] Rabbi Philipson agreed to accept an appointment at Har Sinai only on the condition that he could deliver three sermons in English and one in German, a complete reversal of the prevailing conditions. The congregation acceded to this condition.[172] In the other German congregations the situation was pretty much the same. In 1888 the board of Oheb Shalom addressed a very complimentary letter to its rabbi, Benjamin Szold, who had served the congregation for nearly three decades. The main point of the letter was a request that he support the congregation's engaging an English-speaking assistant rabbi.[173] In the same year Dr. Aaron Friedenwald wrote to his son Harry, "Demand for English preachers is apparently so great, that it matters very little what else [the candidate] may know."[174]

The longevity of German as a language in the synagogue can best be understood if one realizes that in Maryland until World War I

every public law . . . [was] immediately after its passing . . . [to be] published at the expense of the State daily for one week in two daily newspapers of Baltimore, one of which . . . [is] printed in the German language.[175]

Even stronger testimony to the popular status of German comes from Henrietta Szold, who wrote in a letter to her mother:

To me, English, when speaking to you, has not the same meaning as German, although the former is my mother tongue, and I speak the latter but imperfectly, German still has something gemütlich [roughly, good-natured], which like the word standing for that quality, cannot be found in the English tongue.[176]

What was *gemütlich* could not easily be done away with.

The East European congregations had hardly any language problem. They were all Orthodox. Prayers were naturally read in Hebrew, and rabbis just as naturally delivered sermons in Yiddish. By the 1920s, however, English to one degree or another had begun to creep into both the prayers and the sermons of these synagogues also.

Congregation loyalties were very strong. The "temple people," as Har Sinai members were dubbed, and the "Hanover Street *Shul*," as the Oheb Shalom Congregation was called, had "little good religious blood for one another."[177] Nevertheless the time came in 1898 when all German congregations formed a Board of the Jewish Congregations of Baltimore.[178] "The Board," is was agreed, "shall not legislate in matters of ritual or mode of worship."

But aside from ideological problems, there were "matters of mutual welfare," a euphemism for protection of the business end of the synagogues. For this purpose it was agreed that:

1. EVERY CONGREGATION SHALL BE EXPECTED NOT TO DEVIATE FROM ITS FIXED PRICES OF PEWS OR SEATS, OR IN OTHER WORDS NOT TO UNDERSELL ITSELF.
2. IN ORDER TO AVAIL HIMSELF OF THE SERVICES OF ANY RABBI

OR CANTOR AT A WEDDING OR FUNERAL, THE APPLICANT FOR
SUCH SERVICES MUST BE A MEMBER OR A SEAT HOLDER IN
GOOD STANDING OF A CONGREGATION, AND MUST ON DEMAND
PRODUCE A CERTIFICATE TESTIFYING TO THIS FACT. THIS
RULE, HOWEVER, MAY BE WAIVED AT ANY TIME FOR THE
BENEFIT OF OUR POORER CORELIGIONISTS.

3. ONLY CHILDREN OF MEMBERS OR SEAT HOLDERS BE ALLOWED
THE PRIVILEGE OF THE SABBATH SCHOOLS. . . . THIS LAW
ALSO MAY BE WAIVED IN FAVOR OF CHILDREN WHOSE PARENTS
OR GUARDIANS ARE BY FORCE OF CIRCUMSTANCES UNABLE TO
PAY FOR THEIR INSTRUCTION.[179]

Children's Jewish education, marriages, and even the right to be
buried in a Jewish cemetery were all to be dependent upon membership in a synagogue. Despite these strict rules, the unaffiliated could
and did avail themselves of these services as long as they could pay
for them.

It took a full decade before any semblance of unity was achieved
among the East Baltimore synagogues. It was only in July 1908 that
a Federation of Orthodox Jewish Congregations, embracing twenty-
eight downtown synagogues, was organized. Its object, as described in
the agreement, was "promotion of learning and other activities helpful
to Judaism and to advance every interest affecting Orthodox Jews."[180]
The most important item in the agreement was that the newly created
board was entrusted with the thankless task of supervising kosher
butcher shops.

At all times the congregations were concerned with the *shehitah*
problem. Even though being a *shohet* was not a very lucrative occupation, it attracted imposters; as one Baltimore correspondent wrote
in a European Hebrew newspaper:

A simple melamed who knows not even a chapter of Haye Adam
*can come to America, buy himself a black frock coat, grow a beard,
buy a new ritual knife and declare himself a shohet.*[181]

No wonder the rabbis were concerned lest people be fed *tref*. In
1852 it was publicly announced in the Lloyd Street Synagogue that
people be cautioned about buying meat "at the Butcher Banker in
the Lexington market."[182]

Butchers and *shohatim* were favorite, if painful, topics for community discussions. With the mass immigration, they became crucial.
As the community grew larger, religious authorities were able to
exercise less and less control. Butchers felt free to refuse rabbinic

supervision and *shohatim* ceased to be part of the clergy, becoming instead employees of unscrupulous meat-shop owners. "Mosaic butchering" became newsworthy, and *The Baltimore Sun* published two articles under this title.[183] The problem of kosher meat even came up in court, in the form of a *shohet's* suit against a butcher who fired him. Judging by the detailed reports in the *Sun*, it must have been a lively case. Not only was the *Shulhan Arukh* read in the court, not only did rabbis and "Schahets" appear as witnesses, but there were also "many Jews who helped out the interpreter."[184] A series of strikes and counterstrikes—all revolving around the kosher meat problem—began. Women struck against butchers, who in turn struck against packers. The *Sun* reported "little disturbances" in the eastern section of the city, but "police kept watch." One of the striking women, Rebecca Cohen of South Eden Street, was even arrested for "disorderly conduct."[185] The problem of kosher and *tref* meat was disturbing to observant Jews. The publicity given to these affairs in the general press disturbed all Jews, whether they observed dietary laws or not. Rabbis and synagogue leaders proved too ineffectual to bring the whole matter under control.

BALTIMORE'S LATER RABBIS

In all its religious activities Baltimore Jewry was guided by its rabbis. On the seventy-fifth birthday of Benjamin Szold, the scholarly Philadelphia rabbi Morris Jastrow called him

one of those Jewish mountaineers . . . who had to climb from the valley of Talmudic lore to the heights of culture and thought of our age, carrying with them all the time the Jewish learning acquired in childhood and youth, until they were enabled to prove the value of Jewish thought, Jewish law, and Jewish ethics in the full light of the nineteenth century.[186]

The home of this "mountaineer" at 702 West Lombard Street was more than a family residence. It was an institution. The rabbi, his wife, Sophie, and their five daughters always had visitors. The Friedenwalds, young and old, were frequent guests. A number of Jewish students from Johns Hopkins University made it their second home, among them Abraham Flexner, who eventually became head of the Institute for Advanced Study at Princeton University. Joseph Jastrow, later a professor of experimental psychology at the University of Wisconsin, started out as a boarder and ended up as a member of the family when he married Szold's daughter Rachel.

Cyrus Adler, who subsequently became president of both the Jewish Theological Seminary and Dropsie College, lived in Baltimore between 1883 and 1893 and often visited this hospitable home. He recalled that

there was a table which extended the full length of the dining room of their house . . . which was always set, and wayfarers and students dropped in for meals at any hour.[187]

Immigrants, too, came for advice and help, one of whom related his personal experience:

When I arrived in this country ten years ago I was a young man of ambition, but without friends and a teacher. The Doctor [Szold] cheerfully sacrificed his valuable time to give me lessons in English. . . . From his conversations I found hope and encouragement.[188]

Szold was more than a local rabbi or even a man of national prominence. He was widely known in Europe, and many turned to him with scholarly, as well as personal, problems.[189] The most interesting of the latter was an appeal which the Baltimore rabbi received from his former teacher, the great historian Heinrich Graetz. In a series of ten pathetic letters, Graetz asked Szold to help his son Felix, who had left Germany for military reasons. At that time (1886) Felix was living in Baltimore and was suffering from a "dangerous disease." Szold and Henrietta helped the young man, and Graetz wrote:

We are very happy about the beneficial influence which your daughter exercises upon him and hope that she will be kind enough to continue to guide him in the right direction.

The Szolds, father and daughter, busied themselves with the young man, while he wandered about in America.[190]

Szold was considered by Reformers as one of them and was invited to be the main speaker at the first graduation of Hebrew Union College in 1883. Only two years later, after the adoption of the radical Pittsburgh platform of 1885, Szold took a sharp stand against what Wise called the "Declaration of Independence of Reform Judaism." Szold was so incensed with the declaration that he demanded that his congregation withdraw from the Union of American Hebrew Congregations. In this he failed. His Oheb Shalom Congregation refused to comply with the request,[191] perhaps as a result of the rabbi's success in convincing them to join the Reform movement in the first place.

Szold served the community for forty-three years. Busy man that he was, he found the time and energy to write many books for young and old, popular as well as scientific works.[192]

The rabbi who succeeded Szold, William Rosenau (1865–1943), also served the congregation over four decades (1892–1940). He earned a Ph.D. in Semitics at Johns Hopkins University, where he afterward served as associate professor of Semitics. Very active in Jewish and general communal affairs, he also wrote many articles and a number of books.[193]

Among the rabbis of Har Sinai, two deserve special mention. Emil G. Hirsch (1851–1923) came to occupy the pulpit which his future father-in-law, David Einhorn, held in Baltimore. (His father was called to Philadelphia in 1866, also to succed Einhorn.) Although Hirsch served Har Sinai for only eighteen months (1877–1878), he distinguished himself as a champion of social causes. During his ministry and at his insistence, the congregation began to keep its records in English, and more English was introduced into the prayers.[194]

The second prominent rabbi of Har Sinai was David Philipson (1862–1949). A native American, he was a graduate of the first class of the Hebrew Union College. At the age of twenty-one he came to Baltimore, where his public lectures attracted the attention of the entire community, Jewish as well as non-Jewish.[195] He served successfully in Baltimore from 1883 till 1888.[196]

The outstanding rabbi of the Baltimore Hebrew Congregation was Adolf Guttmacher, who led the synagogue from 1891 to 1915. While serving an ever-growing congregation, he received his doctorate in Semitics from Hopkins in 1900. During the years of his service, the temple moved uptown from East Baltimore to Madison Avenue. Dr. Guttmacher has several publications to his credit.[197]

Baltimore made life difficult not only for the first ordained rabbi in the United States, Abraham Rice, but also for the first American-born ordained rabbi, Henry W. Schneeberger, who served the Chizuk Amuno Congregation from 1876 to 1916. Aside from the usual economic problems, Schneeberger was an Orthodox man who had to pacify both the old guard, who opposed any innovations, and those who clamored for changes. Schneeberger's scholarly efforts included an English translation of the book of Ezekiel.[198]

It was not an easy task to be a rabbi in Baltimore. The record of Rabbi William Rosenau suggests what obligations the local rabbinate bore. In 1904, in addition to teaching Bible classes, supervising the congregational school, and attending to other routine duties, Rabbi Rosenau delivered 56 sermons, gave 20 talks in and out of town, performed one conversion and 34 marriages, attended 35 funerals, and made 637 calls with Mrs. Rosenau and 1122 calls by himself.[199] Other spiritual leaders carried an equally heavy load.

Jewish Education

Education had been a primary concern of Baltimore Jewry since the mid-nineteenth century. For a long time education was congregationally sponsored. Hebrew school was a function of the synagogue. Things began to change with the influx of the immigrants.[200] These were not cut from one piece of cloth. Some came from large cities, others from *shtetlekh* and villages. Among them were Ukrainian and Polish *Ḥasidim*, who differed greatly from Lithuanian *Mithnagdim;* both opposed the *maskilim*. There were Galicians and Romanians and many other kinds of Jews. What was the characteristic of this community of communities was flux. Every aspect of life was changing constantly, and, like everything else, it was reflected in the education of children.

EDUCATION IN THE STABLE COMMUNITY

The school was never accorded the status that it deserved, neither was it supported to the extent that it required in order to function properly. Nevertheless, it was apparent to the synagogue leadership that the school was

> not only a religious necessity for the congregation, but a financial one as well, as new friends and patrons are recruited from it by the congregation. Many people will all the more willingly join our congregation if they are offered an opportunity by the religious school. . . . It is therefore highly important that our congregation will open a gratuitous religious school, following the example of all the more important congregations, by which instruction will be given on the Sabbath and on Sunday.[201]

Those parents who wanted their children to receive a Jewish education were forced to join a synagogue by the usual rule that "only children of members and seat holders be permitted to attend."[202]

Although the economic situation of uptown Jewry was very sound and houses of worship excelled in appearance, the schools were not provided with sufficient funds. They had to rely on volunteer teachers. There was no attempt to make teaching in Jewish schools economically attractive. There were often complaints, such as Rabbi Szold's to the school board that "there is no better way to make a mockery of religion" than to depend upon volunteers to carry out the religious instruction of the children.[203]

There has always been ambivalence in the relations of synagogue boards to religious schools. Schools were undoubtedly needed for the future of the community in general and the synagogue in particular. It was inconceivable to have a synagogue without a school. Once the school was established, however, the chief concern of the governing body was not so much education as proper behavior on the part of the pupils.

Another characteristic of the period was resistance to new ideas. The school board of the Baltimore Hebrew Congregation could not agree whether it was desirable to establish a school library.[204] At Oheb Shalom "prolonged discussions" were required before it was decided "to introduce in each classroom one blackboard and one map of Palestine."[205] Three of the five uptown congregations (Baltimore Hebrew, Oheb Shalom, and Har Sinai) conducted only Sabbath and Sunday schools; the other two (Chizuk Amuno and Shearith Israel) had afternoon schools. Only in the last was the school open for two hours, five days a week. At Chizuk Amuno the pupils received their Jewish education in only a couple of hours weekly. The curriculum, consisting of "catechism" (drilling in articles of faith, which the children studied year after year) and ancient Jewish history, was not changed for many decades. It was only in the 1920s that the uninspiring curriculum began to give way to a more meaningful study of Jewish life, past and present.

EDUCATION DOWNTOWN

In the first decade after the arrival of the immigrants, children's education was completely in the hands of old-fashioned *melamdim*. They were usually ne'er-do-wells, people for the most part with no general and very little Jewish knowledge (quite often not beyond an ability to read the *Siddur*). Some established their own *ḥeder* where children came to learn to read the prayer book and eventually to be prepared for the bar mitzvah ceremony. Other *melamdim* went from house to house to impart the little knowledge they could provide. They were a poor lot and were paid pennies for their services. So strong was the tradition of *ḥadarim* and *melamdim* that even after the establishment of well-run Hebrew schools this type of education still persisted. In 1909, for example, when the Jewish population in the city was about 50,000, there were thirty-four Jewish schools. Twenty-two of them were *ḥadarim*, but, since the number of their pupils was relatively small, their 385 students constituted only about 14 per cent of the 2,845 children who were receiving some kind of Hebrew education.[206] Baltimore's first large Hebrew school, the Hebrew Free School, better known as Talmud Torah, was established in 1889. In 1910 it was attended by 900 children. (Education was not all this school provided its pupils. Most of its children came from very poor homes, and the needy scholars were given clothing and shoes along with Torah.)[207]

There were also special schools, where the accent was not primarily on education but on providing pupils with candies and an occasional piece of clothing. These schools were established in order to combat the influence of missionaries, who were very active among the poor. [208] Missionaries had been in Baltimore since the early days of the community, but they found new opportunities in the dire poverty of the new immigrants.

Children were lured to the missionary house by offers of sweets, clothing, and the like. "Rev." Paul Werber, probably from Brody in Galicia, worked in Baltimore from 1882 till 1896, and Philip (Pinhas) Sidersky, from 1900 till about 1920.[209] The missionaries among Baltimore's East European Jews were no more successful than their counterparts in the old country.[210] The distribution of books, candy, and clothing attracted people—especially children—but they did not convert Jews.

The common plight of all schools was a lack of funds. There were always those who fruitlessly complained that the school was the stepchild of the community's religious life. The local weekly wrote that

when the Sabbath schools will receive the attention that our choirs and buildings [synagogues] have heretofore gotten, we should hear less of dearth of competent teachers to have care of them.[211]

Ideology presented additional problems. In 1908 the Talmud Torah underwent a severe crisis. Extreme opponents, the Reform rabbi Rosenau and the Orthodox leader Tanhum Silberman, united successfully on one issue: to replace Yiddish with English in translation of texts. But there were many parents to whom Yiddish meant much more than just a language. Yiddish was *Yidishkayt*, English meant a step toward *goyishkayt*, toward assimilation. These parents removed their children from the school and established a new one, also called Talmud Torah, to which they significantly added the words "Ve-Emuna" (and Faith) [212] to underscore the difference between the new school and the old.

As Baltimore's population increased, many new schools opened, more often because of geography than because of ideology. Children went to the "Hebrew" closest to their homes. Still, since there were many schools, those who cared for ideologies could find schools which taught their points of view.

THE GREAT EXPERIMENTER—
SAMSON BENDERLY (1876–1944) [213]

While visiting Palestine in 1898, Dr. Aaron Friedenwald also went to Syria. In Beirut he met and befriended a young native of Safed (Palestine), Samson Benderly, who was studying medicine at the American University there. The American was impressed by the twenty-two-year-old youth and invited him to come to Baltimore. Benderly agreed.

When he arrived he enrolled in the university and earned a living by teaching Hebrew to the doctor's son, Harry, and to two of Rabbi Szold's daughters, Henrietta and Bertha. In 1900 Benderly received his medical degree and seemed ready for a career in ophthalmology, which was also the field of both Friedenwalds, his patron and his pupil. At that point, however, he made a decision of momentous consequence for Jewish education in the United States. To the astonishment of his friends, he resolved to devote himself to the neglected and unremunerative field of Jewish education. He became the principal of a small Hebrew school run by the Hebrew Education Society. The number of students increased, and in 1903 the society bought a roomy, three-story building on Aisquith and Jackson Streets. This at last gave Benderly the opportunity he had been waiting for to carry out his daring, innovative experiments.

To begin with, he demanded of teachers as well as of pupils something unheard of in those days—cleanliness. That, he insisted, was part of Jewish education.

He felt that the children who attended the bright public schools with . . . plants in the windows would not be attracted by the dingy

*cheder. He related one experience he had in such a "Hebrew." It
was a dirty place and in it he found an admirable young teacher whom
he wanted to engage for his classes. Politely and embarrassedly he
asked: Can you manage to wear a clean collar and—er—clean your
fingernails? The answer consisted of one word: Why? Benderly
was taken aback and approached the matter in a gingerly fashion:
Well, it might be more aesthetic, don't you agree? Aesthetic? queried
the teacher. I am not sure what this has to do with education. Beauty
does not enter into my philosophy of life. Benderly, however, did not
give up. The young man was too good a teacher to be lost in the
dirty cheder. He was taken out of the cellar. Beauty was forced upon
him. He became a party of Benderly's bright world. . . .*[214]

The "bright world" also demanded a washroom with twenty basins
and faucets; the children were made to wash their hands before
entering the classrooms.[215]

This new kind of education emphasized not only books but also
play. In order for children to learn, they had to be happy. This required recreation, which Benderly provided by arranging for play
areas in the school. All these activities were unheard of in Jewish
educational institutions, and the innovations evoked "sarcastic remarks
from every side." Games in Hebrew also met with ridicule.[216] Some
laughed at Benderly's "games"; others fought him tooth and nail. The
Orthodox could not forgive his use of *Lashon Hakodesh* (the Holy
Tongue) for secular purposes.[217]

But there were other reactions. There were those who admired
Benderly's experiments. The influential *Jewish Comment* remarked
editorially:

*Great work . . . has been done by Dr. Samson Benderly for the
cause of Hebrew education. He has accomplished results that must
be considered extraordinary. . . . He has been able successfully to
teach Hebrew as a living language. Recognizing the great need for
competent teachers, he set about training them properly for the work.
He wisely chose Jewish girls (in most cases graduates from our high
schools), who are able intelligently to grasp his ideas. He has succeeded in imbuing them with some of his abundant enthusiasm, and
they are now pursuing advanced studies. It is his plan now to interest
Jewish young men with University training in the study of Hebrew
with a view to becoming enlightened modern teachers of that language,
and he is gratified at the favor with which his approaches have been
received. Dr. Benderly is convinced that the professional Hebrew*

teacher has as bright a future in this country as the teacher of science or of any other language.[218]

A year later the magazine wrote again:

He [Benderly] has shown what extraordinary things may be accomplished by an enthusiastic and comprehending teacher working along modern lines. His classes are among the Jewish attractions of the city.[219]

The Benderly school had about three hundred students. He badly needed teachers, and in his reports to the Board of the Hebrew Education Society, he posed the constant question: "Where can teachers be gotten? This question awaits an answer from the most judicious part of enlightened American Jewry. . . ."[220] In the meantime, the Hebrew Education Society could not wait and had to do its best under the circumstances, which meant utilizing the services of some of the better students for teaching. This was, as Benderly said, the only way for the school "to perpetuate itself."[221]

Benderly went to the board with the basic problems that gave him no rest, and this no doubt disturbed the members, who preferred to hear only good reports. The work of the school was indeed gratifying, but he refused to gloss over existing difficulties. One of his reports asked boldly:

Putting aside meaningless phrases and generalities, what is the aim of Jewish education? Surely no intelligent businessman would equip a plant and employ many workmen without knowing just what he wants to accomplish.[222]

What he was after was a discussion not only of methods, important as they were, but also of the goals of Jewish education. He stressed the point that

the student of Jewish life in this country discerns amidst the chaos in our beliefs and practices an awakening on the part of the more intelligent Jews to the gravity of the Jewish educational problem. This awakening cannot come too soon. . . . Why should Jewish education not have a distinctive aim?[223]

Benderly sought answers to the deeper questions of Jewish education. In the meantime, however, immediate problems were pressing, and there was little time left for reflection. He speculated wishfully that *if all the boards of Jewish educational institutions in this country determined that their duty is merely to find the man in whom they have confidence, and then let him study and learn the best way of doing the work . . . we might be able to bring order out of the chaos.*[224]

He was not given the opportunity "to study and learn." Instead, he became the director of the Bureau of Jewish Education of New York in 1910. His place as principal of the school was taken over by Elias Nathan Rabinowitz, who until then had been the principal of the Talmud Torah. Benderly, however, retained the title of superintendent. In 1912 Rabinowitz became the school superintendent, a post he held until 1918, when he became an army chaplain.

UNITY IN EDUCATION

The number of schools was constantly increasing. They were not communal in the sense of being supported by the Federated Jewish Charities or the United Hebrew Charities; nor were these schools congregational. Each was maintained by its own membership. The result of this state of affairs was chaos. The time had come to do in education what had been done in charity.

Unity came about in 1914, when a board of education was established.[225] Individual schools were jealous of their independence, however. The board was not in a position to supervise education, let alone to deal with the curricula of the schools, appoint teachers, and so on. It took many years before it acquired such authority. In the meantime, it made a humble but very important beginning. It was the Board of Jewish Education which from that time on responded to the constant population shifts by closing old schools and opening new ones.[226]

In spite of all the efforts of both individual schools and the Board of Jewish Education, many children did not receive any Jewish education. Although rabbis and school officials tried hard to enroll all Jewish children, over two thousand did not attend any Hebrew school in 1917.[227] Rabbi Eugene Kohn of Chizuk Amuno asked the Baltimore school board to provide him with a list of the school-children in the vicinity of his synagogue. He hoped that by personal contact with their parents he might induce them to send their children to a Hebrew school. The effort failed when the rabbi's request was rejected because "similar requests might come from every denomination in the city, thus opening the way for classification of children on religious grounds."[228]

Realizing the dearth of properly trained teachers, the newly created central agency converted the school of the Hebrew Education Society into a teachers' training school, which became known as Jewish Teachers' Training School and School for Practice. In 1915 the school had eight trainees, of whom five were also teaching.

For many years Dr. Harry Friedenwald served as president of the Hebrew Education Society, and when the Board of Jewish Education was formed, he became its president. He was always in the forefront of the work for better schools. Dr. Friedenwald was succeeded as president of the society by Isaac Davidson, a substantial German-born businessman, one of the uptowners who took an interest in the affairs of the immigrants.[229]

Day schools, which had been the basis of Jewish education until the middle of the 1870s, came back to life in the second decade of the twentieth century. On February 19, 1917, the Yeshivah Torah Ve-Emuna Hebrew Parochial School of Baltimore City was incorporated. Its founder was Rabbi Abraham Schwartz of Shomrei Mishmereth Hakodesh synagogue. The growth of this school, which opened in 1917 with seven children in grade one, signaled the development of other day schools.[230]

JEWISH HIGHER EDUCATION

The highest Jewish educational institution in the city, the Hebrew College, was established twice, peculiar as it may sound. Many organizations survived only briefly, and later organizations would use the same name even if there was no direct connection between the two. The first college was founded by Benderly in 1902. It was an institution

where adults desirous of pursuing the study of the Hebrew language, Hebrew literature, Jewish history and pedagogies will find every facility for . . . instruction.[231]

The founder's hope was to train women teachers for his school. He could not afford to wait until the young people who entered his teachers' training courses graduated. Brighter girls were given the opportunity to teach and continue their studies for another three years.

Benderly imbued a number of his students with a sense of obligation to teach Hebrew and a belief in the profession. Several of them became teachers in the school, and one of them, Jennie C. Miller, even became his wife. The teachers' classes declined after Benderly left the city, but a dire need for Hebrew teachers later brought them back to life.

The college was reestablished in 1919, with Israel Efros, who subsequently became a noted Hebrew poet, as its dean. The press announced that the purpose of the college was "to keep alive the best of the lore of the ancient Semites."[232] As a matter of fact, the college was much more than the announcement stated. It was not preoccupied solely with Semitic lore. It was from the very beginning a vibrant institution in which every phase of Jewish life was studied and which considered the training of teachers to be its chief function. The Board of directors represented a cross section of the community.[233]

Important as the synagogues and Jewish education were in the life of the community, they were not a unifying force. The two Baltimore Jewries could, and indeed did, work diligently in these areas—but they worked separately. Other forces were eventually to bring them together.

Zionism—A Force for Unity

In breaking down barriers between uptown and downtown Jewries, Zionism played an important role. Strangely enough, the first words in Baltimore about "Zion Restored" came from a non-Jew as far back as 1816. In that year Hezekiah Niles, in his *Niles' Weekly Register*, published a lengthy article about the possibility of the Jews' return to their ancient homeland. The article concluded that

the Jews were once a peculiar people of God, they are yet a peculiar people; though scattered and dispersed in every country and in every clime their future state will no doubt be more glorious than ever. And he who led their fathers through the deserts, has promised to lead them again to their native land. . . . It is probable that the time is not far distant when this great event shall take place . . . and the banners of Israel be unfurled on the walls of Jerusalem the Holy Hill of Zion. The Jews will rebuild their ancestral homeland and those parts of the East so celebrated and sacred . . now so degraded and lost to all that is good and great, may again be the seat of commerce and useful arts. The deserts of Palestine brought into cultivation by patient industry may again blossom as the rose, and Jerusalem miserable as it is, speedily rival the cities of the world for beauty, splendor and wealth.[234]

It was a long time before the prophetic words of the Quaker Niles began to come true. Baltimore contributed much to their realization. Collections were made for the Holy Land as early as 1840, and they continued in one form or another for a long time. In the 1870s Baltimore congregations merited the attention of Sir Moses Montefiore, through whom they sent funds for Palestine. In 1870 and 1879 he sent one Torah Scroll for Shearith Israel and Chizuk Amuno to share, in recognition of their work for the Holy Land.[235] Such fund-raising activities for Palestine were the forerunners of the modern Zionist movement, which began in the 1880s.

When Jews began their mass emigration from Russia, a small group of young people calling themselves BILU (from the Hebrew initials of "House of Jacob, Come and Let Us Go," Isaiah 2:5) left Russia for Palestine. These pioneers paved the way for the restoration of the ancient Jewish homeland. The masses who came to America felt a kinship with this group and with their ideal. While struggling to make a living and to adjust themselves to new conditions of life, they followed with great interest every effort in behalf of Palestine. About two years after the founding of Hovevei Zion (Lovers of Zion) in Russia in 1882, a similar group was organized in New York; and in 1889 a branch was founded in Baltimore by "the very learned, although very young" Rabbi Simon Isaac Halevi Finkelstein.[236]

The organization was eminently successful. In the first year of collecting pennies among immigrants, it raised $234.58. Of this sum only $48.76 was sent to Palestine; the rest was spent on propaganda in Baltimore.[237] Propaganda proved to be a good investment, for the movement attracted attention. A fortunate circumstance brought Palestine closer to home, enabling Baltimore Jews actually to "see" it. After a visit to Palestine, Cyrus Adler, who graduated from the Semitic Department at Hopkins, delivered a lecture "illustrated by stereopticon views."[238]

Baltimore's Lovers of Zion movement grew, and in 1894 a second group was organized under the name Hevrath Zion (Zion Association). Its president, Reuben Aaronson, remained active in the movement for many years. Two of its most active members were Solomon Baroway, who published articles on Baltimore life in *The Jewish Exponent*, and Moshe Falk Mervis, who lived in Baltimore from 1880 till 1960 and wrote about Baltimore in the European Hebrew press. The Zion Association accommodated all Jews who accepted the ideal of rebuilding Palestine. It was quite a progressive step to have a clause in the constitution saying that "the Association will not concern itself with the individual religious and social views of its members."[239] The busy group attended all kinds of gatherings and raised funds for its two pet projects, a school and a library in Jaffa.[240]

Although only a local organization, Baltimore's Zion Association did a great service to American Jewry in 1895 by bringing to this country the famous folk orator Zvi Hirsh Masliansky.[241] No wonder Baltimore was the first American city he visited outside of New York. He was very much impressed by what he saw; in Baltimore he found

a group of devoted Hovevei Zion. . . . I just could not believe that I was in America. I found here a wonderful atmosphere similar to that in Vilna and Bialystok. . . . The Orthodox German Jews like the well-known families, the Friedenwalds and Levys, Dr. Schaffer, Mr. Tanhum Silberman . . . are people of whom Vilna would not be ashamed. . . . Baltimore is the American Bialystok.[242]

In such an atmosphere Zionism was naturally in the ascendancy.

Some of these early Zionists were not satisfied merely to encourage other Jews to settle in Palestine. Their Zionism was more personal. Many who were keenly disappointed with their American "successes," with the long hours and low pay of the sweatshops, began to consider emigration to Palestine. This group was known as Shavei Zion (Returnees to Zion). A meeting of this organization held on May 26, 1892, serves as most eloquent testimony to the interest in *aliyah*. The hall, holding a thousand people, was filled to capacity and many were turned away.[243] Another meeting held three weeks later again attracted several hundred men and women.[244]

The Shavei Zion, while attracting much attention, were not at all successful in realizing their program. True, life in America was hard, but there was hope for a brighter future. They loved Palestine, but they also knew about the hardships of the pioneers in Palestine, where a better lot was not in sight. Moreover, for all its strangeness, there were so many *landslayt in Columbus's Medine* (the land of Columbus, as the United States was usually called by immigrants) that it felt like home, after all. And so the Zionist and especially the Shavei Zion sang songs of love for Zion but remained in Baltimore.

People did not go to Palestine, but nevertheless they worked for the rebuilding of that land. So strong was the movement in Baltimore that in 1897 the only delegate from the United States to the first Zionist Congress in Basel was a Baltimorean, Rabbi Schepsel Schaffer. His reports about the historic gathering attracted thousands. As a result the Zion Association grew to become the largest Zionist group in the country.[245] Two years later, when the World Zionist Organization launched a subscription for the newly established Jewish Colonial Bank, the Zion Association sold the amazingly large number of 1,128 shares.[246]

In the meantime a group of younger people organized the Ezras Hovevei Zion.[247] Its members formed squads, wore white uniforms with the Star of David sewn on them, and marched in military formation down the streets of Baltimore. Their military command was "Aleph, Beth Gimel, Daleth, Hey, Vav, Zayin," the first seven letters of the Hebrew alphabet, with the accent on the last letter, "Zayin," which sounds like Zion. Their marches from Front Street became quite popular. "The Yidn [Jews] loved it and the non-Jews respected the marchers."[248]

The most vigorous Zionist group was Kadima, organized in 1903. It differed from the others in being concerned not only with the restoration, as were all other Zionist groups, but also with local Jewish problems.[249] This was the beginning of a bridge between the Zionist movement and the community as a whole. By 1917 Zionism was so strong in the city that one group, Tifereth Zion, had over five hundred members between the ages of eighteen and thirty.[250] But although Baltimore was a citadel of Zionism, the movement met with some opposition, particularly among Reform elements, who feared the movement was "too nationalistic" and might lead to "dual loyalties."[251] Much stronger was the opposition of the workers' organizations. The anarchists and the Bundists fought against the Zionist "illusion."

A small group of radicals found no conflict between socialism and Zionism. They insisted that a Jewish homeland could be built in Palestine on socialist foundations. The Poalei Zion, as its name indicated, was a movement for a workers' state in Palestine. That Baltimore had a large share in the formation of this movement in North America was in large measure due to one man, Dr. Herman Seidel (1884–1969).

Seidel, already a Labor Zionist, came to the city from Lithuania in 1903. Although only nineteen, he was an "experienced Hebrew teacher" of three years' standing. Seven years after his arrival, Hayim (later Herman) Seidel became a doctor of medicine. During those seven lean years, he taught Hebrew under Benderly and privately tutored Dr. Harry Friedenwald in Hebrew.[252] Busy as the young man was with studying and teaching, he began to organize a Poalei Zion group. Friday nights he used to stand on a soapbox at the corner of Baltimore and Exeter Streets.

The Orthodox did not oppose, even if it was Friday night. I spoke in Yiddish, and I spoke about Eretz Israel, and large crowds would gather.[253]

The Poalei Zion group in Baltimore was small but very cohesive, extremely dedicated to their ideal. Similar groups sprang up in other cities. When the party decided to hold a national convention in 1905, the honors went to Baltimore. Here Seidel "billeted" the twenty-two delegates from eight cities in the homes of the *haverim* (comrades), as members were called. A number of Zionists attended the convention. They thought the Poalei Zion to be a "bunch of *meshugoim* [nuts]," especially since one session lasted for thirty uninterrupted hours. One of those who liked these "stimulating nuts" was Sigmund Sonneborn, who gladly permitted the *haverim* to come to his large clothing factory, deliver a *droshe*, and pass around a can.[254]

As a party in the middle, the Poalei Zion were accused by the general Zionists of being disloyal to Zionism and by the Bund of being disloyal to socialism. Their struggle was especially bitter with the Bundists, with whom they fought "like cats and dogs."[255]

Although Poalei Zion remained small in numbers it had a great many ideological followers. When the Jewish Legion was organized in 1917 to enroll Jewish youth in the British effort to free Palestine from the Turks, Poalei Zion propagandized for it in Baltimore. Dr. Seidel was appointed by the British government as the recruiting officer for Baltimore and Washington. Among the three thousand American volunteers, there were about ninety from Baltimore; one of them, J. O'Brien, was a non-Jew. One of the Legionnaires described the method of recruiting volunteers:

A group of volunteers who had already enlisted would take a position on the corner of a busy intersection in East Baltimore, such as Baltimore and Exeter or Baltimore and High Streets. Sometimes they would sing a Hebrew song or someone would play a musical instrument. When a crowd would gather, one of us would climb on a "Soap Box." He would speak to the audience about the idea of a Jewish homeland. . . . Then he would appeal to the listeners to join the Jewish Legion and fight in a Jewish Army, under a Jewish flag. . . .[256]

Zionist groups were divided not only by socioeconomic ideals; religious differences also played an important role in the movement. In 1917 a branch of the religious Zionist organization, Mizrachi, was formed in Baltimore.[257] Women's activities in behalf of Zionism began with the foundation of a Hadassah organization in the city in 1913. The membership in Hadassah grew continually until it became Baltimore's largest Jewish organization.[258]

East Europeans were not the only Jews active in the movement. They were in the majority, but there were a considerable number of devoted Zionists among the uptown Jews also, including the members of the city's two leading Jewish families, the Friedenwalds and the Szolds. There were enough of them in 1903, in fact, to organize the Theodor Herzl Zionistischer Verein, the first German-speaking Zionist society in America.[259] The ice was broken. German Jews ceased to consider Zionism a movement appropriate only for downtown Jewry but not for them. Even the leading local Reform rabbi, William Rosenau, stated at a conference of his colleagues, "I believe one can be a good reform Jew and be a Zionist."[260]

The Verein attracted more members, and its two founders, Dr. Harry Friedenwald and Miss Szold, were destined to play major roles in the history of Zionism nationally and internationally. Dr. Friedenwald (1864–1950) was a Baltimorean all his life.[261] In 1904 he was elected president of the American Zionist Federation and served in this capacity till 1918. He shared with Dr. Weizmann and Rabbi Magnes the greater part of the work which led to the establishment of the Hebrew University.[262] In 1918 Friedenwald was appointed chairman of the Zionist Commission, which was to undertake necessary measures to implement the Balfour Declaration, to develop the program for creation of a national home in Palestine.[263] Upon his return to Baltimore, after a two-year absence, Friedenwald continued to work in the cause of Zionism till his death on April 9, 1950.

Baltimore's second contributor to Zionism was Henrietta Szold (1860–1945). It cannot be said that she grew up in a Zionistic environment. Far from it. In 1880 her father, Rabbi Szold, wrote:

We are Germans in Germany, Frenchmen in France, Englishmen in England, Americans in America, Russians in Russia, and Turks in Turkey. . . . There is not the least desire on our part to leave our dearly cherished native homes and return to a land that was the home of our forefathers eighteen centuries ago. . . . The modern Israelites . . . feel [themselves] at home everywhere.[264]

By the end of the century Benjamin Szold had changed his views. It was, perhaps, due to the "Russian invasion" of Baltimore. He could not possibly say any longer, "We are . . . Russians in Russia." The escapees from pogroms were not Russians even if they were called by that hateful name. Szold's home became the center of Zionist activity in the city.

His oldest daughter, Henrietta, was not just a "Lover of Zion," satisfied with a colony here and there. Her thoughts were directed to a Jewish state in Palestine. In the same year in which Dr. Herzl wrote his brochure *Der Judenstaat*, which presented his plan for a Jewish state, Miss Szold read a paper in Baltimore on the same topic before the local branch of the Council of Jewish Women. While her beginnings were in Baltimore, Henrietta Szold's great accomplishments were made in Philadelphia, as secretary of The Jewish Publication Society of America, in New York, as founder of Hadassah, and in Jerusalem, as head of Youth Aliyah.[265]

Zionism was extremely popular in the city, especially after the Balfour Declaration in 1917. Yet there were opponents. Some feared it would drain all communal resources, human as well as financial. There was anxiety over its nationalism, which could lead to (or at least bring about an accusation of) dual allegiance. An interesting case was that of Szold's successor, Rabbi Rosenau. In 1904 he believed that reform in religion and Zionism were not mutually exclusive; but by 1917 he had changed his attitude toward the idea of a Jewish national home. In that year, as president of the Central Conference of American Rabbis, he urged a resolution

that the conference reaffirms the fundamental principle of Reform Judaism, that the essence of Israel as a priest people consists in its religious conscience . . . and not in any political or racial national consciousness. And, therefore, we look with disfavor upon the new doctrine of political Jewish nationalism, which finds the criterion of Jewish loyalty in anything other than loyalty to Israel's God and Israel's religious mission.[266]

Baltimore Jewry gained international recognition in 1915, when a thousand tons of food were sent from the port of Baltimore to the starving Jews in Palestine. Not only did the local Jews substantially contribute toward the cost of the shipment, but it also provided the man who was to administer the entire project. Rabbi Szold's son-in-law Louis H. Levin accompanied the collier *Vulcan*, which carried the food. In addition to directing the distribution of the food, Levin had another mission. He was appointed by Secretary of State William Jennings Bryan as "a special agent" to investigate affairs in Turkey.[267]

A Territorial Scheme

In this stronghold of Zionism, a scheme was developed to settle Russian Jews, not in Palestine, but in Mesopotamia. The father of this idea was a non-Jew, Paul Haupt (1858–1926), professor of Semitic languages at Johns Hopkins University.[268] He was very close to a number of Baltimore Jews—Rabbis Guttmacher and Rosenau studied under him, and he was friendly with the Friedenwald family and others. Some of his Jewish friends helped him to publish his Polychrome Bible.[269] Among his closest friends was his first student, who was later his colleague, Cyrus Adler.[270] These associations no doubt evoked in Haupt an interest in various schemes designed to find a territorial solution to the problem of the East European refugees. The result was his pamphlet *Über die Ansiedlung der russischen Juden im Euphrat and Tigris Gebiete* (*Concerning the Settlement of the Russian Jews ·in the Area of the Euphrates and Tigris*) (Baltimore, 1892), in which Haupt sought to prove that "the best region for the settlement of the Russian Jews is undoubtedly the country between the Euphrates and Tigris. . . ." The pamphlet was discussed by American Jewish leaders, who corresponded on the subject with European leaders. Adler forwarded the pamphlet to Dr. Herzl.[271] But it was Zionism, not territorialism, that brought about the creation of a Jewish state.

Many Baltimore Jews gave much of themselves to Zionism. Among them were Jews with different points of view about religion and socioeconomic problems, Jews of different extractions. Zionism united all of them.

Combatting Anti-Semitism

Just as hopes for a brighter Jewish future brought together people of different backgrounds, so did the menace of anti-Semitism. American Jews reacted like a seismograph to discrimination and persecution everywhere. A Jew in America felt threatened even when his people were persecuted thousands of miles away. But bad news came not only from abroad. True, America was different. It was a country without historical links between Church and State. One might have expected the complete absence of anti-Semitism in a land of religious diversity and ethnic multiplicity. But there was anti-Semitism in "the

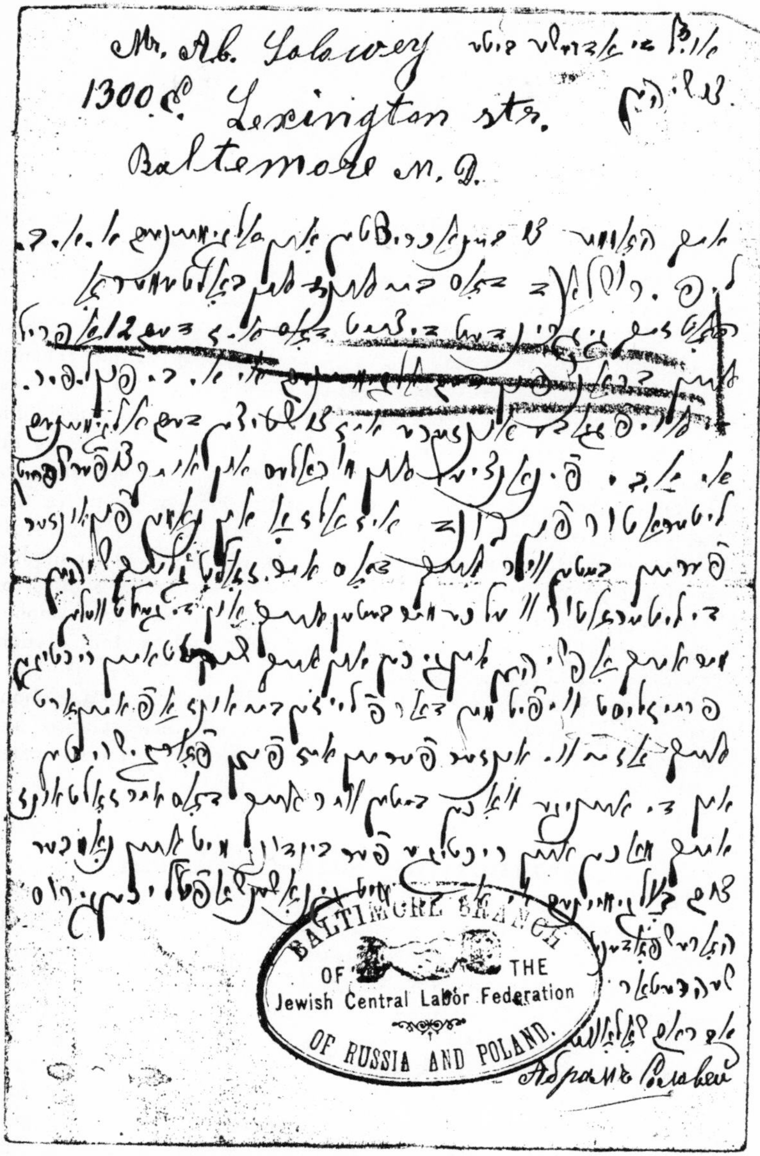

Mr. Ab. Solowey
1300 E. Lexington str.
Baltemore M. D.

BALTIMORE BRANCH OF THE Jewish Central Labor Federation OF RUSSIA AND POLAND.

Абрамъ Соловей

Bund comes to Baltimore; first report of the formation of a "Baltimore Branch of the Central Labor Federation of Russia and Poland."

Courtesy of the Bund Archives.

The Friedenwalds:

Jonas Friedenwald, 1801–1893, founder of the leading Baltimore Jewish family of community workers and physicians.
Courtesy of the Jewish Historical Society of Maryland.

Dr. Aaron Friedenwald, 1836–1902, community leader, professor.
Courtesy of the Associated Jewish Charities.

Dr. Harry Friedenwald, 1864–1950, leading Zionist, professor.
Courtesy of the Associated Jewish Charities.

Letter from Joseph Friedenwald to his nephew Harry Friedenwald about the lot of "our brethren in faith in that hellish country Russia" (1903).
Courtesy of the Jewish Historical Society of Maryland.

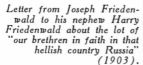

land of the free," even if it was not rampant or accompanied by violent outbreaks like Russia's pogroms. Baltimore Jews were naturally very sensitive to any anti-Jewish incidents in their own city and reacted to such events wherever they occurred.

ON THE LOCAL SCENE

The first recorded anti-Jewish act in the city occurred in 1855. The anti-Semitic cry of "Hep-Hep," so popular in Germany in 1819, had been resurrected in Baltimore by a German, Herr Knorr, who took pleasure in harassing a Jewish peddler with that ugly cry. The poor peddler did what so many Jews have done in similar situations—he "appealed to the Hebrew merchants and residents for relief." But America was different. Here one could turn for protection to the authorities, and Baltimore Jews did just that. The mayor ordered the arrest of anyone crying or mocking any person with the taunt "Hep."[272]

This is the only *Hep-Hep* incident on record, but attacks on Jews by the Catholic press were recurrent and inflammatory. The *Katholische Volkszeitung*, a Democratic paper founded in 1860, specialized in reprinting anti-Semitic articles from the press of the *Vaterland* and warned its readers against the Jews, "the ruination of the body and soul of the German nation."[273] This paper even introduced anti-Semitic propaganda into the presidential campaign of 1900, attacking McKinley as "a puppet of international Jewry."[274] The presidential inauguration provided another opportunity for an attack on Jews. The festivities were described as the "crowning of an emperor of America" that was attended by forty people bearing the name Rosenfeld—an obvious allusion to Vice-President Theodore Roosevelt and family.[275] Similar if more sophisticated articles appeared in the Catholic papers *The Freeman* and *The Catholic Mirror*.[276]

Rabbis Einhorn and Szold responded in sermons and articles to the vicious Catholic press.[277] The attacks continued until 1877, when James Gibbons came back to his hometown as archbishop and, after 1886, cardinal. Born in Baltimore in 1834, Gibbons was ordained in 1861. He served as bishop in Richmond, Virginia (1872–1877), where he became a friend of Rabbi Aaron Bettelheim, later rabbi of the Baltimore Hebrew Congregation. Upon his return to the city he continued his friendly relations with a number of Jews and was especially close to Joseph Friedenwald, Rabbi Rosenau, and Jacob Epstein. On many occasions Gibbons lent the authority of his office to the repudiation of anti-Semitism.[278]

On one occasion Gibbons joined the rabbis in taking issue with the Baltimore school board over Bible reading in public schools, saying:

I am opposed to this, as it gives the teacher the opportunity to make such selections and comments as may offend the religious beliefs of the scholars. It is an entering wedge that might lead to great abuse.[279]

There were other problems with the school board. Jews insisted that Christian hymns had no place in a public school. School authorities disagreed. Jews even threatened to withdraw their children if the practice did not stop. A compromise was reached: hymns were still sung, but children were "not compelled" to sing them.[280] Jewish parents protested with some success against a devout Catholic teacher at the public school on High Street who taught Catholics prayers to the children, most of them Jewish, and instructed them to recite these prayers before going to bed.[281]

Jews met with another kind of discrimination in education. Public schools had poor scholastic standards, and many Jews wanted their children to attend one of Baltimore's excellent private schools. They found themselves excluded.[282] Some wealthy Jews then opened the "nonsectarian" private Park School.[283]

Things became worse before they became better. In 1892 Baltimore Jews felt obliged to organize for self-defense against German and Negro gangs, who often attacked them on the streets.[284] The Baltimore Hebrew weekly *Hapisga* reported in 1892 that Mayor Latrobe had received an anonymous warning that "many citizens" intended to dynamite the Russian-Jewish neighborhood, because the Jews were "the shame of the country and rob our bread." The editorial ended ominously, saying, "only God knows what is going to happen to us."[285] One legislator, a Mr. Owen, even introduced a bill in the General Assembly "to keep out Chinese, Negroes and Jews from neighborhoods where they were not wanted."[286]

The Jewish neighborhood was not dynamited. A ghetto was not instituted. Attacks on the Jews in the streets diminished and eventually disappeared completely. Minor incidents, such as efforts by three Polish women to organize a boycott of Jewish stores, were settled in court.[287] B'nai B'rith's request to the Board of Motion Picture Censors and theater managers, to "eliminate as much as possible the objectionable characterization of the Jews," elicited a promise to comply.[288]

These were all relatively unimportant incidents. Although they were not ideal, relationships with the neighbors were on the whole good. There remained (as it does to this day) one Maryland law which unintentionally discriminated against Jews by forbidding "any work or bodily labor on Sunday."[289] Jews were actually arrested for working on Sunday in their own homes.[290] The Society of Sabbath Observers protested to the lawmakers. They insisted that the law made it impossible for Orthodox Jews to make a living, since they were unable to work two days a week.[291] In the course of years the Sunday blue laws have been amended, but the basic statute is still the law of Maryland.[292]

At times there were left-handed compliments to Jews in the press. In reporting on the meeting of the Union of American Hebrew Congregations held in Baltimore in 1917, the *Sun* noted:

We see now that the Jew is not merely a genius in the line of money making, not only a sharp bargainer who overreaches the duller "heathen" around him but a force in the realm of thought, morals and government of which we must take notice.[293]

But Baltimore Jews were not in need of testimonials. They knew their own worth and were standing guard in defense of their rights. Anti-Semitism was a menace, and they did all they could to prevent this evil from raising its head in their city.

IN THE NATION

In 1861 Baltimore Jewry joined Jews throughout the nation in responding to anti-Jewish discrimination in the chaplaincy of the armed forces. The chaplaincy was established by the Continental Congress in 1775. Until the Mexican War (1846), all chaplains were Protestants. In that year the Catholics succeeded in securing the right to have chaplains of their own faith. In 1861 various Jewish communities sent petitions to Washington requesting Jewish chaplains. The *Sun* reported that

the Israelites of this city are now preparing a petition to be presented to Congress for a modification of the Act of 1861 which ordains that there can be no chaplain . . . except a regularly ordained minister of some Christian denomination.[294]

The Baltimore petition was signed not only by Jews but also by several hundred Christians and proved to be the largest in the entire country.[295] The petitions were effective, and on July 17, 1862, Jews gained the right to have their own chaplains.

Instances of discrimination against Jews in America never demanded the concerted response of all Jewish communities, for anti-Semitic occurrences were of a local character and were dealt with locally. The case of Leo Frank, sentenced to death in Georgia in 1914 on trumped-up charges, may be cited as an exception. When the distinguished lawyer and outstanding Jewish leader Louis Marshall became interested in the case, he solicited the help of two Baltimoreans, Dr. Harry Friedenwald and Professor Jacob Hollander.[296]

In another case, similar to the Swiss treaty controversy over the rights of American Jews to live in that country, Baltimore Jewish leaders played a very important role. In 1832 the United States and Russia concluded a treaty by which the citizens of each country had the right "to sojourn and reside in all parts [of the other country] whatsoever." In spite of this clause, Russia imposed upon American Jews the same restrictions under which Russian Jews lived. Protest resolutions introduced in Congress against the conduct of Russian authorities were buried in committee. Finally in 1911 the American Jewish Committee stepped into the picture.

At this juncture a number of Baltimore Jews provided much assistance in bringing about the abrogation of the treaty. A delegation of the Baltimore branch of the American Jewish Committee visited the two United States senators from Maryland.[297] Two members of the delegation, Jacob Hollander and Harry Friedenwald, played an especially important role in the treaty fight. Their relationship with the Maryland senator Isidor Rayner, himself a Jew, was a very close one. It was to Hollander that Rayner wrote, "No man living feels more deeply upon the subject than I do."[298]

Senator Rayner (1850–1912) was a son of one of Baltimore's Jewish pioneers and communal leaders, William S. Rayner. Although a member of Har Sinai, the senator was never involved in Jewish affairs. He was married to a Christian woman, brought up his only son as a Christian, and was buried in a Christian cemetery, although he never converted and remained all his life a member of the Har Sinai Congregation.

Nevertheless, Rayner's moving address in the Senate demanding the abrogation of the treaty was the outcry of a suffering Jew. He did not limit himself to the question of discrimination against American Jews. He spoke of persecutions of Jews in Russia who

have committed the same crime which their forefathers committed and which their posterity will continue to commit to the remotest generations. They have worshipped God according to the tradition of their faith. . . . For centuries their ancestors spurned the faggot and the flame, and these people, emulating their heroic fortitude, will bear up under affliction. . . . They will defy imprisonment . . . rather than compromise with their tormentors.[299]

A year after Rayner's address, the United States abrogated (on January 1, 1913) the treaty with Russia.

IN DEFENSE OF JEWS ABROAD

The role of Baltimore Jewry in the Swiss treaty and Mortara cases has already been related. With the outbreak of pogroms in Russia in the 1880s, Baltimore Jewry knew no rest in protesting atrocities, collecting funds for victims, and transmitting funds for self-defense.[300] A mass protest meeting of Baltimore Jews was held on May 28, 1891, to express their "indignation . . . against the Czar's dealing with his Hebrew subjects."[301] There were many more protest meetings. Baltimore Jews had no difficulty in getting Cardinal Gibbons to join them in protesting against the Russian atrocities. On December 15, 1890, the cardinal wrote to Benjamin H. Hartogensis:

I cannot well conceive how Christians can entertain other than most kindly sentiments toward the Hebrew race, when I consider how much we are indebted to them.[302]

No event abroad aroused American Jewry more than the pogrom in Kishinev, which began on Easter Sunday, April 19, 1903, coinciding with the last day of Passover. It lasted for two days. American Jews responded as one does when his own flesh and blood is being butchered. Natives and immigrants alike bitterly protested the murder of forty-seven innocent victims, the injuries inflicted upon five hundred others, and the destruction of hundreds of Jewish homes.

Baltimore Jews came to the largest meeting in their history. Over three thousand people filled the Academy of Music. Among the speakers was the mayor of the city, Thomas G. Hayes, who denounced the fact that "the Russian police stood idly by" while women and children were "butchered."[303]

The most moving speech by all accounts was delivered by a young Russian-born medical student, Samuel Wolman. Like the others he spoke of the pogroms, but the major concern of his address was Russian Jewry's high intellectual standards. He concluded with these words:

When a Russian Jew seeks a husband for his daughter, it is the champion of the school who commands the largest dowry. For his is the only community where learning alone obtains the letters patent to noble work. No more sacred title can [be] bestow[ed] than that of Rabbi-teacher. What an index is all this of the intellectuality of the Russian Jew.[304]

Wolman's speech was a historic one. It marked the first time that a new kind of Russian-born Jew was presented to a cross section of the community, Jew and non-Jew alike. Here was not the stereotyped Jewish peddler or even a merchant prince. This was an intellectual, who pointed with pride to his kin in Russia as a noble people who held learning above all else. Wolman was a harbinger of many others.

Cardinal Gibbons sent a message that "only enforced absence" from the city prevented his coming to the meeting. He wanted his Jewish friends to know that he deplored the Russian atrocities and regarded them to be a "blot upon civilization."[305]

An important note was struck by Senator Rayner. In his message he asked the assemblage not to limit their activities to relief and resolutions but to resort to political action. He expressed his belief that

an earnest appeal from this government emanating from its legislative branches . . . could bring about the desired result and every effort ought to be made to obtain this action. It has been done at other times in our history, and it will be done now if a combined pressure is brought upon Congress to take action in the matter.[306]

It was the senator who reminded his constituency that legislators were sensitive to its pressure.

Baltimore Jewry followed Rayner's advice only in part. It did not press its chosen representatives to act in the matter, but the resolution did call upon the United States "in all available ways to bring such influence to bear on the Russian government as may tend to bring about a cessation of these inhumanities." The Baltimore Jews assembled at the mass meeting also issued an appeal "to the people of the United States to call upon their Representatives in Congress" to protest against "the outrage to which the Jews of Russia have been subjected."[307] The local press unanimously joined in denouncing the Russian government for tolerating such massacres.[308] Baltimore Jewry began a financial appeal for the pogrom victims at the meeting. Three thousand dollars was raised that night.[309]

The Baltimore Committee of the Alliance Israélite Universelle forwarded four thousand dollars to Paris "for the Kishinev sufferers."[310] The organization of such a committee was first suggested to Rabbi

Benjamin Szold in a letter from the Central Committee of the Alliance. In it the parent organization pointed out that

the movement of intolerance . . . has developed with . . . strong intensity recently, and the incessant attacks to which Judaism has been exposed, impose upon the Jews the urgent necessity of mustering all their forces and of lending fraternal support.[311]

Baltimore Jewish leaders were well attuned to such appeals. A committee consisting of Dr. Aaron Friedenwald, president, Rabbi Benjamin Szold, vice-president, Mendes Cohen, treasurer, Hugo Steiner, secretary, and Cyrus Adler, Simon Dalsheimer, Rev. Alois Kaiser, and William Rayner became very active in the community in behalf of the Alliance. Indeed due to the high caliber of its leaders it became "one of the best organized committees in the United States. . . . The Committee was conspicuous in its personnel and . . . made many friends for the Alliance."[312]

NATIONAL DEFENSE ORGANIZATIONS

Events at home and abroad pointed to the need for a representative body which could speak in the name of American Jewry when Jewish rights were threatened. In 1906 such an organization, the American Jewish Committee, came into being. Its stated objective was "to prevent the infraction of the civil and religious rights of the Jews in any part of the World." This, however, was not a representative body. It was an organization of a few important, established leaders of the old German families who believed that they were entitled to speak in the name of all American Jews. Two leading Baltimore Jews, Harry Friedenwald and Jacob Hollander, played a very important role in the organization's activities. Because of their connections with prominent Americans, the two were often entrusted by the American Jewish Committee with very delicate assignments. The relationship between the national office in New York and the Baltimore branch was cemented by Herbert Friedenwald. A Baltimorean and a first cousin of Dr. Harry Friedenwald, he served as the secretary of the organization during the first seven years of its existence.[313]

The first major issue in which the American Jewish Committee involved Baltimore Jews was the Literacy Test Bill. It was the intent of those who introduced this measure in Congress to curtail immigration by banning illiterates. A bill to that effect was first introduced in 1897. It passed both houses but was vetoed by President Cleveland, and his veto was sustained. The same bill in a much stricter form was reintroduced in 1913. Herbert Friedenwald, in his capacity as secretary of the American Jewish Committee, wrote on January 24, 1913, that if adopted this bill would

exclude from the country thousands whose sole offense is that they have been denied the benefits of an education, but whose brawn and muscle and energy are essential to the development of the country.

Friedenwald pointed out the Jewish aspect of the bill. If it passed, it would "exclude a large portion of our coreligionists." Consequently, he asked Hollander to secure signatures of the opponents of the bill and forward them to the president.[314] A similar letter was addressed to Dr. Friedenwald. The two men complied.[315] They also obtained a statement in support of their position from Cardinal Gibbons which read:

I am not in favor of any educational test as applied to immigrants desiring to enter the United States. Such a law, if passed, would in my opinion work great harm; for illiteracy is by no means always ignorance. . . . The schemer is, in more ways than one, more dangerous than the honest workman, even though he be illiterate.[316]

In spite of all opposition the bill passed, but it was vetoed by President Taft. The bill passed again the following year. Again it was vetoed, this time by President Wilson. It finally became part of the Immigration Act of 1917.

Jewish reaction against devices to curb immigration points up the change of attitude toward Russian immigration in the American Jewish community generally and in Baltimore specifically. Only four decades had passed snce American Jewry had bitterly opposed the entrance of Russian Jews into America. Now they were moving heaven and earth to facilitate it. In fact attitudes toward immigrants had begun to change much earlier. As early as 1891 Jewish organizations from several American cities, including Baltimore, petitioned the secretary of the treasury to facilitate the admission of Russian refugees. They argued that

to deny [the refugees] a resting place on God's footstool, because temporarly devoid of material wealth, would be an endorsement of cruelty and encouragement to its continuity. . . . About ten years since . . . a very large number of Russian Jews sought this land of liberty as a haven of rest. They have been assimilated in the mass of citizenry, and, so far as can be ascertained, not a single one has become a public burden.

The reply to this and subsequent pleas was always very ambiguous. Yes, the government would facilitate immigration, but it must not be "excessive or threatening."[317]

The position of the American Jewish community also remained constant, although in direct opposition to the policy of the government. The Jews insisted that anyone escaping persecution be admitted. In all the petitions and protests in behalf of persecuted Jews anywhere in the world, it was the American Jewish Committee that stood in the forefront of American Jewry. A growing resentment toward the committee developed, however, because of both its methods and its leadership.

THE GREAT SPLIT

Many Jews were opposed to the policy of petitions instituted by the American Jewish Committee. They balked at entreating the government, believing that as Americans they had the right to demand, rather than plead that their government act in a way which they considered just. They were unhappy with the diplomacy used by the American Jewish Committee in its relationship with authority. They believed that if only the leaders of the organization were elected and not self-appointed, things would be different. This conviction grew among East European Jews, especially among those of the second generation, native Americans. Since change from within did not seem possible, they felt it was imperative to establish a new national organization. After a great deal of time and planning, the American Jewish Congress was formally organized on December 15, 1918.

On the national scene Louis D. Brandeis, a German Jew, became the leader of those who wanted to see more democracy in Jewish life. In Baltimore their spokesman was also a German Jew, Harry Friedenwald. Though he had been very active in the affairs of the American Jewish Committee, he resigned from that organization and helped found the new movement. His letter of resignation best explains the ideological differences between the two organizations. He wrote:

The issues have become clearer and clearer. A class of Jewry is ranged against the overwhelming masses—the unorganized masses which have so long been silent. . . . I wish to remove all doubt as to which side has my sympathy. Those of us who feel that their life is part of the throbbing, anxious, suffering Jewish life, belong to that body which is now seeking self-expression in the [American Jewish] Congress movement. I find no difficulty in making my choice. I am obliged to resign from the American Jewish Committee.[318]

The split between the American Jewish Committee and the American Jewish Congress was not one of national origin, not Russian versus German. It was rather one of ideology, the democratic versus the aristocratic, and of two opposing attitudes toward Zionism. The American Jewish Congress was committed to the Zionist ideal; the American Jewish Committee was opposed. In Baltimore Harry Friedenwald lent prestige to the new organization and the promising young lawyer Simon Sobeloff became its first president. The American Jewish Congress quickly became a major organization in the city.[319]

Symphony in Agony—
The First World War

Jews may have been divided on many issues, but they acted as one in the face of Jewish suffering. The First World War brought much distress to large masses of Jews in Russia. Help was needed immediately, and all united in an effort to provide the help. The Jewish War Relief Fund called upon Baltimore Jewry to provide "bread for the hungry and shrouds for the dead." United by the slogan "We have our own Belgium," the factory owners and their workers, the Russians and the Germans, the uptown ladies and the Workmen's Circle all worked together to raise $50,000 in 1915 and a year later, another $200,000.

The climax of the campaign was two huge mass meetings held simultaneously in two different halls. Both meeting places were filled to capacity and thousands of people were turned away. Two speakers addressed each audience. One was the beloved local Orthodox rabbi, Rabbi Reuben Rivkin, who spoke in Yiddish. As he spoke there was heard in the hall

a low wail, . . . a huge composite sigh coming from the heart and going to the heart. . . . The entire audience melted into a unit of horror and pity. Sobs heard before here and there throughout the house now became general.

Rabbi Rivkin was followed by the renowned New York rabbi Judah Magnes, who spoke of the "conspiracy of silence" which tried to keep from American Jews the story of the sufferings of millions of Jews in war-torn Europe. His appeal for funds electrified the audience. Money, pocketbooks, rings, watches, all kinds of jewelry flowed to the speakers' stand.[320] A note received by the chairman of the campaign, William Levy, characterized the mood of the community:

Dear Sir:

Inclosed you will find $1 for the Jewish Relief Fund to aid the Jewish Sufferers in this war, which is contributed by Joseph Hirshman of 1708 Eutaw Place and myself. It is part of the money we received for singing in the Chizuk Amuno Boy's Choir. Last month I sent in $1 but could only send to you 90¢ this month. With the glad feeling that I have done something to help my fellow Jews.

Yours truly,
Master Arthur Bronstein[321]

Not only Jews, but also non-Jews participated in the campaign. In a letter to Rabbi Magnes dated January 18, 1916, Dr. Harry Friedenwald wrote:

I have always opposed the idea of making direct appeal to the "goyim" for help. But I have worked quite hard to bring about an interest on the part of the goyim and have tried to make this as spontaneous as possible. . . All our newspapers have written leading editorials and appeals for non-Jewish help.

And a few days later (January 23, 1918) Friedenwald informed Magnes that "very generous contributions" were made by non-Jews and that the Scottish Rite Masons "are going to contribute one thousand dollars." (These letters are in the Magnes Archives of the Jewish Historical Society in Jerusalem.)

Toward an Organized Community

Zionism and anti-Semitism had each had a share in breaking down the barriers between Baltimore's two Jewries. More was needed, however, to bring about unity. This could come—in fact did come—only when the immigrant group became economically strong and socially important. In addition, the breakup and reorganization of the complex institutional organization of the community was necessary. It was to this goal that the best minds of Baltimore Jewry turned their attention. On the agenda was a united Jewish community in Baltimore.

Much was accomplished by those who worked tirelessly for various communal causes. Yet some knew that much more could be achieved if work were more rationally organized, if the well-meaning competition among various groups were to come to an end. But consolidation might have jeopardized the positions of entrenched organizational leaders. The situation at the beginning of the twentieth century was similar to that in 1888 when a local correspondent wrote:

What Baltimore badly needs is a few more representative men and women to take a managerial hand in its charities. The same names and faces invariably appear whenever funds must be raised for some good purpose.[322]

Despite the similarity to the earlier time, there was also a difference. True, there was still no cooperation, but now there was a growing awareness that something must be done in behalf of the community as a whole. This realization came first to the uptown Jews and brought about a meeting of the representatives of ten organizations in order to coordinate their activities.[323] Even though the desired goal was not achieved at that gathering, the meeting was a breakthrough in the history of Baltimore Jewry; a beginning in the direction of creating a central communal organization was made. The meeting was followed by others and after four years of discussions a central communal agency, the Federated Jewish Charities (generally known as the Federation) came into being.[324] The first step toward unification had been accomplished. The many organizations of the uptown community had coordinated their activities.

From the first, the central body was fortunate in its president, Jacob Hollander. A native Baltimorean, Hollander (1871–1946) was already a man of distinction at the time he assumed office. He had a Ph.D. in economics from Hopkins and became a professor at his alma mater. Author of many books in his field, he enjoyed high repute and was entrusted by the government with many important assignments, including an appointment by President McKinley in 1900 as treasurer of Puerto Rico. He had an active interest in American Jewish history, as shown both by his service in the Council of the American Jewish Historical Society and by his writings on the history of the Jews in Maryland. Hollander was equally concerned, active, and involved with the American Jewish present.[325]

On the basis of his economic studies the professor concluded that poverty was not a "social necessity" but rather "an economic consequence . . . remediable, even preventable, not by [the] panacea of upheaval, but by unerring determination of causes and devoted application of correctives."[326] He believed that "some day future generations will look back on the poverty of our own day with the same astonishment that we feel in contemplating slavery."[327]

Hollander found a kindred soul in the Federation's secretary, Louis H. Levin (1866–1923). Born in Charleston, South Carolina, Levin was the son of a poor peddler, one of fourteen children. He worked by day and studied by night to graduate from law school. In Baltimore he worked as a bookkeeper and lawyer in addition to being the Baltimore correspondent of the Philadelphia *Jewish Exponent*. In 1899 he became editor of *The Jewish Comment*, a weekly Baltimore journal.

At all times Levin exhibited a keen interest in Jewish communal affairs. His marriage to Rabbi Szold's daughter Bertha brought him even closer to the center of Jewish activities. When the Federation was founded, Levin joined with Hollander to bring order to the affairs of the Jewish community. So great was his contribution that Levindale, the home for the aged, was named after him. He is the only man after whom a communal institution has been named.[328]

The Federation was crowned with success from its very beginning.[329] Charity contributions rose in the first year from $46,682 to $70,-734.50.[330] In his second annual report, Hollander spoke of the "creditable record" of the organization:

There have been no bazaars, benefit performances, nor ticket peddling, with the incidents of misdirected efforts and needless waste. . . . Individual directorates have been relieved completely from all anxiety and exertion as to monetary affairs, and have been free to devote undivided energy and attention to their institutional cares. Finally, there has been an element of responsible control over the general charitable activities of the community. . . . Less tangible, but certainly not less important, is the dignity and effectiveness with which the Federation has represented the Jewish community in the general charitable interests of the city.[331]

Hollander was proud to report that the Federation was, indeed, so successful that

a distinctive fillip has been given to the organization—administrative and fiscal—of non-Jewish charities by the really notable results achieved by the Jewish organizations, through the application of skilled intelligence and thoroughgoing business methods.[332]

It was more than natural that downtown Jewry was also duly impressed. Charity activities among the immigrants were completely disorganized, largely because of overorganization. There was no end to

the "specialized" agencies; each *landsmanshaft* was in fact a federation in itself, doing all kinds of charitable work with little regard to the
efforts of other organizations. Difficult as it was to attain unity in such
a climate, it was accomplished, at least in part, in December 1907,
when the seven major downtown groups[333] formed a central agency,
the United Hebrew Charities, generally referred to as the United.

The first president of the newly formed organization was a wealthy
clothing manufacturer, himself a Russian immigrant, Solomon
Ginzberg.[334] After he served only one year the unexpected happened
—he was succeeded by an uptowner, William Levy. Levy had inherited from his father, Michael, not only a prosperous straw hat business, but also a zeal for community work. In his new position he learned
to know the immigrants more intimately. He found them

to be earnest and industrious workers in the cause of charity . . .
frequently compelled to neglect their duties to their families, as well as
their own interests, in order to provide for the needs of constituent
societies.[335]

The Federation and the United brought some order to the affairs of
the community. Many leaders knew that much more could be accomplished if the two organizations would unite, but in the words of
Hollander, "the time for this far-reaching reform is obviously not yet
arrived."[336] In the meantime both organizations worked for the same
causes—sometimes in harmony, other times at cross purposes; and very
often their work overlapped.[337]

THE FEDERATED JEWISH CHARITIES

The Federation not only reorganized the existing agencies and expanded their activities, it also created new ones. Distressed by the
"excess of litigation among the poor classes and generally among those
who have not had the benefit of a long residence in this country," the
Federation established the Jewish Court of Arbitration in 1912, hoping
that it would serve as "a forum in which disputes may be considered
and justice rendered without delay, expense or unnecessary publicity."[338] The expectations were fulfilled. In the first two and a half
years the court handled 351 cases. From the first, its verdicts were
generally accepted; only 10 per cent of the litigants (thirty-five in all)
refused to abide by the court's decision.[339]

Many kinds of cases came before the "judges." Problems from the
smallest debts to the most serious crimes were brought for their decision.
In his report of 1915, the clerk of the court reported that there was a

"remarkable increase in the number of domestic relations cases." His inability to see the cause of that increase[340] suggests an amazing blindness to the extreme poverty, often accompanied by tuberculosis, which was breaking up Jewish family life.

The Court of Arbitration, like other agencies of the Federated Jewish Charities, testifies to the fact that in spite of its name the Federation was much more than a central charity organization. It was an American version of the old *ḳahal*. Although voluntary, its decisions were generally accepted, and its activities embraced many phases of communal life, of which charity in the strict sense of the word was only one, although an important one.

WORK FOR YOUTH

Louis H. Levin was ahead of his time when he pointed out to the directors of the Federation that the most serious problem the community had to face was juvenile delinquency: "The number of Jewish boys in the Maryland School for Boys [a state school for juvenile delinquents]," he noted, "would surprise this assemblage if I were to mention it; and we have far too many Jewish children in the juvenile court."[341] He stressed not merely the large number of delinquents, but their constantly growing rate. Levin saw a solution to this menace only in a new communal approach to charity. Traditional institutions—hospitals, orphan asylums, benevolent societies, and the like—were, in his opinion, powerless to stem the tide. He insisted that

what is needed is social contact with the children before they are tempted into small crime, and even firmer contact after they have developed harmful tendencies. To this need we need a social center or settlement as well equipped and as up-to-date as our hospitals, for the social disease cannot otherwise be properly treated.[342]

He knew, of course, that good, charitable people wanted to give only aid whose results "they could see with their own eyes." They could not as yet think in terms of preventive social medicine, which was the essence of their secretary's plea. Levin warned them:

At no great time in the future we shall have to address ourselves seriously to this task, when, very likely, conditions will be more difficult to control than they are now.[343]

As a matter of fact a primitive begining had been made in this direction by a few foresighted ladies almost two decades earlier. In

1890 the Daughters in Israel, one of the city's many charitable organizations, took note of the single Jewish immigrant girls who could hardly sustain themselves on wages of about five dollars a week and too often became the "wayward girls" that were frequently discussed at Federation meetings. These girls needed decent housing. The Daughters in Israel were anxious to do much, but for the "lack of means" could only afford to open a home for fifty girls.[344] In 1896 an organization of young men, the Maccabeans, opened club rooms for boys. The battle between the club and the street was long and bitter, but as time passed it became obvious that the club would be the victor. By 1908 over a thousand boys were regularly attending the Maccabean House.[345]

The success of the Maccabeans and the Daughters in Israel suggested how much more could and should be done for Baltimore's Jewish youth. In 1909 these two pioneer organizations in Jewish settlement work united and formed the Jewish Educational Alliance, which, in the words of one of its workers, was a "blessed refuge for youth and adult . . . an anchorage, a fountain of life and light."[346] For the first five years the JEA (as the Jewish Educational Alliance was generally called) accomplished little. Its quarters were too cramped for all those young people who preferred club rooms to street corners.

A great change in its development came in 1914, when the brothers William and Julius Levy presented a spacious building on East Baltimore Street to the JEA in memory of their parents.[347] For about four decades, until it closed its doors in 1952, this building built, maintained, and largely staffed by German Jews fulfilled many functions. First, it provided a second home for the East Baltimore youth. Second, it brought together some of the uptown people with those from downtown.

The philanthropists of the northwest gave more than money. They and their daughters were enrolled as volunteer workers, either as leaders of clubs, as teachers . . . of the various societies organized for literary as well as athletic development. These sons and daughters were not "aloof-menshen." They came as friends. They came not to command but to coach. . . . To the aspiring youth of East Baltimore their friends from the Eutaw Place area were the archetype of aristocracy.[348]

Strangely enough this institution, a creation of the German Jews, brought together East European Jews stemming from different countries. *Landsmanshaftn* remained strong, but the beginning of an amalgam was made within the walls of the JEA; it was a melting pot of its own for East Baltimore Jewry. It would eventually make possible another and much more difficult task, the consolidation of this group with the German Jews—the hope of the best minds of the community, to be fulfilled only in the future. In the meantime, in the beehive of the JEA Jews from different countries and of different ideologies sat side by side at concerts and lectures and attended classes to learn all kinds of trades. The JEA building at 1204 East Baltimore Street was a second home for many Jews of East Baltimore.[349]

The JEA had to face one very difficult problem of unity which was never resolved, the problem of Jew-Gentile relations in the JEA. The neighborhood was a mixed one. In school, on the streets, and in dance halls Jewish youngsters mingled with non-Jews. When the JEA introduced dances, the problem of "mingling" was immediately on the agenda. The resolution on this delicate question was, as might be expected, double-talk, although the mood of the board was quite clear. "We do not encourage," they resolved, "in fact, we seldom permit non-Jewish people on our floor."[350] The "seldom" in the resolution did not clarify the situation. This case illustrates only one aspect of the complex problem of being both integrated and distinct at the same time.

The Jewish Educational Alliance was a settlement house serving a primarily immigrant group. But a considerable number of American-born children of immigrants who no longer lived in East Baltimore had grown up. They too needed a center but not a settlement house. When a national organization of Young Men's Hebrew Association was formed in 1913, Baltimore was not included in the roster, for there was no YMHA in the city at that time (although the first Young Men's Hebrew Association in the country was organized in Baltimore in 1854 and was active for a few years). In 1916 William Levy called together a few young men and proposed to them the formation of a YMHA. The response was enthusiastic, but the opposition found its spokesman in the person of Rabbi Rosenau. He wrote to the initiator of the project, William Levy:

I am opposed to the formation of a Young Men's Hebrew Association in this city or anywhere else because these deflect the interests of young people from the synagogue.[351]

Rosenau, like many others, saw no need for any institution other than the synagogue. To be sure the people who wished to establish a "Y" did not oppose the synagogue. They did not, however, consider the two institutions to be mutually exclusive.

Plans for the center were shelved—not because of rabbinical objections but because the year was 1917, the year in which the United States entered the First World War. Thousands upon thousands of young Jews who came to America were deserters from military service in Russia. They were not considered citizens of that country, and they in turn did not consider it as their homeland. Not so America. *Die naye heim* (the new home) was *home* and the young men had only one thing on their mind. They knew that before long they would be in uniform and would probably be shipped "over there," as indeed they were. At least 1,033 Baltimore Jews responded to the call and participated in the war. Of these, 54 were killed in action and 271 were wounded. Many were decorated for bravery. Eight were promoted to the rank of major, and one, Charles H. Lauchheimer, became a brigadier general.[352]

It was only after the war that the "Y" project was revived. This time the initiative came from young women in the community. They formed a Young Women's Hebrew Association, which quickly attracted over a thousand members. On August 9, 1920, representatives of thirty-eight young men's clubs launched a campaign for a Young Men's Hebrew Association. This time it proved to be a success. The organization enrolled 1,400 members and its energetic president, Harry Greenstein, raised funds for a suitable building on Madison Avenue.[353] The old JEA continued to serve East Baltimore Jewry until 1952.

The Immigrants

CRIME IN EAST BALTIMORE

Crime among the young of East Baltimore was becoming a major community problem. The decent, hard-working people of the neighhood could not allow such a situation to continue indefinitely. People forgot their religious differences, political affiliations, and socioeconomic groupings and all joined hands to fight crime to the finish. East Baltimore rose as one. A large mass meeting was addressed by such adversaries as the Orthodox rabbi Avrum Schwartz and the Labor Zionist leader Dr. Herman Seidel.[354] Demands that they clean up the neighborhood were presented to the police.

Again it was the well-organized and influential Federation that stepped into the picture to help create decent surroundings for decent people. In 1914 the Big Brother League was organized by the Federation to give a helping hand to youths in trouble with the law.

How badly this service was needed becomes clear from its annual reports. One report, that for 1917, lists 1,046 cases.[355]

THE ECONOMIC GROWTH OF THE IMMIGRANTS
In 1887 the perceptive Louis H. Levin observed that

when they [the immigrants] just arrived they seemed to be an unpromising lot and their coreligionists wrung their hands in despair at their uncouth manners, their seeming disinclination to work, and the bright prospect of supporting them for years to come. How quick the change. . . . There is scarcely a branch of trade at present in which they are not making themselves felt. The gradual creeping up of unpronounceable names into the business section of the directory testifies to the activity of those residing in the city. For these people I predict a great future.[356]

The "great future" was late in coming, but come it did.

The development of the Baltimore Jewish tailor did not follow the textbook. He did not, as might be expected, advance from the ranks of the very low-paid unskilled workers to those of the better-paid skilled ones and remain there. Many did not remain in the ranks even after they became proficient in their trades but continued to move up, and many others skipped this process entirely and moved directly into the middle class. The chief characteristic of the Jewish tailors and employees in other crafts was that they left the ranks of the working class in droves.

Changing conditions in the city made the shifts both possible and profitable. Baltimore was a rapidly growing city. From a population of 332,130 in 1880 it grew to 508,500 in 1900[357] and to 555,485 in 1910.[358] It increased by nearly 200,000 in the next decade, reaching 733,826 in 1920.[359]

The constant increase in population, and especially the boom period of World War I, offered ever-greater economic opportunities. Many former immigrants and even newly arrived Jews took advantage of the situation. Those who left the shops entered the middle class as merchants, real estate men, jobbers, and even as professionals. All but the last of these usually required only a little money, which the immigrants somehow managed to scrape together. Even more important than money was business acumen. They possessed this in full measure. Refugees brought with them various skills and traditions. One of these was business experience which they gained as tradesmen in the large cities, in the smaller towns, or even in the villages of the old country.

Becoming a professional was another matter. This required not business acumen but another tradition which the Jewish immigrant also brought with him: the tradition of education, so prevalent in Eastern Europe and continued in the new country. The yeshiva bench was exchanged for the university bench. The contemporary phrase "my son, the doctor" was common also in those days, but in a different form—"my *ḥosn* [fiancé] the doctor." Many a girl worked long days and late into the night to enable her future husband to go to school and become a professional. Many young workers attended night school and a considerable number of Jewish doctors, lawyers, and accountants could look back on earlier careers as pressers, cutters, or operators. There were, moreover, many parents who denied themselves the most essential things to send their offspring through college.

Morris Wolman and his wife, Rosa, are a case in point. Morris was in his early twenties when he came to Baltimore in 1885, leaving his wife and two small children behind in his native Poland. He started out as a peddler, became a buttonhole maker, and brought over his family. In time he developed a buttonhole-making shop, which was later ruined by the competition of the automatic buttonhole-making machine. In the meantime the Wolman famly was increased by four more children and fell upon hard times. In their small house lived the parents, six children, and the inevitable immigrant "cousins, uncles, and aunts" (probably euphemisms for boarders or lodgers). Three sons of this modest family received advanced degrees from Hopkins and subsequently became outstanding men in their respective fields. Samuel, a heart specialist, joined the faculty of his alma mater in 1905. Leo, an economist, also began to teach at Hopkins in 1915. They were followed by their brother Abel in 1918.[360]

The Wolmans were perhaps an exception in terms of achievement, but it was quite common for a presser, a cutter, a cabinet maker, or any other poor immigrant worker or small merchant to have a daughter who was a schoolteacher and a son in the professions. With great pride immigrant parents called these children of theirs *gantze Yenḳis* (one hundred per cent Americans). This new breed of Jews, most of them American-born, became socially, economically, and culturally an integral part of the general community, as much so as the German Jews. But like their American-born sons and daughters, the immigrants themselves underwent a change—at a slower pace.

They were adjusting themselves to their children and grandchildren. And even if their English was far from perfect, the feeling of being a stranger disappeared. They were no longer greenhorns. They felt themselves to be Baltimoreans rather than *Vilner* or *Odesser*. The new country ceased to be *Columbus's Medine* (the land of Columbus). Instead it became *die naye heim* (the new home), and this was said with unmistakable pride.

Economically, too, the Russian immigrant of former days came into his own. In the beginning of the century, 75 per cent of the German Jews in Baltimore were engaged in mercantile pursuits, while among the immigrants 60 per cent were artisans.[361] Two decades later, in 1924, its Jewish population of about 67,500[362] presented a different picture. There was not much of an occupational distinction between German and Russian Jews. The former were generally much wealthier, but the occupational distribution of the two groups was about the same. There were even a number of Russian Jews who surpassed the Germans in wealth.

In the 1920s one could already discern the contours of the future oil empire of the Blausteins, father and son. The father, Louis, who came to Baltimore as a poor immigrant in 1888, started out by selling kerosene to stores, which was the modest beginning of a giant enterprise. He was assisted by his son Jacob, a graduate engineer (1912). By 1926 the Blausteins were wealthy enough to contribute twenty-five hundred dollars (a substantial sum in those days) to the Jewish charities in the city.[363]

One of the wealthiest men in the city was the immigrant Jacob Epstein. The saga of this man is the remarkable story of an immigrant who became a merchant prince. As a penniless youth of seventeen Epstein came to Baltimore from his native town of Tarragon in Lithuania in 1882. He started as a peddler, but before long he opened a small store on Barre Street and developed it into a great venture by introducing catalogues and establishing it as a mail-order business. It became the most important jobbing concern for the entire South. By 1910 it employed a thousand people and was doing over a million dollars' worth of business a month.[364] Epstein was not only a millionaire, he also knew the art of giving on a grand scale. A younger community worker in speaking of him called him "the man who taught the city how to give,"[365] which he indeed did. From 1917 to his death in 1945 he was by far the largest contributor to Jewish charities in the city.[366] It was, however, not only by his generosity, but also by the manner of his giving that Epstein earned the esteem of the community. His attitude toward charity is best expressed in one of the many stories he was so fond of telling:

Two brothers were walking and the elder one sprained his ankle, and his younger brother was carrying him home and a minister approached the younger brother and said to him, "Let me help you carry him, he is too heavy for you," and the answer was, "He is not heavy, he is my brother."[367]

In the social world in which Epstein lived bankbooks spoke louder than birth certificates. The German Jews could not allow themselves to snub Epstein or treat him with contempt merely because he was of Russian extraction. This applied also to other immigrants with the same "blemish" who made good even if they were not millionaires. Not all Russian Jews were of Epstein's class, but neither were all German Jews in the some class with Sonneborn. American-born Jews of Russian extraction did not have to overcome the inferiority complex so characteristic of the immigrant. In the business world, in the professons, and in the halls of higher learning, they were to be found in ever-increasing numbers.

With the economic restratification of the immigrant came a change in their attitude to radical ideologies, which also contributed to the easing of the relations between uptown and downtown Jews. No more could one speak of the immigrants as anarchists. They were becoming more and more a substantial group, active in all phases of the city's life.

Jews in the General Life
of Baltimore

IN CIVIC AFFAIRS

As a rule it was those Jews who were active in the Jewish community who were also involved in the affairs of the general community. It would seem that one supplemented rather than excluded the other. Many excelled in community work, but only a few outstanding individuals can be mentioned here.

One of these was the prominent Jewish community leader, successful businessman, industrialist, and landowner Joseph Friedenwald, who served for twenty-one years as a member of the board and as president of Baltimore's almshouse, the Bay View Asylum. It was he who prevailed upon the board of the institution to have a Catholic

Historic communal buildings:

Jewish Educational Alliance.
Courtesy of the Associated Jewish Charities.

Hebrew Orphan Asylum.
Courtesy of the Associated Jewish Charities.

Hebrew Hospital.
Courtesy of the Associated Jewish Charities.

Betsy Levy Memorial Home.
Courtesy of the Associated Jewish Charities.

Ladies' apartment in the Hebrew Friendly Inn and Aged Home.
Courtesy of the Associated Jewish Charities.

Some present-day communal buildings:

Baltimore Hebrew College.
Courtesy of the Baltimore Hebrew College.

Associated Jewish Charities.
Courtesy of the Associated Jewish Charities.

Lloyd Street Synagogue Museum.
Courtesy of the Lloyd Street Synagogue Museum.
Photo by Sussman-Ochs.

Jewish Community Center.
Courtesy of the Jewish Community Center.

Plaque awarded to the Lloyd Street Synagogue Museum by the City of Baltimore, November 8, 1964.
Courtesy of the Lloyd Street Synagogue Museum. Photo by Hughes.

chaplain for the institution.[368] Another of the most active Jewish community workers, David Hutzler, occupied many civic posts. He was the treasurer of the State Relief Committee after the great Baltimore fire of 1904. The conflagration, which continued for thirty hours, burned out seventy blocks in the city and destroyed 1,343 buildings. Many Jews lived in the area destroyed by the fire, and consequently the suffering in the Jewish community was great.[369]

The city showed great stamina in its ability to restore itself. Along with the rest of the city the Jewish community responded to the needs of the burned area. As treasurer of the relief committee, Hutzler contributed much to the rehabilitation of the city. Despite all his other civic activities he remained most active in Jewish community affairs.[370] William Levy, a great force in shaping Jewish life in Baltimore and at one time president of the large Chizuk Amuno Congregation, also served on the State Board of Charities.[371]

The most prestigious civic position in the city was that of president of the Maryland Historical Society; the city's regard for Jews can perhaps best be measured by the fact that a Jew was chosen for this post. It was only natural that such an office should be occupied by a member of an old family in the city, and the man chosen was Mendes Cohen (1831–1915), a scion of the first Cohens in the city. A president of the American Society of Civil Engineers, member of the Municipal Art Commission of Baltimore, trustee of the Peabody Institute, he served as secretary of the Maryland Historical Society for twenty years, from 1884 to 1904, and for the following ten years as its president.[372] Along with his interest in Maryland history, Cohen had a keen interest also in American Jewish history. He was one of the founders of the American Jewish Historical Society and served as one of its vice-presidents. Although not an official in any Jewish organization, he was a contributor to various Jewish causes.[373]

There were those who feared that Jews would be suspected of trying to further Jewish interests by having one of their own appointed to a civic post. They felt the need to allay these suspicions. When the active Jewish communal worker Eli Frank was appointed commissioner of the Baltimore school board in 1911, for instance, an influential local Jewish weekly commented:

Jews are not interested to have a Jew on the School Board. There are no Jewish problems there. . . . We are glad that Eli Frank was appointed commissioner. We are glad because he is a good man, not because he is a Jew.[374]

At times the apologetics became absurd—for instance, a remark made by a rabbi at a banquet of the Hebrew Benevolent Society, an affair attended by a few invited non-Jews. In his talk Rabbi Samuel Sale of Har Sinai Congregation said: "We do not come here as Jews, nor as Hebrews [whatever this might have meant to the rabbi] but as men."[375] Apologists notwithstanding, Jews were involved in Jewish charities because they were Jewish, and they were proud that their Jewish leaders honorably discharged their civic responsibilities.

IN EDUCATION

Jews not only attended schools and colleges in high percentages, but also became prominent as teachers on all educational levels. By the 1920s many taught in the public school system, and one, David Weglein, was the principal of the large Western High School, a post he held from 1906 to 1921.[376] There was also a significant number of Jews on the faculties of institutions of higher learning.

The first Jewish professor at Hopkins was the mathematician James Joseph Sylvester, whom President Gilman brought over from England when the university was founded in 1876.[377] In 1877 he started the *American Journal of Mathematics*, of which another Jewish professor at Hopkins, Abraham Cohen, later became co-editor.[378] There were many other Jews on the Hopkins faculty, among them Fabian Franklin in mathematics, David Simon Blondheim in Romance languages, Maurice Bloomfield in Sanskrit, Cyrus Adler and William Rosenau in Semitics, Hollander in political economy, and Florence E. Bamberger, the first woman professor at Hopkins, in education.[379]

Other institutions of higher learning in Baltimore also had Jewish professors. Eli Frank was professor of law in the University of Maryland. A highly respected lawyer, Frank was president of the Baltimore Bar Association and, as mentioned, a member of the Baltimore school board.[380] He also served the Jewish community faithfully—he was president of the Baltimore Hebrew Congregation, of the Federated Jewish Charities, and of the Hebrew Hospital. A perfectly "integrated" American Jew, Frank, like many others though not all, encountered no conflict between his Jewish activities and those of the general community. He was at home in both. The three Friedenwald brothers, Harry, Julius (1867–1941), and Edgar (1879–1966) taught medicine in the College of Physicians and Surgeons, and there were many more Jews among Baltimore's academicians, especially in medicine.

For a better understanding of the situation in the Jewish community it is important to single out a few professors who either themselves were born in Eastern Europe or were the first generation of American-born of that extraction. Among these were Aaron Ember, professor of Egyptology, born in Kovno, Lithuania; David Macht, professor of pharmacology; and the three Wolman brothers, mentioned above, of whom the oldest, Samuel, was born in Poland. These and others of the same origin mingled freely with Jewish professors of German extraction. The measure of importance was not place of birth but scientific achievement. As in the business world, in academe also the importance of genealogy was continually diminishing.

Some of the academicians showed little or no interest in Jewish affairs. Of them it was said that they "no longer count themselves among the Jews, who belong to no Jewish organization . . . to whom even a pogrom can't penetrate in their non-Jewish seclusion."[381] In a similar vein Rabbi Rosenau complained eight years later that the students did not identify themselves with the Jewish community and were estranged from the synagogue.[382] As against these there were others who took a keen interest in Jewish affairs generally and in those of the local community specifically. Professor Blondheim was a lifelong Zionist and translated some Zionist classics from German into English. Aaron Ember was very active in the local Hebrew Education Society, and in 1912 David Macht organized a Union of Jewish Academicians, whose objective was "to encourage the study of Torah . . . to enlighten and give moral and religious support to fainthearted and otherwise erring Jewish academic men."[383]

While some Jews served as teachers, others contributed to educational institutions in another manner. In 1884 Mendes Cohen presented Hopkins with the "Cohen Collection of Egyptian Antiques," a large number of valuable articles brought back by his uncle Mendes I. Cohen from his trip to Egypt in 1829.[384] A collection of rabbinics was given to Hopkins by Leopold Strouse, and a collection of ceremonial objects donated by Henry Sonneborn and one of Semitics from the families of Professors Ember and Blondheim were among other important gifts to the university. The Rayner fellowship in Semitics was established by William Rayner's children after his death in 1899, and a chair in political economy endowed by Abram G. Hutzler in 1925. Benjamin Henry Hartogensis, one of the most devoted community workers, established a Jewish legal section in the Baltimore Law Library.[385] All in all, in one way or another many Baltimore Jews were quite prominent in all fields of education.

IN THE ARTS

A leading Baltimore artist of the period was Ephraim Keyser (1850–1937). Upon graduation from the Maryland Institute of Art, Keyser studied abroad. He returned to Baltimore in 1893 as an artist with an established reputation. Among his best-known works are a statue of General de Kalb on the Annapolis State House grounds and the tomb of President Chester A. Arthur in Albany, New York. Of particular interest to Jews are his bronze plaque of Rabbi Einhorn and a number of tombstones in the cemetery of the Baltimore Hebrew Congregation.[386]

While Keyser taught at the Maryland Institute of Art he assisted two gifted Jewish students, both immigrants from Lithuania. Eventually both of them—Saul Bernstein (1872–1905) and Louis Rosenthal (1888–1964)—distinguished themselves, the first as painter and the second as sculptor of miniatures.[387]

As with the universities, a great number of collections were presented to the Baltimore Museum of Art by Jewish art-lovers in the community. Among its founders and original trustees were Julius Levy and Jacob Epstein. Their interest in this great art institution, which was incorporated in 1914 and opened its doors in 1922, was constant. They were the first Jews, but by no means the last, to show their great interest in the museum by making magnificent contributions.[388]

IN POLITICS

By 1920 almost a century had passed from that all-important year for the Jews in Maryland—1826—when they were given political equality in the state and the two proponents of the "Jew Bill," Solomon Etting and Jacob I. Cohen, were elected to the City Council. Much had changed in the political life of Baltimore Jews. In the twentieth century a considerable number of Baltimore Jews occupied political positions, both elective and appointive, on local, state, and federal levels.

The most bitter fight on the local level took place in 1903 for a place on the City Council. All the elements of political drama were involved in that election on Baltimore's East Side. To divisions by party affiliation, Democrats versus Republicans, was added the problem of the "Jewish vote." Only one of the candidates was a Jew. And on top of this the downtown group was fighting for independence from uptown leadership. The chief culprit in the af-

fair was a man whom we have met before in so many different connections—Joseph Friedenwald. Friedenwald never ran for office
himself, but he was a meddler in politics. He supported the Democrat
Albert S. Gill against the Republican Joseph Seidenman, a Jewish
immigrant from Russia.

Harry Friedenwald's mother might have been right when she
described "Uncle Joe's" relationship with the immigrant community
in 1888: "You can form no idea of what an influence he has and
how well he uses it, particularly for our Russians."[389] But if this
was the situation in 1888, it was not so in 1903. The immigrant
asserted himself; his vote could not be delivered anymore. In abusive
language Friedenwald was savagely attacked for "using the synagogue
for political purposes." The Jewish issue was exploited to the limit.
The Seidenman election committee published leaflets which read in
part:

*The great idol of uptown, who preaches that he is a special friend of
the Russo-Polish Jews . . . and gives charity for them . . . this creature
who calls himself a Jew, speaks in the synagogues before a Jewish
audience [and tells them] that he is a friend of the Russian Jews
and wishes them success and at the same time sends out letters to
Russian Jews [urging] that they vote for a gentile, not a Jew.*

Friedenwald was not a man to take such insults lying down. Not
only did he publish a counterattack (all in Yiddish) but he brought
from New York the folk orator Masliansky and the poet Morris
Rosenfeld to influence the masses for his candidate. Even this did
not help. Seidenman's final call read:

*We as Jews as defenders of our honor and faith whether Repub-
licans or Democrats must show our independence . . . and vote for
Seidenman.*[390]

The Jewish issue, coupled with that of independence, won for Seidenman the seat for the Fifth Ward on the City Council.[391]

The Seidenman case was the first one in which the "Jewish vote"
question was so openly discussed. The outcome was not lost on the
politicians. A pattern was established; as a general rule a Jew was
the candidate in a Jewish neighborhood. There was nothing unusual
in this—similar election fights with similar results were characteristic
of other ethnic groups also.

Over the years there were many Jews who became members of
the City Council and of the Maryland House of Delegates and

Senate.[392] Harry B. Wolf served in the U.S. House of Representatives in 1908 and 1909.[393]

The most colorful political personality on the state level was Jacob M. Moses (1873–1968). An uptown Jew who was one of the early Zionists, a most active protagonist of the American Jewish Congress, Moses showed great interest in the lives of the sweatshop workers, by offering them not charity but understanding. The topic of his thesis, presented at his graduation from the University of Maryland Law School in 1895, was *The Law Applicable to Strikes;* in it he pointed out the rights of striking workers. Moses became the darling of East Baltimore Jewry and was elected by their votes to the state Senate in 1902 and again in 1904. In 1908 he was appointed judge of Juvenile Court. He went on to become, as we mentioned, the leading arbitrator in the needle industry, trusted and respected by both employers and employees. During his long life (he died at the age of ninety-five) Moses remained active in the liberal movement as well as in Jewish affairs.[394]

The highest elective office held by a Baltimore Jew was that of United States senator, an honor held by Isidor Rayner (1850–1912). Prior to his election to the Senate he held several political positions in the state—he served in the House of Delegates and was attorney general. Rayner was elected as United States senator in 1904 and later reelected. He died in 1912 while in office.[395]

A new political figure came on the scene during the first two decades of the twentieth century. The political career of Simon Sobeloff (1893–   ) began when as a lad of fourteen he became a page boy in the House of Representatives. From 1919 to 1923 he served as assistant solicitor of Baltimore. From then on his rise was meteoric, and he eventually became solicitor general of the United States. At all times Judge Sobeloff remained very active in Jewish affairs and occupied important offices in community institutions. Among these were the presidency of the Board of Jewish Education and the chairmanship of the Board of Trustees of the Baltimore Hebrew College. Nationally, Sobeloff was especially active in the Zionist movement and in the American Jewish Congress.[396]

In Rabbi Szold's archives there is an interesting document written in 1876 which testifies to the changed attitudes of Jews toward American politics. During the Civil War years Szold, a newcomer to this country, showed little interest in American life outside the Jewish sphere. But like others before him and others since, the rabbi changed.

Children were born to him, he learned the language, he ceased to be
a stranger; although only seventeen years had passed since he came
to America he adapted himself to his adopted land and began to
taken an interest in politics. The presidency of the United States was
his business. The year 1876 was a presidential election year. Republican Rutherford B. Hayes and Democrat Samuel J. Tilden were
the candidates. Szold cared enough about the election to issue a "call
to the inhabitants of this land." In sharp words, so uncharacteristic of
the Szold of Civil War days, he called upon the people to do away
with "Grantism." The call read:

*The day that we hoped for is approaching. Everyone looks to
you. It is you who will decide between the two warring sections competing for the Presidency of this country. Those who are for the
democrats are called upon to elect Tilden and his reform program, and
their opponents call for the election of Hayes and the continuation of
the policy of Grant.*

*Those who want to continue and strengthen the policy of President
Grant, who for seven years imposed a heavy yoke on us and burdened
us with high taxes so that he made the poor poorer and the rich
richer, and in addition, made other nations hate us . . . who wish to
increase violence in this country should vote for Hayes. . . . Samuel
Tilden is the only one who can bring peace and prosperity to this
country.*

*Whoever looks forward to a change for the better will on the
seventh day of November cast his ballot for Tilden. But, beware
not to be caught in the net of swindlers who change and falsify the
ballots.*[397]

The call was written in Hebrew, and there is no record as to
whether it was published. But published or not it tells much about the
feeling of security and the sense of belongingness to *die naye heim*
among German Jews beginning with the 1870s. Szold's feeling of belonging, of being at home, was repeated in the 1920s by the later immigrants, the Russians.

The Final Step toward Unity

It is strange that while there was hardly any distinction left between Jews of different extractions in public life, they could not
unite into one inter-Jewish activity. The German and East European

Jews—or rather their descendants, all born in America—continued to work through two separate charity organizations, the Federated Jewish Charities and the United Hebrew Charities, in spite of appeals of many leaders that the separation was an anachronism which must be done away with. In 1904 Rabbi Rosenau had sought to dispel the notion of the German Jews that their brothers from the East were cultural outcasts. The rabbi even went a step further and said: "What these people [the Russian Jews] can give us is infinitely greater in value than what we give them."[398] The rabbi's plea did not help much. The two groups remained separate.

William Levy, the uptown Jew who worked closely with the Russian Jews as president of their charity organization, said in 1910:

The kindly feelings now existing among the Jewish charitable organizations of our city will ultimately lead to one large and stronger federation. . . . I join with my friend, Mr. Eli Frank, the president of the Federated Jewish Charities, in trusting that the time is not far distant when this will be accomplished.[399]

This too did not help. There was "kindly feeling," but not enough of it to bring about something which was considered essential for the community—a united charity organization. At every meeting of the Federation such pleas were made, but they were of no avail.

Eight years passed after Levy's first call for unity as president of the downtown charities. In 1918, as president of the uptown charities, he again renewed his plea:

I desire to call to your attention . . . the bringing together of the Federated and United Charities. My very able predecessor—Dr. Harry Friedenwald—three years in succession urged the union of the two organizations. The reasons for it are so manifest that it is unnecessary to enter into the details at present, but the main and most essential one, I think, is the belief that one organization will perform the work more economically than two, prevent duplication, and also be more representative of Jewish communal life. . . . If all our strength were combined in one unit . . . it would result in greater benefit to all.[400]

This call and many similar ones remained cries in the wilderness as long as a substantial number of officeholders considered their positions to be of greater importance than the needs of the community. Speaking of such people, Hollander remarked:

The directorate, nominally elective, acquired a formal rigidity on the basis of generous contributions, quasi-tribal representation and available leisure. . . . The officers . . . developed a proprietary relation and a permanent tenure . . . once elected, nothing short of death could remove them.[401]

Another obstacle to unity was the sense of superiority which permeated both Jewries. German exclusiveness was matched by that of many Russians. The latter were, in their language, *Yidn;* the former, *Yahudim.* The two terms (the first in Yiddish and the second in Hebrew) which originally meant the same—Jews—came to mean two different things to the Russian Jews. *Yidn* meant good, wholesome, truly Jewish, while *Yahudim* carried with it a connotation that was anything but good. What the word, always pronounced with a sneer, was supposed to convey was "assimilated Jews."

There were good psychological reasons for downtown Jews to oppose unity. Insults die slowly. There can be no doubt that Betsy Wiesenfeld, for example, was a kind soul. She surely meant well when she, the wife of one of the richest men in the community, walked the streets of East Baltimore wearing a long apron with deep pockets. These were filled with small coins and sweets which she distributed freely among young and old. People grabbed the pennies and the candies.[402] Those who "enjoyed" these gifts were poor. Little did people of Mrs. Wiesenfeld's kind realize the resentment and bitterness they instilled in the poor whom they tried to help in such a manner.

Hollander, one of those who looked deeper into the relationship between the two groups, remarked:

What he [the immigrant] received was given to him too often, neither in the form to which he was accustomed, nor in the spirit to which he was entitled. . . . Had the older community been wise, it would have strained every nerve to have included within its resources this new force, whose potentiality in economic capacity and philanthropic impulse was not then, and not even now, fully appreciated. . . . We took their money only when it could be given in the form in which we have been accustomed to assess it. We were slow to elect the newcomers to membership, and we were averse to giving even the foremost of them place on the institutional directorate.[403]

The insults were not forgotten by the Russians. They did not care to form a union with those who were "averse" to giving due recognition even to the "foremost" among them.

There was also another reason for their opposition. They feared that they would be intimidated when they met the *Yahudim*, who were so much wealthier, spoke a good English, and enjoyed superior standing in the community. A Baltimore Yiddish newspaper no doubt expressed the prevailing mood of East Baltimore when it wrote editorially:

Uptown Jews want to unite all charities. We are against it. Before long they will swallow us. What is badly needed is to unite all down- town charities, but not to merge with the uptown charities.[404]

Fortunately for the community, Hollander, Friedenwald, Levy, and Levin persisted in their pleas for unity. They must have had their counterparts among the East European Jews, although their names are not known to us because the records of the United were lost. The wealthy elements among the immigrants and the younger "Russians," native Americans, had no fear of intimidation. They knew that they would not be "swallowed up." After long debates the more reasonable minds in both groups prevailed. The long division came to an end in 1920. The legacy of the Federation was expressed by its last president, Walter Sondheim:

We have reached a point where it is no longer sufficient or satisfy- ing to furnish food and clothing to those needing and desiring it, but we must make up our minds to diagnose carefully each family condi- tion and supply time and money to make that family self-sustaining to the extent . . . that it may live a normal life.[405]

This was the philosophy that the Federation brought to the new united organization, the Associated Jewish Charities, more commonly known as the Associated,[406] the name by which it is still known. Just as was the case of the Federation, however, the name did not describe the real functions of the organization. The Associated took on the mandate to make all people "self-sustaining" in the broadest sense of the word. Along with aid to the needy, it included education, a court of arbitration, and an employment bureau; and it quite naturally as- sumed a role as guardian of Jewish rights. In brief, it embraced all aspects of the community except the synagogues, which at all times remained the province of their worshipers—a Jewish version of the separation of Church and State.

Like the Federation, the Associated was blessed from the beginning with two exceptionally able and devoted leaders. Louis H. Levin, who contributed so much to the community, served as its first executive director, and after a short interval he was followed by Harry Green-stein in the same capacity.

With the formation of the Associated a new chapter in the history of Baltimore Jewry began. Its first president, A. Ray Katz, was a symbol of that era. Himself a wealthy German Jew, Katz was the son-in-law of a wealthy Russian Jew, Jacob Epstein. At first unity between the Germans and the Russians was a clumsy one. It took years to do away with long-inbred prejudices. And yet even if not united socially, both groups worked hand in hand in communal affairs. It was not, nor was it ever intended to be, a monolithic community. There were differences in religion (even though all were Jewish), in politics, in approaches to social problems; but division by country of national origin was steadily declining.

By the 1920s the 65,000 Baltimore Jews[407] had far more important concerns than where their ancestors had come from. The Immigration Act of 1921 drastically curtailed immigration from Eastern Europe. As we have said, this was accomplished by limiting the number of aliens admitted to the United States annually to 3 per cent of the number of foreign-born persons of any nationality living in this country in 1910. In 1921 there were 119,036 Jewish immigrants. This number was reduced to 53,424 in the following year and was reduced to a trickle in the year after the passage of the Johnson Act of 1924.[408] American Jewry could no longer depend on European immigrants to provide the stimulus for vitality and distinctiveness. From then on it had to rely on its own resources.

It was this challenge with which the Jews of Baltimore, no less than Jews throughout America, were now faced. No longer uptown and downtown Jews, a united community turned to the challenge and in turning to it together, rose to it as well.

EPILOGUE

HALF A CENTURY LATER

It is not possible to do justice to the last fifty years of Baltimore's Jewish community without examining those years in great detail. This is a task for the future. What follows here is a kaleidoscopic view of the community in 1970 and, barring world-shaking events similar to those which occurred in the past fifty years, a prediction of its future.

Fifty years is a significant period of time. The community has grown from 65,000 in 1920[1] to 106,300 by 1968.[2] The predominantly immigrant Baltimore Jewry has changed to a predominantly native-born community.[3] Synagogues have multiplied and become quite elaborate, if not extravagant, structures with an affiliation of 64 per cent of the Jews in the city.[4] There are three rabbinical associations,[5] two agencies which supervise Jewish education in the city,[6] and two institutions of higher learning.[7] Thousands of children attend Jewish elementary Sunday and afternoon schools and the three day schools, at a cost of slightly under three million dollars in 1970.[8] The needy are taken care of by various charity agencies,[9] the sick are hospitalized,[10] and big sums are forwarded for Jewish overseas needs.[11]

Large funds are needed to provide for all the activities mentioned here and for the many more which are not mentioned.[12] Baltimore Jews are in a position to furnish these; on the whole the community is affluent. A full 35 per cent of the Jewish families make over fifteen thousand dollars a year (but 14 per cent make less than five thousand dollars a year).[13] The East Baltimore ghetto for the poor is dimly remembered by some. To most Baltimore Jews who live today in a different kind of a ghetto, a gilded one in Baltimore's suburbs, the stories about the old ghetto sound like a bad fairy tale. Forty-two per cent of the Jews over the age of twenty-five are college graduates and 84.5 per cent of the population between the ages of eighteen and twenty-one are in college.[14]

These well-to-do, well-educated men and women give not only money. In 1967 twenty-one thousand of the adult population contributed to the campaign of the Associated Jewish Charities, and twenty-five hundred worked as volunteer solicitors.[15] There are thousands upon thousands of men and women, young and old, who work for all kinds of worthy Jewish and nonsectarian causes.

241

The greatest accomplishment by far in the past half a century, however, has been the amalgamation of the two Jewries, the uptown and downtown. The first years of the Associated were trying ones. There was much cooperation but just as much suspicion and jealousy. The "Germans" were chagrined when a "Russian" was elected to a high office in the organization, just as the latter were elated by such a promotion, which did not occur too often. But three factors led to increasing cooperation and eventually to nearly total amalgamation.

First, the experience of working together served to reduce suspicion and to increase interaction. As people met, as they shared experiences with one another, they ceased to view each other chiefly as representatives of different cultures, but rather as people with common interests and diverse abilities. One was not elected to office either *because* or *in spite* of the fact that he was from one or the other of the two communities.

Second, and more important, as the number of natives increased, *yiḥus* (pedigree) took on less and less significance. The American-born cared little, if at all, which country their grandfathers and great-grandfathers had come from. It was of little consequence in their own lives and was still less relevant to their community work. Although it was true that for a considerable period the wealthy German Jews held the leadership, in 1970 wealth in the Jewish community is no longer limited to German Jews. Although wealth still remains a mark of leadership, the country of origin is of no consequence.

Important as working together and being of American birth were in the forming of one community, there were two events that were far more significant in creating a united community. The Holocaust and the birth of Israel profoundly altered the character of Jewish life throughout the world. It was these two events more than anything else that made people speak of the "oneness of our community"[16] and realize that "our community knows no borders."[17]

In 1939 the community formed a special agency, the Baltimore Jewish Community Council, to combat anti-Semitism. This evil force, which served to knit Jews together, is hardly a problem in Baltimore in 1970, and the main activity of the organization is in the field of civil rights.[18]

Today there is a united Baltimore Jewish community. Much is being accomplished by it, and measured by conventional standards it seems to be a healthy body. Yet conventional measures do not accurately assess the real situation, the situation in depth. And in depth there is uneasiness. Beneath the affluence, beneath edifices, beneath the busy world of organizations and institutions, beneath the security, there is the gnawing question: What of tomorrow?

As the community enters the 1970s it enters the most challenging period in its long history. On the agenda are alienation of the young, the insufficiency of Jewish education, the centrifugal forces which tend to destroy old established forms. There will be less and less interest in private charity work in a state which becomes more and more welfare oriented.

The ever-increasing load of the Big Brother League, an agency of the Associated that was founded in 1916 to deal with delinquency problems, is perhaps the darkest cloud on the horizon. In 1966 the league interviewed 1,103 persons who came to the agency with "problems." One year later the figure jumped to 1,629.[19] Use of marijuana has reached dangerous proportions among Jewish youth.[20]

As against this dark side of the picture there is the great vibrancy of the community, the reservoir of accumulated experience and wisdom. It has overcome many crises in the past—even the crisis of the alienation of the first native-born generation, which rejected its foreign-born parents and their style of life.

Now, two generations later, the "gap" is again high on the agenda of the American Jewish community, even as it is with the general American society. Yet the past is not entirely dead. It is not dead even to those who deny it and reject it. If the past is any measure of the future, one may prognosticate that in the 1970s, as in the 1920s, there will be many tensions, although much severer ones than those of a half a century ago. There will be, as in the past, much compromising—again, more than in the past. But armed with a wealth of experience, with a remarkable degree of devotion and zeal from so many of its members, with a strong will to live, the Baltimore Jewish community is prepared to meet all the difficulties and enjoy all the advantages of living in a pluralistic society.

appendix i

MARYLAND TOLERATION ACT OF 1649

[The following version of the Toleration Act has been transcribed from the Assembly Journal now at the Hall of Records in Annapolis. Most seventeenth-century forms of capitalization, punctuation, and spelling have been retained.]

Acts of Assembly of the 21th of Aprill 1649 Confirmed by the Lord Proprietary by an instrument vnder his hand & seale dated 26th of August 1650. Philip Calvert.

ACTS AND ORDERS OF ASSEMBLY AS- SENTED VNTO Enacted and made at a genāll Sessions of the said Assembly held at St Maries on the one and twentieth Day of Aprill Anno Dm̄ 1649 as followeth viz:

An Act concerning Religion

fforasmuch as in a well governed and x̄pian Com̄on Wealth matters concerning Religion and the honor of God ought in the first place to bee taken into serious consideracōn and endeavoured to bee settled Be it therefore ordeyned and enacted by the right Hoble Cecilius Lord Baron of Baltemore absolute Lord and Proprietary of this Province with the advise and consent of this Generall Assembly That whatsoever pson or psons within this Province and the Islands therevnto belonging shall from henceforth blaspheame God, that is, curse him or deny our Saviour Jesus Christ to bee the sonne of God, or shall deny the holy Trinity the ffather sonne and holy Ghost, or the Godhead of any of the said three psons of the Trinity or the Vnity of the Godhead, or shall vse or vtter any reproachfull speeches words or language concerning the said Holy Trinity, or any of the said three psons thereof shalbe punished with death and confiscacōn or forfeiture of all his or her lands and goods to the Lord Proprietary and his heires. And bee it also Enacted by the authority and with the advise and assent aforesaid That whatsoever pson or psons shall from henceforth vse or vtter any reproachfull Words or Speeches concerning the blessed Virgin Mary the mother of our Saviour or the holy Apostles or Evangelists or any of them shall in such case for the first Offence forfeit to the said Lord Proprietary and his heires Lords and Proprietaries of this Province the Suṁe of ffive pounds sterling or the value thereof to bee levyed on the goods and chattells of every such pson soe offending, but in case such Offender or Offenders shall not then have goods and chattells sufficient for the satisfyeing of such forfeiture, or that the same bee not otherwise speedily satisfyed that then such Offender or Offenders shalbe publiquely Whipt and bee ymprisoned during the pleasure of the Lord Proprietary or the leive^t or cheife Governor of this Province for the time being. And that every such Offender or Offenders for every second offence shall forfeit tenne pounds sterling or the value thereof to bee levyed as aforesaid, or in case such offender or Offenders shall not then haue goods and chattells within this Province sufficient for that purpose then to bee publiquely and severely Whipt and imprisoned as before is expressed And that every pson or psons before mencōned offending herein the third time shall for such third Offence forfeit all his lands and goods and bee for ever banished and expelled out of this Province. And bee it also further Enacted by the same authority advise and assent that whatsoever pson or psons shall from henceforth vppon any occasion of Offence or otherwise in a reproachfull manner or Way declare call or denominate any pson or psons Whatsoever inhabiting residing traffiqueing trading or comerceing within this Province or Within any the Ports Harbors Creeks or Havens to the same belonging an heritick, Scismatick, Idolator, puritan, Independant, Prespiterian, popish priest, Jesuite, Jesuited papist, Lutheran, Calvenist, Anabaptist, Brownist, Antinomian, Barrowist, Roundhead, Separatist, or any other name or terme in a reproachfull manner relating to matter of Religion shall for every such Offence forfeit and loose the sōme or [of] tenne shillings sterling or the value thereof to bee levyed on the goods and chattells of every such Offender and Offenders, the one half thereof to bee forfeited and paid vnto the person and persons of whom such reproachfull words are or shalbe spoken or vttered, and the other half thereof to the Lord Proprietary and his heires Lords and Proprietaries of this Province, but if such pson or psons whoe shall at any time vtter or speake any such reproachfull Words or language shall not haue goods or chattells sufficient and overt within this Province to bee taken to satisfy the penalty aforesaid, or that the same bee not otherwise speedily satisfyed, that then the pson or persons soe offending shalbe publickly whipt, and shall suffer imprisonm^t without baile or maineprise vntill hee shee or they respectively shall satisfy the party soe offended or grieved by such reproachfull language by asking him or her respectively forgivenes publiquely for such his Offence before the Magistrate or chiefe Officer

or Officers of the Towne or place where such Offence shalbe given
And bee it further likewise Enacted by the authority and consent
aforesaid That every person and persons within this Province that
shall at any time hereafter pphane the Sabbath or Lords day called
Sunday by frequent swearing drunkennes or by any vncivill or disorderly recreacōn or by working on that day when absolute necessity
doth not require it shall for every such first offense forfeit 2ˢ 6ᵈ sterling
or the value thereof and for the second Offense 5ˢ sterling or the
value thereof, and for the third offence and soe for every time hee
shall offend in like manner afterwards 10ˢ sterling or the value thereof
And in case such Offender and Offenders shall not haue sufficient
goods or chattells within this Province to satisfy any of the said Penal-
ties respectively hereby imposed for prophaning the Sabbath or Lords
day called Sunday as aforesaid That in every such case the p̄tie soe
offending shall for the first and second offence in that kinde bee imprisoned till hee or shee shall publickly in open Court before the
chiefe Commander Judge or Magistrate of that County Towne or
precinct where such offence shalbe committed acknowledg the Scandall
and offence hee hath in that respect given against God and the good
and civill Governemᵗ of this Province And for the third offence and
for every time after shall also bee publickly whipt. And whe[reas]
the inforceing of the conscience in matters of Religion hath frequently
fallen out to bee of Dangerous consequence in those common wealthes
where it hath beene practised, And for the more quiett and peaceable
governemᵗ of this Province and the better to pserve mutuall love and
amity amongst the Inhabitants thereof Be it herefore also by the Lo:
Pr[o]prietary with the advise and consent of this Assembly Ordeyned
& enacted (except as in this psent Act is before Declared and sett
Forth) That noe person or psons whatsoever within this Province or
the Islands Ports Harbors Creeks or Havens therevnto belonging
professing to beleive in Jesus Christ shall from henceforth bee any waies
troubled molested or disconteñaced for or in respect of his or her
religion nor in the free exercise thereof within this Province or the
Islands therevnto belonging nor any way compelled to the beleife or
exercise of any other Religion against his or her consent, soe as they
bee not vnfaithfull to the Lord Proprietary or molest or conspire against
the civill Governemᵗ established or to bee established in this Province
vnder him or his heires And that all & every pson and psons that shall
presume contrary to this Act and the true intent and meaning thereof
directly or indirectly either in person or estate willfully to wrong dis-
turbe trouble or molest any person Whatsoever within this Province

professing to believe in Jesus Christ for or in respect of his or her religion or the free exercise thereof within this Province other than is provided for in this Act, that such pson or psons soe offending shalbe compelled to pay treble damages to the party soe wronged or molested, and for every such offense shall alsoe forfeit 20ˢ sterling in money or the value thereof, half thereof for the vse of the Lo: Proprietary and his heires Lords and Proprietaries of this Province, and the other half for the vse of the party soe wronged or molested as aforesaid, Or if the ptie soe offending as aforesaid shall refuse or bee vnable to recompense the party soe wronged or to satisfy such ffyne or forfeiture then such Offender shalbe severely punished by publick whipping & imprisonmᵗ during the pleasure of the Lord Proprietary or his Leivetenāt or cheife Governor of this Province for the tyme being without baile or maineprise And bee it further alsoe Enacted by the authority and consent aforesaid That the Sheriff or other Officer or Officers from time to time to bee appointed & authorized for that purpose of the Country Towne or precinct where every particular offence in this psent Act conteyned shall happen at any time to bee comitted and wherevppon there is hereby a fforfeiture ffyne or penalty imposed shall from time to time distraine and seise the goods and estate of every such pson soe offending as aforesaid against this psent Act or any pt thereof and sell the same or any part thereof for the full satisfaccōn of such forfeiture ffine or penalty as aforesaid Restoring vnto the ptie soe offending the Remainder or Overplus of the said goods or estate after such satisfaccōn soe made as aforesaid.

> The ffreemen haue assented. Tho: Hatton
> Enacted by the Governor Willm Stone

appendix ii

MEMORIAL BY MARYLAND JEWS TO THE GENERAL ASSEMBLY OF MARYLAND, 1824

TO THE HONORABLE THE GENERAL ASSEMBLY OF MARYLAND. THE MEMORIAL OF THE SUBSCRIBERS, CITIZENS thereof, RESPECTFULLY REPRESENTS:

Your Memorialists are of that class of the Citizens of Maryland, long subjected to the pressure of political disqualifications, by the operation of a religious test in the Constitution of the State; and they approach your Honorable Body with this their prayer, that an Act passed the 29th of Janaury 1823 "to extend to all the citizens of Maryland the same civil rights and religious privileges that are enjoyed under the Constitution of the United States," may be confirmed by the present session, becoming thereby part of the Constitution.

Your Memorialists, feeling it incumbent on them at this stage of the proceeding, address themselves on the subject, to your Honorable body, in the honest confidence, which the American is educated to entertain in his fellow citizens, and in the legislative guardians of his rights. It is not their wish to obtain from your honorable body, a grant of exclusive privilege; because such a privilege would be hostile, not only to the principles of our institutions, but to the express provisions of that charter which we have all alike, sworn to support; but it is equal rights which they petition; their voice is not raised in favor, but in opposition, to exclusive privilege; they ask an equality of rights with their fellow citizens. If the disqualifications under which they labor, were imposed as the penalty of law for civil delinquencies, for habits of social intemperance, or a disregard of the obligations of religion, they would blush to murmur; but it is, as they humbly apprehend, the retribution for a too honest perseverance in conscientious faith, unmindful of political disqualifications, of social inconvenience, and of individual contumely; and this same manly and virtuous constancy, which, exerted in the causes of their Country, would entitle them to be honored as patriots exposes them to proscription, when exercised in the service of the acknowledged God. They firmly flatter themselves, and have at length some reason to believe, that your enlightened Councils will suffer no longer, those strange anomalies to endure—that the period has arrived at last, when conscience and reason, the peculiar gifts of an Omnipotent benevolence, will be respected, and persecutions be abandoned to the Inquisitor and the Bigot. Are their doctrines immoral? They are the foundation of the general faith. Are they dangerous? It is no part of them to work conversions. Are they new? Ancient as the revelation of Almighty truth. Your Memorialists, with all humility, are at a loss to understand what there is so peculiarly exceptionable in these their tenets, as to have induced a solitary, but persevering departure, from the sublime system of our American political jurisprudence: why even at this moment, when the whole American pulse throbs with indignation at the civil and religious proscriptions, renewed and asserted in the old world, the good people of Maryland alone, should find it necessary or expedient, to continue for a moment, the disqualification of any class of their fellow Citizens. Your Memorialists beg leave to remind your Honorable Body, that the honors of office in our happy Republic, are not assumed, but conferred; not usurped by guilty ambition, but bestowed directly or indirectly, by popular confidence; that to disqualify any class of your citizens, is for the people to disqualify themselves; can it be necessary, can it be wise or politic at this day, for the people to disqualify themselves on the score of opinion only, from consulting merit in the selection of their public servants?

Your Memorialists do not here propose, a voluminous discussion of the great principles involved in the question, which they desire to bring before you; because it is one, as they apprehend, at this day, almost universally understood. It is the same which has agitated like a tempest, the human family from its earliest existence; has armed the hands of men in wide and desolating wars; has strained nations and families with intestine crime; trampled the charities of life; and driven societies from their natural homes, to seek an asylum more hospitable, on the billows of the deep or amid the recesses of the desert: a question which, as it mainly contributed to populate this our common Country, was here first and fully understood: and one, the liberal and happy results of whose true nature, our own Maryland, though too long misled upon the subject, evinced at the last session of her Legislature, and as your Memorialists trust, will again prove to the world on the present occasion, are deeply felt and thoroughly appreciated.

America, instructed in the school of adversity and oppression, and warned by the calamities of nations, has attained the haven of political happiness, by the guide of political wisdom. Moderate in her might, she has never sought to find in power, the foundation of new rights, but metes out to the weak the same measure with the strong. It was reserved for her to discover, that true policy consists in Justice, which, whilst it secures the confidence and devotion of her own Sons, entitles her to the reciprocity of the stranger. Above all, America has been the first to respect opinion and the human mind, that mysterious and sacred relation of sublunary Man to Celestial Wisdom; nor has thought to control the measureless elasticity of that principle, which created for exclusive allegiance to the Omnipotent alone, is beyond the reach of temporal restraints. America has wisely relinquished it to the insidious policy of regal governments, to make an instrument of religion; she has forever sundered the spiritual from the temporal concerns of men, and convinced mankind that disqualifications and persecution are only fruitful of disunion and hate;—toleration and equal rights, of good will and peace on earth.

Your Memorialists humbly apprehend that a peculiar and most important crisis hath occurred in the political world, and in the history of man; and if in the eastern hemisphere, his struggles for civil and religious liberty, hitherto ineffectual, have been smothered in their birth, it is now particularly important that, successful throughout the west, no speck should endure upon the purity of that code, sublime in its nature, as in its origin, it is confessedly divine.

As fellow citizens of Maryland, as Brethren of the same human family; for the honor of the State, for the great interests of humanity; your Memorialists humbly pray at your hands, that the Bill before you may be confirmed.

appendix iii

THE MARYLAND "JEW BILL"
introduced on January 5, 1826; passed on February 26, 1826

Sec. 1. Be it enacted by the General Assembly of Maryland, that every citizen of this state professing the Jewish Religion, and who shall hereafter be appointed to any office of public trust under the State of Maryland, shall in addition to the oaths required to be taken by the constitution and laws of the State or of the United States, make and subscribe a declaration of his belief in a future state of rewards and punishments, in the stead of the declaration now required by the constitution and form of government of this state.

Sec. 2. Be it enacted, that the several clauses and sections of the declaration of rights, constitutional and form of government, and every part of any law of this state contrary to the provisions of this act, so far as respects the sect of people aforesaid, shall be, and the same is hereby declared to be repealed and annulled on the confirmation hereof.

Sec. 3. And be it enacted, that if this act shall be confirmed by the General Assembly of Maryland, after the next election of delegates in the first session after such new election as the constitution and form of government directs, in such case this act and the alterations of the said constitution and form of government shall constitute and be valued as a part of the said constitution and form of government to all intents and purposes, anything therein contained to the contrary notwithstanding.

appendix iv

News items about Jews, primarily about events in the Baltimore Jewish community, appeared in The Baltimore Sun *(1882–1920) on the following dates:*

1882 April 4, June 12.
1886 Sept. 18.
1891 Aug. 4, 5, 20, 21, 26, 27.
1892 Sept. 4, 9.
1894 May 28, 29, Aug. 18, Oct. 31, Dec. 27.
1895 Jan. 2, 12, April 19, May 26, Nov. 18. Dec. 2, 30.
1896 April 6, Aug. 21, Nov. 10, 16, 17, 18, 20, Dec. 1, 2.
1897 Jan. 7, 25, 27, 28, 29, Feb. 1, 13, May 6, 22, 25, June 14, 15, 21, 24, July 8, 27, 28, Aug. 6, 11, 30, Sept. 4, 9, 13, 21, Nov. 2, Dec. 20, 21, 24, 27, 28, 30, 31.
1898 Jan. 7, 31, Feb. 8, 28, April 4, May 3, June 18, July 7, 8, 12, 21, Sept. 9, 13, 14, 20, Oct. 12, 15, 20, 24, Nov. 14, Dec. 6, 7, 8, 9, 20, 27.
1899 Jan. 24, 26, 28, 30, Feb. 9, 11, 22, 25, March 2, 8, 10, 11, 14, 15, 16, 17, 18, 23, 27, 30, April 26, May 2, 19, 20, 25, June 3, July 11, 18, August 4, 7, 16, 19, 22, Sept. 18, 25, Oct. 20, 24, Nov. 20, 28, Dec. 27.
1900 Jan. 1, 2, 24, 29, 30, Feb. 19, 26, March 14, 21, 26, April 10, 30, June 11, 12, 13, 14, July 9, Aug. 6, 14, 15, 25, Oct. 8, 9, 15, 26, Nov. 11, 17, 25, 28, 30, Dec. 3, 9, 18, 27, 31.
1901 Jan. 15, 30, Feb. 7, 11, 21, 25, March 12, 14, 18, 23, April 15, 24, May 8, 20, 25, 29, June 3, 17, 21, July 1, 3, 5, 8, 9, 29, Aug. 5, Oct. 7, 28, Dec. 15, 23, 27, 29.
1902 Jan. 5, 6, 9, 27, 29, 31, Feb. 10, March 4, 13, 15, 26, May 16, 18, 19, 29, June 13, July 20, Aug. 5, 18, Sept. 18, 20, 21, 24, 27, Oct. 17, Nov. 10, 21, 26, Dec. 23, 28, 29.
1903 Jan. 12, Feb. 9, 13, March 30, July 2, 3, 4, 5, 13, 15, 28, Sept. 20, 28, 30, Oct. 5, 12, 19, Dec. 4.
1904 May 3, 25, June 28, Sept. 7, Oct. 3, 15, 27, Dec. 1, 5, 8.

1905   Jan. 9, 11, 16, 18, Feb. 12, 13, 23, March 19, April 21, 24, 29, May 1, 13, 22, 23, July 1, 3, 5, 6, 7, 8, 9, 20, Aug. 1, 3, 4, 5, 19, 20, 26, 27, Sept. 17, Oct. 2, Nov. 14, 16, 18, 19, Dec. 25.

1906   Jan. 3, Feb. 12, 28, April 6, 16, May 8, 11, 14, 21, June 5, July 2, 4, 5, 6, 7, Aug. 29, Sept. 3, Oct. 28, Nov. 8, Dec. 17, 25.

1907   Jan. 21, 28, Feb. 11, March 1, 4, April 15, 28, May 13, July 15, 23, Sept. 9, Nov. 7, 11, Dec. 2.

1911   Jan. 3, Nov. 19, 25.

1912   Nov. 10.

1913   Oct. 12.

1914   Sept. 30.

1916   Jan. 8, 27.

1918   March 10.

1919   Dec. 3.

1920   Nov. 18, Dec. 20.

appendix v

News items about Maryland Jews (for all practical purposes, Baltimore Jews) published in The Occident. List, prepared by Frank M. Waldorf, is found in the American Periodical Center, Cincinnati.

Vol.   7, pp. 178, 226, 449, 475, 573, 575.
Vol.   8, pp. 56, 428, 480, 575 f., 614, 620.
Vol.   9, p. 272.
Vol. 10, pp. 46, 112, 148, 171, 187, 360, 362, 413 f., 502, 504.
Vol. 11, pp. 10–16, 122–123, 123–156, 186, 187, 235, 238, 257–61, 267, 279, 285, 327 f., 391–394, 423, 503, 506–11, 526, 540, 581, 599, 613 f.
Vol. 12, pp. 30, 117, 168, 227, 228, 263 f., 325, 374, 404, 477, 576, 579.
Vol. 13, pp. 102, 195, 196, 206, 209, 213, 270, 311 f., 358, 393, 448–453, 512, October 1855, 2a, 525–536, 549–552, 586–588, 602, March, April, May 1856, 3a, 2a.
Vol. 14, pp. 33 f., 73, 81 f., 185, 229–235, 252–257, 307, 310, 357, 403 f., 406–408, 409, 411, 448 f., July, August, September, March, April, May, 2a, 3a, May, June, July 1858, 4a.
Vol. 15, pp. 42, 43, 103 f., 118, 201, 202, 205–214; 224; 243, 246, 303, 351 f., 355–357, 403–406; 423–428, 431 f., 433–435, 453, December 1857, 2a, 505–513.
Vol. 16, pp. 54, 69–71, 72, 132–144, 222, 258, 309, 346 f., 355, 357–359, 360, 400, 426, 455, June, July, August, September, October, 3a, 4a, January, February, 6a, 533, 550, 555, 563 f.
Vol. 17, pp. 5, 16, 29 f., 33 f., 86, 88, 108, 119, 125 f., 143 f., 168, 174, 185, 194, 198, 214, 220, 224 f., 227, 240, April, May, June, July, August, 2a, November, December, 2a, 246, 253, 259, 269, 275, 277 f., 287 f., 297 f.,

Vol. 18, pp. 4, 42, 74, 82, 108, 130, 140, 180, 209 f., 217 f.,
222, 232, 240, May, June, July, 2a, November, 2a,
August, September, 2a, 248 f., 262, 268, 292, 310,
313.

abbreviations
USED IN THE NOTES AND BIBLIOGRAPHY

AJA . . . . *American Jewish Archives* (magazine)
AJAR . . . American Jewish Archives (Cincinnati)
AJHQ . . . *American Jewish Historical Quarterly*
AJYB . . . *American Jewish Year Book*
Am Heb . . . *American Hebrew*
AOJD . . . *Americans of Jewish Descent* (Cincinnati, 1960)
AZJ . . . . *Allgemeine Zeitung des Judenthums*
BCD . . . . *Baltimore City Directory*
BSA . . . . Benjamin Szold Archives (JHSM)
BSVG . . . *Baltimore Seine Vergangenheit und Gegenwart*
CCMHS . . . Cohen Collection, Maryland Historical Society
           (Baltimore)
CZAJ . . . Central Zionist Archives (Jerusalem)
DNB . . . . *Dictionary of National Biography*
FA . . . . Friedenwald Archives (JHSM)
HA . . . . Hollander Archives (JHSM)
HSA . . . . Henrietta Szold Archives (JHSM)
Isr . . . . . *The American Israelite*
JC . . . . . *Jewish Comment*
JE . . . . . *Jewish Encyclopedia*
J Exp . . . . *Jewish Exponent*
JHSM . . . Jewish Historical Society of Maryland
           (Baltimore)
J Mess . . . *The Jewish Messenger*
JSS . . . . Jewish Social Studies, New York
JTS . . . . Jewish Theological Seminary
LA . . . . Levy Archives (JHSM)
LCDC . . . Leeser Collection, Dropsie College
MBBHC . . . Minute Books, Baltimore Hebrew Congregation
           (at congregation, Baltimore, copy in AJAR)
MBCAC . . . Minute Books, Chizuk Amuno Congregation (at
           congregation, Baltimore)
MBHSC . . . Minute Books, Har Sinai Congregation (at con-
           gregation, Baltimore)

MBOSC . . . Minute Books, Oheb Shalom Congregation (at congregation, Baltimore)

MBSMC . . . Minute Book, Shomrei Mishmereth Congregation (at JHSM)

Md Arch . . . *Maryland Archives*

MHM . . . *Maryland Historical Magazine*

MHR . . . Maryland Hall of Records (Annapolis)

MHS . . . . Maryland Historical Society

Occ . . . . *The Occident*

PAJHS . . . *Publications of the American Jewish Historical Society*

RC . . . . Rice Collection (Jewish Theological Seminary of America)

RFJC . . . . *Report, Federated Jewish Charities of Baltimore*

SHGM . . . Society for the History of the Germans in Maryland, *Reports*

Sun . . . . *The Baltimore Sun*

YBCCAR . . *Year Book, Central Conference of American Rabbis*

notes

For complete references, see Bibliography

THE PIONEERING AGE: THE COLONIAL PERIOD

1. George Alzop, *A Character of Maryland* (London, 1666), reproduced in Clayton Colman Hall, ed. *Narratives of Early Maryland, 1633–1684* (New York, 1910), p. 364.
2. John Leeds Bozman, *The History of Maryland from the Settlement in 1633 to the Restoration in 1666* (Baltimore, 1837), II, 73.
3. Ibid., pp. 78–79.
4. *Md Arch*, XXV, 602–603.
5. Wilbur F. Coyle, *First Acts of Baltimore Town and Jones' Town, 1729–1797* (Baltimore, 1905), p. ix.
6. Ibid., p. x.
7. Avery O. Graves, "Soil Exhaustion as a Factor in the Agricultural History of Virginia and Maryland," *University of Illinois Studies in the Social Sciences*, XIII, No. 1 (Urbana, 1925), 29–32. By far the best studies on Maryland's economy in the colonial period are those of Clarence P. Gould: "Money and Transportation in Maryland, 1720–1765," *Johns Hopkins University Studies in History and Political Science Series*, XXXIII, No. 1 (Baltimore, 1915); "The Land System in Maryland, 1720–1765," ibid., XXXI, No. 1 (Baltimore, 1913); "The Economic Causes of the Rise of Baltimore," *Essays of Colonial History* (New Haven, 1931), pp. 225–271.
8. *Charter of Maryland*, sections I and XXI.
9. "Calvert Papers," *MHM*, XXVIII (1933), 220.
10. "Act of Assembly of the 21st of April 1649," *Md Arch*, I, 244–247.

In spite of the common belief that Maryland is called "Free State" because of the Toleration Act, that nickname has nothing to do with the act. It is of recent vintage and refers, not to religious tolerance, but to prohibition in Maryland. The phrase was coined by Hamilton Owen, editor of *The Baltimore Evening*

Sun. H. L. Mencken, *The American Language: Supplement* (New York, 1948), II, 602–603.

11. Some of the laws of the original Toleration Act and the amendments of 1723 are still on the books of Maryland, although with reduced punishments. The present blasphemy law reads: "If any person by writing or speaking shall blaspheme or curse God, or shall write or utter any profane words of and concerning our Savior Jesus Christ, or of and concerning the trinity, or any of the persons thereof, he shall on conviction be fined not more than one hundred dollars, and imprisoned not more than six months, or both. . . ." *Maryland Annotated Code,* Crimes and Punishments, Section 20, Article 27.

The most recent instance of "blasphemy" took place in 1968. The accused was imprisoned and fined for using profane language, namely, saying "God damn." *Sun,* July 17, 1968.

The Sunday Law, too, is still on the books, although local ordinances have introduced exceptions. *Maryland Annotated Code,* Article 27, sec. 492–543 c; Articles 2B, sec. 28 (a), 90–106; Article 66 c, sec. 132 (d), 698 (d). Court decisions have stressed that "ours is a Christian community . . . [and Sunday] is the day consecrated by the resurrection of our Saviour. . . ." *Kilgour* v. *Miles,* 6 Giles and Johnson 268; *Judenfind* v. *State,* 78 Md. 510, 514, 28A. 405, 406 (1894).

The author is obliged to Mr. Carl N. Everstine, director of the Department of Legislative Reference of the State of Maryland for his assistance in clarifying the points discussed above.

It is worth noting that only in 1927 did marriages consecrated by rabbis become legal. The legislature amended the original law—which gave authority to solemnize marriages only to "ministers of the Gospel"—by adding the words "or official of a religious order or body authorized by the rules and customs of said order." *Maryland Code,* Chapter 380, Acts of 1927.

For a detailed discussion of the subject, see B. H. Hartogensis, "Unequal Religious Rights in Maryland since 1776," *PAJHS,* XXV (1917), 93–107.

The intolerance of the Toleration Act notwithstanding, an official brochure published by the state, *Maryland at a Glance* (Annapolis, 1968) states: "The original settlers, Catholics, Protestants and Jewish, all practiced religious tolerance."

12. J. H. Hollander, "The Civil Status of the Jews in Maryland, 1634–1776," *PAJHS,* II (1893), 33–44. On Jewish rights

in various colonies, see Stanley F. Chyet, "The Political Rights of the Jews in the United States, 1776–1840," *AJA*, X (1958), 14–75.

13. Raphael Semmes, *Crime and Punishment in Maryland* (Baltimore, 1938), 166–167. In correspondence with the author, the following specialists in this area expressed the opinion that Lumbrozo was the only individual to be tried under the Toleration Act: Dr. Morris L. Radoff, director of the Maryland Hall of Records, John J. Szymasky, legislative analyst of the State of Maryland, and Prof. Ashley Ellefson, whose doctoral dissertation was on "The Provincial Court and County Courts of Maryland."

14. For detailed studies on Lumbrozo, see J. H. Hollander, "Some Unpublished Material Relating to Dr. Jacob Lumbrozo of Maryland," *PAJHS*, I (1893), 25–39; Abram Vossen Goodman, *American Overture* (Philadelphia, 1947), pp. 134–145; Semmes, *Crime and Punishment*, passim.

15. Leon Hühner, "Jews in the Legal and Medical Profession in America," *PAJHS*, XXII (1914), 158.

16. *Md Arch*, LIII, 355 f.

17. Ibid., LIV, 291 f.

18. *Provincial Court Records* (Maryland), Liber 5 (1658 to 1662), Judgements, folio 159–160; *Md Arch*, XLI, 202–204, 258.

19. *Record of Wills*, MHR, Liber I, folio 249–250.

20. *Md Arch*, LIII, 319.

21. Ibid., X, 473.

22. Samuel Oppenheim, "The Early History of Jews in New York, 1654–1664," *PAJHS*, XVIII (1909), 1–91, passim.

23. *Maryland Journal and Advertiser*, December 16, 1773.

24. Edwin Wolf, 2nd, and Maxwell Whiteman, *The History of the Jews of Philadelphia from Colonial Times to the Age of Jackson* (Philadelphia, 1956), p. 78; also Samuel Oppenheim, "Notes," *PAJHS*, XXV (1917), 143.

25. E. D. C., "Notes," *PAJHS*, XXXIV (1937), 271–273. Morris did not avail himself of Levy's hospitality. He remained in Philadelphia while the Continental Congress was sitting in Baltimore from December 12, 1776, until March 4, 1777. This information based on Morris's diaries was graciously supplied by John D. Kilburne, curator of the Historical Society of Philadelphia.

26. Ibid. The letter was dated July 26, 1789.
27. B. H. Hartogensis, "Notes on Early Jewish Settlers in Baltimore," *PAJHS*, XXII (1914), 194.

Burial in a Christian cemetery is not to be construed as a sign of conversion. There is a record of an active member of the first Jewish congregation in Baltimore, Levy Collmus, who was buried in a Christian cemetery "according to the full Orthodox ritual." This in spite of the fact that a Jewish burial ground had existed in the city since 1786. Rachel Levy's case is, however, suspicious. On page 114 of the rare book *Memoirs of the Dead and Tomb's Remembrancer*, published by "Editors" (Baltimore, 1806), we find: "Mrs. Rachel Levy d. November 11, 1794, age 55, E." (Episcopalian). This establishes that at least Rachel Levy, if not her husband, did convert. In this booklet we find other entries with the letter "J" alongside the names of deceased, for example, "Zepporah Mordeica" (no doubt Mordecai), wife of Mordecai Mordecai.
28. Mikveh Israel Archives, cited in Wolf and Whiteman, *Jews of Philadelphia*, p. 128.
29. County Judgements, ISB2, f. 238, June Court, 1752, MHR.
30. *Md Arch*, LV, 300.
31. Max J. Kohler, "Incidents Illustrative of American Jewish Patriotism," *PAJHS*, IV (1896), 94–96.
32. Matthew Page Andrews, *History of Maryland Province and State* (New York, 1929), p. 131.
33. Jacob R. Marcus, *Early American Jewry* (Philadelphia, 1953), II, 52.
34. Guido Kisch, "German Jews in White Labor Servitude," *PAJHS*, XXXIV (1937), 30–47.
35. Thomas W. Griffith, *Annals of Baltimore* (Baltimore, 1833), p. 32.
36. *The Federal Gazette and Baltimore Advertiser*, December 9, 1799, gives figures indicating the economic rise of the city. In 1790 the export was slightly over two million dollars, and by 1799 it reached the sum of sixteen million dollars.
37. William Eddis, *Letters from America, Historical and Description, Comprising Occurrences from 1769 to 1777 Inclusive* (London, 1792), p. 96.
38. U. S. Census, 1790.
39. Ibid., 1800.
40. Hall, *Narratives*, I, 56.
41. Ira Rosenswaike, "An Estimate and Analysis of the Jewish

Population of the United States in 1790," *PAJHS*, L (1960), 25.

42. Isidor Blum, *The Jews of Baltimore* (Baltimore-Washington, 1910), p. 3.

43. *BCD*, passim.

44. For a long, although in many respects incomplete, study of Solomon Etting, see Aaron Baroway, "Solomon Etting, 1764–1847," *MHM*, XV (1920), 1–20. There is also an Etting collection in the Jewish Theological Seminary, New York, and a wealth of original materials in the Maryland Historical Society, Baltimore, mss. Nos. 57, 104, 373, 538, 539.

45. Isaac Rivkind, "Early American Hebrew Documents," *PAJHS*, XXXIV (1937), 66–69.

46. Samuel Oppenheim, "The Jews and Masonry in the United States before 1810," *PAJHS*, XIX (1910), 41, 42, 44, 46.

47. *Baltimore Advertiser*, January 4, 1791.

48. CCMHS, ms. 251.

49. *General Advertiser*, June 13, 1794, cited in Wolf and Whiteman, *Jews of Philadelphia*, pp. 192, 437, n. 36.

50. William D. Hoyt, Jr., "Civilian Defense in Baltimore, 1814–1815, Minutes of the Committee of Vigilance and Safety," *MHM*, XXXIX (1944), 199–224, 293–309; ibid., XL (1945), 7–23, 137–163, and passim.

51. Robert Fulton to Solomon Etting, New York, November 27, 1814. Ms., Fulton Papers, Library of Congress. The project was a fiasco because the banks subscribed only $86,000, while the sum needed was $150,000.

52. Louis P. Henninghausen, *History of the German Society of Maryland* (Baltimore, 1909), p. 171.

53. Solomon Etting to Samuel D. Ingham, secretary of the treasury, cited in Joseph L. Blau and Salo W. Baron, *The Jews of the United States, 1790–1840: A Documentary History* (Philadelphia, 1963), I, 62–63.

54. *Address of the Maryland State Colonization Society, to the People of Maryland, with the Constitution of the Society* (Baltimore, 1831).

55. *DNB*, XI, 27–28.

56. Aaron Stopack, "The Maryland State Colonization Society," *MHM*, LXII (1968), 275–279; William D. Hoyt, Jr., "The Papers of the Maryland State Colonization Society," *MHM*, XXXII (1937), 247–271.

57. Rosenswaike, "An Estimate," 20.

58. Isaac Leeser, "The Jews and Their Religion," cited in *PAJHS*, VI (1897), 143–144.
59. Hyman B. Grinstein, *The Rise of the Jewish Community of New York, 1654–1860* (Philadelphia, 1945), p. 143.
60. *Occ*, V (1847), 320.
61. Subscription list of Mikveh Israel, November 8, 1818. Ms., Mikveh Israel Archives, as cited by Wolf and Whiteman, *Jews of Philadelphia*, pp. 361, 496, n. 7.
62. Grinstein, *Jewish Community*, p. 588, n. 24.
63. Ira Rosenswaike, "The Jewish Population of the United States as Estimated from the Census of 1820," *AJHQ*, LIII (1963), 138. The figure given for Baltimore in 1820 is one hundred and twenty, hence the rough estimate of about a hundred for 1817.
64. *Baltimore Land Records*, WK 1103-04-05, WG72, Folio 1–2, December 2, 1801, in MHR.
65. MBHSC, January 15, 1843.
66. Ms. copy in CCMHS, ms. 251; see also Walter H. Liebmann, "The Correspondence between Solomon Etting and Clay," *PAJHS*, XVII (1909), 87–88.
67. It is rather strange that the wealthy Etting's entire estate, outside of real estate, was only $9,605.26. The real estate was worth only $13,551.73. See Inventories, Book 58, Folio 339 in MHR. The value of his library was set at $23.85. Three books dealing with the Hebrew language, inscribed SOLOMON ETTING, NO. 15 CALVERT ST., BALTIMORE, 1791, are to be found in the JTS. His copy of David Levy's *A Defense of the Old Testament, in a Series of Letters Addressed to Thomas Paine* (New York, 1797) is in the library of the Gratz College, Philadelphia. It is worth noting that one of the two executors of Etting's will was his son Bernard, the other was a non-Jew, yet both swore "on the holy Evangely of the almighty God," and this twenty-one years after the Jews were granted equality in Maryland in 1826.
68. Reuben Etting is not to be confused with his namesake, another Baltimorean, who served in the Revolutionary army; see Solomon Solis-Cohen, "Note concerning David Hays . . . ," *PAJHS*, II (1894), 66.
69. *BCD*, 1802.
70. *Occ*, VII (1897), 227; Blum, *Jews of Baltimore*, p. 4.
71. Although he was appointed in 1801, Etting worked in the

sheriff's office at least a full decade prior to his appointment. One document bearing his signature as marshal of Maryland is dated September 17, 1791. The National Archives, group 56, Document No. 213. See also photostat copy of documents dated September 17, 1791, and November 23, 1791, signed "Reuben Etting, Marshal of the State under Jefferson," in JHSM.

72. In addition to these there is also a miniature of Solomon Etting in the Pennsylvania Academy of the Fine Arts (artist unknown; formerly attributed to James Peale). Important comments about some of these portraits were made by Hanna R. London, *Miniatures of Early American Jews* (Springfield, Massashusetts, 1933), p. 33.

73. The family disappeared from the Jewish scene. Intermarriage took its toll. The first of the Ettings to marry a non-Jew was Elizabeth Solomon Etting's only sister to survive infancy, who married Robert Mickle.

74. Herbert T. Ezekiel and Gaston Lichtenstein, *The History of the Jews of Richmond* (Richmond, 1917), pp. 29–31.

75. On the Cohens in Baltimore see Aaron Baroway, "The Cohens of Maryland," *MHM*, XVIII (1923), 355–375; XIX (1924), 54–77; also the Cohen Collection in JTS. There is a wealth of material on the Cohens in the MHS, especially mss. 251, 251.1, 251.3, 251.4.

76. All Cohen brothers used the middle initial "I.," which is omitted in this work.

77. Jacob I. Cohen, Jr. and Brothers to Levi Woodbury, secretary of the treasury, May 27, 1835, cited in Blau and Baron, *Jews of the U.S.*, I, 149–150.

78. Proceedings of the Committee to Promote the Trade and Commerce Interests of the City of Baltimore, December 22, 1834, unidentified clipping in MHS, ms. 251.4.

79. Henninghausen, *German Society*, pp. 98, 171, and passim.

80. Wolf and Whiteman, *Jews of Philadelphia*, p. 496, n. 8; *Occ*, II (1844), 144; Morris U. Schappes, *A Documentary History of the Jews in the United States, 1654–1875* (New York, 1950), p. 229.

81. William S. Rayner, *Address Containing the History of the Har Sinai Congregation of Baltimore City* (Baltimore, 1892), p. 5; similarly, *Sinai*, II (1857), p. 445.

82. B. H. Hartogensis, "The Sephardic Congregation of Baltimore," *PAJHS*, XXIII (1915), 146.

83. MHR, *Baltimore Land Records*, WK1103-04-05, WG72, Folio 203. *Land Records of Baltimore County*, Liber W. G. No. 206, Folio 421 and Liber No. 210, Folio 558. For further details see CCMHS, folders 47128A, 47969 (Old Classification); also *Baltimore Evening Sun*, May 30, 1911, and *Sun*, September 4, 1915, and June 27, 1926. Although the Etting private cemetery was the *second* in Baltimore, the legend on the bronze tablet affixed on its gate reads: "ETTING CEMETERY, FOUNDED 1799. The oldest Hebrew Burial Ground in Baltimore." Following the last burial in this cemetery in 1881, Mendes Cohen took care of it; after his death in 1915 it was turned over for perpetual care to the Baltimore Free Burial Society.

84. Hartogensis, "Unequal Religious Rights," 101.

85. Letter of Joshua Cohen to Governor Bradford, May 17, 1864, CCMHS.

86. See note 11.

87. The collection, consisting of 417 rare volumes, was catalogued by Cyrus Adler and printed privately in 1887. It is presently located in the Dropsie College, Philadelphia.

88. *The National Medical Journal* (Washington), I, No. 4, (January 1887).

89. CCMHS, ms. 251.3. Of special interest are Cohen's descriptions of Jewish life in Palestine in his letters of September 28 and 29, 1832.

90. Hartogensis, "Sephardic Congregation," 146.

91. J. Thomas Scharf, *The Chronicles of Baltimore* (Baltimore, 1874), p. 121.

92. Isaac F. Nicholson, *Baltimore Stock Exchange, Historical Sketch* (Baltimore, n.d.), ii.

There were many later Cohens. Each of them played a role in the general community. Most were also active in Jewish affairs. The last of this distinguished family was Eleanor Septima Cohen (1857–1937). Interested in art, she was a liberal contributor to the Baltimore Art Museum. Under the influence of her friend Dr. Harry Friedenwald she also endowed scholarships at the Jewish Theological Seminary of America in New York and the Shulamith School of Music in Tel Aviv. The Maryland Historical Society, of which a cousin of hers, Mendes Cohen, served as president, received many valuable gifts from her during her lifetime and was bequeathed additional gifts after her death. The beautiful Cohen Room of the Maryland Historical Society, with its superb furniture, rugs, family portraits, and silver, serves as a memorial to this family. Here there are eight large oil paintings, eight miniatures, and three pastels of different members of the Cohen family (full record is to be found in the JHSM).

She bequeathed real estate and rents worth $107,828 to the Associated Jewish Charities in Baltimore and the Hebrew University in Jerusalem, appointing as executors Dr. Harry Friedenwald and Justice Brandeis. See Hayim Margalith's, "The Transmigration of a Law," *American Journal of International Law*, XL (April 1946), 411–414, 483–490. The case was argued before the Maryland Court of Appeals, October term, 1943, No. 53, 182 Md. 432.

Throughout her life she mingled with non-Jews and counted them among her "close friends," but she was a strictly observant Jew. Not only did she observe *kashrut* in all its detail, but she blessed candles on Friday night even when she was a house guest at the home of a gentile friend. She would never allow a non-Jew to touch the body of a deceased member of her family.

Yet Miss Cohen was cremated. In a letter to this writer dated November 4, 1968, Samuel J. Fisher, a personal friend and attorney of Eleanor Cohen, wrote: "She [E.C.] wanted to be buried beside her father, and, in view of the fact that no separate adjacent lot was available, she decided that she wanted to be cremated."

93. Wolf and Whiteman, *Jews of Philadelphia*, p. 148.
94. *Votes and Proceedings of the House of Delegates of the State of Maryland, November Session 1797, Being the First Session of This Assembly*, 69, 71–72. For a detailed history of this case see E. Milton Altfeld, *The Jew's Struggle for Religious and Civil Liberties* (Baltimore, 1924); Joseph L. Blau, "The Maryland Jew Bill . . . ," *Review of Religion* (1944), pp. 227–239.
95. Hartogensis, "Unequal Religious Rights," 96.
96. Oppenheim, "Jews and Masonry," pp. 55–78. Oppenheim listed twenty-four Jewish Masons in Maryland.
97. Leon Hühner, "Jews in the War of 1812," *PAJHS*, XXVI (1918), 186–188. An interesting account of the battle of Fort McHenry was related by Col. Mendes Cohen, a participant in the battle. CCMHS, ms. 251.4.
98. Blau, "Maryland Jew Bill," presents a most interesting treatment of Kennedy from this point of view.
99. Altfeld, *The Jew's Struggle*, p. 17.

100. Ms. copy in CCMHS, ms. 251.4.
101. Hartogensis, "Unequal Religious Rights," 95.
102. *JC*, October 31, 1915.
103. The full texts of speeches delivered in favor of the Jew Bill, except a five-hour speech of McMahon's, which was not published, are found in *Sketch of the Proceedings in the Legislature of Maryland, December Session, 1818, on What Is Commonly Called the Jew Bill* . . . (Baltimore, 1819); *Speech of Thomas Kennedy, Esq. in the Legislature of Maryland, on the Bill respecting Civil Rights and Religious Privileges* (Annapolis, 1823); *Speeches on the Jew Bill in the House of Delegates of Maryland, by H. M. Brackenridge, W. G. D. Worthington, and J. S. Tyson, Esquire* . . . (Philadelphia, 1829); *Speech of W. G. D. Worthington on the Confirmatory Act Abolishing the Religious Test* . . . (Baltimore, 1824). Much material on the Jew Bill is also found in CCMHS, ms. 251.4.
104. *Sketch of Proceedings*, 68.
105. *The Herald of Hagerstown*, August 18, 1823, reprinted in *Niles' Weekly Register*, XXV, September 26, 1823.
106. *Copy in JHSM*
107. *Constitution of Maryland*, Article 70, Section 9.
108. *Niles' Weekly Register*, LXIX (1846), 284.
109. Ibid., XXIII (1823), 33; ibid., 336, and passim. (For a detailed study of Niles's attitude to Jews see Isaac M. Fein, *"Niles' Weekly Register* on the Jews," *PAJHS*, L (1960), 3–22.)
110. *Niles' Weekly Register*, XXIX (1826), 308.
111. Jacob Cohen to Mordecai M. Noah, letter dated February 2, 1819, CCMHS, ms. 251.
112. Ibid.
113. *Isr.* July 13, 1855.
114. Blau and Baron, *Jews of the U. S.*, I, 78; Simon Wolf, *The American Jew as Patriot, Soldier and Citizen* (Philadelphia, 1895), pp. 72–80.
115. CCMHS, as cited by Blau and Baron, *Jews of the U. S.*, I, 246, n. 83.
116. Letters dated February 3, 1830, and March 2, 1830, CCMHS, ms. 251.3.
117. *Isr*, July 20, 1855.
118. Since then a Jew, Philip H. Goodman, a native of Poland, was mayor of the city in 1962 and 1963, and at the time of this

writing (1970) another Jew, Marvin Mandel, is serving as governor of the state of Maryland.

119. Rosenswaike, "The Jewish Population of the U. S.," 150.

120. Ibid., p. 32.

121. In connection with Rosenswaike's important studies on the Jews in the country on the basis of the censuses of 1790 and of 1820, note the article by Malcolm H. Stern, "Some Additions and Corrections," *AJHQ*, LII (1964), 285–288, and Rosenswaike's "Comments on Dr. Stern's Additions and Corrections," ibid., pp. 289–292.

122. U. S. Census, 1790.

123. Ibid., 1820, gives the population of New York as 123,706, Philadelphia, 63,802, and Baltimore, 62,738. In the next few years Baltimore earned two "firsts." In 1816 it became the first city in the country to be lit by gas (and, incidentally, the Cohen home was the first private home to use the new method of lighting). A few years later, in 1827, the Baltimore and Ohio Railroad was organized. As has already been mentioned, two of its directors were Solomon Etting and Jacob Cohen.

124. *BCD*, 1817.

125. Rosenswaike, "An Estimate," 40. The names listed in the census and the number of members in the families are:

Jacobs Moses, family of seven
Levy Benjamin, family of three
Myers Jacob, family of nine
Solomon Elkin, family of four
Solomon Isaac, family of seven

Rosenswaike overlooked Bernard Jacob, a family of three; see Stern, "Some Additions," p. 288.

126. Rosenswaike, "An Estimate," pp. 25, 36.

127. Malcolm H. Stern, "Two Jewish Functionaries in Colonial Pennsylvania," *AJHQ*, LVII (1967), 29–35. Another strange oversight, on the part of the census enumerators, was the omission of the name of Shinah Etting, who had lived in the city since 1780. Blum, *Jews of Baltimore*, p. 3, quoting Shinah Etting's grandson, not further identified.

128. Wolf and Whiteman, *Jews of Philadelphia*, p. 413, n. 10.

129. Deed Book D, 228–232, MHR.

130. Stern, "Two Jewish Functionaries," pp. 35–48.

131. This idea was suggested to the writer by Malcolm H. Stern. Russell had ten children, five of these were born in Baltimore, *AOJD*, p. 184.
132. *BCD* (1810), p. 86.
133. Wolf and Whiteman, *Jews of Philadelphia*, p. 275.
134. Elias Polack file in AJAR. Elias's wife, Polly, died in February 1806 at the age of 41. In the *Memoirs of the Dead* . . . she is listed as "J" (Jewish).
135. Rosenswaike, "Jewish Population of the U. S.," 162–163.
136. Ibid., p. 162.
137. Blum, *Jews of Baltimore*, p. 9.
138. *JE*, II, 479. "H.S." (Henrietta Szold) wrote about the *minyan* "according to the recollection of one participant still living."
139. *Occ*, VII (1849), 226.
140. Ezekiel and Lichtenstein, *Jews of Richmond*, pp. 37–40.
141. Blau and Baron, in *Jews of the U. S.*, give two different dates for Rhine's arrival in Baltimore According to I, 298, n. 124, he came in 1828 or 1829, but in III, 987, n. 212, the date of his coming to Baltimore is given as 1812.
142. Adolf Guttmacher, *A History of the Baltimore Hebrew Congregation* נדחי ישראל *1830–1905* (Baltimore, 1905), p. 20.
143. Ibid., p. 17.
144. Charter, Baltimore Hebrew Congregation. Guttmacher is in error in giving the date as February 19.

THE FORMATIVE YEARS: 1830–1855

1. Blum, *Jews of Baltimore*, p. 255.
2. In transliteration, the Hebrew name of the congregation became Nitgy Israel, instead of Nidhei Israel. See *Constitution and By-Laws of the Hebrew Congregation Nitgy Israel of Baltimore, 5590* (Baltimore, 1930). This constitution served as a model for the Buffalo congregation, Beth El, organized in 1847. Selig Adler and Thomas E. Connolly, *From Ararat to Suburbia* (Philadelphia, 1960), p. 59.
3. In the preface to Guttmacher's history of the congregation, *Baltimore Hebrew Congregation*, (Chapter I, n. 146), he notes that "the congregational records for the first decade (1829–39) are very fragmentary." At present records before October 21,

1851, are nonexistent. After that date the Minute Books are in excellent condition.

Guttmacher's volume, inadequate as it is, remains the primary source for the period 1830–1851.

4. Ibid., pp. 28–29.
5. *BCD*, 1830, 1835, 1837.
6. Guttmacher, *Baltimore Hebrew Congregation*, pp. 20–21.
7. Ibid., 29–31; see also "Trail Blazers of the Trans-Mississippi-West," *AJA*, VIII (1956), 71–72.
8. Guttmacher, *Baltimore Hebrew Congregation*, p. 31.
9. They included Joseph Osterman, S. Eytinge, S. Hunt, and Joseph Simpson, who had been members of Mikveh Israel in Philadelphia before they came to Baltimore.
10. Alexandra Lee Levin, *Vision: A Biography of Harry Friedenwald* (Philadelphia, 1964), passim.
11. Guttmacher, *Baltimore Hebrew Congregation*, pp. 26, 27. This was a copper cent of U. S. coinage, also called "fip" or "levy" or "fippenny bit," valued at half a shilling.
12. *Occ*, X (1847), 468.
13. MBBHC, April 12, 1852; June 6, 1862, and passim.
14. Ibid., October 7, 1852.
15. Ibid., April 1, 1852.
16. Ibid., September 17, 1854.
17. Ibid., December 4, 1853.

"Shew" for chew, "suit" for sue, and similar errors in spelling the most common English words should not be surprising. These Jews were newcomers, and English was a foreign tongue. In addition, most of the Bavarian immigrants were people without any education, and it was often difficult for them to learn a new language. Their German, too, was rather poor, and when writing the Hebrew names of months, holidays, or ceremonial objects, they spelled phonetically. On the very limited knowledge of Hebrew by early Jewish immigrants, see M. Arthur Oles, "The Henry Joseph Collection of the Gratz Family Papers at the American Jewish Archives" in *Essays in American Jewish History* (Cincinnati, 1958), pp. 99–122.

18. MBBHC, May 2, 1869.
19. Ibid., July 14, 1861.
20. Ibid., July 4, 1852.
21. MBHSC, June 15, 1874.
22. MBBHC, January 28, February 4, 1855. Jonas Friedenwald

left a legacy of five thousand dollars as a perpetual Matzah Fund.

23. Ibid., October 21, 1851; February 14, 1852, and passim.
24. Ibid., October 21, 1851; October 6, 1853, and passim.
25. Ibid., December 11, 1851.
26. Guttmacher, *Baltimore Hebrew Congregation*, p. 24.
27. MBBHC, August 20, 1853; also *Occ*, XI (1853), 423.
28. Copy in JHSM.
29. Salo W. and Jeannette M. Baron, "Palestinian Messengers in America, 1849–1879," *Jewish Social Studies*, V (1943), 127.
30. MBBHC, March 3, 1861.
31. *Occ*, XXI (1854), 264; XI, (1853), 279, and passim.
32. MBBHC, February 18, 1855.
33. Ibid., October 5, 1862.
34. M. Jastrow at a public meeting of the Jewish Ministers' Association in Baltimore, October 26, 1885, as reported in *J Mess*, October 30, 1885.
35. Rayner, *Address*, p. 5.
36. Ibid., p. 4.
37. *Occ*, X (1852), 362.
38. Ibid., III (1845), 365.
39. Guttmacher, *Baltimore Hebrew Congregation*, p. 37; Rayner, *Address*, p. 6.
40. MBBHC, March 6, 1853.
41. Ibid., September 7, 1854.
42. Ibid., December 4, 1853; July 13, 1856.
43. *Occ*, V (1855), 452.
44. Rayner, *Address*, p. 6.
45. An attempt to organize "The Reformed Society of the Israelites" in 1824 in Charleston, South Carolina, had failed. It ceased to exist in 1833. See Charles Resnikoff and Uriah Z. Engelman. *The Jews of Charleston* (Philadelphia, 1950), 123–134.
46. *Occ*, VI (1849), 178.
47. RC.
48. August 24, 1851, LCDC.
49. *Sun*, February 25, 1845; *Occ*, III (1845), 97.
50. Rice to Leeser, August 1848, LCDC.
51. MBBHC, June 3, 1855.
52. May 15, 1849, LCDC.
53. *Occ*, VII (1849), 223.

54. The last missionary house closed only in 1966.
55. Spring, 1862, RC.
56. Letter from Hazan Leucht, husband of Rice's adopted daughter, to Dr. Harry Friedenwald, January 16, 1904, RC.
57. Harry Friedenwald, *Life, Letters, and Addresses of Aaron Friedenwald, M.D.* (Baltimore, 1906), p. 23. Similarly, Henrietta Szold, *JE*, II, 479.
58. *Occ*, XX (1862), 432.
59. Correspondence from Baltimore in *AZJ*, June 14, 1850.
60. Shearith Israel, Trustee Minutes, V (28 November, 1841), 231.
61. Guttmacher, *Baltimore Hebrew Congregation*, p. 23. An erroneous report stated that this contribution was $1,700, *Sun*, June 27, 1905.
62. *Occ*, IV (1846), 359.
63. Ibid., III (1845), 362.
64. William Harvey Hunter, Jr. (director of Peale Museum in Baltimore), *The Lloyd Street Synagogue* (mimeographed, Baltimore, 1963).
65. The two synagogues built before this one which are still standing are the Touro Synagogue in Newport, Rhode Island, completed in 1763, and Beth Elohim in Charleston, South Carolina, built in 1841, which replaced an earlier one destroyed by fire in 1840.
66. For a most detailed report on the consecration of the synagogue, see, *Occ*, III (1845), 361–367. This description and a few photographs served as the basis on which the synagogue was restored in 1964 by the Jewish Historical Society of Maryland. On April 15, 1965, the city authorities affixed a plaque on a wall of the building reading:

HISTORIC BALTIMORE
LLOYD STREET SYNAGOGUE
FIRST SYNAGOGUE ERECTED IN MARYLAND
DEDICATED SEPTEMBER 26, 1845
RESTORED BY JEWISH HISTORICAL SOCIETY
AS A HISTORIC SHRINE, NOV. 8, 1964
AWARDED BY THE CITY OF BALTIMORE
PLAQUE PRESENTED ON APRIL 15, 1965
THEODORE R. MCKELDIN, MAYOR

67. *Occ*, III (1845), 367.
68. May, 1851, LCDC.

69. *Occ*, IV (1847), 564.
70. MBBHC, January 1, 1854. The date of the meeting also tells a tale. Those were the days when meetings could still be held on New Year's Day.
71. There are two conflicting dates given for the founding of this congregation. According to Blum, *Jews of Baltimore*, p. 9, the congregation was founded in 1838. Benjamin Friedman, "Synopsis of the History of the Baltimore Fell's Point Hebrew Friendship Congregation," JHSM, gives 1843 as the date of its founding.
72. *Acts of Maryland*, 1846, Chapter 53; passed, February 12, 1847. Phillip Emerich, Jacob Gasan, Phillip Herzberg, Mark Pollock, Julius Kahn, and Charles Strasburger were the incorporators.
73. Friedman. The "Synopsis" is in the main a history of the cemetery rather than of the congregation. While the synagogue functioned only until 1902, the cemetery, one of the largest in the city, is still a going concern. It is managed by a nonprofit stock company and is not affiliated with any synagogue.
74. *Occ*, VII (1849), 444–453, 475.
75. Rayner, *Address*, p. 7.
76. N. Taylor Phillips, "Items Relating to the History of the Jews of New York," *PAJHS*, XI (1903), 158–159.
77. Ibid., 160.
78. *Isr*, February 27, 1857.
79. MBHSC, August 3, 1845.
80. *The American and Commercial Daily Advertiser*, September 8, 1849.
81. Joshua Bloch, "Isidor Rayner (1850–1912)," *PAJHS*, XL (1951), 288–295.
82. MBHSC, August 4, 1844. The pages of the Minute Book of the Har Sinai Congregation between September 10, 1846, and May 30, 1873, are missing.
83. *Sun*, October 30, 1853.
84. Blum, *Jews of Baltimore*, p. 195.
85. The organizational meeting was attended by Moses Oettinger, Julius Stiefel, Emanuel Hess, L. Einstein, Louis Dreshfield, Nisan Frank, S. Herman, Solomon Oettinger, Seligman Bernei, Simon Bass, Simon Ramer, Jacob Strauss, Simon Cohen, M. Einstein, Herman Sachs, Moses Pollack, Mendel Steibel, M. H. Weil, Daniel Katz, Phillip Herzberg, and Samuel Katz.

This was the only meeting of the new congregation that Herzberg attended. For some unknown reason he did not join it, but became very active in the Lloyd Street Synagogue. His name does not appear in the Minute Books of Oheb Shalom, but does appear in those of the Baltimore Hebrew Congregation.

86. MBOSC, November 20, 1853.
87. *Sun*, November 27, 1853.
88. Louis F. Cahn, *History of Oheb Shalom, 1853–1953* (Baltimore, 1953), p. 21.
89. MBOSC, November 30, 1853.
90. Ibid., March 12, 1854.
91. Ibid., September 21, 1854.
92. MBHSC, June 11, 1843.
93. Rayner, *Address*, pp. 12–13.
94. Guttmacher, *Baltimore Hebrew Congregation*, p. 67.
95. MBBHC, October 25, 1856.
96. Ibid., March 28, 1852.
97. Original in JHSM.
98. MBBHC, August 15, 1852.
99. Ibid., August 26, 1845.
100. *Occ*, XI (1853), 186–187.
101. Ibid., III (1845), 363.
102. Ibid., X, (1852), 171.
103. MBHSC, August 26, 1845.
104. Ibid., April 5, 1846.
105. In 1855 there were between twenty and thirty Jewish orphan children in Baltimore. *Isr*, July 27, 1855.
106. *Sinai*, II (1857), 662; III (1858), 887–888.
107. Bernard Steiner, *History of Education in Maryland* (Baltimore, 1894), pp. 53–68.
108. *Laws of Maryland*, XII, Chapter 13e. An oral tradition speaks of an earlier organization called *Irische Chevra*. Blum, *Jews of Baltimore*, pp. 7–8.
109. *Sinai*, I (1855), 386.
110. D.P., "Jacob Ezekiel," *PAJHS*, IX (1901), 160–163. See 1734 in AJAR.
111. The booklet, which covers the period from January 4, 1834, to January 13, 1835, was given to the JHSM by Collmus's descendants, none of them any longer Jewish. The booklet was written in a Germanized Yiddish.
112. *Laws of Maryland*, Chapter 86, Act of 1838.

113. *Acts of Maryland,* 1840, Chapter 139.
114. *Occ,* VI (1848), 510.
115. Original charter in JHSM.
116. *Baltimore American,* February 21, 1856.
117. Scharf, *Chronicles of Baltimore,* p. 516.
118. Kohler, "Incidents," 95–96. Dr. Phineas J. Horwitz's war record is to be found in Record Group 52: *Records of the Bureau of Medicine and Surgery, U.S. Navy,* National Archives, I, 412; II, 32; see also, *Dictionary of American Medical Biography,* ed. H. A. Kelley (Philadelphia, 1923), p. 599.
119. M. Vaxer, "The First Hebrew Bible Printed in America," *Journal of Jewish Bibliography,* II (1940), 20–26.
120. U. S. Census, 1850.
121. *AZJ,* June 14, 1850.
122. *Occ,* XVII (1859), 29; similarly, [I. J.] Benjamin, *Three Years in America* (Philadelphia, 1956), II, 305.
123. Henninghausen, *German Society,* p. 106.
124. Isaac M. Wise, *Reminiscences,* David Philipson, ed. (Cincinnati, 1901), p. 182.
125. *Occ,* VIII (1851), 576.

YEARS OF DISSENSION AND EXPANSION: 1855–1880

1. U. S. Census, 1880.
2. *Isr,* November 16, 1855.
3. Estimate of Union of American Hebrew Congregations, cited by David Sulzberger, "Growth of the Jewish Population in the United States," *PAJHS,* VI (1897), 144.
4. *Manufacturers' Record, A Weekly Southern Industrial and Financial Newspaper* (Baltimore, 1882), Supplement, 2.
5. The biographical data presented here are based on Einhorn's biography written by his son-in-law Kaufmann Kohler in Kaufmann Kohler (ed.), *David Einhorn Memorial Volume* (New York, 1911), pp. 403–455.
6. In the original, *Das Prinzip des Mosaismus und dessen Verhältniss zum Heidenthum und rabbinischen Judenthum* (Leipzig, 1854).
7. The sermon was translated by one of Einhorn's most devoted followers, Dr. Abraham B. Arnold (Baltimore, 1855). It sold for 12½ cents. *Sinai,* II (1857), 470. Full text of sermon,

Sinai, II (1857), Appendix I, 1–14. (German); Appendix II, 1–15 (English).

8. *Occ*, III (1845), 470.
9. *Occ*, II (1845), 599–600.
10. On various attempts to create union among American Jews, see Joseph Buchler, "The Struggle for Unity," *AJA*, II (1949), 21–46.
11. *Isr*, October 26, 1855.
12. *Sinai*, I (1856), 27–29.
13. *Sinai*, VII (1862), 312.
14. *Occ*, XIII (1855), 450–453.
15. *Occ*, XIII (1856), 549–552.
16. Bertram Wallace Korn, *Eventful Years and Experiences* (Cincinnati, 1954), pp. 57–58.
17. *Sinai*, I (1856), 259.
18. Ibid., 354–355.
19. Ibid.
20. The biographical sketch of Benjamin Szold in Europe is based on Alexandra Lee Levin's *The Szolds of Lombard Street* (Philadelphia, 1960) and a wealth of manuscript material located at JHSM.
21. Boruch Szold's will is to be found in the JHSM.
22. Among the recommendations was also one from the leader of the ultra-Orthodox Rabbi Gedalya Tiktin. In his letter this rabbi praised young Szold, who, he wrote, promised him faithfully that he "would not make any changes in laws established by the sages of Israel nor deviate from the established norms even the breadth of a hair." This recommendation was never shown by Szold to any congregation. It is to be found together with the others in the BSA.
23. Kurt Wilhelm, "Benjamin Szold and the Rabbinic Post in Stockholm," *Historia Judaica*, XV (1953), 49–58.
24. MBOSC, February 6, 1858.
25. Original letter in JHSM.
26. Moshe Davis, *Yahadut Amerika Be-Hitpathutah (The Shaping of American Judaism)* (New York, 1951), p. 46.
27. *Inaugural Sermon*, Benjamin Szold (1859), translated by Sophie and Henrietta Szold, 1909. Copy in JHSM.
28. *Sinai*, IV (1859), 321–339.
29. This type of language was characteristic of the age. Wise and Rice, for example, did not stop hurling much invective at each

other. Wise wrote: "Mr. Reis [Rice] and others . . . consider themselves learned, while actually they know very little. Rice is very little known outside Baltimore and in Baltimore, too well known to be regarded." *Isr*, September 10, 1858. And Rice wrote: "About Mr. Wise, may his name be obliterated [שמו ימח]. We know no more dangerous man than he for our religion. He is a bad man and a great heretic." Rice to Leeser, April 24, 1861, LCDC.

30. Copy in JHSM.
31. *Sinai*, V (1860), Supplement, 1–28.
32. For a detailed study of the subject, see Isaac M. Fein, "Baltimore Jews during the Civil War," *AJHQ*, LI (1961), 67–96.
33. *Isr*, August 17, 1860.
34. *Deutsche Correspondent*, May 13, 1861.
35. *Der Wecker*, June 18, 1861.
36. *Isr*, January 15, 1864.
37. Korn, *Eventful Years*, p. 190, nn. 69, 70.
38. Ibid., p. 275, n. 23.
39. MBOSC, October 1, 1861; MBBHC, October 11, 1864.
40. MBBHC, April 6, 1862.
41. MBOSC, March, 1861; MBBHC, June 29, 1861.
42. Letter dated 1862, RC.
43. Full text of sermon in *Occ*, XVIII (1861), 267–268.
44. Benjamin Szold, "Peace and Concord," *Isr*, January 11, 1861.
45. In Emanuel Herz, *Abraham Lincoln: The Tribute of the Synagogue* (New York, 1927), pp. 39–47.
46. Levin, *The Szolds*, p. 49; Fein, "Baltimore Jews," pp. 74–75.
47. Benjamin Szold, "Passover Sermon," *The Jewish Chronicle*, April 6, 1877.
48. *Occ*, XVIII (1859), 444–453; XVIII (1861), 236.
49. *Sinai*, I (1856), 259.
50. Ibid., VII (1867), 187.
51. Ibid., VI (1861), 2–20; VI (1861), 45–50, 60–61; VI (1861), 99–100.
52. This discourse, "The Bible View of Slavery," was delivered at the B'nai Jeshurun Synagogue in New York on the occasion of the National Fast Day, January 4, 1861.
53. *Sinai*, VI (1861), 30. As if describing today's Judaism, he went on: "There are enough synagogues and temples, but there is very little religion, little morality . . . here [among the Jews]. Everything is empty, everything is glimmer. . . . Here, too, all

feelings of the heart and dreams are concentrated only on acquiring [things]. There is only one thought: to make as much as possible."

54. Ibid., 95.
55. Bertram Wallace Korn, *American Jewry and the Civil War* (Philadelphia, 1951), p. 18.
56. Max J. Kohler, "The Jews and the American Anti-Slavery Movement," *PAJHS*, V (1897), 151.
57. *Sinai*, VI (1861), 367.
58. *Sinai*, VII (1862), 185.
59. *Sinai*, VI (1861), 32.
60. Kohler, *David Einhorn*, p. 120.
61. Korn, *American Jewry*, p. 152.
62. *Sun*, April 6, 1861.
63. *Sinai*, VI (1861), 135–142.
64. Ibid., VII (1862), 392. Einhorn served as rabbi of Knesseth Israel in Philadelphia from 1861 until 1866, and from August 1866 until 1879 he was rabbi of Adath Jeshurun Congregation in New York. The title of his last sermon delivered on July 12, 1879, was עברי אנכי (I am a Hebrew). A few months later, at the conclusion of the Yom Kippur services, Einhorn died.
65. Einhorn-Oppenheimer correspondence in AJHS. Oppenheimer, like his rabbi, favored open discussion on political as well as religious questions. He published a protest against a resolution of the Richmond Young Men's Literary Association that "political and religious questions of any kind are out of order." *Sinai*, I (1856), 69.
66. H. Spitz in Marcus, *Memoirs of American Jews, 1775–1865* (Philadelphia, 1955), I, 299.
67. Bertha Friedenwald (wife of Dr. Aaron Friedenwald, one of Jonas's sons), *Memoirs*. The original manuscript of this important document covering the period 1862–1895 is located at the JHSM.
68. Ibid.
69. Letter from Berlin, February 1861, FA.
70. Ibid., date and place illegible, April or May 1861.
71. Bertha Friedenwald, *Memoirs*.
72. Ibid.
73. Mrs. Joseph Wiesenfeld, memorandum, AJAR, March 7, 1861; Fein, "Baltimore Jews," pp. 90–91.

74. *Proceedings and Speeches at a Public Meeting of the Friends of the Union* (Baltimore, 1861), p. 1.
75. Many important original documents pertaining to this case are located in the JHSM.
76. Wolf, *The American Jew*, pp. 199–200, 412, lists for all of Maryland eleven Jews in the Union army.
77. *History and Roster of Maryland Volunteers* . . . (Baltimore, 1892), I, 179, 181. Many documents and an oil painting of Blumenberg were presented to the JHSM by his descendants, none of them Jewish.
78. *Sun*, September 7, 1861.
79. Marcus, *Memoirs*, III, 324.
80. *Sun*, August 9, 1861.
81. H. Spitz in Marcus, *Memoirs*, I, 300.
82. *Sun*, August 21, 1861.
83. Simeon Hecht (1824–1872), "Memoirs" (typed ms.), 41–42. Original with Hecht family, copy at JHSM.
84. *AZJ*, 1865, p. 940.
85. MBBHC, June 2, 1861.
86. Ibid., August 10, 1865.
87. Jacob Hollander, *The Financial History of Baltimore* (Baltimore, 1899), p. 201.
88. *Occ*, XVI (1858), 139, 146.
89. *Isr*, July 27, November 16, 1855.
90. *Occ*, XIV (1856), 357.
91. *Sinai*, II (1857), 663.
92. Ibid., 664.
93. Ibid., II (1857), 698.
94. *Isr*, November 13, 1857.
95. Sol M. Strook, "Switzerland and American Jews," *PAJHS*, XI (1903), 7–52.
96. Bertram Wallace Korn, *The American Reaction to the Mortara Case: 1858–1859* (Cincinnati, 1957).
97. *Sinai*, III (1859), 1170.
98. *Sun*, January 6, 1859. The signatories were Rabbis A. Günzburg, H. Hochheimer and D. Einhorn. The others were Mendes Cohen, Abraham B. Arnold, S. N. Carvalho, S. Stein, L. G. Putzel, B. A. Franklin, William S. Rayner, S. Hess, G. Rosenstock, Joseph Sachs, and A. Nachman.
99. On Buchanan's political considerations, see Korn, *Mortara Case*, pp. 79–93.

100. *Sun*, January 26, 1859; similarly, *Baltimore American*, November 16, 1858.
101. *Sinai*, I (1856), 354.
102. Ibid., IV (1859), 2.
103. Ibid., IV (1859), 1147.
104. Levin, *The Szolds*, p. 52.
105. *Occ*, XVI (1858), 346–347.
106. Solomon R. Kagan, *Jewish Contributions to Medicine in America* . . . (Boston, 1939), pp. 27, 517, n. 58.
107. *Sun*, January 20, 1845.
108. Ibid., January 27, 1845.
109. Letter Dated October 1, 1894. Friedenwald Microfilms in the JHSM.
110. Kagan, *Jewish Contributions*, pp. 29–30.
111. Letter dated January 15, 1877. Microfilm, JHSM.
112. *Isr*, January 15, 1864.
113. *Sinai*, I (1856), 406.
114. *Occ*, XIV (1856), 406.
115. *Occ*, XVI (1858), 360; Shearith Israel Trustee Minutes, vol. 6, p. 328.
116. *Occ*, XVII (1859), 108. For details about the congregation, see Hartogensis, "Sephardic Congregation," pp. 141–146; *Sun*, September 17, 1857.
117. Resnikoff and Engelman, *Jews of Charleston*, p. 132.
118. *Occ*, XVII (1859), 2A.
119. The volume, with an excellent introduction and biographical data of the Carvalho family by Bertram Wallace Korn, was republished under the original title by The Jewish Publication Society of America (Philadelphia, 1954).
120. Carvalho's letters to Leeser are located in the LCDC.
121. "An Inventory of Portraits and Paintings by Solomon Nunes Carvalho," in Carvalho, *Travel and Adventure*, pp. 327, 328.
122. *Occ*, XVIII (1860), 180.
123. Samples of this work were published in *The Occident*, XIII (1856), 252–257, and XVIII (1860), 288. Scholarship and versatility seem to have run in the family. Toward the end of the nineteenth century Solomon's son, David, a handwriting expert, was the first authority to establish that important documents in the Dreyfus case were forgeries. Korn, in Carvalho's *Travel and Adventure*, p. 50.
124. *Isr*, January 15, 1864.

125. Blum, *Jews of Baltimore*, p. 62; author's interview with Mendel Feldman, rabbi of Shearith Israel.
126. Letter from Rabbi Henry W. Schneeberger to the Chizuk Amuno Congregation dated July 3, 1887, in the archives of the congregation.
127. MBCAC, November 6, 1881.
128. Ibid., July 3, 1892.
129. Ibid., October 7, 1896.
130. *The Jewish Chronicle*, January 8, 1875.
131. MBBHC, February 26, 1856.
132. MBHSC, May 21, 1876.
133. Ibid., June 1, 1876.
134. *Jewish Times* clipping, not dated, BSA.
135. MBHSC, July 17, 1878.
136. Letter of September 5, 1876. This letter and a wealth of original correspondence about the Mayer affair between Szold, Hochheimer, and many people in the United States and abroad is to be found in the JHSM.
137. *Occ*, XIV (1856), No. 1, 2A, and passim.
138. Guttmacher, *Baltimore Hebrew Congregation*, p. 71.
139. MBOSC, October 8, 1854.
140. *AZJ*, August 14, 1896, app. 4.
141. MBBHC, April 9, 1855; May 20, 1865.
142. Ibid., May 25, 1854.
143. *Sinai*, I (1856), 257.
144. Kohler, *David Einhorn*, p. 417.
145. *Sinai*, III (1858), 824.
146. Kohler, *David Einhorn*, p. 453.
147. *Sinai*, IV (1859), 29.
148. Part of the elaborate Ninth of Av service in Einhorn's prayer book, *Olat Tamid* (Baltimore, 1856), p. 396, as translated in Davis, *Yahadut Amerika*, p. 309.
149. MBHSC, October 1, 1874.
150. MBBHC, August 6, 1845.
151. Ibid., April 1, 1860.
152. Transcripts of both the application for an injunction and the injunction itself in JHSM.
153. MBBHC, March 27, 1857.
154. *Occ*, XVII (September 8, 1859).
155. Ibid., (1860), 209.
156. MBBHC, May 12, 1861.

157. Ibid., June 9, 1861.
158. Constitution of October 8, 1861.
159. MBBHC, October 5, 1862.
160. Ibid.
161. *Isr*, August 17, 1860.
162. MBBHC, June 1, 1865.
163. There is no record of the *rabbiner's* reply. The pages from December 2, 1861, to January 3, 1861, were torn from the Minute Book.
164. MBHHC, January 2, 1870.
165. Ibid., July 10, 1870.
166. The following appealed for the injunction: Jonas Friedenwald, his two sons—Joseph and Moses, Louis Goodman, Isaac Arnold, H. Hable, B. Stern, S. Grinsfelder, H. Blondheim, S. Halle, A. Rothschild, A. Neuberger, N. Greenbaum, H. Oppenheimer, L. Heilner, L. Engel, P. Herzberg, H. L. Heusler, S. Harman, and A. Rosenfeld. The defendants were the officers of the congregation and the Board of Managers: Bernard Himmelreich, president; Joel Seliger, vice-president; Joseph Schenthal, treasurer; Levi Bar, Jacob Rice, Moses Rosenthal, Moses Keyser, J. Greenbaum, Henry Nussbaum, trustees.
167. MBBHC, September 10, 1873.
168. Ibid., October 9, 1873.
169. Ibid., February 2, 1879.
170. *Occ*, XVI (1858), 356.
171. MBOSC, August 1, 1858.
172. Ibid., August 3, 1858.
173. Letter dated November 12, 1859, published in *Isr*, VI, No. 21, 165.
174. MBOSC, October 20, 1867.
175. Ibid., August 15, 1869.
176. MBCAC, April 2, 1871.
177. Ibid., July 17, 1876.
178. MBBHC, November 10, 1876. Friedenwald must have been afraid of *shaatnez*.
179. MBCAC, November 5, 1876.
180. *Sun*, August 19, 1876, a detailed report of the dedication.
181. In 1947 it officially became a Conservative congregation.
182. The presidents of Chizuk Amuno were Judah Rosenwald (1871 to 1879), Jonas Friedenwald (1879 to 1892), his son Dr. Aaron Friedenwald (1892 until his death in 1902), Michael

S. Levy (1902 to 1911) and Jonas Friedenwald's grandson Dr. Harry Friedenwald (1911 to 1920).

183. Israel M. Goldman, "Henry W. Schneeberger: His Role in American Jewry," *AJHQ*, LVII (December 1967), 153.

184. Benjamin, *Three Years*, p. 305.

185. *Occ*, XVIII (1859), 198.

186. MBBHC, August 16, 1857.

187. *Isr*, June 27, 1857.

188. Kohler, *David Einhorn*, pp. 427–428.

189. Einhorn's prayer book served as the basis for the *Union Prayer Book of the American Reform Congregations*. See *YBCCAR*, XVIII (1908), 137 f.

190. *Occ*, XVII (1858), 359.

191. For an excellent comparison of all the prayer books used in those days, see Davis, *Yahadut Amerika*, pp. 307–312, 315–317.

192. Benjamin Szold, *Abodath Israel* (Baltimore, 1873), p. 589, as translated in Davis, *Yahadut Amerika*, p. 309.

193. *Isr*, August 17, 1860.

194. MBBHC, March 26, 1860.

195. Many of these are to be found in the JHSM.

196. MBBHC, July 26, 1868.

197. MBHSC, September 14, 1873.

198. MBCAC, October 21, 1878.

199. MBBHC, November 1879.

200. MBCAC, June 23, 1878.

201. *Isr*, March 3, 1857.

202. *Sinai*, II (1857), 433, 437–446.

203. *Isr*, March 3, 1857. See also Hartogensis, "Sephardic Congregation," pp. 145–146.

204. *Occ*, XIV (1857), 497–498.

205. *Sinai*, II (1857), 442–443.

206. Ibid., 433.

207. *Occ*, XVII (1859), 119.

208. *Sun*, April 15, 1867.

209. Minute Book, Hebrew Religious School, (at JHSM), March 14, 1869.

210. Ibid., November 25, 1868.

211. Ibid., January 26, 1868.

212. MBOSC, May 4, 1874.

213. Ibid., April 2, 1871.

214. MBHSC, February 1, 1877, August 20, 1878, and passim.

215. Ibid., January 28, 1877.
216. MBCAC, March 30, 1878.
217. A full list of Jewish students who attended Loyola College is to be found in the JHSM.
218. Levin, *Vision*, p. 37.
219. *Report, Baltimore School Commissioners*, VIII (Baltimore, 1873) and XXV, (Baltimore, 1893).
220. H. L. Mencken, *Happy Days* (New York, 1955), pp. 23–25.
221. *Isr*, August 17, 1860.
222. Charter of the Hebrew Benevolent Society, E. D. No. 3, folio 30 VC. Original charter in JHSM. The sixteen "managers" whose signatures appear on the charter were William S. Rayner, president; Dr. Joshua I. Cohen, vice-president; Samuel Dellevie, treasurer; A. Matger, secretary, and Jonas Friedenwald, Magnus Polack, Isaac Hamburger, Henry Lauer, Emanuel Hess, Ignatius Lauer, John Rosenhaupt, Phillip Herzberg, Charles Weiller, E. Freidenrich, S. Hartman, Joseph Obendorf. The Hebrew name of the Society was חברה שוחרי תושיע
223. *Sinai*, I (1857), 384–385.
224. *Occ*, XIX (1861), 38–39; Blum, *Jews of Baltimore*, p. 133. The Friedenwalds were always active in charitable affairs. The last surviving member of the family, Mrs. Julia Friedenwald Potts, daughter of Dr. Harry Friedenwald, was most active in bringing over refugees from Germany. See Samuel L. Frank, "German Refugees and Their Adjustment in Baltimore," typescript, 1942, in JHSM.
225. *Isr*, January 13, 1860.
226. *Occ*, XXI (1864), 566–567.
227. *Laying of the cornerstone of the Baltimore Asylum for Israelites, Beth Machase Umisthor* (Baltimore, 1867), pp. 5–7.
228. Eugene L. Leopold (chairman of the Medical Board of Sinai Hospital), *History of Sinai Hospital*. The original name, Hebrew Hospital and Asylum (בית מחסה ומסתור) was changed on July 26, 1926, to its present one, Sinai Hospital.
229. The other officers were B. F. Ulman, Levi Straus, and Ignatius Lauer.
230. Leopold, *Sinai Hospital*.
231. *RFJC* (1913), 42; similarly in other reports of the Federated Jewish Charities.
232. Blum, *Jews of Baltimore*, p. 19; The Hebrew Free Burial So-

ciety is still in existence, but, as in many other cases, its name does not necessarily describe its activities. In addition to free burials, of which there have been about thirty in the last few years, it also provides poor people with artificial limbs and eyeglasses.

233. In 1876 Rabbi Hofmann left for Richmond, where he became rabbi at Beth Abraham Congregation. A collection of his sermons was presented to the Jewish Historical Society of Maryland by his grandson Hugo Dalsheimer, a founder and the first president of the society.

234. *Am Heb*, October 30, 1885. Records of the society are located in the JHSM. It is worth noting that these records are presently accepted as valid documentation in establishing the date of birth of individuals who do not have birth certificates. This is a problem not only for immigrants who arrived in this country a long time ago, but also for native Baltimoreans—mandatory registration of births in Baltimore went into effect only in 1875 but for a long time was not strictly observed.

235. *Occ*, XVIII (1861), 43; *JC*, December 24, 1897.

236. *J Mess*, March 18, 1876.

237. Goody Rosenfeld (1837–1924) was born in England and brought by his parents to Baltimore as an infant. He became a clerk and then a junior partner in Wiesenfeld's clothing enterprise. He, too, was arrested during the Civil War on suspicion of doing business with the South. He was, however, released soon after his detention. The information about him was given by his son, Moses W. Rosenfeld. Blum, *Jews of Baltimore*, p. 121. Reports of the Purim Association are to be found in the JHSM.

238. It is strange to read that non-Jewish Germans took credit for the charity work done by the Jews for the Jews. There were reports that the Jewish Orphan House was "established by the Germans in the city" and that "the Jewish Hospital of East Baltimore is another evidence of *German* [italics in text] humanity."

It took a long time for Jews, who either themselves came from Germany or whose progenitors did, to begin thinking of themselves as just Jews and not as German Jews. It took equally long for Baltimore non-Jews to stop thinking of Jews as Germans. The process of psychological dissociation with Little Germany was a long and painful one, but as the years passed the separation became complete. *Eighth Annual Report of the Society for the History of the Germans in Maryland* (Baltimore, 1895).

239. *Isr*, March 14, 1856.
240. Edward E. Crusd, *B'nai B'rith* (New York, 1966), pp. 30, 31.
241. *The Jewish Chronicle*, May 25, 1875; *Occ*, XXII (1866), 742; XXIV (1866), 183, and passim.
242. Constitution and Bylaws of Beacon Light Literary and Pleasure Association are to be found in the JHSM.
243. *Sun*, April 4, 1878.
244. The call was issued under the signature of E. Goldman, chairman, and M. B. Blumenthal, corresponding secretary. *Occ*, XXII (1864), 444.
245. *Isr*, January 15, 1864; *Occ*, XXII (1864), 523; *Isr*, May 20, 1864. For details on the project, see letters from one of the prime movers, Leon Dalsheimer, to Rabbi William Rosenau, dated May 25, 1901. Copies in the JHSM.
246. Preamble to the constitution of the YMLA, in the JHSM.
247. *Isr*, October 26, 1854.
248. Minute Book of the Young Men's Literary Association, February 1 and 8, 1857. These reports are to be found in their entirety in the JHSM.
249. Benjamin Rabinowitz, "The Young Men's Hebrew Association (1854–1913)," *PAJHS*, XXXVII (1947), 226.
250. *Isr*, January 16, 28, 1870.
251. Letter of January 24, 1870, in JHSM.
252. *Isr*, April 25, 1856.
253. Baltimore's Harmony Circle did not have one problem that its namesake in New York had to contend with. The New York group had as its slogan "More polish and less Polish." There were not as yet any East European Jews who aspired to become members of such a club. Hyman B. Grinstein, "The Efforts of East European Jewry to Organize Its Own Community in the United States," *PAJHS*, XLIX (1959), 76.
254. Blum, *Jews of Baltimore*, p. 27.
255. John Higham, "Social Discrimination against Jews in America, 1830–1930," *PAJHS*, XLVII (1957), 13.
256. *Archive Israelite* (1865), 940–944.
257. On this phase of Baltimore's development, see Charles Hirschfeld, *Baltimore, 1870–1900: Studies in Social History* (Baltimore, 1941), pp. 32–83.
258. *Baltimore: The Gateway to the South, the Liverpool of America* (Baltimore, 1898); *Baltimore: the Trade Queen of the South* (Baltimore, 1902); John Randolph Bland, *A Review of the*

Commerce of the City of Baltimore . . . (Baltimore, 1886), pp. 46–83; George W. Howard, *The Monumental City* (Baltimore, n.d.), pp. 106 ff.

259. *Twelfth Census (1910), Statistics of the Population,* VIII, CCXXXVI.

260. M. Wiesenfeld, stock account, in possession of Henry Wiesenfeld, son of Moses's brother, David, copy in the JHSM.

261. Private stock account, M. Wiesenfeld, B. Stein, Joseph Friedenwald, Moses Friedenwald.

262. *Illustrated Baltimore, The Monumental City* (New York, 1890), p. 89; interview with Jacob Edelman, leading labor lawyer in Baltimore, February 13, 1963, himself at one time a worker in the Greif factory. Typescript of the interview at the JHSM.

263. Blum, *Jews of Baltimore,* p. 165; *A History of the City of Baltimore, Its Men and Institutions* (Baltimore, 1902), p. 172.

264. William T. Brigham, *Baltimore Hats, Past and Present* (Baltimore, 1890), pp. 99, 104–105.

265. *Illustrated Baltimore,* p. 86.

266. Louis H. Levine, "David Hutzler," *PAJHS,* XXV (1917), 152–156.

267. Carrie Baumgarten Wallenstein, "Selig Baumgarten," *PAJHS,* XXVI (1918), 248.

268. Memorial of the late Moses Wiesenfeld, containing the services and addresses at his funeral, February 26, 1871, in JHSM.

269. Blum, *Jews of Baltimore,* pp. 133–143.

270. Private stock account, in JHSM. The shares of the other partners were B. Stern, $172,806.82, Moses Friedenwald, $126,-532.75, and Ike Friedenwald, $64,720.33.

271. Joseph Friedenwald file, JHSM.

272. Sermon by Rabbi Szold published in *The Jewish Chronicle* (Baltimore), August 25, 1876.

FROM DISCORD TO UNITY: 1880–1921

1. Benjamin, *Three Years,* I, 305. Benjamin states that the congregation was founded in 1852, but there is no other record of this synagogue.

2. MBBHC, June 18, 1865.

3. Ibid.

4. *Records of Baltimore City*, Liber 17, Folio 475.
5. *AJYB*, I (1899–1900), 146.
6. *Diamond Jubilee Program, B'nai Israel Congregation*, May 23, 1948.
7. Computed on the basis of Aaron Antonovsky, *The Early Jewish Labor Movement in the United States* (New York, 1961), Table 4, p. 352.
8. *AJYB*, I (1899–1900), 152.
9. *Mikro Kodesh, Beth Israel, Calendar, 1963–1964* (Baltimore, 1963).
10. Computed on the basis of information given in *AJYB*, I (1899–1900), 142–155.
11. Samuel Joseph, *Jewish Immigration to the United States from 1881 to 1910* (New York, 1914), Table XXIX, p. 173.
12. *Appendix to the Congressional Record*, 46th Congress, 2nd Session, May 21, 1880, p. 306. Cox explained that "the signatures of this remarkable document are withheld . . . only because their names would be the signal for persecution, exile and death."
13. For details, see Simon S. Dubnow, *History of the Jews in Russia and Poland* (Philadelphia, 1918), II, 243–323.
14. Archives of the Alliance Israélite Universelle, cited by Zosa Szajkowski, "The Attitude of American Jews to East European Immigration (1881–1893)," *PAJHS*, XL (1951), 225.
15. Ibid., 226.
16. Ibid., 232.
17. Ibid.
18. United States Department of Justice, *Our Immigration* (Washington, 1912), p. 15.
19. Ibid.
20. Ibid.
21. Joseph, *Jewish Immigration*, Table XXX, p. 174.
22. Jacob Lestchinsky, *Jewish Migration for the Past Hundred Years* (New York, 1944), Table III, p. 14.
23. Harry S. Linfield, "Statistics for Jews," *AJYB*, XXVIII (1926), Table XXII, p. 416. Approximately the same numbers came in the succeeding years: in 1923 there were 49,719 and in 1924, 49,989.
24. The quotas allotted by this act for the countries with a large potential of Jewish immigrants were as follows: Poland—6,524; Russia—2,712; Austria—1,413; Hungary—869; Lithuania

—386; Romania—377; Latvia—236. By comparison, the quota for Great Britain and Northern Ireland was 65,721 and that for Germany, 25,957. These figures are taken from United States Immigration and Naturalization Service, *Annual Report*, for year ending June 30, 1947, Table 7. On restrictive immigration laws and their effects on Jewish immigration to the United States, see Max J. Kohler, *Immigration and Aliens in the United States* (New York, 1936), passim.

25. Joseph, *Jewish Immigration*. Table VIII, p. 162. According to this table Jews from the Russian Empire made up 69.9 per cent of all Jews who came in 1881–1900 and 72.1 per cent of those who came between 1901 and 1910.
26. Szajkowski, "The Attitude," p. 239.
27. *J Mess*, October 18, 1882.
28. Ibid.
29. *Sun*, August 27, 1891.
30. Ibid., August 4, 20, 21, 1891.
31. *Hamaggid*, January 20, 1903.
32. *Sun*, August 27, September 7, 1891; *JC*, August 29, 1902.
33. *Am Heb*, November 5, 1886.
34. Friedenwald, *Aaron Friedenwald*, p. 120.
35. Joseph, *Jewish Immigration*, Table III, p. 159.
36. In the official document the classification "Hebrew" was used only between 1899 and 1943. The figures of the local charity organization are, however, completely reliable.
37. *RFJC* (1908), p. 25.
38. Ibid. (1909), p. 25.
39. Ibid, (1910), p. 47.
40. Samuel Joseph, *History of the Baron de Hirsch Fund* (Philadelphia, 1935), p. 246.
41. *RFJC* (1915), p. 20.
42. *Niles' Weekly Register*, VII (1817), 359.
43. For the history of Am Olam, see A. Menes, "The Am Olam Movement" in *History of the Jewish Labor Movement . . .* (Yiddish), ed. E. Tcherikower (New York, 1945), II, 203–238.
44. Alexander Harkavy (1863–1939) became a leading philologist of Yiddish and author of textbooks for foreigners. He also compiled a Hebrew-Yiddish-English dictionary. Itzak Rivkind, "Alexander Harkavy, Pioneer and Veteran" (Yiddish), *Tzukunft* (June 1933), 312–314.
45. *J Mess*, November 2, 1882.

46. Eli Ginsberg, "The Jewish Colony in Waterview," *The Virginia Magazine of History and Biography* (October 1958), pp. 460–462.
47. *Charles County Land Records.* BSG #5 (CR558), pp. 451–457, in MHR.
48. *Sun,* June 12, September 4, 9, 1882.
49. *Sun,* August 3, 1906. See also Richard E. Singer, *The American Jew in Agriculture, Past History and Present Conditions* (unpublished Prize Essay, Hebrew Union College, Cincinnati, 1941), pp. 342–343.
50. Henrietta Szold's description of this colony, *JC,* May 31, 1901.
51. *J Exp,* August 4, 1893.
52. *Occ.* XIII (1855), 102.
53. *Israel's Herald,* May 25, 1849.
54. Joseph, *Hirsch Fund,* 246.
55. *AJYB,* VII (1905–1906), 39–40.
56. Levin, *The Szolds,* p. 261. Some original records of the Baron de Hirsch Fund activities in Baltimore are to be found in JHSM.
57. Many of the original records of the Hebrew Benevolent Society in the JHSM.
58. *RFJC* (1917), p. 13.
59. Ibid. (1918), p. 16
60. Reports of assistance rendered: *RFJC* (1911), p. 21; (1912), p. 20; (1917), p. 30; (1918), p. 36. Similarly, (1913), p. 27; (1915), p. 35; (1919), p. 18.

1911

	NUMBER OF FAMILIES	NUMBER OF PERSONS
Sickness	72	351
Physical Defects	8	34
Old Age	37	73
Insufficient Earnings	46	259
Lack of Work	44	210
Death of Husband	83	254
Wife Desertion	53	182
Tuberculosis	62	335
Incompetency	26	166
Insanity	4	24
Imprisonment	2	9
Totals	437	1,897

1912

	NUMBER OF FAMILIES	NUMBER OF PERSONS
Sickness	57	274
Physical Defects	10	42
Old Age	38	74
Insufficient Earnings	49	286
Lack of Work	56	300
Incompetency	24	152
Death of Husband	79	248
Wife Desertion	51	186
Tuberculosis	56	328
Insanity	7	32
Imprisonment	2	12
Totals	429	1,934

1915

	NUMBER OF FAMILIES	NUMBER OF PERSONS
Lack of work	230	1,113
Insufficient earnings	112	721
Illness	110	498
Death of Husband	91	321
Tuberculosis	60	304
Wife Desertion	48	188
Old Age	24	50
Incompetency	14	89
Physical Defects	14	62
Mental Defects	4	15
Totals	707	3,361

1917

	NUMBER OF FAMILIES	PER CENT OF FAMILIES	COST	PER-CENTAGE OF COST
Widows	766	28	$10,417.76	28.0
Tuberculosis	469	18	7,489.18	20.0
Desertion	408	15	6,407.54	17.0
General Illness	338	12	5,785.23	16.0
Low wage	167	6	1,265.51	3.0
Lack of Parental Care	128	4	1,400.80	4.0
Old Age	105	4	784.80	2.0
Physical Defects	96	3	1,033.81	3.0
Incompetency	80	3	543.21	1.0
Insanity	79	3	1,647.22	4.0
Transients	63	2	131.00	0.4
Unemployment ...	37	1	234.89	0.6
Imprisonments	21	1	338.10	1.0
Totals	2,757	100	$37,479.05	100.00

1918

	NUMBER OF FAMILIES	PER CENT OF FAMILIES	COST	PER-CENTAGE OF COST
Transient	192	17.4	$ 137.92	0.38
Sickness	184	16.6	5,755.60	15.10
Tuberculosis	171	15.4	7,429.46	19.50
Widowhood	134	12.1	13,390.07	35.20
Insufficient Earnings	98	8.9	930.09	2.40
Desertion, Separation, Divorce	83	7.6	5,386.19	15.00
Domestic Difficulty	59	5.4	—	—
Lack of Parental Care . .	48	4.3	1,707.20	4.30
Old Age	36	3.3	580.78	1.50
Incompetency	24	2.1	256.70	0.70
Juvenile Delinquency . . .	24	2.1	—	—
Unemployment . . .	17	1.5	123.42	0.30
Physical Deficiency	16	1.4	888.75	2.30
Insanity	16	1.4	1,414.76	3.30
Imprisonment	4	0.3	9.00	0.02
Inebriety	2	0.2	—	—
Totals	1,108	100.0	$38,009.94	100.00

61. See records of the Baltimore Hebrew Orphan Asylum.
62. *RFJC* (1910), p. 20.
63. *Am Heb*, February 19, 1886.
64. *Sun*, November 19, 1905.
65. *RFJC* (1910), p. 39.
66. See Hospital *Reports* at JHSM and Sinai Hospital, present-day name of Baltimore's Jewish hospital.
67. *RFJC* (1917), p. 19. This policy of giving free care is still being continued.
68. *RFJC* (1918), p. 22. The nonsectarian policy is also observed at present.

69. Computed on basis of *RFJC* (1910), p. 9.
70. Computed on basis of *RFJC* (1910), Table G, p. 129.
71. *RFJC* (1916), p. 128.
72. See annual reports of *RFJC*.
73. Michael Aaronsohn, *Broken Lights*, (Cincinnati, 1946), pp. 13–29. In the foreword Aaronsohn wrote: "The incidents recorded are authentic almost in every detail. The characters portrayed are nonfictional, though in some instances the names are the invention of the author." In a letter to the author dated March 19, 1968, Rabbi Aaronsohn asserted that "the only fictional inventions are some of the names—Fernal for example. Otherwise, all the rest is unvarnished reality. . . ." In addition to this volume, the Minute Book of the Hebrew Orphan Asylum for May 1893 to October 1905, located in JHSM, was used in the writing of this section.
74. Aaronsohn, *Broken Lights*, pp. 114–115.
75. In addition to the Minute Book of the asylum, see also *J Exp*, December 21, 1877, and July 13, 1882.
76. Friedenwald, *Aaron Friedenwald*, p. 95, n. 3.
77. Letter dated June 19, 1882, in the Morais Collection in the Dropsie College, cited by Goldman, "Henry W. Schneeberger," p. 179.
78. Michael Miller, *Fifty Years of Achievement, 1890–1940, Hebrew Home for the Aged and Infirm at Levindale* (no place or date of publication), n.p. The Friendly Inn was the forerunner of the present-day home for the aged, Levindale.
79. United Hebrew Charities *Report* (1910), n.p.
80. Eugene Kaufman, *A Half a Century of HIAS in Baltimore, 1903–1953* (Baltimore, 1953), n.p. See also Mark Wischnitzer, *To Dwell in Safety* (Philadelphia, 1948), p. 122.
81. *AJYB*, I (1899), 145.
82. Ibid., p. 146.
83. Minute Book of the Free Loan Association; see also *AJYB*, I (1899), 147.
84. *Souvenir of the Hebrew Sick Relief Association, Baltimore, 1888–1963* (Baltimore, 1963).
85. Henry Sonneborn, Jr., *Family Memoirs* (Baltimore, 1966).
86. Baltimore American, *A History of the City of Baltimore* (Baltimore, 1902), pp. 213–214.
87. H. Sonneborn Company employed 5,000 workers; L. Greif and Brother Company, 3,500; J. Schoeneman Company, 2,000; Isaac Hamburger & Sons Company, 1,000; Schloss Brothers,

4,000; Strouse & Bros., 2,500; Philip Kahn and Company, "the overcoat king of America," 1,000 workers. This and much additional information about labor conditions in this period was given to the author by Jacob Edelman, at present a leading labor lawyer and member of the Baltimore City Council since 1939, himself a "graduate" of some of these factories, where he worked as a youth at the beginning of the century (see Note 262 of Part III).

88. Information of personal experiences was graciously related to the author by Mrs. Stanford Z. Rothschild, Sr., who came out in 1921. The morning after the ball, on Thanksgiving Day, the Baltimore *Sun* published a photograph of the debutantes with the caption EIGHT HEBREW MAIDENS.

There is a record of the fourteen debutantes in 1907. Six of them lived on Eutaw Place and the rest on the adjoining streets. See *Social Register, A Compendium of Names and Addresses of Members of the Jewish Community of Baltimore* (Baltimore, 1907–1908), 9.

89. Blum, *Jews of Baltimore*, p. 87. Detailed materials on the history of the club, from its inception in 1886 till its dissolution in 1951, are to be found in the AJAR, boxes Nos. 2251 and 2251A.

It is worth noting that from the beginning the club has had a rule that anyone who did not contribute an appropriate sum to Jewish charities was not eligible for membership.

90. Aaronsohn, *Broken Lights*, pp. 39–40.

91. *J Exp*, August 19, 1887.

92. *RFJC* (1913), p. 104. See similar reports in *JC*, May 23, and June 6, 1902.

93. From the diary of David Philipson, *AJA*, XVIII (April 1966), 134–135.

94. Letter by Mrs. Aaron Friedenwald to her son Harry quoting Schneeberger's sermon, cited by Goldman, "Henry W. Schneeberger," p. 171.

95. Ibid.

96. Cited in Marvin Lowenthal, *Henrietta Szold, Life and Letters* (New York, 1942), p. 41

97. Of these, 506 involved youths below the age of sixteen. Delinquents among the 460 who were over sixteen were found guilty of gambling, larceny, trafficking in dope, begging, and receiving stolen goods. *JC*, March 17, 1916.

98. *RFJC* (1918), p. 38.
99. Ibid. (1913), p. 20.
100. *JC*, May 15, 1916.
101. Ibid., March 16, 1906.
102. Lowenthal, *Henrietta Szold*, p. 45.
103. James Ryder Randall, *Constitutionalist* (Augusta, Ga.), cited in Levin, *The Szolds*, p. 189.
104. *Sun*, September 7, 1891.
105. Ibid., August 4, 1891.
106. Friedenwald, *Aaron Friedenwald*, p. 121.
107. *Sun*, July 13, 1892.
108. *J Exp*, May 25, 1882.
109. Ibid., March 23, 1888.
110. *Sun*, January 1, June 12, and July 1, 1885; Bland, *Commerce of Baltimore*, p. 86.
111. *Tenth Annual Report*, B.I.S., pp. 142–147.
112. Immigrants' declarations that they were tailors in the old country were not necessarily true. They knew that such declarations might open the gates to America, and anyone who could hold a needle called himself a tailor. In 1909–1910, 36.6 per cent of all Jewish males claimed to be tailors, and 10.3 per cent of the women said they were seamstresses. Joseph, *Jewish Immigration*, Table LIX, p. 108.
113. *JC*, December 14, 1890.
114. *Tenth Annual Report*, B.I.S., pp. 142, 147.
115. From a talk, reported in the *Jewish Daily Forward*, February 6, 1955.
116. *Baltimore Amerikaner* (Yiddish), May 20, 1908.
117. Bland, *Commerce of Baltimore*, 102.
118. Blum, *Jews of Baltimore*, 273.
119. *Sun*, September 18, 1886.
120. *Folkstzaytung*, February 8, 1889.
121. Ibid.
122. Louis Levine, *The Women's Garment Workers* (New York, 1924), p. 34.
123. *Yiddishe Gazetn*, July 8, 1892.
124. *Sun*, September 18, 1886.
125. *Fifth Annual Report*, B.I.S., pp. 147–151.
126. Levine, *Women's Garment Workers*, p. 105.
127. See author's interview with Jacob M. Moses, October 30, 1963, in JHSM. Moses (1873–1968), a former state senator and

judge, distinguished himself as a perennial arbitrator in the needle trade.

128. Among those especially active on behalf of the strikers were Elizabeth Gilman, daughter of the first president of the Johns Hopkins University (henceforth referred to as Hopkins) and Dr. Kinsolving, pastor of one of Baltimore's most aristocratic churches, Brown Memorial Church. The rabbis of the city, however, remained aloof.

129. For details, see interview with Jacob Moses and *Family Memoirs* by Henry Sonneborn, Jr., both in JHSM.

130. Moses interview.

131. Sidney L. Nyburg, *The Chosen People* (Philadelphia, 1917), pp. 239–240.

132. See letter from the manager of the Jewish People's Relief Committee to A. Golomker, secretary of the Jewish National Workers Alliance, February 7, 1917, in American Jewish Historical Society.

133. *Sun*, September 29, 1890. Cohn wrote up the debate, his arrest, and his treatment in solitary in *Die Fraye Arbeiter Shtime*, February 1 and 20, and May 27, 1891.

134. *Hapisga*, October 11, 1890. For more details about the anarchists in Baltimore, see S. Garson (Slobodkin), *In Kamf Tzvishn Tzvei Ideologies*. Ms. in YIVO.

135. *Hapisga*, October 11, 1890.

136. H. Lang, "Hymns and Prayers" (Yiddish), *David Edelstat Book*, ed. B. J. Bialostotzky (New York, 1953), pp. 423–424.

137. Reports of Bund activities in Baltimore in Bund Archives, New York.

138. See especially the testimony of the Bund's sharpest opponent, Dr. Herman Seidel, in interview, October 9, 1966; taped interview in JHSM.

139. *Der Amerikaner Yid*, May 6, 1908.

140. Information supplied by Mr. William Braiterman and Drs. Samuel Neistadt and Herman Seidel, leaders of different radical movements in the city.

141. Interview with Simon Cohen, one of the founders of the Workmen's Circle in the city, May 21, 1966; Dr. Samuel Neistadt, one of its leaders, May 14, 1966; and Harry Cohen, for many years secretary of the organization, May 23, 1966. All in JHSM.

142. Information supplied by a number of members of the *Farband*,

chiefly Dr. Herman Seidel, one of the founders of the organization in Baltimore. The author also had the privilege of examining material on the subject in the Labor Archives in Tel Aviv.

143. *Laws of the State of Maryland*, 1894, ch. 302; 1896, ch. 467; 1898, ch. 123.

144. See announcements in the local Yiddish press.

145. *JC*, December 28, 1906.

146. Information supplied by Mr. Simon Cohen in interview cited above. He was present when the incident took place.

147. The weekly *Jewish Chronicle*, "A journal dedicated to contemporary history, poetry and literature," was published for two years, 1876–1878, in English and German. There were a considerable number of newspapers in Yiddish. One of them, *Baltimore Fraye Presse*, published by the nationally prominent labor leader Joseph Barondess, lasted only for four issues (1899). The only one that existed for a considerable period of time (1901–1910) was Dr. Maurice Hidekel's *Der Vegvayzer*. On Hidekel, see *Biographical Dictionary of Modern Yiddish Literature* (Yiddish) (New York, 1960), III, 725–726. *Der Yidisher Progres* and *Baltimore Yid* were of short duration. A few random copies of these newspapers are found in JHSM.

148. In this magazine the famous Hebrew poet Shaul Tschernikhovski published his first poem, "Ba-Halomi" (In My Dream), on December 9, 1892.

149. The editors were Max Mayers, Clifton Harry Levy, Tobias Shanfarber, William Rosenau, Abraham B. Arnold, A. Guttmacher, Louis Manheimer.

150. While the news in these publications was generally reliable, it verged at times on the fantastic. Such a news item was published in 1895, for instance. It related that in one Baltimore synagogue a telephone had been installed connecting the house of worship with the homes of some well-to-do members, making it possible for them to listen to the services without attending the synagogue. *Hamaggid L'Israel*, June 27, 1895. The telephone company has assured the author that such service did not exist at that time.

151. The name was an acronym formed from the initials of the father of Haskalah (Jewish Enlightenment movement) in Russia, Reb Itzchak Baer Levinsohn.

152. The committee consisted of the following: Dr. Aaron Friedenwald, chairman, Edward H. Wise, Moses R. Walter, Benjamin H. Hartogensis, Rev. Alois Kaiser, Max Hochschild, Leopold Strouse, Simon Dalsheimer, Albert Rayner, Dr. Joseph

Blum, David Oppenheimer, Samuel Tahl, Henrietta Szold, Solomon Baroway, secretary.

153. By 1897 Henrietta Szold was already in Philadelphia, where she had become the editor of the Jewish Publication Society in 1893. The Baltimore chapter of her life was closed. With her away from the city, the finances of the school deteriorated. The school was then taken over by the city. Thus the creation of the RIBAL society and Henrietta Szold's school opened a new chapter in night classes for adults in Baltimore. In her work Miss Szold was especially assisted by Benjamin H. Hartogensis, Miss Grace Bendam, and Miss Rose Summerfeld, who succeeded her as superintendent of the school. For more details about the institution, see Benjamin H. Hartogensis, "The Russian Night School of Baltimore," *PAJHS*, XXXI (1928), 225–228, and Alexandra Lee Levin, "Henrietta Szold and the Russian Immigrant School," *MHM*, Vol. 57 (1962), 1–15.

154. Levin, "Henrietta Szold," *MHM*, p. 15. On Benjamin H. Hartogensis, see Ezekiel J. Londow, "Benjamin Henry Hartogensis," *PAJHS*, XXXVII (1947), 469–470.

155. *Congressional Record* (March 8, 1960), Vol. 106, No. 43, Appendix P.A. 2018 cited in Levin, "Henrietta Szold," p. 15.

156. Unidentified newspaper clipping at JHSM.

157. *Sun*, May 9, 1905.

158. Michael Miller, *The Origin and Early Years of Menorah Lodge in Baltimore* (from January 1, 1915, to December 31).

159. Circular of the society in JHSM (n.d.).

160. *Constitution of B'rith Sholom*, 1902. Some of the minutes of this organization are to be found in JHSM.

161. The temple, built at a cost of $150,000, remained in use for six decades. It was finally sold to a church, and in 1951 the congregation moved into a more spacious building on the northwest section of the city. The Baltimore Hebrew Congregation has at the time of this writing (1968) the largest membership of any synagogue in the city.

162. It is the only East European congregation whose records were preserved. These were written in a Yiddish that shows the inroads of English in a corrupt form. MBSMC at the JHSM.

163. MBSMC, 1905 (n.d.).

164. MBSMC, April 1910.

165. Aaronsohn, *Broken Lights*, p. 66. On details of Rabbi Schwartz's biography, see memorandum by his son Dr. Joseph Schwartz in JHSM.

166. Records of sale at JHSM.
167. Information supplied by Rabbi Israel Tabak of Shaarei Zion.
168. Beth Tfiloh Congregation, *15th Anniversary Memorial History* (Baltimore, 1936).
169. *RFJC* (1913), p. 99. This report, incidentally, shatters the argument that "three-day-a-year" Jews were only found among the Reform.
170. MBHSC, December 4, 1881.
171. Ibid., September 9, October 18, 1883.
172. Philipson's, diary p. 29.
173. BSA, May 6, 1888.
174. FA, Reel #2, August 5, 1888.
175. *Acts of Maryland*, March 1868.
176. HSA, July 7, 1878.
177. Philipson's diary, pp. 32–33.
178. The following congregations formed the board: Baltimore Hebrew Congregation, Chizuk Amuno, Oheb Shalom, Har Sinai, Shearith Israel, and Oheb Israel (the old Fell's Point Congregation, which was still lingering downtown). Copy of the agreement in JHSM.
179. Part of the agreement.
180. Copy of this agreement in JHSM.
181. *Hamelitz*, May 1, 1890.
182. MBBHC, April 15, 1852.
183. *Sun*, April 3 and 6, 1897.
184. Ibid., April 7, 8, 1897. The *shohet*, Isaac Soloveitschek, could not speak English, although he had been in the country for twenty-three years. The ghetto was to many an island where one could live for decades without learning the language of the country.
185. Ibid., March 25, 1910.
186. Cited in Levin, *The Szolds*, p. 352.
187. Cyrus Adler, *I Have Considered the Days* (Philadelphia, 1941), p. 56.
188. Unidentified newspaper clipping in BSA.
189. BSA.
190. The last communication on the subject is a letter from Mrs. Graetz (Marie), dated Breslau, July 19, 1889. In it she asked the rabbi to forward an enclosed letter to her son, whose address the parents did not know. Correspondence in BSA.
191. MBOSC, October 8, 1886.
192. Among Dr. Szold's writings the following are of special interest:

I. WORKS ON LITURGY AND RELIGIOUS EDUCATION

Abodath Israel, 1st ed., 1863, 2nd ed., 1864; Eng. transl., 1865; 3d ed., 1873.

Hegyon Lebh (for private devotion), 1867.

Sefer Hachayim, 1887. In this book are included:
"Urim Vethumim"—system of Judaism
"Reshith Da'ath"—catechism.
"Mikrae Kodhesh"—selections from the Bible.
"Imre Bhinah"—proverbs of Solomon.
"Mikra Beth Hassefer"—abridgment of the Bible with Vocabulary; a Hebrew Primer.

Andachtsbüchlein—a prayer book for children in three languages: Hebrew, German, and English.

II. PUBLISHED SERMONS

Vaterland und Freiheit (in memory of President Lincoln), June 1, 1865.

The Sabbath, 1888.

III. WORKS ON THE BIBLE

Commentary on Job, 1886.

"Commentary on Book of Daniel," Ch. XI, in *Semitics Studies in Memory of Alexander Kohut*, 1897.

In Szold's archives are also a few poems in Hebrew and German-Yiddish which he wrote before he came to America.

193. Among Rabbi Rosenau's books are the following: *Hebraisms in the Authorized Version of the Bible* (1901), *Jewish Ceremonial Institutions and Customs* (1903). He also contributed a number of articles to *The Jewish Encyclopedia* and wrote *A Brief History of Congregation Oheb Shalom* . . . (1903). Much material by and about Rosenau at AJAR, Boxes No. 1017–19 and X-1.

194. S. D. Schwartz, "Emil Gustave Hirsch," *AJYB*, XXVII (1925–1926), 230-237; Shusterman, *The Legacy of a Liberal* (Baltimore, 1967), pp. 35–36.

195. The lectures were later published as *The Jew in English Fiction* (Cincinnati, 1889).

196. On his ministry in Baltimore, see Shusterman, *Legacy*, p. 41; Philipson's diary, pp. 31–45.

197. Guttmacher contributed a number of articles to *The Jewish Encyclopedia*. His doctoral dissertation was published under

the title *Optimism and Pessimism in the Old and New Testament* Baltimore, 1903). He also published *A History of the Baltimore Hebrew Congregation.* See William Rosenau, "Adolf Guttmacher," *PAJHS*, XXV (1917), 150–152.

198. Included in the English Bible, published by the Jewish Publication Society in 1917. For an excellent study of Schneeberger, see Goldman, "Henry W. Schneeberger," 153–190.

199. *JC.* October 3, 1913.

200. The situation has changed again in the past two decades. Now practically all Jewish schools are affiliated with synagogues.

201. MBOSC, July 4, 1886.

202. Oheb Shalom *Constitution* (1893), Article XIV, Sec. 10.

203. August 19, 1891, BSA.

204. MBBHC, April 27, 1898.

205. MBOSC, April 23, 1893.

206. *Statistical Data of the Jewish Religious Schools of Baltimore, Maryland and Pittsburgh, Pennsylvania for 1908–1909*, ed. J. H. Greenstone (Philadelphia, 1909), p. 4.

207. *Yiddishe Gazetn* (New York), November 29, 1892.

208. *Isr*, March 26, 1885; *Am Heb*, February 19, 1886; *J Exp*, July 27, 1888.

209. Author's interview with Dr. Henry W. Einspruch, the head of the last mission in the city. A highly educated man, translator of the New Testament into a masterful Yiddish, Einspruch headed the mission house until its closing in 1966.

210. On missionary activities in Eastern Europe, see Isaac M. Fein, "The London Missionary Society in Russia in the Nineteenth Century" (Yiddish), *YIVO Bleter*, XXIV (1944), 27–46.

211. *JC*, October 4, 1901.

212. *Baltimore Amerikaner* (Yiddish), April 3, 1908.

213. For a detailed study on Benderly, see J. Nathan H. Winter, *Jewish Education in a Pluralistic Society: Samson Benderly and Jewish Education in the United States* (New York, 1966). Some observations presented here are based in part on the author's three interviews in 1967 and 1968 with Mrs. Samson Benderly.

214. Memoirs about Benderly written for the author by Mrs. Judah Magnes in Jerusalem on November 23, 1964. Ms. in possession of the author.

215. Rebecca A. Brickner, "As I Remember Dr. Benderly," *Jewish Education*, XX (1949), 54.

216. Interview, October 9, 1966, with Dr. Herman Seidel (see note 138), who taught at Benderly's school in Baltimore and whom the master took along to New York in 1910. Taped interview in JHSM.
217. Ibid.
218. *JC*, July 18, 1902.
219. Ibid., November 20, 1903.
220. *RFJC* (1908), p. 101.
221. Ibid.
222. Ibid. (1910), p. 116.
223. Ibid.
224. Ibid. (1911), p. 120.
225. Ibid. (1914), p. 119.
226. Ibid., p. 120.
227. *RFJC* (1918), p. 48.
228. *Am Heb*, August 8, 1913.
229. Blum, *Jews of Baltimore*, p. 253.
230. In 1968 the school enrolled about 500 pupils— boys only— in its three divisions: kindergarten, elementary school, and high school. A girls' school, Bais Yaakov (kindergarten through high school), founded in 1941, had a registration of about 500, and one coed school, maintained by the Beth Tfiloh Congregation (pupils from kindergarten through the ninth grade) had an enrollment of about 250.
231. *JC*, October 31, 1902.
232. *Sun*, December 28, 1920.
233. The following served as members of the first board of the college: Bessie S. Cone, Sadie J. Crokin, Harry Friedenwald, Julius Levy, and Jacob M. Moses, with Isaac Davidson as president.
    Since 1930 the college has been under the direction of its president, Dr. Louis L. Kaplan. In the course of years it has developed into a major educational institution In addition to the college department, it maintains a large high school division and adult education classes. Its total enrollment in 1968 was about eight hundred persons.
234. *Niles' Weekly Register*, XI (1816), 680.
235. Montefiore's wish was that the synagogues use the Scroll in rotation. There were disputes on this score, and appeals were made to the donor in London about it. Correspondence in JHSM.
236. *Hamelitz*, September 27, 1889. Nothing further is known about Rabbi Finkelstein.

237. *Report,* Hovevei Zion (Baltimore, 1889), JHSM.
238. Maxwell Whiteman, "Zionism Comes to Philadelphia," *Early History of Zionism in America,* ed. Isidore S. Meyer, p. 209, n. 15.
239. *Constitution* of the Zion Association, Article III, par. 6, n.p. (Baltimore, 1894), in JHSM.
240. *Report of the Zion Association* (Baltimore, 1894), at JHSM.
241. David Panitz, *Memoirs of Zion* (Hebrew) (Baltimore, 1903), p. 47.
242. H. Masliansky, *Memoirs* (Yiddish) (New York, 1924), pp. 207–208.
243. *Hapisga,* June 3, 1892.
244. *Der Israëlite,* June 24, 1882.
245. *Hamelitz,* 1897, No. 44, p. 2.
246. *Hatehia,* IV, December 2, 1899.
247. The leaders of the organization were Morris D. Robinson, Jacob Ettelman, Morris Spector, and L. Katz. Unidentified newspaper clipping (Hebrew) in JHSM.
248. Interview with Herman Seidel, cited above.
249. Author's interview with Simon Levin, secretary of the Baltimore Zionist Council from 1912 till 1922, March 4, 1968.
250. Ibid. This was more than merely an ideological club. It became in addition a social club with a high rate of marriages among its members.
251. Rabbi Charles Rubenstein of Har Sinai Congregation in *Sun,* December 2, 1917.
252. Benderly discouraged Seidel from becoming a doctor. When the former left for an educational post in New York in 1910, he took the young physician along. Seidel subsequently returned to Baltimore and became an eminent physician. In relating this episode nearly six decades later, Seidel remarked wryly: "And maybe Benderly was right after all."
253. Seidel interview, cited above.
254. Ibid. Sigmund Sonneborn, a member of a large clothing firm, was an ardent Zionist. He was the author of a volume, *The Book of the Baal Shem Mishpot* (Baltimore, 1913), in which he expressed in blank verse ideas gathered from Psalms.
255. Seidel interview.
256. William Braiterman, *Memoirs of the Palestine Jewish Legion in 1917* (Baltimore, 1967), pp. 2–3.
    Following is a partial list of Baltimore boys who enlisted with

the Jewish Legionnaires. Due to the fact that many Baltimore boys enlisted in Philadelphia, it was impossible to secure a complete list. It is estimated that ninety Baltimoreans were enlisted with the Jewish Legion: Harry Alkover, Harry Alperson, Jacob Beider, Nahan Berlin, Carlin, Louis Cohen, Benjamin Director, David Discount, Jacob Eiseman, Frank Finkelstein, Samuel Garekol, Isidor Goldman, Harry Goulin, Ardig Kasan, Harry Kramer, Morris Kramer, Jacob Khanoovsky, Morris Leiberman, Joe Lieberman, Charles Liesner, Henry Luerie, Michael Margolis, Sam Margolis, Sam Mishel, Isidor Mosgin, Isidor Narberg, Jacob Piper, William Pleet, Sam Rodman, brother of artist Rosenthal, Hyman Rubenstein, Max Rudoff, Ruthenberg, Julius Sare, Satanovski, Solomon Savitz, Isidor Schaffer, Zalkino Schein, Benjamin Shannon, Abraham Shapiro, Sol Shapiro, Shenovovitch, Siegel, J. Silverman, Soibel Simche, Ellis Stein, Dave Wichman, Isidor Wolfston, Milton Zalich. *The Jewish Times,* February 20, 1920.

257. Materials about Mizrachi in Baltimore at JHSM.
258. See Hadassah materials in Hadassah Archives, Baltimore and JHSM.
259. *JC,* October 16, 1903.
260. *YBCCAR,* XV (1904), 68.
261. Dr. Friedenwald, a leading ophthalmologist, left his great collection of incunabula and rich medical library to the Hebrew University in Jerusalem. His important works on Jewish contributions to medicine include *The Jews in Medicine* (Baltimore, 1944) and *Jewish Luminaries in Medical History and Catalogue* (Baltimore, 1946). His son Jonas (1897–1955) was also an outstanding ophthalmologist. For a detailed biography of Dr. Friedenwald, see Levin, *Vision.*
262. FA, Reel #23.
263. For two years he worked with the top Jewish leadership and with representatives of the British government in Palestine. Those were trying days for the Zionist veteran. The ugly mood of the Arabs and the duplicity of the British at times brought him to the brink of despair. On May 1, 1919, he wrote to his son Jonas: "I have never felt so discouraged and so pessimistic. . . . I am disturbed. . . . Our cousins [the Arabs] have become presumptuous and encouraged in a degree that makes me exceedingly concerned. Indeed, I should like you to indicate to "Uncle Louis" [Louis D. Brandeis] how very anxious I am and how far I

fear he is from understanding the possible danger—perhaps, I might say, the inevitable, if this is not changed by very prompt action."

On the same day he warned Brandeis directly about the "deep anxiety [and] constantly increasing fear has come over me and the other members of the commission." FA, Reel #9.

264. Cited in Irving Fineman, *A Woman of Valor* (New York, 1961), pp. 98–99.

265. For Henrietta Szold's early life, see Levin, *The Szolds*. For a full-length biography, see Fineman, *Woman of Valor*.

266. *YBCCAR*, XXVII (Cincinnati, 1917), 132.

267. National Archives, Group 59; Decimale File 867, 48/1888.

Years later, another much more famous boat was refitted, staffed, and equipped in Baltimore for a mission of saving Jews. This was the Chesapeake Bay steamer *Governor Warfield*, renamed the *Exodus*.

268. Hopkins was the first institution of higher learning in the country to introduce Semitic studies, and Haupt was the first professor. See Cyrus Adler, "The Beginnings of Semitic Studies in America," in *Oriental Studies in Honor of Paul Haupt* (Baltimore, 1926), pp. 317–328.

269. *JC*, March 3, 1891.

270. Adler, *I Have Considered*, passim.

271. Moshe Perlman, "Paul Haupt and the Mesopotamian Project, 1892–1914," *PAJHS*, XLVII (1958), 154–175.

272. Hecht, *Memoirs*, p. 18.

273. *Katholische Volkszeitung*, July 19, 1879; September 11, 1880.

274. Ibid., May 19, 1900.

275. Ibid., March 9, 1901.

276. See, for instance, the editorials of February 18, 1859, in *The Freeman*; May 31, 1851, November 29, 1859, in *The Catholic Mirror*.

277. *Sinai*, VII (1862), 31–36; *The Jewish Times* (New York), February 4, 1876.

278. William Rosenau, "Cardinal Gibbons and His Attitudes toward Jewish Problems," *PAJHS*, XXXI (1928), 219–224.

279. Ibid., 222. Even the prestige of the cardinal did not help. Bible reading remained part of the school program and remained a bone of contention between the Jewish community and school boards in Baltimore until the Supreme Court's ruling against Bible reading in the schools.

280. *Sun,* December 19, 1913.
281. *Yiddishe Gazetn,* December 2, 1892.
282. Lewis Levin to Henrietta Szold, May 3, 1912, HSA.
283. *JC,* June 14, 1912.
284. *Yiddishe Gazetn,* October 5, 1892. There was never a "Jewish approach" to Negroes. One document relates the attitude of one leading Jewish personality in the city. When a "committee" called on Dr. Harry Friedenwald to help protect the neighborhood in which he lived from a "Negro invasion," he refused to join and wrote on October 22, 1929, to his son Jonas: "Our people have had such a long experience in the particular question of segregation, that I would never actively promote such a movement. . . . I consider any such restrictions based upon class, whether of color, race or religion as the manifestation of such injustice that I could not take a hand in it. . . . This country could not endure permanently a caste system with a caste of untouchables." FA, Reel #9.
285. *Hapisga,* April 29, 1892.
286. *JC,* December 3, 1905.
287. *Sun,* June 14, 1919.
288. *Sun,* March 26, 1912; Minute Book, B'nai B'rith, Menorah Lodge, September 21, 1896.
289. *Maryland Annotated Code,* Article 21, Section 402. See Part I, note 10.
290. *JC,* May 6, 1904.
291. *Baltimore Amerikaner,* May 8, 1898. On subsequent protests, see, for instance, *Sun,* October 1, 1911; March 24, April 1, 1914.
292. Maryland was not the only state with laws restricting work on Sunday. See Albert M. Friedenberg, "The Jews and the American Sunday Laws," *PAJHS,* XI (1903), 101–115.
293. *Sun,* January 7, 1917.
294. Ibid., December 12, 1861.
295. Korn, *American Jewry,* p. 66.
296. Letter to Friedenwald, December 9, 1914, FA, Reel #9. Letter to Hollander, May 16, 1915 in HA.
297. *JC,* December 1, 1911. The committee, according to this news item, consisted of Jacob Hollander, Harry Friedenwald, Moses Walter, Mendes Cohen, Eli Frank, William Levy, Jacob Epstein, the rabbis, and others.
298. Undated handwritten letter in HA.

299. *Addresses of Hon. Isidor Rayner*, ed. by J. Frederick Essary (Baltimore-New York, 1914), pp. 287–288.
300. The author found material on the subject in the Ussishkin Archives in the Central Zionist Archives in Jerusalem.
301. *Sun*, March 28, 1891.
302. Rosenau, "Cardinal Gibbons," p. 220.
303. *The Voice of America on Kishineff*, ed. Cyrus Adler (Philadelphia, 1904), pp. 16–39.
304. Ibid., p. 37.
305. Ibid., pp. 19–20.
306. Ibid., pp. 27–29.
307. Ibid., p. 32.
308. Ibid., pp. 242–264.
309. Although he was vacationing at that time in Wiesbaden, Germany, Joseph Friedenwald sent in a contribution of $150. In a letter to his nephew, Harry Friedenwald, he expressed his "great pleasure" with the latter's involvement in matters "connected with our faith and race." Letter dated July 2, 1903. FA, Reel #9.
310. *JC*, XVII, no. 7, p. 14.
311. Letter (in French) in JHSM.
312. Z. Szajkowski, "The Alliance Israélite Universelle in the United States, 1860–1949," *PAJHS*, XXXIX (1950), 412–413.
313. Harry Schneiderman, "Herbert Friedenwald," *PAJHS*, XXXVII (1947), 463–466.
314. Letter in HA. Friedenwald did not exaggerate the danger of the bill to Jews. A full 26 per cent of Jewish immigrants fourteen years of age and older were unable to read or write the language of their native countries. See Joseph, *Jewish Immigration*, Table LX, p. 192.
315. FA, Reel #9.
316. Cited by Rosenau, "Cardinal Gibbons," pp. 222–223.
317. *Official Correspondence Relating to Immigration of Russian Exiles*, Washington, 1891, as cited Wischnitzer, *To Dwell in Safety*, p. 77.
318. Letter of June 12, 1916, FA, Reel #9.
319. Many records of the Baltimore branch of the American Jewish Congress are to be found in JHSM.
320. *JC*, January 7, 1916.
321. LA.
322. *J Exp*, February 24, 1888.

323. *Sun*, January 13, 1902. The societies which were represented at the meeting were Hebrew Benevolent Society, Hebrew Orphan Asylum, Hebrew Hospital and Asylum Association, Daughters in Israel, Council Milk and Ice Fund, Jewish Educational Society, Hebrew Ladies' Sewing Society, Maccabeans, Hebrew Ladies' Aid Society, Hebrew Free Burial Society.

324. *Act of the General Assembly of Maryland, Chapter 264*, April 2, 1906. The incorporators were Jacob Hollander, Bernard Wiesenfeld, William Levy, Eli Frank, and Leon Greenbaum. The eight organizations that formed the Federation were the Hebrew Hospital and Asylum Association, Hebrew Ladies' Sewing Circle, Hebrew Orphan Asylum, Hebrew Ladies' Orphan Aid Society, Maccabeans, Hebrew Free Burial Society, Hebrew Ladies' Sewing Society, Council Milk and Ice Fund, Hebrew Education Society, and Daughters in Israel. *RFJC* (1908), pp. 11–12.

325. Rosamond H. Weisberger, "Jacob Harry Hollander," *PAJHS*, XXXVII (1947), 471–473; HA. In becoming president of the Federation, Hollander followed the lead of the president of his university, Daniel C. Gilman, who headed the first united charities in the city, the Charity Organization Society of Baltimore, founded in 1881.

326. Jacob Hollander, *Forces and Tendencies of Jewish Charities* (Baltimore, 1910), p. 9.

327. Letter from Hollander to Joseph Fells, quoted by the latter in a letter to Hollander of March 13, 1911, HA.

328. Harry Friedenwald, "Louis Hiram Levin," *PAJHS*, XXIX (1925), 176–178. Levin served as the secretary of the Federation throughout the fifteen years of its existence (1906–1921).

329. On the formation of the Federation, see *RFJC* (1908), pp. 9–10. The following served as its presidents: Jacob Hollander (1906–1908), Eli Frank (1909–1910), Simon H. Stein (1912–1913, died in office), S. H. Lauchheimer (1913–1914), Harry Friedenwald (1915–1916), Julius Levy (1917–1918), A. Ray Katz (1919–1920).

330. *RFJC* (1908), p. 10.

331. Ibid., pp. 4–5.

332. Hollander, *Forces*, p. 16.

333. They were The Hebrew Sheltering and Protective Association, The Friendly Inn and Aged Home, Hebrew Free School, Hebrew Free Loan Association, Immigration Protective Asso-

ciation, Young Ladies' Protective Society, and Ladies' Auxiliary Society.

334. Blum, *Jews of Baltimore*, p. 211.
335. From Levy's presidential address, 1910, LA.
336. *RFJC* (1908), p. 8.
337. The only available records of the United Hebrew Charities are the minutes of its annual meeting of 1910 (in LA) and occasional references to its activities in the reports of the Federation. A complete set of the latter is to be found in the Archives of the Associated Jewish Charities of Baltimore.
338. *RFJC* (1913), p. 7. The arbitration court is still functioning almost six decades after its founding.
339. *RFJC* (1916), pp. 34–35.
340. Ibid., p. 34.
341. Ibid. (1908), p. 13.
342. Ibid., p. 14.
343. Ibid.
344. Ibid., pp. 81–85.
345. Ibid., p. 87. See full report on the activities for the year 1907, ibid., pp. 87–93.
346. Aaronsohn, *Broken Lights*, pp. 44–45.
347. *In Memoriam, Michael Simon Levy and Betsy Levy* (Baltimore, 1912), pp. 72–77.
348. Aaronsohn, *Broken Lights*, pp. 44–45.
349. See reports on the "headworkers" of the Jewish Educational Alliance in the published reports of the Federation.
350. *RFJC* (1917), p. 41.
351. Rosenau to William Levy, January 15, 1917, LA.
352. *Sun*, February 24, 1919; *Jewish Times*, February 20, 1920.
353. The information about the formation of the YMHA and YWHA was graciously given to the author by Harry Greenstein, who played a decisive role in all these events and in the history of the community generally for the past half century. He served in leading local, national, and international posts, both Jewish and general. See a full-length biography of him by Louis L. Kaplan and Theodor Schuchat, *Justice Not Charity: A Biography of Harry Greenstein* (New York, 1967). See also Greenstein's diaries and scrapbooks in JHSM. For additional information about the "Y" see Rose Esterson, "History of the Young Men's and Young Women's Hebrew Association of Baltimore" in *YM-YWHA of Baltimore, 5691–1930*, pp. 31–40.

354. *Sun*, December 30, 1911.
355. *RFJC* (1918), p. 20. See also reports for other years.
356. *J Exp*, May 7, 1887. The correspondence from Baltimore is signed "Label," the pen name of Louis H. Levin.
357. United States Census Office, *Census Reports of the United States*, I (Washington, 1900), p. 430.
358. *13th Census of the United States* (Washington, 1910), p. 848.
359. *14th Census of the United States* (Washington, 1920), III, 427.
360. The author acknowledges with thanks the information about the Wolman family given to him by Prof. Abel Wolman.
    Among the many important posts in which Prof. Wolman serves at present (1969) are United States chairman of the National Water Resources Board and chairman of the board of consultants on Israel's water problem (a post he has held since before Israel became independent).
361. George E. Barnett, "The Jewish Population of Maryland," *AJYB*, IV (1902), 58.
362. Lindfield, "Statistics," *AJYB*, XXIX (1927–1928), 243.
363. A detailed biography of the Blaustein business in JHSM. Jacob Blaustein became not only the wealthiest Jew in the United States, but one of the richest men in the country. In addition to being a leading industrialist he became an important leader on a national and international scale, both in Jewish and general affairs. He served as president of the American Jewish Committee and delegate to the United Nations and held many other prominent positions.
364. Blum, *Jews of Baltimore*, pp. 181–187. See also many newspaper clippings dealing with Epstein at the JHSM.
365. Lester S. Levy in 1944, on the occasion of Epstein's eightieth birthday. See Levy's paper on *Jewish Charities in Baltimore*, delivered in 1964, in JHSM.
366. In 1916 Epstein contributed to Jewish charities $2,500, *RFJC* (1917), p. 75; in 1917 $3,500, ibid., (1918), 79; and by 1926 it reached a full $20,000.
367. *Bulletin* of the Associated Jewish Charities, 1921, n.p.
368. Later Joseph Friedenwald became a close friend of Cardinal Gibbons and in his will bequeathed two thousand dollars to his "good friend." *Sun*, December 25, 1910.
369. *JC*, February 12, 1964.
370. Levin, "David Hutzler," *PAJHS*, 152–156.
371. LA.

372. Harold R. Manakee, *Mendes Cohen as President of the Maryland Historical Society*. Typescript in JHSM. Mr. Manakee is director of the society, and his paper is based on original documents available at its archives.
373. Cyrus Adler, "Mendes Cohen," *PAJHS*, XXV (1917), 145–147. See also Mendes Cohen file at JHSM.
374. *JC*, January 13, 1911.
375. *Am Heb*, December 24, 1880.
376. From this position he became superintendent of the entire Baltimore school system, a post he held from 1925 till 1946.
377. David Halstead, "Sylvester at Hopkins," *The Johns Hopkins University Magazine*, IV (March 1916), 188.
378. Blum, *Jews of Baltimore*, p. 149.
379. See unpublished paper by Joseph Feld, *The Jews at the Johns Hopkins University, 1876–1901*, in JHSM.
380. In 1922 Mr. Frank was appointed judge of the Superior Court and in 1926 to the board of Hopkins, the first Jew to hold such a position. Blum, *Jews of Baltimore*, p. 157; *Tercentenary History of Maryland* (Baltimore, 1925), III, 356.
381. *JC*, November 30, 1906.
382. Ibid., January 30, 1914.
383. Ibid., January 21, 1912.
384. Baroway, "Cohens of Maryland."
385. Londow, "Benjamin Henry Hartogensis," 469–470.
386. Joseph Gutmann, "Jewish Participation in the Visual Arts of Eighteenth- and Nineteenth-Century America," *AJA*, XV (1963), 47; Blum, *Jews of Baltimore*, p. 157.
387. Much material on both artists is available in JHSM.
388. A number of Baltimore Jews have presented the museum with outstanding collections and large funds. Especially outstanding were the contributions of Jacob Epstein, the sisters Dr. Claribel and Miss Etta Conn, and Sadie A. May. See *The Baltimore Museum of Arts, News* XXV (1962), 6–7; *The Baltimore Museum Annual* (1962), pp. 6–11; ibid., (1967), pp. 17–21.
389. Levin, *Vision*, p. 89.
390. Materials on this campaign in JHSM.
391. Seidenman was a picture-frame maker. He served in the City Council for three years. In the 1906 election he was defeated, but politics paid off. According to the *Baltimore City Directory* of that year, he was no longer in the picture-frame business. He was already a deputy sheriff. Information about Seidenman's

campaigns and career was supplied by the Department of Legislative Reference of the City of Baltimore, August 18, 1969.

392. Lewis Putzel, "The Jew in Political Life" in Blum, *Jews of Baltimore*, pp. 57–58.

393. Ibid., p. 57.

394. Author's interview with Judge Moses and a wealth of material about him in JHSM.

395. For details of Rayner's career in the Senate as well as a full record of his speeches, see Rayner, *Addresses;* see also a collection of scrapbooks at the University of North Carolina, Chapel Hill.

396. Sobeloff presently (1969) serves as United States Circuit Judge for the Fourth District. Material about Judge Sobeloff available in the JHSM. Besides Sobeloff, another Baltimore Jew was appointed solicitor general of the United States—Philip B. Perlman (1890–1960) held this position from 1947 till 1952.

397. Original of Rabbi Szold's call in BSA.

398. *YBCCAR*, XV (1904), 68.

399. *Sun*, December 9, 1910.

400. RFJC (1918), p. 9.

401. Hollander, *Forces*, p. 12.

402. The episode with the apron was related to the author by Mrs. Stanford Z. Rothschild, Sr., who is a great-granddaughter of Betsy Wiesenfeld. See also "An Account of Mrs. Betsy Wiesenfeld and Her Father Jonas Friedenwald" reprinted from *The Jewish Exponent* of February 14, 1890, in Blum, *Jews of Baltimore*, pp. 133–143.

403. *RFJC* (1908), p. 7.

404. Clipping from local Yiddish newspaper (in JHSM), date not identified.

405. *RFJC* (1920), p. 10.

406. It was incorporated on January 13, 1921. The following were the corporate names of the constituent agencies that formed the Associated: Big Brother League, Board of Jewish Education: Baltimore Talmud Torah Society, Hebrew Education Society, Isaac Davidson Hebrew School, Western Talmud Torah, South Baltimore Talmud Torah, Southwestern Talmud Torah, Council Milk and Ice Fund of Baltimore City, Daughters in Israel, Hebrew Benevolent Society of Baltimore, Hebrew Free Burial Society, Hebrew Free Loan Association of Baltimore City, Hebrew Friendly Inn and Aged Home, Hebrew Home for In-

curables, Hebrew Immigrant Aid Society, Jewish Children's Bureau, Jewish Children's Society, Jewish Court of Arbitration, Jewish Educational Alliance, Jewish Home for Consumptives (Mount Pleasant), Sinai Hospital of Baltimore Inc. (formerly Hebrew Hospital and Asylum Association), Woodland Country Home, and Young Ladies' Benevolent Society.

407. An estimated figure based on Linfield, "Statistics," in *AJYB*, XXVII (1926), 385, which gives the figure of 60,000 for 1917–18 and that of *AJYB*, XXIX (1928), 243, with the figure 67,500 for Baltimore in 1924.

408. Wischnitzer, *To Dwell in Safety*, Table I, p. 289. In the next few years Jewish immigration was reduced much more sharply. In 1924 only 10,292 Jewish immigrants were reduced to 2,755 in 1932. (Ibid.)

EPILOGUE

1. Linfield, "Statistics," *AJYB*, XXVII (1926), 385, and *AJYB*, XXIX (1928), 243.

2. *The Jewish Community of Greater Baltimore: A Population Study* (Baltimore, 1968), 11, Table 1. This study, which in further notes will be referred to as *Study*, was conducted for the Associated Jewish Charities by a team of specialists in conducting such surveys.

3. A full 98 per cent of those under the age of fifteen are native born. *Study*, 31, Table 14.

4. Ibid., 75, Table 58. The distribution of members among the three branches of Judaism is about equal: 66 per cent Orthodox, 63 per cent Conservative, and 69 per cent Reform. See *Study*, 76, Table 59.

5. Rabbi Herbert Birnbaum, president of the Orthodox Association, letter dated March 31, 1970. The three groups are composed as follows: One association is composed of all Reform and Conservative rabbis, and rabbis of the leading Orthodox congregation. The other two associations are composed of Orthodox rabbis, one of the younger elements and the other of "old-timers." Letter from Rabbi Herbert Birnbaum, president of the Orthodox Association, dated March 11, 1970.

6. Ibid.

7. The Baltimore Hebrew College, a subsidiary of the Associated, had an enrollment in 1969 of 764 students. Of these, 253 at-

tended classes in the high school department, 76 in the college, 343 in various adult education classes, 32 in the Washington branch of the college, and 60 in the teachers' in-service courses. Mr. Raymond Bloom, registrar of the college, supplied this information.

The other institution of higher learning is the Ner Israel Rabbinical College with 480 students from all over the world. This institution is completely supported by friends all over the United States. This information was given by Rabbi Herman N. Newberger, executive director of Ner Israel, in a letter dated March 30, 1970.

8. There are 5,860 pupils who attend the Sunday and afternoon schools affiliated with the Board of Jewish Education, and 684 attend those affiliated with the Hebrew Education Association. In addition, 1,293 attend all-day schools. Information was supplied by Dr. Sidney L. Esterson, director, Bureau of Jewish Education, April 1970, and a letter dated May 1, 1970.

9. *Chairman's Manual . . . 1970 Campaign,* passim (hereafter referred to as *Manual*).

10. Ibid., 16–17.

11. In 1698 the Jewish Welfare Fund raised $1,869,700 primarily for overseas needs, in addition to the Israel Emergency Fund of $2,150,000. *Currents,* "News of Interest to the Baltimore Jewish Community," February 1969 (n.p.). The projected campaign for 1970 for overseas needs, including the Israel Emergency Fund, is $3,646,600. *Manual,* 61.

12. *Manual,* passim.

13. *Study,* 50, Table 34. This compared with 13.9 per cent of the white general population in the northeast who make above fifteen thousand dollars a year and 20.3 per cent whose income is less than five thousand dollars a year. *Statistical Abstract, U.S.,* 1969, 322, Tables 475 and 322.

14. *Study,* 46, Table 30.

15. Letter of December 21, 1967, from Robert I. Hiller, executive vice-president, Associated Jewish Charities and Welfare Fund.

16. Report of the president of the Associated Jewish Charities, October 23, 1969.

17. Report, president, Jewish Welfare Fund, 1968, (n.p.).

18. My informant is Leon Sachs, executive director, Baltimore Jewish Community Council, March 19, 1970.

19. Jewish Big Brother League, *Report* (1967), Baltimore, 6.

20. Ibid. (1968–1969), 3.

glossary

ALIYAH (pl. ALIYOT). Literally, "ascent"; immigration to Israel; honor of being called up to the Torah-reading at divine services

BAAL MELOKHE. Artisan

DROSHE (pl. DROSHES). Sermon(s), speech(es)

GABBAI (pl. GABBAIM). Officer(s) of a synagogue

GEMILUT HASADIM. Acts of kindness; applied to lending money without interest

GOYISHKAYT. Non-Jewishness

GREENER. In American Yiddish, an immigrant, one who has not yet been Americanized

HAPHTARAH (pl. HAPHTAROT). Portions from the Prophets read in the synagogue

HASID (pl. HASIDIM). Member(s) of a pietist, mystic movement which arose in Eastern Europe in the middle of the eighteenth century

HASKALAH. Englightenment movement among the Jews of Europe

HAVER (pl. HAVERIM). Comrade(s)

HAZAN (pl. HAZANIM). Cantor(s)

HAZIR MARKET. Literally, pig market; name given by immigrants to area where the hiring of labor took place

HEDER (pl. HADARIM). Jewish religious school for younger children in Eastern Europe

HEIMISH. Intimate

HEP, HEP. Anti-Semitic slogan especially popular in Germany in the nineteenth century

HEREM. Excommunication

HOL HA-MOED. Days between the first two and the last two days of both Passover and Succoth

HOVEVEI ZION. Early Zionist societies

KAHAL. Governing body of a Jewish community

KOSHER. Food prepared in accordance with Jewish ritual

KASHRUT. Dietary laws practiced by observant Jews

KEHILLAH (pl. KEHILOT). Jewish community (communities)

KIND (pl. KINDER). Child(ren)

KLAL ISRAEL. The totality of Jewry

LANDSMAN (pl. LANDSLAYT). Immigrant(s) from the same town or region in Europe

LANDSMANSHAFT (pl. LANDSMANSHAFTN). Society (societies) of immigrants from the same locality

LITVAK. One who comes from Lithuania

MASKIL (pl. MASKILIM). Follower(s) of the Haskalah movement

MATZAH (pl. MATZOT). Unleavened bread eaten on Passover

MELAMED (pl. MELAMDIM). Teacher of children in a *heder*

MESHULAH (pl. MESHULAHIM). Collector(s) for Jewish institutions, especially those in the Holy Land

MIKVE (pl. MIKVOT). Ritual bath house(s)

MINHAG (pl. MINHAGIM). Custom(s)

MINYAN (pl. MINYANIM). Quorum(s) of ten males above the age of thirteen required for public worship

MITHNAGED (pl. MITHNAGDIM). Opponent(s) of Hasidism

MITZVAH (pl. MITZVOT). Commandment(s); good deed(s)

MOHEL (pl. MOHALIM). One(s) who perform(s) the rite of circumcision

PIYUT (pl. PIYUTIM). Poetic selection(s) in prayer books

REBBE (pl. RABBEIM). Hasidic leader(s); teacher(s) in *heder*

ROSH HASHANAH. Jewish New Year

SEPHARDIC. Of Spanish or Portuguese origin or order of prayers

SHAATNEZ. Mingled wool and linen, which must not be worn according to Mosaic law

SHABBES GOY (pl. GOYIM). Non-Jew(s) who perform(s) chores forbidden to Jews on the Sabbath

SHOHET (pl. SHOHATIM). Ritual slaughterer(s)

SHTETL (pl. SHTETLEKH). East European small town(s)

SHTIBL (pl. SHTIBLEKH). Small Hasidic house(s) of worship

SHUL (pl. SHULN). Synagogue(s)

SHULHAN ARUKH. Code of Jewish law compiled in the sixteenth century

TALLIS. Prayer shawl

TALMUD TORAH. Elementary religious school, traditionally free

TISHA BEAV. Fast day commemorating the destruction of the Temple

TREF. Nonkosher food

YAHUDI (pl. YAHUDIM). Hebrew for Jew(s); applied as a term of derision by East European Jews referring to German Jews

YID (pl. YIDN). Jew(s)

YIHUS. Pedigree

YIDISHKAYT. Jewishness

YOM KIPPUR. Day of Atonement

bibliography

The following is a selected bibliography. Minor articles, letters, and brief organizations' reports have been omitted. These are to be found in the pertinent notes. A few books and articles which are not mentioned in the notes but are important for a better understanding of the problem at hand are listed here. (The abbreviations used here are the same as those used in the Notes.)

I. MANUSCRIPT MATERIAL

Cohen Family Collection (MHS).

Etting Family Collection (MHS, The Historical Society of Pennsylvania).

Fulton, Robert, Fulton Papers (Library of Congress).

Garson, S. (Slobodkin). *In Kamf Tzvishn Tzvei Ideologies.* Unpublished memoirs of a leader of the anarchists in Baltimore (YIVO Archives, New York).

Lesser Collection (Dropsie College).

Levy Family Papers (JHSM).

The Mayer affair (a large collection of letters, newspaper clippings, etc. in JHSM).

Rice Collection (JTS).

Szold, Benjamin. Over a thousand sermons, letters, etc.

Szold, Boruch (Rabbi Szold's father). Will (JHSM).

Wiesenfeld, M. Stock account, in possession of Henry Wiesenfeld, son of Moses's brother, David.
Documents related to Wiesenfeld's arrest in 1861 (JHSM).

II. PERSONAL STATEMENTS

(Unless otherwise noted this material is in JHSM. Much of the material about the Workmen's Circle, the Bund, and labor conditions is based on the interviews with Neistadt and H. and S. Cohen mentioned in Part IV, note 139.)

1. *Interviews*

Benderly, Mrs. Samson. Wife of Dr. Samson Benderly. 1967–1968.

Braiterman, William. Leading member of the Labor Zionist movement. October 26, 1965.

Edelman, Jacob. Prominent labor lawyer. February 6, 1963.

Einspruch, Henry W. Missionary. November 12, 1968.

Levin, Simon. Secretary of the Baltimore Zionist Council, 1912–1922. March 4, 1968.

Magnes, Mrs. Judah. Friend of Dr. Samson Benderly. November 23, 1964, in Jerusalem.

Moses, Jacob M. Former state senator and labor mediator. October 30 and November 12, 1966.

Rothschild, Mrs. Stanford Z., Sr. Prominent civic leader. February 12, 1967.

Seidel, Dr. Herman. Founder of the Poalei Zion in the United States. October 9, 1966.

2. *Memoirs*

Friedenwald, Bertha. *Memoirs*, 1862–1895.

Friedenwald family papers. Most of these on microfilm.

Hecht, Simeon, *Memoirs*, 1824–1872.

Hollander, Jacob. Papers, letters in mss. and typescript.

Rayner, Isidor. Scrapbooks. University of North Carolina, Chapel Hill.

Schwartz, Joseph. Memorandum on the life of his father, Rabbi Abraham Schwartz. Typescript. (JHSM).

Sonneborn, Henry. *Family Memoirs*. Baltimore, 1966. Typescript.

Szold, Henrietta. Large collection of letters, notes, etc., in addition to Miss Szold's archives on microfilm.

III. OFFICIAL DOCUMENTS

(Unless otherwise noted the documents are in MHR).

1. *In Manuscript*
Acts of Maryland.
Records of Baltimore City.
Baltimore Land Records.
Calvert Papers (MHS).
Charles County Land Records.
Deed Books.
Inventories.
Laws of the State of Maryland.
Maryland Annotated Code.

Maryland Court of Appeals Records.
Provincial Court Records.
Record of Wills.

2. *Printed*

Baltimore School Commissioners' *Reports.*
Bureau of Industrial Statistics of Maryland. *Reports* for 1893–
    1903. Pratt Library, Baltimore.
Charter of Maryland.
Congressional Record.
Constitution of Maryland.
Laws of Maryland.
U. S. Census.
United States Immigration and Naturalization Service, *Annual
    Report,* for Year Ending June 30, 1947.

IV. SYNAGOGUE MATERIAL

1. *Minute Books and Other Records* (in manuscript)

Baltimore Hebrew Congregation. Minute Books. (In congre-
    gation, Baltimore, and AJAR).
Baltimore Hebrew Congregation. *Constitution,* 1861.
    (JHSM).
Baltimore Hebrew Congregation. *Constitution and By-Laws,*
    January 18, 1874. (JHSM).
Baltimore Hebrew Congregation. Records of Marriages,
    Funerals and Confirmation, 1889–1915. (JHSM).
Beth Israel. *Mikro Kodesh, Calendar, 1963–1964* (Balti-
    more, 1963).
Chizuk Amuno Congregation. Minute Books. (In congrega-
    gation, Baltimore).
Har Sinai Congregation. Minute Books. (In congregation,
    Baltimore, and JHSM).
Oheb Shalom. *Constitution,* 1893. (In congregation, Balti-
    more).
Sharei Israel. Minute Books. (New York).
Shomrei Mishmereth Hakodesh. Minute Book, 1906.
    (JHSM).

2. *Published Congregational Histories*

BALTIMORE HEBREW.

*Constitution and By-Laws of the Hebrew Congregation Nitgy
    Israel of Baltimore, 5590.* Baltimore, 1930.

Guttmacher, Adolf. *A History of the Baltimore Hebrew Congregation, 1830–1905.* Baltimore, 1905.

Hunter, William Harvey, Jr. *The Lloyd Street Synagogue.* Baltimore, 1963. Typescript, JHSM.

BETH TFILOH.
15th Anniversary Memorial History. Baltimore, 1936.

B'NAI ISRAEL.
Diamond Jubilee Program. Baltimore, 1948.

CHIZUK AMUNO.
Diamond Jubilee Banquet. Baltimore, 1946.

FELL'S POINT HEBREW FRIENDSHIP CONGREGATION.
Friedman, Benjamin. *Synopsis of the History. . . .* Typescript, 1910.

HAR SINAI.
Rayner, William S. *Address Containing the History of the Har Sinai Congregation of Baltimore City.* Baltimore, 1892.

Rubenstein, Charles A. *History of the Har Sinai Congregation.* Baltimore, 1918.

Shusterman, Abraham. *The Legacy of a Liberal: The Miracle of Har Sinai Congregation.* Baltimore, 1967.

OHEB SHALOM.
Cahn, Louis F. *History of Oheb Shalom, 1853–1953.* Baltimore, 1953.

Rosenau, William. *A Brief History of Congregation Oheb Shalom, Baltimore, Md., 1853–1938.* Baltimore, 1903, 1928, 1938.

V. ORGANIZATIONS' DOCUMENTS

(Unless otherwise noted, the documents are in JHSM).

Associated Jewish Charities. Reports, Bulletins.

Baltimore Hebrew Religious School Association. Record Book, 1868–1871.

Baron de Hirsch Fund. Records, ms.

Beacon Light Literary and Pleasure Association. *Constitution and By-Laws.*

B'nai B'rith. Miller, Michael. *The Origin and Early Years of the Menorah Lodge in Baltimore.* Typescript.

B'rith Sholom.
    Constitution and Minutes, ms.
    Brith Sholom, ms. 1911–1915.
    Ledger Book. Menorah Lodge, ms. 1915–1917.

Bund Archives. New York.

Federated Jewish Charities. Reports, 1908–1921. (In the archives of the Associated Jewish Charities, Baltimore.)

Free Loan Association Minute Book, ms. (In office of the association.)

Hebrew Benevolent Society.
    Charter (1856), ms.
    Minute Book, 1877–1879.

Hebrew Hospital and Asylum (now Sinai Hospital).
    Laying of Cornerstone in 1866, ms.
    Leopold, Eugene L. *History of Sinai Hospital*, (n.d., n.p.), typescript.
    Reports (typescript).

Hebrew Ladies' Orphan Aid Society.
    Charitable Gifts, Record, 1887–1908, ms.
    Legacies, 1869–1916, ms.
    Minute Book, 1882–1901, ms.
    Record Book, 1892–1901.

Hebrew Orphan Asylum.
    Charitable Gifts, Record, 1897–1906.
    Memorial Book, 1877.
    Record Book, 1905–1919, ms.

Hebrew Sick Relief Association, 1888–1963. *Souvenir* (1963).

Hovevei Zion. *Report*, 1889.

Jewish Big Brother League, *Report*, 1967.

Loyola College. List of Jewish students in the middle of the nineteenth century. Typescript.

Maryland State Colonization Society. *Address to the People of Maryland, with the Constitution of the Society.* Baltimore, 1831.

United Hebrew Charities. *Report*, 1910, ms.

Young Men's Literary Association. Minutes, 1856–1858. Photocopy.

Zion Association. *Constitution.* 1894.

VI. NEWSPAPERS AND PERIODICALS

Lack of sources is painful to the historian. The United Jewish Charities, the central charity agency of East European Jews, was in existence from 1907 until 1920, yet only the minutes of one meeting are available. There was a Yiddish secular school in the city, but all that is known about it is that it was founded in 1919 and existed for a "few" years. (See Benjamin Laikin, Memoirs of a Practical Dreamer *[New York, 1970], 110–111.) These are only two instances— there are many similar ones. No wonder one is pleasantly surprised and appreciative of the many references to Baltimore Jewry found in the local, national, and even European press.*

The local Jewish periodicals were published in four languages— German, English, Yiddish and Hebrew—and are, naturally, the most important source for the daily life of Baltimore Jews. There is also, however, much material on the subject in the local non-Jewish press. This is especially true of The Baltimore Sun *(see Appendix IV).*

The national press also provides much information on the subject. The most important source in this group is The Occident *(see Appendix V).*

1. UNITED STATES

A. LOCAL

The American and Commercial Daily Advertiser.
Der Amerikaner Yid. (Yiddish).
Baltimore Advertiser.
Baltimore American.
Baltimore Evening Sun.
Baltimore Amerikaner. (Yiddish).
The Baltimore Sun.
Baltimore Seine Vergangenheit und Gegenwart. (German).
The Catholic Mirror
Der Deutsche Correspondent. (German).
The Federal Gazette and Baltimore Advertiser.
The Freeman.
General Advertiser.
Hapisga. (Hebrew).
Der Israëlite. (Yiddish).
The Jewish Chronicle. (German and English).
The Jewish Comment.

The Jewish Times.
Katholische Volkszeitung. (German).
Manufacturers' Record, A Weekly Southern and Financial Newspaper.
Maryland Archives.
Maryland Historical Magazine.
Maryland Journal and Advertiser.
Niles' Weekly Register.
Sinai. (German).
Der Vegvayzer. (Yiddish).
Der Wecker (German).

B. Out of Town

The American Hebrew. (New York).
American Jewish Archives. (Cincinnati).
American Jewish Historical Quarterly. (New York, Waltham).
American Jewish Year Book. (New York).
The Asmonean. (New York).
Folkstzaytung. (Yiddish). (New York).
Forverts (Jewish Daily Forward) (Yiddish). (New York).
Fraye Arbayter Shtime (Yiddish). (New York).
The Israelite (or *The American Israelite*). (Cincinnati).
Jewish Exponent. (Philadelphia).
The Jewish Messenger. (New York).
The Jewish Record. (Philadelphia).
The Maccabean. (New York).
The Occident. (Philadelphia).
Publications of the American Jewish Historical Society.
Die Tzukunft. (Yiddish). (New York).
Yiddishe Gazetn. (Yiddish). (New York).

2. EUROPEAN

Allgemeine Zeitung des Judenthums. (Berlin).
Der Freitag Abend (Frankfurt on the Main).
Hamaggid. (Lyck).
Hamelitz. (Saint Petersburg).
Hazefirah. (Warsaw).
Hayehudi. (London).
Der Israelite. (Mainz).
Israelitische Wochenschrift. (Berlin).
Die Welt. (Vienna).

VII. BOOKS AND PAMPHLETS

1. ANONYMOUS AND COLLECTIVE

Annual of the American Branch of the Yiddish Scientific Institute, Jacob Shatzky, Alexander Mukdoni, ed. I, 1938; Leibush Lehrer, Yudl Mark, II, 1939 (New York).

Baltimore City Directories. (MHS).

Baltimore: The Gateway to the South, the Liverpool of America. Baltimore, 1898.

Baltimore: The Trade Queen of the South. Baltimore, 1902.

Biographical Dictionary of Modern Yiddish Literature. Yiddish. New York, 1960.

Dictionary of National Biography.

A History of the City of Baltimore, Its Men and Institutions. Published by the *Baltimore American.* Baltimore, 1902.

History and Roster of Maryland Volunteers, War 1861–1865. Baltimore, 1892.

Illustrated Baltimore, The Monumental City. New York, 1890.

Jewish Encyclopedia. 12 vols. New York, 1901–1905.

Maryland at a Glance (Annapolis, 1968).

Memoirs of the Dead and Tomb's Remembrancer. Baltimore, 1806. Rare book. In Pratt Library, Baltimore.

Memorial of Moses Wiesenfeld, February 26, 1871.

In Memoriam, Michael Simon Levy and Betsy Levy. Baltimore, 1912.

Proceedings and Speeches at a Public Meeting of the Friends of the Union. Baltimore, 1861.

Report of the Zion Association (Baltimore, 1894), at JHSM.

A Sketch of the Proceedings in the Legislature of Maryland . . . December, 1818. Baltimore, 1819.

Social Register. A Compendium of Names and Addresses of the Jewish Community of Baltimore. Baltimore, 1907–1908.

Speech of Thomas Kennedy, Esq. in the Legislature of Maryland. . . . Annapolis, 1823.

Speeches on the Jew Bill, in the House of Delegates of Maryland by H. M. Brackenridge, Col. W. G. D. Worthington, and John S. Tyson, Esquire. Philadelphia, 1829.

Tercentenary History of Baltimore. Baltimore, 1925.

United States Department of Justice, *Our Immigration* (Washington, 1912), p. 15.

Votes and Proceedings of the House of Delegates of the State of Maryland, November Session 1797, Being the First Session of This Assembly, 69, 71–72.

YIVO. *Annual of Jewish Social Sciences*. I–XIV (New York, 1946–1969), passim.

2. BY AUTHORS

Aaronsohn, Michael. *Broken Lights*. Cincinnati, 1946.

Adler, Cyrus. *I Have Considered the Days*. Philadelphia, 1941.

————, ed. *The Voice of America on Kishineff*. Philadelphia, 1904.

Adler, Selig and Thomas E. Connolly. *From Ararat to Suburbia*. Philadelphia, 1960.

Altfeld, E. Milton. *The Jew's Struggle for Religious and Civil Liberties*. Baltimore, 1924.

Alzop, George. *A Character of Maryland*. London, 1666.

Andrews, Matthew Page. *History of Maryland Province and State*. New York, 1929.

Antonovsky, Aaron. *The Early Jewish Labor Movement in the United States*. New York, 1961.

Barker, Charles Albo. *The Background of the Revolution in Maryland*. New Haven, 1940.

Benjamin [I.J.]. *Three Years in America*. Philadelphia, 1956.

Bland, John Randolph. *A Review of the Commerce of the City of Baltimore*. Baltimore, 1886.

Blau, Joseph L. and Salo W. Baron. *The Jews of the United States, 1790–1840: A Documentary History*, 3 vols. Philadelphia, 1963.

Blum, Isidor. *The Jews of Baltimore*. Baltimore-Washington, 1910.

Bozman, John Leeds. *The History of Maryland from the Settlement in 1633 to the Restoration in 1666*. 2 vols. Baltimore, 1837.

Braiterman, William. *Memoirs of the Palestine Jewish Legion in 1917*. Baltimore, 1967.

Brigham, William T. *Baltimore Hats, Past and Present*. Baltimore, 1890.

Burgin, Herz. *The History of the Jewish Labor Movements in America, Russia and England*. New York, 1915.

Carvalho, Solomon Nunes. *Incidents of Travel and Adventure in the Far West*. Bertram Wallace Korn, ed. Philadelphia, 1954.

Coyle, Wilbur. *First Acts of Baltimore Town and Jones' Town, 1729–1797*. Baltimore, 1905.

Crusd, Edward E. *B'nai B'rith*. New York, 1966.

Cunz, Dieter. *The Maryland Germans*. Princeton, 1948.

Davis, Moshe. *Yahadut Amerika Be-Hitpathutah (The Shaping of American Judaism)*. New York, 1951.

Dubnow, Simon S. *History of the Jews in Russia and Poland*. Philadelphia, 1918.

Eddis, William. *Letters from America, Historical and Description, Comprising Occurrences from 1769 to 1777 Inclusive*. London, 1792.

Einhorn, David. *Ausgewählte Predigten und Reden*. (German). New York, 1880.

————. *Olat Tamid*. Baltimore, 1856.

————. *War with Amalek*. Philadelphia, 1864.

Ezekiel Herbert T. and Gaston Lichtenstein. *The History of the Jews of Richmond*. Richmond, 1917.

Feld, Joseph. *The Jews at the Johns Hopkins University, 1876–1901*. Baltimore, 1969. Typescript in possession of author.

Fineman, Irving. *A Woman of Valor*. New York, 1961.

French, John C. A. *A History of the University Founded by Johns Hopkins*. Baltimore, 1946.

Friedenwald, Harry. *Life, Letters, and Addresses of Aaron Friedenwald, M.D.* Baltimore, 1906.

Glanz, Rudolf. *Jews in Relation to the Cultural Milieu of the Germans in America up to the 1880's*. New York, 1947.

Glushakow, Abraham D. *Maryland Tercentenary Book*. Baltimore, 1934.

————. *A Pictorial History of Maryland Jewry*. Baltimore, 1955.

Goodman, Abram Vossen. *American Overture*. Philadelphia, 1947.

Gould, Clarence P. *The Land System in Maryland, 1720–1765*. Baltimore, 1913.

————. *Money and Transportation in Maryland, 1720–1765*. Baltimore, 1915.

Greenstone, J. H., ed. *Statistical Data of the Jewish Religious Schools of Baltimore . . . , 1908–1909*. Philadelphia, 1909.

Griffith, Thomas W. *Annals of Baltimore*. Baltimore, 1833.

Grinstein, Hyman B. *The Rise of the Jewish Community of New York, 1654–1860*. Philadelphia, 1945.

Hall, Clayton Colman, ed. *Narratives of Early Maryland, 1633–1684*. New York, 1910.

Hansen, Marcus L. *The Atlantic Migration, 1607–1860*. Cambridge, 1940.

Hapgood, Hutchins. *The Spirit of the Ghetto*. New York, 1909.

328

Hartogensis, Benjamin H. *Studies in the History of Maryland*. N. p., n.d.

Henninghausen, Louis P. *History of the German Society of Maryland*. Baltimore, 1909.

Hirschfeld, Charles. *Baltimore, 1870–1900: Studies in Social History*. Baltimore, 1941.

Hollander, Jacob. *The Financial History of Baltimore*. Baltimore, 1899.

————. *Forces and Tendencies of Jewish Charities*. Baltimore, 1910.

Hourwich, Isaac A. *Immigration and Labor*. New York, 1912.

Howard, George W. *The Monumental City*. Baltimore, n.d.

Joseph, Samuel. *History of the Baron de Hirsch Fund*. Philadelphia, 1935.

————. *Jewish Immigration to the United States from 1881 to 1910*. New York, 1914.

Kagan, Solomon Robert. *Jewish Contributions to Medicine in America from Colonial Times to Present*. Boston, 1939.

Kaplan, Louis L. and Theodor Schuchat. *Justice Not Charity: A Biography of Harry Greenstein*. New York, 1967.

Kaufmann, Eugene. *A Half a Century of HIAS in Baltimore, 1903–1953*. Baltimore, 1953.

Kelly, H. A., ed. *Dictionary of American Medical Biography*. Philadelphia, 1921.

Kohler, Kaufmann, ed. *David Einhorn Memorial Volume*. New York, 1911.

Kohler, Max J. *Immigration and Aliens in the United States*. New York, 1936.

Korn, Bertram Wallace. *American Jewry and the Civil War*. Philadelphia, 1951.

————. *The American Reaction to the Mortara Case: 1858–1859*. Cincinnati, 1957.

————. *Eventful Years and Experiences*. Cincinnati, 1954.

Lestchinsky, Jacob. *Jewish Migration for the Past Hundred Years*. New York, 1944.

Levin, Alexandra Lee. *The Szolds of Lombard Street*. Philadelphia, 1960.

————. *Vision: A Biography of Harry Friedenwald*. Philadelphia, 1964.

Levine, Louis. *The Women's Garment Workers*. New York, 1924.

Levy, Lester S. *Jewish Charities in Baltimore*. Baltimore, 1964. Typescript.

London, Hanna R. *Miniatures of Early American Jews*. Springfield, Massachusetts, 1933.

Lowenthal, Marvin. *Henrietta Szold, Life and Letters*. New York, 1942.

Manakee, Harold R. *Mendes Cohen as President of the Maryland Historical Society*. Baltimore, 1962.

Marcus, Jacob R. *Early American Jewry*. Philadelphia, 1951–1953.

———. *Memoirs of American Jews, 1775–1865*. 3 vols. Philadelphia, 1955–1956.

Masliansky H. *Memoirs*. (Yiddish). New York, 1924.

Mencken, H. L. *The American Language: Supplement*. New York, 1948, II, 602–603.

———. *Happy Days*. New York, 1955.

Nicholson, Isaac F. *Baltimore Stock Exchange, Historical Sketch*. Baltimore, n.d.

Nyburg, Sidney L. *The Chosen People*. Philadelphia, 1917.

Panitz, David. *Memoirs of Zion*. (Hebrew). Baltimore, 1903.

Perry, Thomas W. *Public Opinion, Propaganda and Politics in Eighteenth Century England: A Study of the Jew Bill of 1753*. Cambridge, 1962.

Philipson, David S. *My Life as an American Jew*. Cincinnati, 1941.

Rayner, Isidor. *Addresses*. J. Frederick Essary, ed. Baltimore-New York, 1914.

———. *Essay of Isidor Rayner*. Baltimore, 1914.

Resnikoff, Charles and Uriah Z. Engelman. *The Jews of Charleston*. Philadelphia, 1950.

Rischin, Moses. *The Promised City: New York's Jews, 1870–1914*. Cambridge, 1962.

Schaffer, Schepsel. *Twenty-five Years of Activity in the Cause of Orthodox Judaism*. Baltimore, 1918.

Schappes, Morris U. *A Documentary History of the Jews in the United States, 1654–1875*. New York, 1950.

Scharf, J. Thomas. *The Chronicles of Baltimore*. Baltimore, 1874.

———. *History of Baltimore City and County*. Philadelphia, 1881.

Seidman, Joel. *The Needle Trades*. New York, 1942.

Semmes, Raphael. *Crime and Punishment in Maryland*. Baltimore, 1938.

———. *John H. B. Latrobe and His Times, 1803–1891*. Baltimore, 1917.

Singer, Richard E. *The American Jew in Agriculture, Past History and Present Conditions*. Unpublished Prize Essay, Hebrew Union College, Cincinnati, 1941.

Sobeloff, Simon E. *Zionism in Baltimore.* Baltimore, 1967.

Steiner, Bernard. *History of Education in Maryland.* Baltimore, 1894.

Stern, Malcolm. *Americans of Jewish Descent.* Cincinnati, 1960.

Stiffman, Jeffrey B. *Prolegomena to the Study of the History of the Jewish Community of Baltimore, Maryland.* Typescript. Cincinnati, 1965. Copy at JHSM.

Szold, Benjamin. *Abodath Israel.* Baltimore, 1873.

———. *Der Enthülte Einhorn (Einhorn Unmasked).* Baltimore, 1860.

———. *Inaugural Sermon.* Baltimore, 1859. Translated by Sophie and Henrietta Szold, 1909.

———. *Vaterland und Freiheit.* (In memory of President Lincoln). Baltimore, 1865.

Tcherikower, E., ed. *History of the Jewish Labor Movement in the United States,* I, New York, 1930; II, New York, 1945.

Winter, J. Nathan H. *Jewish Education in a Pluralistic Society: Samson Benderly and Jewish Education in the United States.* New York, 1966.

Wischnitzer, Mark. *To Dwell in Safety.* Philadelphia, 1948.

Wise, Isaac M. *Reminiscences.* David Philipson, ed. Cincinnati, 1901.

Wolf, Edwin, 2nd, and Maxwell Whiteman. *The History of the Jews of Philadelphia from Colonial Times to the Age of Jackson.* Philadelphia, 1956.

Wolf, Simon. *The American Jew as Patriot, Soldier and Citizen.* Philadelphia, 1895.

Worthington, W. G. D. *Speech of W. G. D. Worthington.* Baltimore, 1824.

VIII. ARTICLES

Adler Cyrus. "The Beginnings of Semitic Studies in America," *Oriental Studies in Honor of Paul Haupt* (Baltimore, 1926), 317–328.

Barnett, George E. "The Jewish Population of Maryland," *AJYB,* IV (1902), 46–62.

Baron, Salo W. and Jeannette M. Baron, "Palestinian Messengers in America, 1849–1879," *Jewish Social Studies,* Vol. V, No. 2 (April 1943), 115–162; No. 3 (July 1943), 225–292.

Baroway, Aaron. "The Cohens of Maryland," *MHM,* XVIII (1923), 355–375.

———. "Solomon Etting, 1764–1847," *MHM,* XV (1920).

Blau, Joseph L. "The Maryland Jew Bill," *Review of Religion* (1944), 227–239.

Bloch, Joshua. "Isidor Rayner (1850–1912)," *PAJHS*, XL (1951), 288–295.

Brickner, Rebecca. "As I Remember Dr. Benderly," *Jewish Education*, XX (1949), 53–58.

Buchler, Joseph. "The Struggle for Unity," *AJA*, II (1949), 21–46.

Chyet, Stanley F. "The Political Rights of the Jews in the United States, 1776–1840," *AJA*, X (1958), 14–75.

Cunz, Dieter. "The Baltimore Germans and the Year 1848," *American German Review*, X (1943), 30–33.

Davis, Moshe. "Hazofeh ba-Arez ha-Hadashah: A Source for the History of East European Jews in the United States," (Hebrew), *Sefer ha-yovl li-ḳevod Alexander Marx* (New York, 1950), 115–141.

D. P. "Jacob Ezekiel," *PAJHS*, IX (1901), 160–163.

E.D.C., "Notes," *PAJHS*, XXXIV (1937), 271–273.

Einhorn, David. "Abvertigung . . ." (Final Rejoinder, dealing with Rabbi Szold), *Sinai*, V (1860). Supplement 1–28.

―――. "The Cleveland Conference," *Sinai*, I (1856), 25–30.

―――. "The Departure of the Publisher," *Sinai*, VI (1861), 136–142.

―――. "Dr. Raphall's Speech." *Sinai*, VI (1861), 2–20; 45–50; 60–61; 99–100.

―――. "The Fate of the Oheb Shalom Congregation in Baltimore," *Sinai*, IV (1859), 325–339; V (1860).

―――. "Inaugural Sermon," *Sinai*, II, Appendix I (1857), 1–14 (German); Appendix II, 1–15 (English).

Esterson, Rose. "History of the Young Men's and Young Women's Hebrew Association of Baltimore" in *YM-YWHA of Baltimore, 5691–1930*, pp. 31–40.

Fein, Isaac M. "Baltimore Jews during the Civil War," *AJHQ*, LI (1961), 67–96.

―――. "The London Missionary Society in Russia in the Nineteenth Century" (Yiddish), *YIVO Bletter* XXIV (1944), 27–46.

―――. "*Niles' Weekly Register* on the Jews," *PAJHS*, L (1960), 3–22.

Friedenberg, Albert M. "The Jews and the American Sunday Laws," *PAJHS*, XI (1903), 101–115.

Friedenwald, Harry. "Louis Hiram Levin," *PAJHS*, XXIX (1925), 176–178.

Ginsberg, Eli. "The Jewish Colony in Waterview," *The Virginia Magazine of History and Biography* (October 1958), 460–462.

Glanz, Rudolf. "Notes on Early Jewish Peddling in America," *JSS*, VII (1945), 119–136.

Goldberg, Nathan. "Dynamics of the Economic Structure of the Jews in the United States" in Davis and Myer, eds. *The Writing of American Jewish History* (New York, 1957), 233–256.

Goldman, Israel. "Henry W. Schneeberger: His Role in American Judaism," *AJHQ*, LVII (December 1967), 153–190.

Goodman, Abraham. "An American Jewish Peddler's Diary," *AJA*, III (1951), 81–111.

Gould, Clarence P. "The Economic Causes of the Rise of Baltimore," *Essays of Colonial History* (New Haven, 1931), 225–271.

Graves, Avery O. "Soil Exhaustion as a Factor in the Agricultural History of Virginia and Maryland," *University of Illinois Studies in the Social Sciences*, XIII, No. 1 (Urbana, 1925), 29–52.

Grinstein, Hyman B. "The efforts of East European Jewry to Organize Its Own Community in the United States," *PAJHS*, XLIX (1959), 73–89.

Gutmann, Joseph. "Jewish Participation in the Visual Arts of Eighteenth- and Nineteenth-Century America," *AJA*, XV (1963), 21–57.

Halstead, David. "Sylvester at Hopkins," *The Johns Hopkins University Magazine*, IV (March 1916), 3.

Handlin, Oscar and Mary F. Handlin. "A Century of Jewish Immigration in the United States," *AJYB*, L (New York, 1949), 1–84.

Hartogensis, Benjamin H. "Notes on Early Jewish Settlers in Baltimore," *PAJHS*, XXII (1914), 191–195.

———. "The Russian Night School of Baltimore," *PAJHS*, XXXI (1928), 225–228.

———. "The Sephardic Congregation of Baltimore," *PAJHS*, XXIII (1915), 141–146.

———. "Unequal Religious Rights in Maryland since 1776," *PAJHS*, XXV (1917), 93–107.

Henninghausen, Louis P. "The Redemptioners and the German Society of Maryland," *SHGM*, II (1888), 31–54.

Higham, John. "Social Discrimination against Jews in America, 1830–1930," *PAJHS*, XLVII (1957), 1–33.

Hollander, J. H. "The Civil Status of the Jews in Maryland, 1634–1776," *PAJHS*, II (1893), 33–44.

————. "Some Unpublished Material Relating to Dr. Jacob Lumbrozo of Maryland," *PAJHS*, I (1893), 25–39.

Hoyt, William D., Jr. "Civilian Defense in Baltimore, 1814–1815 . . . ," *MHM*, XXXIX (1944), 199–224, 293–309; XL (1946), 7–23, 137–163.

————. "The Papers of the Maryland State Colonization Society," *MHM*, XXXII (1937), 247–271.

Hühner, Leon, "Jews in the War of 1812," *PAJHS*, XXVI (1918), 173–200.

————. "Jews in the Legal and Medical Profession in America," *PAJHS*, XXII (1914), 147–165.

Kisch, Guido. "German Jews in White Labor Servitude," *PAJHS*, XXIV (1937), 11–47.

————. "The Revolution of 1848 and the Jewish 'On to America' Movement," *PAJHS*, XXXVIII (1949), 185–234.

Kohler, Max J. "Incidents Illustrative of American Jewish Patriotism," *PAJHS*, IV (1896), 81–99.

————. "The Jews and the American Anti-Slavery Movement," *PAJHS*, V (1897), 137–155.

Korn, Bertram W. "Isaac Mayer Wise on the Civil War," *Hebrew Union College Annual*, XX (1947), 635–658.

————. "Jewish 48'ers in America," *AJA*, II (1949), 3–20.

Lang, H. "Hymns and Prayers" (Yiddish). In *David Edelstadt Book*, B. J. Bialostotzky, ed. New York, 1953, 423–424.

Leeser, Isaac "The Jews and Their Religion," cited in *PAJHS*, VI (1897), 143–144.

Levin, Alexandra Lee. "Henrietta Szold and the Russian Immigrant School," *MHM*, LVII (1962), 1–15.

Levine, Louis H. "David Hutzler," *PAJHS*, XXV (1917), 152–156.

Liebmann, Walter H. "The Correspondence between Solomon Etting and Clay," *PAJHS*, XVII (1909), 81–88.

Linfield, Harry S. "Statistics of Jews," *AJYB* (various years).

Londow, Ezekiel J. "Benjamin Henry Hartogensis," *PAJHS*, XXXVII (1947), 469–470.

Margalith, Hayim. "The Transmigration of a Law," *American Journal of International Law*, XL (April 1946), 411–414, 483–490.

Menes, A. "The Am Olam Movement," *History of the Jewish Labor Movement in the United States* (Yiddish), E. Tcherikower, ed. (New York, 1945), II, 203–238.

Miller Michael. *Fifty Years of Achievement, 1890–1940, Hebrew Home for the Aged and Infirm at Levindale* (no place or date of publication), n.p.

Oles, Arthur. "The Henry Joseph Collection of the Gratz Family Papers . . . ," *Essays in American Jewish History* (Cincinnati, 1958), 99–122.

Oppenheim, Samuel. "The Early History of Jews in New York, 1654–1664," *PAJHS*, XVIII (1909), 1–91.

———. "The Jews and Masonry in the United States before 1910," *PAJHS*, XIX (1910), 1–94.

———. "Notes," *PAJHS*, XXV (1917), 142–143.

Perlman, Moshe. "Paul Haupt and the Mesopotamian Project, 1892–1914," *PAJHS*, XLVII (1958), 154–175.

Philipson, David. "Strangers to a Strange Land," *AJA*, XVIII (1966), 133–138.

Phillips, N. Taylor. "Items Relating to the History of the Jews of New York," *PAJHS*, XI (1903), 149–161.

Rabinowitz, Benjamin. "The Young Men's Hebrew Association (1854–1913), *PAJHS*, XXXVII (1947), 221–326.

Rivkind, Isaac. "Alexander Harkavy, Pioneer and Veteran" (Yiddish), *Tzukunft* (June 1933), 312–314.

———. "Early American Hebrew Documents," *PAJHS*, XXXIV (1937), 51–74.

Rosenau, William. "Cardinal Gibbons and His Attitudes toward Jewish Problems," *PAJHS*, XXXI (1928), 219–224.

Rosenswaike, Ira. "Comments on Dr. Stern's Additions and Corrections," *AJHQ*, LII (1964), 289–292.

———. "An Estimate and Analysis of the Jewish Population of the United States in 1790," *PAJHS*, L (1960), 23–67.

———. "The Jewish Population of the United States as Estimated from the Census of 1820," *AJHQ*, LIII (1963), 131–178.

Schneiderman, Harry. "Herbert Friedenwald," *PAJHS*, XXXVII (1947), 463–466.

Solis-Cohen, Solomon. "Notes concerning David Hays . . . ," *PAJHS*, II (1894), 63–72.

Steiner, Walter R. "A Contribution to the History of Medicine in the Province of Maryland, 1636–1671," *Johns Hopkins Hospital Bulletin*, XIII (August/September, 1902, 137–138).

Stern, Malcolm H. "Some Additions and Corrections," *AJHQ*, LII (1964), 285–288.

————. "Two Jewish Functionaries in Colonial Pennsylvania," *AJHQ*, LVII (1967), 29–35.

Stopack, Aaron. "The Maryland State Colonization Society," *MHM*, LXII (1968), 275–279.

Strook, Sol M. "Switzerland and American Jews," *PAJHS*, XI (1903), 7–52.

Sulzberger, David. "Growth of the Jewish Population in the United States," *PAJHS*, VI (1897).

Szajkowski, Z. "The Alliance Israélite Universelle in the United States, 1860–1949," *PAJHS*, XXXIX (1950), 389–443.

————. "The Attitude of American Jews to East European Jewish Immigration (1881–1893)," *PAJHS*, XL (1951), 221–280.

————. "How the Mass Migration to America Began," *Jewish Social Studies*, IV, No. 1 (October, 1942), 291–310.

Szold, Benjamin. "Passover Sermon," *The Jewish Chronicle*, April 6, 1877.

————. "Peace and Concord," *Isr*, January 11, 1861.

"Trail Blazers of the Trans-Mississippi-West," *AJA*, VIII (1956), 59–129.

Vaxer, M. "The First Hebrew Bible Printed in America," *Journal of Jewish Bibliography*, II (1940), 20–26.

Wallenstein, Carrie Baumgarten. "Selig Baumgarten," *PAJHS*, XXVI (1918), 248.

Weinryb, Bernard D. "Jewish Immigration and Accommodation to America: Research Trends, Problems," *PAJHS*, XLVI (1957), 366–403.

Weisberger, Rosamond H. "Jacob Harry Hollander," *PAJHS*, XXXVII (1947), 471–473.

Whiteman, Maxwell. "Zionism Comes to Philadelphia," *Early History of Zionism in America*. Isidore S. Meyer, ed. (New York, 1958), 191–218.

Wilhelm, Kurt. "Benjamin Szold and the Rabbinic Post in Stockholm," *Historia Judaica*, XV (1953), 49–58.

Williams, J. T. C. "Washington County Maryland," *MHM*, II (1907).

index

Compiled by Paula Kasper

339